# Tasting Life

# Tasting Life

## My Story

**Barbie Rieger**

Copyright © 2021 by Barbie Rieger

All rights reserved. No part of this book may be reproduced by any mechanical, photographic or electronic process or in the form of a phonographic recording; nor may it be stored in a retrieval system, transmitted or otherwise be copied for public or private use—other than for "fair use" as brief quotations embodied in articles and review—without prior written permission of the publisher.

Books may be purchased in bulk by contacting the publisher or author at:
Support@QuantumShiftMedia.com

ISBN: 978-1-955533-05-8 (Paperback)
Library of Congress Control Number: 2021912873

Quantum Shift Media
2645 S. Wadsworth Circle
Lakewood, Colorado 80227
www.quantumshiftmedia.com

Editing, book design and cover design by Quantum Shift Media

Printed in the United States of America

# Dedication

To my wonderful family.

# Table of Contents

Chapter 1 - The Early Years . . . . . . . . . . . . . . . . . . . . . . . . . . 1
   A Scary Time. . . . . . . . . . . . . . . . . . . . . . . . . . . . . . . . . . . 3
   The DoodleBug Train-Grandma and Grandpa's Farm . . . 6
   A Bigger House . . . . . . . . . . . . . . . . . . . . . . . . . . . . . . . . 12
   Hard Times . . . . . . . . . . . . . . . . . . . . . . . . . . . . . . . . . . 14
   My First Real Job. . . . . . . . . . . . . . . . . . . . . . . . . . . . . . 20
   The Girl who Loved to Sing . . . . . . . . . . . . . . . . . . . . . . 22
   My Highschool Years. . . . . . . . . . . . . . . . . . . . . . . . . . . 24

Chapter 2 - A Wonderful Day in May . . . . . . . . . . . . . . . . . 29
   An Enchanting Evening. . . . . . . . . . . . . . . . . . . . . . . . . 31
   A Day at Sandy Beach . . . . . . . . . . . . . . . . . . . . . . . . . . 33
   Caught in a Whirlwind . . . . . . . . . . . . . . . . . . . . . . . . . 36
   Surprise in the Glove Compartment. . . . . . . . . . . . . . . . 39

Chapter 3 - Life Changing Events . . . . . . . . . . . . . . . . . . . . 41
   No Goodbyes. . . . . . . . . . . . . . . . . . . . . . . . . . . . . . . . . 45

Chapter 4 - Chappell & Julesburg . . . . . . . . . . . . . . . . . . . . 49
   Our Wedding Day. . . . . . . . . . . . . . . . . . . . . . . . . . . . . 55
   Meeting the Parents . . . . . . . . . . . . . . . . . . . . . . . . . . . 58

Visiting the Harvest Field – The Woman from India . . . 60

Chapter 5 - The New Bride Returns to Wichita . . . . . . . . . . 63
    Uncle Sam Knocking on the Door. . . . . . . . . . . . . . . . 70
    Life's Little Challenges . . . . . . . . . . . . . . . . . . . . . . . . . 72

Chapter 6 - Army Life in Virginia . . . . . . . . . . . . . . . . . . . 85
    A New Job in Washington, D. C.. . . . . . . . . . . . . . . . . 89
    Surprising Visit. . . . . . . . . . . . . . . . . . . . . . . . . . . . . . 92
    New Apartment and New Friends . . . . . . . . . . . . . . . 93
    Happy News . . . . . . . . . . . . . . . . . . . . . . . . . . . . . . . 96
    My Mother's Visit. . . . . . . . . . . . . . . . . . . . . . . . . . . 102
    A Child is Born . . . . . . . . . . . . . . . . . . . . . . . . . . . . 103

Chapter 7 - Farewell to Army Life . . . . . . . . . . . . . . . . . . 127
    New Beginnings in Wichita. . . . . . . . . . . . . . . . . . . 128

Chapter 8 - Life on The Farm. . . . . . . . . . . . . . . . . . . . . 139
    A Special House Guest. . . . . . . . . . . . . . . . . . . . . . 142
    A Blissful Event . . . . . . . . . . . . . . . . . . . . . . . . . . . 144
    Unexpected News. . . . . . . . . . . . . . . . . . . . . . . . . . 153
    Raising My Family on The Farm . . . . . . . . . . . . . . 155
    Road Trips in the New Car . . . . . . . . . . . . . . . . . . 162
    Life's Surprising Changes. . . . . . . . . . . . . . . . . . . . 167
    The Big Auction. . . . . . . . . . . . . . . . . . . . . . . . . . . 170

Chapter 9 - City Life - A New Home in Town. . . . . . . . . . 173
    Our First Really Big Vacation. . . . . . . . . . . . . . . . . 180
    Christmas Puppies . . . . . . . . . . . . . . . . . . . . . . . . . 184
    Leaving Wichita. . . . . . . . . . . . . . . . . . . . . . . . . . . 193

Table of Contents

Chapter 10 - A New Life Unfolds in Boulder . . . . . . . . . . . . 197
    The Seventies . . . . . . . . . . . . . . . . . . . . . . . . . . . . . 203
    A Hole in One . . . . . . . . . . . . . . . . . . . . . . . . . . . . 206
    Real Estate World by Rieger. . . . . . . . . . . . . . . . . . . 210
    Remarkable Resilience . . . . . . . . . . . . . . . . . . . . . . 212
    My Children – The Graduates . . . . . . . . . . . . . . . . . 216
    An Aspiring New Career . . . . . . . . . . . . . . . . . . . . 217
    The Chinook Winds. . . . . . . . . . . . . . . . . . . . . . . . 220
    A Special Celebration. . . . . . . . . . . . . . . . . . . . . . . 225
    Wonderful Happenings . . . . . . . . . . . . . . . . . . . . . 229

Chapter 11 - The Eighties. . . . . . . . . . . . . . . . . . . . . . . . . . 235
    Special Times with Friends and Family . . . . . . . . . . . 238
    Becoming Grandy . . . . . . . . . . . . . . . . . . . . . . . . . 242
    South America Journey . . . . . . . . . . . . . . . . . . . . . 250
    Embarrassing Real Estate Moments . . . . . . . . . . . . . 258
    A Time to Rejoice . . . . . . . . . . . . . . . . . . . . . . . . . 260
    Santa's Visit on Christmas Eve . . . . . . . . . . . . . . . . . 264
    Sponsoring Miss Colorado. . . . . . . . . . . . . . . . . . . . 266
    If only . . . . . . . . . . . . . . . . . . . . . . . . . . . . . . . . . 267

Chapter 12 - The Nineties . . . . . . . . . . . . . . . . . . . . . . . . . 271
    A Blessed Event . . . . . . . . . . . . . . . . . . . . . . . . . . 274
    Turn of Events . . . . . . . . . . . . . . . . . . . . . . . . . . . 276
    Little Bump in The Road . . . . . . . . . . . . . . . . . . . . 283
    Time to Build a New House. . . . . . . . . . . . . . . . . . . 297
    Life is Full of Surprises. . . . . . . . . . . . . . . . . . . . . . 304
    An Essay for My Sister . . . . . . . . . . . . . . . . . . . . . . 308

    Fun in Bigfork . . . . . . . . . . . . . . . . . . . . . . . . . . . . . 310

Chapter 13 - Turn of the Century 2000 . . . . . . . . . . . . . . . . 313
    Close Call in Barcelona . . . . . . . . . . . . . . . . . . . . . . 326
    Determination and Amazing Skills . . . . . . . . . . . . . . 336

Chapter 14 - A New Decade – 2010 and Beyond . . . . . . . . 339
    Special Events. . . . . . . . . . . . . . . . . . . . . . . . . . . . . . 342
    Girl's Trip to The Big Apple . . . . . . . . . . . . . . . . . . . 347
    Randy and Erin's Visit . . . . . . . . . . . . . . . . . . . . . . . 350
    Celebrating Sixty Years Together . . . . . . . . . . . . . . . 351
    Great Accomplishments . . . . . . . . . . . . . . . . . . . . . . 358
    A Time to Hang in There. . . . . . . . . . . . . . . . . . . . . 363
    A Joyful Event . . . . . . . . . . . . . . . . . . . . . . . . . . . . . 369
    2017 – An Eventful Year. . . . . . . . . . . . . . . . . . . . . . 386
    Transitioning Forward . . . . . . . . . . . . . . . . . . . . . . . 392
    Becoming Great-Grandy . . . . . . . . . . . . . . . . . . . . . 394
    The Clock was Ticking. . . . . . . . . . . . . . . . . . . . . . . 395

Chapter 15 - 2020 – A Doozy of a Year . . . . . . . . . . . . . . . 407
    All Things Are Possible. . . . . . . . . . . . . . . . . . . . . . . 408
    Take Nothing for Granted . . . . . . . . . . . . . . . . . . . . 410
    Zoom Thanksgiving. . . . . . . . . . . . . . . . . . . . . . . . . 415
    Miracles Do Happen . . . . . . . . . . . . . . . . . . . . . . . . 416

About the Author. . . . . . . . . . . . . . . . . . . . . . . . . . . . . . . . 419

# Chapter 1

# The Early Years

A glowing sun fills the sky on the day this story begins – the day I was born, the day my life begins. My little body emerges from my mother's womb. When I enter the world, my tiny fingers are curled in my hands, my lungs fill with air and my voice cries out "I'm here!" The day is September 1, 1936. I'm the second of five children and my parents are Leona and Allen Winter. They proudly chose my name and I became Barbara Anne Winter. My big sister was two years old and I don't know how she felt about having a baby sister, but there I was. I came home from the hospital to a brand-new house. Grandma Kinsley and my sister were there waiting. Grandma had travelled from Okeene, Oklahoma to help Mama with cooking and things. The new house wasn't very big but it was a cute house with four rooms – the living room, dining room, kitchen, one bedroom plus a bathroom. The dining room served well as a kid's bedroom, but it didn't have a door. Our house was located in the midwestern city of Wichita, Kansas. My first address was 422 West 26th Street, and that's where I lived for twelve years.

My family lived a simple life and we were a happy little family. In those days, there was no television, no internet or computer, no Facebook or Twitter, and no cell phones to consume our time. My parents didn't have a car but that didn't seem to be a problem because we had two modes of transportation. First was the bus and next – our legs. My Daddy was a nurse and he rode the bus to work while Mama stayed home to look after us kids. When I was old enough to play, my sister, Mary, and I became best pals, mud pie pals, we were called. We didn't have very many store-bought toys, but we used our imagination and we had fun together. Mary and I loved to make mud pies in the backyard. We played house, and sometimes we played hide and seek. I liked hiding in the corn field between our house and the neighbor's house, but Mama used to tell me I shouldn't go in the corn field.

There wasn't any snow, but it was Christmas morning and Santa's reindeer had managed to find our house. I remember how excited I was to discover two dolls sitting under the tree. I jumped up and down and shouted "Santa was here!" Mary liked the brown-eyed doll and I was happy to have my very own dolly with blue eyes that opened and closed. I took that dolly to bed with me for many years. Mary and I liked to watch Mama sort clothes and do the laundry. She had a wringer washing machine and I was fascinated by the wringer and how it squeezed the water out of the clothes. One day, Mary and I were playing in the basement and we tried to climb on top of the washing machine. Oops! … That's when it toppled over and fell on top of me. Mary screamed for Mama, and somehow Mama got that heavy washer off me. She picked me up and rushed to the neighbor's house, and the neighbor drove us to the hospital. I wasn't hurt badly, but later on, my mama told me that I was unconscious and she was scared. I have no memory of this event because I was only three years old, but I do remember hearing stories about the accident and I still have the newspaper article telling what happened.

## Chapter 1

Daddy usually got home from work around dinnertime, and my big sister and I liked to watch for Daddy's bus to arrive. The bus stop was a long block from our house, and Mama would tell us when it was about time for Daddy's bus. Then we went outdoors to wait at the edge of our yard by the mailbox where we could see the bus. The minute Daddy stepped off the bus, we ran to meet him. When we went back in the house, Daddy always commented about the yummy smell coming from the kitchen. Mama liked having a nice meal ready when Daddy got home from work. But then one day, something happened at our house. It must have been Sunday, because Daddy was home and he was reading the Sunday comics to my sister and me. I looked forward to those times when we could snuggle up on Daddy's lap and look at the pictures in the newspaper while he read to us. Back then, the comics were called the "funnies." Earlier in the day, Mama said she wasn't feeling well and she went to lie down in the bedroom. I thought Mama was sleeping, but suddenly, I heard her scream for Daddy to come quick, and then, I heard Mama crying. We scooted off Daddy's lap and he rushed to Mama and closed the bedroom door. Mary and I sat waiting quietly for our parents to come out of the bedroom. When I saw Mama, she seemed okay. Then, later that day I saw my Daddy holding the Folgers Coffee can and I heard Mama say, "Don't let the kids see that." I think Daddy made a grave somewhere in the backyard for the little brother we would never meet.

### A Scary Time

I stood at the front window with my face pressed to the glass. It felt cool against my skin as rain pelted the window. It rained steadily for several days and I was begging to go outside, but Mama said I had to stay indoors until the rain stopped. Then my sister asked, "But when will the rain stop?" Mama said she was tired of the rain too, but we need to be patient. Later that day, Daddy came home from work and when he walked in, he shook the rain from his coat and said, "If this rain keeps up, the creek might overflow." After supper, the rain let up and Daddy decided to walk over to the creek. Mama asked Daddy to take us kids with him saying, "Maybe they'll burn off some energy." It was sprinkling when we left the house and we were happy to be outdoors. I skipped along-side Daddy, splashing in puddles along the way. When we got to the creek, people were standing around bundled in raincoats. I noticed a crew of men placing bags around the creek and I asked, "Why are they doing that, Daddy?" He said the sand bags would help keep the water from spilling out. Daddy went over and talked to a few of the men but then it began raining again and we hurried home.

The next morning, I looked out the window and saw that it was still raining and the sky was gray as it could be. Unfortunately, the sand bags the men put around the creek couldn't hold the water and the creek overflowed. Water gushed out and down the street and soon it was coming into our yard. It wasn't long until we couldn't see our yard or the street. Water was everywhere and it was scary. Mama was worried it might get into our house. Daddy was at work and we were by ourselves. Mama stood looking out the front window and was surprised to see a horse-drawn hay wagon approaching. "Well, look at that!" she said. I looked out the window and saw a man sitting on a bench seat on a hay wagon. He was holding onto some straps that were attached to the horse. Mama opened the door and stepped out onto the porch. "Whoa!" I heard the man say, and the horse stopped. Then the man climbed down from the wagon. He waded through the

## Chapter 1

water and came over to our porch. I noticed he was wearing tall rubber boots. The man spoke to Mama and said he could take us to a safe shelter. Mama was scared and said that was a good idea, but was he suggesting we ride on the hay wagon? Apparently so, and Mama asked if she could grab a few things from the house. "Yes, ma'am." He said, and he waited for Mama. When Mama returned, he carried my sister and lifted her onto the hay wagon and told her to stay there. Then he came back and picked me up. I put my arms around the man's neck and held on tight. After that, he picked up Mama, and he carried her too! He lifted her up onto the hay wagon and Mama sat down. She leaned against a bale of hay and cuddled us close. Then the man climbed up and took his seat on the bench and nudged the horse forward. I don't know how he could tell where the street was, but he seemed to know how to guide that horse through the water. He said he would take us to a school shelter that had been set up by the Red Cross.

When we arrived at the school, the nice man helped us down from the hay wagon. I heard Mama thank him for helping us. I will always remember that nice man with the horse and hay wagon. Other families had been rescued and were already in the school gym. When we walked in, I quickly noticed the big Red Cross sign on the wall. During our stay at the school, I got sick with the flu and was taken to the County Hospital. I remember feeling very weak and I heard Mama say I had a high fever. When I was well enough to go home, the nurses at the hospital gave me a new dress and a new pair of shoes. By the time I got home the flood water had drained away from our house, but our basement was filled with water. I remember the noisy pump Daddy used to drain the water out. Mama said we were lucky because the water was within one inch of getting into the house.

## The DoodleBug Train
## Grandma and Grandpa's Farm

It was summertime, and I was very excited. Mama, Mary and I were going on a vacation to visit Grandma and Grandpa Kinsley! Our grandparents lived on a farm in Okeene, Oklahoma. Okeene is best known for the Annual Rattlesnake Hunt. People came from near and far to participate in this event. I'm glad I wasn't in Okeene during the rattlesnake hunt because I don't like snakes! Mama packed our suitcases and when we were ready to go, a taxi took us to the Wichita Train Depot. When we arrived at the depot, there were lots of people coming and going in every direction. I can still hear the hustle-bustle of that noisy place. My sister and I stood next to Mama as she bought our tickets, then we found a place to sit. After a while, it was time to board the train. The friendly conductor helped Mama with our suitcases and the three of us climbed aboard. People called the train "The DoodleBug," perhaps because it didn't go very fast. Mama found our seats and Mary and I giggled as we settled in. Each row had two bench seats facing each other with enough space for four people, and that allowed my sister and I to have window seats. I loved the adventure of riding the train and I liked gazing out the window counting cows and horses, and playing little games. The DoodleBug made a loud screeching sound whenever it stopped to pick up passengers. Then, when it was ready to leave, the engineer pulled a chain to sound the loud whistle and away we went chugging along.

The DoodleBug slowed down as it approached the train depot in Okeene. I looked out the window and stretched my neck, trying to find Grandpa. When I spotted his car, I giggled with excitement and shouted "There's Grandpa, there's Grandpa!" After

## Chapter 1

the train came to a complete stop, we got off and Grandpa was right there to help Mama with our bags. When we climbed into Grandpa's car, Mama gave us instructions to "sit still and behave." Grandpa put our bags in the back of the car and off we went. Our grandpa was a serious kind of man and he didn't say much, but I think he was glad to see us. Grandpa had the bluest blue eyes and he had false teeth, but he didn't wear his teeth very often. I noticed that he munched his mouth together to hide his gums. Years later, I realized that's why he didn't smile a lot. It wasn't long until we arrived at my grandparent's house. I could see Grandma standing in the doorway as we got out of the car. She was smiling and rushed out to hug us and kiss us. She made us feel welcome. She always wore an apron over her pretty flower-print dress. She enjoyed baking special treats for us and she always remembered which ones were our favorites. Grandma's house always smelled like fresh-baked bread. We had no sooner stepped inside, when Grandma handed us a thick slice of her wonderful bread saying "I'll bet you kids are hungry." It was delicious just plain bread, but with Grandma's homemade butter and jam on top of that bread – oh my goodness, it was so yummy! Grandpa fixed homemade ice cream for us using a hand crank machine. Sometimes we got to help Grandpa turn the crank while he added more salt and ice around the metal container. When the ice cream was softly frozen and ready, Grandpa pulled out the beater and handed it to my sister and me – he knew how to put a smile on our faces. Grandpa's homemade ice cream was the best!

My grandparent's house was a typical farm house – cozy and comfy. Whenever we visited them, Grandma made a special bed on the floor for us kids. One year, my California cousins were visiting at the same time – Larry, Bobby, Donny and Wesley. Mary and I slept on the floor with those four rambunctious boy cousins! We had fun whispering back and forth before closing our eyes. I loved my grandparent's house, but one thing seemed weird – it didn't have a toilet. Of course, that wasn't weird at all for a farmhouse in 1941, but I was used to a toilet inside our house in Wichita. I thought it was funny that they had to go outdoors to a tiny shed they called "The Outhouse," and at night, they brought in a large pot and sat it on the floor. My grandparents didn't have a refrigerator either. Instead, they had a wooden ice box, and ice was delivered to their house on a regular basis. This too, seemed silly to me, but was common in rural farming communities. But their house did have a small bathroom – literally, a "bath" room with a bathtub, but the bathtub didn't have a faucet. Bath water had to be heated on the kitchen stove, then carried to the bathtub. But they didn't seem to mind this routine, and Grandma made sure us kids got our baths. My grandma was amazing and she could do almost anything. She had a butter churn and used it to make her own butter. Grandma and Grandpa had a garden at their farm where they planted vegetables. Grandma canned vegetables and fruit, and stored the glass jars underground in their storm cellar.

One day, Grandpa came rushing into the house. "Storm's brewing – might be a twister" he shouted. "We need to get to the storm cellar right away!" I had heard the word "tornado" and wondered if a twister was like a tornado. It looked dark outside, almost like nighttime, and the sky was filled with big scary clouds. Grandma, Mama, Mary and I followed Grandpa to the cellar. The cellar had a wooden door that laid flat on the ground covering the opening. Grandpa grabbed hold of the handle and raised the big door up. The wind was blowing hard and Grandpa held tight onto the door while we hurried down the steps into the cellar. After we were safe inside, Grandpa pulled the door down over the opening and latched it shut. The cellar was dark inside and smelled musty, but Grandma lit the lantern and that made a nice glow. The cellar seemed to be the perfect place for Grandma to store her canned fruits and vegetables. I remember how colorful and pretty the jars looked, all lined up on the shelves Grandpa had built. While we were in the cellar, I saw a furry tarantula crawling on the dirt floor. I was frightened by the huge spider and climbed on Grandma's lap. She said the spider wouldn't bite and it wouldn't hurt me, but I pulled my feet up off the ground anyway. When Grandpa thought the storm was over, he climbed up the steps to release the door hatch. He held onto the inside handle while raising the cellar door slightly to peek out, then he said, "Storm's gone." He opened the door all the way and laid it over onto the ground. I squinted as I looked up to see the bright daylight. We climbed up the steps and went back to the house. I didn't like that cellar but it kept us safe from the storm.

Grandma saved all of her big colorful flour sacks. She could sew better than anyone and the material came in handy to make her aprons and other things. I think she had an apron for every day of the week! The flour sacks were made of pretty material with colorful flowers and designs. Grandma enjoyed making pretty dresses and things for her grandkids. After we got there, she surprised us with new sunsuits. The sunsuits were the most adorable pull-on shorts with a front bib. They had two straps that criss-crossed in the back, and the straps came forward over each shoulder and attached to the buttons on the front bib – so cute! It was a hot afternoon, and Mary and I couldn't wait to try on our new sunsuits. We were excited and ran outside to play. Grandma and Mama followed us outdoors. I remember hearing sounds in the distance that sounded like music. When I asked my Grandma about the noise, she tilted her head to listen then replied in her kind voice "Why, that's the dove mating call. The pretty birds are calling out for a playmate." I loved listening to the doves; they always seemed to be there whenever we visited the farm.

It was fun exploring things at my grandparent's farm. My big sister wanted to check out the chicken coup so I followed her inside. The chickens began flapping their wings and scurried about as we chased them. We both giggled as we tried to catch one of those chickens. Grandma came looking for us and she found us in the chicken coop. She told us that she was going to fetch a chicken for dinner and asked if we wanted to help her. Grandma didn't have any problems catching a chicken. She quickly grabbed hold of that chicken with one hand - she made it look so easy. We followed Grandma outside and watched as she flopped it down onto the chopping stump, and "swoosh" – she cut off that chicken's head! I thought the chicken was dead and didn't understand how it could flutter about without a head, but that's what it did. My sister and I thought that chicken looked silly flopping around and we couldn't stop laughing. But then, Grandma picked up that chicken and held onto its feet as she dunked it up and down in a bucket of water. After that, she showed us how to pull the feathers off the chicken. I didn't like that job, but us kids pulled all the feathers off that chicken.

Visiting Grandma and Grandpa at their farm is one of my fondest childhood memories. My sister and I were having such fun, but all too soon our vacation was over and it was time to go home. "I don't want to go home," I remember saying. "But you'll get to ride the DoodleBug." Grandma said. I did love that train, so I climbed into the back seat of the car with Mama and Mary. Then Grandma and Grandpa drove us to the train depot. After we arrived, we waited inside the depot until it was time to leave. Grandma and Grandpa kissed us goodbye, and I hugged both of them tight. We climbed aboard the DoodleBug, and Mama

## Chapter 1

guided us to our seats. I sat down by the window and looked out at Grandma and Grandpa standing near the train. They waved to us and I waved back. I felt sad to leave, and wanted to get off the train and hug them again. But I sat there and watched as the train slowly left the depot. I kept looking out the window until I could no longer see Grandma and Grandpa. The train chugged through the little town of Okeene, then it picked up speed and all I could see was farm fields. I must have fallen asleep on the train, because Mama was waking me and my sister, saying we were home and needed to get off the train.

After we got home from our vacation, Mary and I got sick with whooping cough. The Sedgwick County Health Department posted a sign on our house that read "Under Quarantine." Mama told us the sign was put there to alert people we were sick, and they should stay away to avoid getting exposed. We were pretty sick kids and we sure did cough a lot. Sometimes, we coughed so hard that our food came up in a mess on the floor. I can still see my Mama rushing to help us, when she slipped on our mess and fell flat on her back. Mama and Daddy were concerned because Mama was pregnant with my baby sister. Luckily, Mama was okay and the baby didn't get hurt either. A few months later, adorable Paula was born. My parents set up a baby bed in the dining room-bedroom where Mary and I slept. I was five and a-half years old at the time and Mary was seven.

It was the first day of school and Mama told me I was a big girl now – going to first grade. She said I could walk to school with my big sister. But I didn't feel like a big girl; I was scared and I wanted Mama to take me to school. Mama said she needed to stay home with baby Paula, and I had to go with Mary, so we walked to St. Patrick's School by ourselves. In those days, it was customary for Catholic students in elementary school to attend Mass before school. The church was located next door to the school and when Mary and I got there, she guided me to the church pew where the first graders were sitting. My sister left me there and went to sit with her classmates. Then the priest walked down the aisle and the thirty-minute church service began. Everyone stood up and I glanced at the other first graders. I didn't know anyone and I was scared. I turned around to look for my sister – I wanted to sit with her, but I couldn't find her. All of a sudden, I felt a warm trickle run down my legs as I wet my pants. I looked down and saw the puddle around my feet. The nun noticed what happened and when church was over, she asked me why I did that. I looked up at the nun then I lowered my eyes in shame and said, "I don't know." I can still remember how icky I felt all day with wet pants. It never happened again!

## A Bigger House

Two years after Paula was born, James arrived, and fourteen months later Michael was born. Michael was a premature baby, barely weighing five pounds. He was a frail skinny kid, but such a lovable cutie with his curly blonde hair. Michael had asthma when he was little and seemed to be sick a lot. He had a speech impediment and stuttered during his early years, but he outgrew all those things and grew up strong enough to join the military after graduating high school. After the boys came along, Mary and I became Mama's helpers. We had to change the baby's diapers, rinse the dirty diapers in the toilet, and I got stuck with the endless task of toilet-training those toddlers. Our bedroom (the dining room) was soon filled with five kids. One day I decided to find another place to sleep, so I grabbed my pillow and took possession of the living room couch and that became my new bed.

# Chapter 1

The little one-bedroom house at 422 was bursting at the seams, no surprise there, and the kitchen table became smaller as we all crowded 'round. My parents knew they could no longer delay getting a bigger house, so Daddy went searching for a house with more space. It didn't take long for him to find a house that was better suited to our needs. My parents bought a 3-bedroom ranch-style house with a finished basement. One of the bedrooms was in the basement, along with a half-bath. The main level of the house had two bedrooms with a full bathroom in-between. The living room was a good size and at one end, there was space for a dining table. The kitchen was bigger than our kitchen at 422 and it even had space for a table. This place also had a detached one-car garage. I didn't understand why my parents bought a house with a garage when they didn't have a car, but it was part of the property, and I heard them mention that it would be good storage space.

It was a nice sunny day when my dad took me to see the new house. The bus stopped at the corner of Douglas and Athenian. Douglas was a main through-street that ran east to west across Wichita. I was excited when we got off the bus and made our way across the busy street to Athenian. I looked up the street, wondering which house was ours. Most of the houses sat way back away from the street with big front yards. I hoped that one of those houses would be our new home. But Daddy stopped at the very first house, the one sitting next to the sidewalk, and not far from the brick building at the corner. The house had a big front porch, and I thought that was nice, but there was no back yard. Our little house at 422 had a big backyard. There was a side yard in front of the garage and I guess my parents thought the kids could play in that area. I liked having a sidewalk and thought it would be fun to roller skate. We didn't go inside the house that day because another family was still living there.

Moving day came and it was hustle-bustle at our little house. It was 1948, and I had lived in the house at 422 since I was born. I don't remember feeling any sad emotions about leaving the little house, and I was excited about having a bedroom with a closet and a door, and I looked forward to making new friends. The moving guy arrived and he loaded our things onto his truck and moved our belongings across town to 111 South Athenian. It was fun exploring the inside of our new house. My parents took the front bedroom, Mary and I shared the back bedroom and Paula, James and Michael occupied the basement bedroom. My little brothers were three and four years old at the time, Paula was seven, Mary was fourteen, and I was twelve. As the boys got older, they became "Jim and Mike." Each of us kids got settled into our new space and it wasn't long until it felt like home. Our new school was St. Joseph's Catholic School, and I was in seventh grade that fall. We always walked to elementary school – rain or shine. But my big sister, Mary, was a freshman in high school that year and St. Mary's High School was too far to walk, so she began taking the bus to school.

## Hard Times

When I was a young girl, I had a vague idea about money and that some families had more than others. I noticed how other kids lived and dressed, and I knew we had less. My dad struggled to make ends meet, and it seemed there was never enough money to go around. My dad did the grocery shopping and he bought two-day-old bread and other groceries marked with a sale tag. He kept tabs on the money and every penny was accounted for. But, of course, that's what he had to do – buy as much food as he could with a limited amount of money; he had a family of seven to feed and care for, plus paying the mortgage and other bills. My dad worked at the Veteran's Hospital in Wichita. He was a nurse, and in those days, a male nurse was called an Orderly. Before my parents met, my mom was a student at St. Francis Nursing School, studying to be a Registered Nurse. At that time, my dad also worked at St. Francis Hospital, and that's where my parents met and fell in love. After my parents were married, my mom got pregnant with my big sister and she quit her nursing job. She became a stay-at-home mom and she took good care of us kids, but I think she became a little overwhelmed after the fifth baby arrived.

Shortly after moving into the house on Athenian, Mama went back to work to help pay expenses. She worked the day shift at St. Francis Hospital, and my dad worked the late shift at the VA Hospital. That allowed them to keep tabs on us five kids, with one parent home most of the time. Since my parents didn't have a car, they used the local bus for grocery shopping and going back and forth to work. One day, however, my dad decided to buy a scooter, thinking it would be an easy mode of transportation on good weather days. But when my dad took the scooter out for a test ride, he accidentally hit a curb and was thrown off. Luckily, my dad wasn't hurt, other than a few scrapes, but he was so frightened by the accident that he never rode that scooter again and he never bought another motor vehicle for the rest of his life; he continued walking or riding the bus. When us kids were old enough, we learned how to use public transportation and that's how we got around town.

After Mama started her job, things suddenly became much different at our house. Going back to work was no doubt a difficult transition for Mama, and it was especially hard for us kids. When I came home from school, my mom wasn't there. Her job took nine hours out of her day and that didn't leave much time for cooking and laundry. Daddy worked during the evening and was no longer home for supper, and we rarely had meals together as a family. Us kids learned how to take care of ourselves and we began fixing our own meals, or snacking, and doing our own laundry. Some might say that was a good experience, and I guess it was, but I wanted my mom back. Our parents were busy and there didn't seem to be enough time to help us with our homework. After working all day, my mom was tired when she got home. We soon got used to our new way of fending for ourselves, and from then on, that's how life was at the house on Athenian.

Being raised Catholic, I attended Catholic schools which were much different from the public school system. During the elementary school years, the first subject of the day was Catechism – teaching the beliefs of the Catholic faith. The Catechism session lasted about one hour. Over the school year, students had to memorize certain sections of the Catechism book, then recite by memory in front of the class. I found Catechism to be quite boring and I was always glad when that class was over. During those elementary school years, attending Mass, followed by Catechism is what I was accustomed to. I was taught by nuns, and most of the nuns were very strict teachers, but excellent teachers. Each nun had a reputation at school and the students knew who was who, and which nuns to look out for. However, I have to say, I am grateful for the wonderful education I received in the Catholic school system.

The day began as an ordinary day but turned out to be a "shame on me" day. I sang in the church choir during seventh and eighth grade at St. Joseph's. I loved to sing and enjoyed being part of the choir. But one day during choir practice, I was taken by surprise when the choir nun slapped me. Her slap jolted me and I swayed into the girl standing next to me. I squeezed my eyes shut

## Chapter 1

as I felt tears start to form. I managed to regain my composure while everyone else stood stiff and stared. Moments before, I had whispered something to the girl in front of me. I shouldn't have done that as it obviously upset the nun. Looking back, I realize I was being disrespectful in doing that, but perhaps the nun could have given me a warning or asked me to leave the practice session. After the incident, the nun didn't say one word to me or anyone else. She simply walked back around to her position in front of the students and motioned with her hands to resume singing. Catholic nuns were known for punishing kids with a slap or hitting fingers with their pointer stick. You're probably wondering, "Did I quit the choir?" No, I did not. In fact, I remained in the church choir through eighth grade. But I will say this: If a lesson was to be learned that day – be assured, I learned it!

It was a chilly day in March, and school was out for the day. As I left the building, I noticed a sign posted on the door and I turned around to read it – "Sign-up for Girls Softball." I would be graduating from eighth grade that May, but thought, "It might be fun to play ball during the spring and summer." I went back inside and headed for the school office to inquire. The secretary handed me the sign-up sheet for the girls' softball team. I noticed that several girls had already signed up to join the team. Without hesitation, I added my name to the list and left with a big grin on my face. The team practiced every day after school, and usually played games on Fridays and weekends. The coach was great in giving each girl the opportunity to play every position. I didn't like playing the outfield position, but when it was my turn, I did it without complaint. I even got to try my hand at pitching but soon realized I needed more practice if I wanted to pitch. My favorite position was first, second or third base, and I got excited with every opportunity to bat. The girls were good sports and I loved playing ball with a team where no one was better than anyone else. It was great fun and a wonderful experience for me.

Keeping up with five sets of growing feet must have been a huge chore for my parents. One day, I heard my dad tell Mom that he was going downtown to visit the second-hand shoe store. I shuddered to think what Daddy might come home with. My shoes were worn out and I wanted a "new" pair of shoes, not someone else' shoes worn on stinky feet. When Daddy came home that day, he was carrying a large bag. The guy at the shoe store had given Daddy a good deal and that bag was filled with shoes. Daddy figured there would surely be a pair to fit each of us. He sat the bag on the floor in the living room and us kids gathered around. I held my breath, hoping there would be something cute for me. I watched Daddy reach into the bag and pull pair after pair out of the bag and line them up on the floor – and no, there was nothing in the bag that I would consider putting on my feet. I was horrified when I saw the shoes my dad handed to me. They looked like men's shoes and were the ugliest pair of shoes I had ever seen. I said I wouldn't wear them and I stormed out of the room. I stayed in my room and pouted most of the afternoon. But later that day, when I looked at my old shoes with holes in the soles, I realized I had no choice. I went back into the living room and the ugly shoes were still sitting on the floor. I hated those shoes but they fit my big feet and I had to wear them. Walking into my classroom the next day, I was self-conscious and felt sure the kids were looking at my ugly shoes. However, I don't remember anyone making fun of me. But I do remember thinking about my babysitting job and vowed to save every dollar. I would buy my own cute shoes!

It was the week before Thanksgiving when a truck pulled up in front of our house. I peeked out the window and saw a guy get out and go around to the back of the truck. I recognized him – he was

## Chapter 1

a boy from my class. He was carrying a large bag of groceries and he was coming to my house! I quickly hid in the hallway hoping the boy wouldn't see me. I was embarrassed and didn't want him to know that my family was one of the poor needy families. My mom was home and she went to the door. She graciously accepted the bag of groceries and invited the boy to come in. Thankfully, the boy said he had other deliveries and couldn't stay. My mom thanked him for the gift and he left. I breathed a sigh of relief but later wondered if he knew I lived there.

Birthdays were never a big deal at my house, and they came and went without much notice. But I do have fond memories of how special my Aunt Eleanor made me feel when I was a little girl and it was my birthday – she always sent me a present! Aunt Eleanor was my dad's sister and she was my Godmother. She was married to Uncle Ed, and they had two kids – a boy and a girl. I didn't get to know my cousins very well because they didn't live in Wichita, however, they did come to visit us occasionally. Aunt Eleanor was a pretty lady with a friendly smile. She wore pretty dresses, and I remember she always wore a hat.

My little sister, Paula, was about to turn eight years old, and I thought it would be fun to have a birthday party for her. I adored my little sister and wanted her to feel special on her birthday. When I asked Paula if she would like to have a party, her eyes lit up and she smiled saying "Oh goodie!" I asked Paula who she would like to invite to her party. She wrote down the names of her friends and I began making plans. We didn't have games at our house so I just made things up, such as "Hide the Rock" and "Pin the Nose on the Snowman." I found a white pillow case and hoped my mom wouldn't miss it because I was going to draw a snowman on it. I used my black marker to draw a jolly face with big eyes and a wide smile, and I made a black circle for the nose.

Then I made several circles down the front of the snowman's belly. Paula's birthday arrived and I could see how excited she was. I was excited too — it was fun! One by one, her friends arrived, carrying presents for Paula. Paula was having a good time with her friends and she was a happy little girl. I was amazed at the fun those kids had with that silly snowman. After playing games, I served the girls cake and milk, and we sang Happy Birthday to Paula. Hearing the little girls' giggle, and seeing the smile on my sister's face, I knew the party was a success.

## My First Real Job

Eighth grade graduation was over and I was excited about starting high school in the fall. I decided to look for a real job. I already had several babysitting jobs in our neighborhood but I wanted a full-time summer job. And, I could still babysit in the evening. The first place I thought about was St. Francis Hospital, so I hopped on the bus and went downtown. When I arrived at the hospital, I was greeted by a lady in the main lobby. I told her I would like to apply for a job and she directed me to the employment office at the end of the hallway. I walked into the office where a friendly lady said hello and asked if she could help me. I said that I wanted to apply for a job. She could see I was young, and asked if I had a Social Security number. I shook my head and said I didn't know what that was. The lady was very nice and explained it to me, then she gave me the address for the Social Security Office. She said they would assign a number to me and issue a card with my personal number. I remember her telling me that I would have that same number for the rest of my life, and no one else would have that number. I didn't understand what all that meant at the time, but it sounded important. The kind lady said I could come back to fill out an application after I had my Social Security card.

## Chapter 1

The Social Security office was located across town. I reached into my purse to check the bus schedule and saw that I would need to change buses in order to get there. I was anxious to have that special card and decided to go to the Social Security Office that very day. When I got there, I was given a form to complete. I wrote my information on the form and when I handed it back, the man said I would receive my card within a week or two. I checked the mail every day and when my card arrived, I was excited. It gave me a feeling of importance, and I remembered the lady telling me that I would have the same Social Security number for the rest of my life. I wasted no time in going back to the employment office at the hospital. The same lady was on duty and she gave me the application form to fill out. The only job reference I had was my babysitting jobs and I wrote those names and addresses on the form. I took the form back to the lady and she quickly looked it over, then she asked me if I would like to work in the diet kitchen. St. Francis Hospital is where I was born, it's the hospital where my mom worked. I was excited and said, "yes, I would love to work in the diet kitchen!" Of course, I would have taken any job just to work there!

It was my first day on the job and I made sure to be on-time. My duties involved washing dishes, wrapping silverware in napkins, filling salt and pepper shakers, cleaning and stacking food trays, and various other things. Later on, I was allowed to deliver meals to the patients. I must say, I became quite good at delivering those meals. I learned how to carry the tray with one hand, perfectly balanced above my shoulder to the side of my head. It was amazing, and I don't think I ever dropped a tray! The diet kitchen housed a large freezer. The first time I opened the freezer, I quickly spotted a special treat. The vanilla ice cream was wrapped in a single-serving size – just perfect. A few times – or more, I quietly opened the freezer door and reached inside for one of those yummy ice cream treats. I don't think the nun in charge minded one little bit that I helped myself to the ice cream.

My job was fun and easy and I loved working in the diet kitchen. When payday rolled around, I looked at my paycheck and beamed with joy. It had my name on it and I couldn't wait to spend it on a new pair of shoes! Everyone was nice to work with at the hospital, and I especially enjoyed delivering food to the patients. One day, I had a little accident while washing dishes. I shouldn't have put my whole hand inside the tall glass and twist with the towel. The glass broke and punctured a vein on the top of my right hand. Blood shot in the air like a fire hose! The nun rushed over and wrapped my hand in a towel. She told me to hold tight and apply pressure, and she sent me downstairs to the Emergency Room. The doctor on duty inserted a large needle into the top of my hand. He waited a bit, then stitched my wound together. The doctor covered my injury with a bandage and I went back upstairs to work – it was no big deal. I still carry a small scar on my right hand and I consider it a nice memory of my first real job.

## The Girl who Loved to Sing

When I was a kid in my early teens I loved to sing. I listened to the radio a lot, trying to mimic the talented singers. When one of my favorite songs was being played on the radio, I listened carefully and quickly jotted the words on a piece of paper. And every time I heard that same song, I jotted down more words until I finally had all the words to the song. Then I sang that song over and over, trying to sound like the singer on the radio. This must have driven my family crazy, but they never complained. Then one day, I was surprised when my mom said "Barbara, you should sing one of your pretty songs on that radio program." She was

# Chapter 1

referring to a live radio program broadcast each week for young hopeful talents. The following week, I tuned-in and listened to the broadcast. There were young kids just like me – some were singing and one played an Accordion. It sounded like a fun thing to do, so I told my mom I would do it. My mom wasted no time in calling the radio station, and she made arrangements for an interview. The following week Mom and I boarded the city bus and we went downtown to the radio station. We took a seat in the lobby and waited to be called. After a few minutes, we were taken to a small room where we met with a friendly man who seemed to be in charge. It was all very casual – there was no microphone, and I just stood in front of the man's desk and sang one of my songs. I assume the interview went well because I was scheduled to sing on the program in two weeks. Meanwhile, my mom excitedly called all the relatives to let them know that "Barbara is going to sing on the radio!"

Two weeks passed quickly and the day arrived. I had memorized all the lyrics to the song and I practiced the melody over and over – I was ready. I got dressed and soon my mom and I were on our way to the radio station. We arrived a few minutes early and were directed to the studio. When we walked into the room, I noticed other kids were already there; some looked much older than me. Then I saw the small platform and the microphone. The room looked totally different from where I had interviewed. We took our seats and all of a sudden, I felt nervous and scared, and wanted to leave. My mom turned her head and smiled as she patted my hand. She could tell that I was nervous. I sat watching as each kid took their turn. And then, I heard the announcer call my name. I walked over and stepped onto the platform like the other kids had done, and I stood in front of the microphone. Everyone was looking at me as I waited for the signal to begin. Then the man gave me a nod. I opened my mouth to sing but my throat felt like it was frozen, and no sound came forth. The announcer was patient but finally said that I could try again next week. I left feeling embarrassed and I'm sure my mom was too – after calling all those relatives.

I had one week to get rid of my stage fright. During that week, my mom offered her support with words of encouragement when she said, "Barbara, just sing like you do at home." As I practiced, I thought about what my mom said and I told myself, "She's right – I'm not afraid to sing at home, so why should I be afraid to sing in front of a silly microphone?" Soon the waiting was over and it was time to head back to the radio station. I put on my best dress and I felt pretty. I was determined to sing my song and I kept thinking about what my mom said, "Just sing like you do at home." When we arrived at the radio station, I still felt a little nervous but I put on a smile and that seemed to help me relax. When it was my turn, I walked over to the platform and once again stood in front of the microphone. As I waited for the signal to start, I gently swayed my body back and forth and that seemed to take away the tension of standing still. My signal came and I started to sing my song. After the first few lyrics, I heard my voice become stronger and I knew I would finish. As I stepped down from the platform, I breathed a sigh of relief. I looked over at my mom and felt a happy smile spread across my face. While I didn't win a prize, I gained a lot of confidence that day and I left the radio station feeling proud.

## My Highschool Years

High school was a happy time in my life. I had finally learned to appreciate and enjoy school. I attended Mount Carmel Academy, an all-girls Catholic Boarding School in Wichita. I was fortunate to attend that school, and it happened just by luck. The first time

## Chapter 1

I visited the campus, I was awed by the beautiful grounds and the small lake where ice skating was allowed during frozen winter months. After my eighth-grade graduation in May, there was a little party for the graduates. My good friend, Charlotte, was at the party and she's the one who told me about Mount Carmel. Charlotte seemed excited when she told me that she had already registered as a day-student. Even though it was a boarding school, Charlotte said you could still live at home. Most of our classmates at St. Joseph's Elementary School would attend St. Mary's High School; that's where my big sister went. But, after hearing Charlotte describe Mount Carmel, I was intrigued and wondered if I could go to a school like that. But then, my friend went on to say it was a private school and you had to pay tuition to attend. She said the teachers were nuns, just like other Catholic schools. Well, I knew my parents couldn't afford to pay for a private school, so I told Charlotte that it probably wouldn't work for me but I would think about it.

A couple days later, Charlotte called to invite me to visit her new school. She said the school was within walking distance and she was going there that afternoon. I told her I'd love to go and we walked over together. The campus was very inviting with old stately buildings, lots of big trees and a pretty little lake. Charlotte showed me around, and after seeing the campus and touring the school building, I wanted that school – but how could I go there? I told Charlotte I would love to attend Mount Carmel, but my parents couldn't afford to pay tuition. But then she said, "There might be a tuition assistance program. You should ask." That sounded encouraging and I said I would go back another day to inquire.

I couldn't stop thinking about that beautiful school. A few days later, I went back to Mount Carmel by myself to meet the administration nun. I asked if they had a tuition assistance program. The nun was very nice and welcoming. She told me they do offer an assistance program for qualifying students, and just by chance, they had one opening left for the fall semester. The nun explained how a student could work at the school in various capacities in lieu of paying tuition. The nun went on to say that they still had a kitchen job available, if I was interested. I told her about my experience working in the diet kitchen at the hospital, and I think that impressed her. Without hesitation, I said I was interested. I wanted to attend high school at Mount Carmel Academy.

When I got home, my dad was there and I told him about Mount Carmel, and that I had met with the administrative nun. I think my dad was impressed when I explained how the nun said I could work at the school and that would take care of the tuition. My dad was further impressed that it was a Catholic girls' school. He was probably thinking, "Humm, a girl's school – no boys, that's a good thing!" I told my mom about the school when she got home from work, and she too was impressed that I had taken that on by myself, and that I had agreed to work for free tuition. My application for tuition assistance was approved! When school started that fall, I began my job working in the school cafeteria. I got to know many of the students by name and I made a lot of new friends. I felt lucky to attend such a fine school and I was proud to wear the navy-blue uniform. Working at school kept me quite busy, but I didn't mind. Later on, I managed to get a few free voice lessons by working an extra shift now and then. I was on the girls' basketball team and I also participated in the theatre program and the annual play. While I was a busy student, I still found time to ice skate on that pretty little lake whenever I could borrow my friend's skates. Fortunately, the school had designated

## Chapter 1

uniforms and that was the dress code, so there were no worries about what to wear – everybody looked the same.

When I was a Sophomore, Charlotte invited me to go on a trip with her to Carroll, Iowa. Her cousin was having a birthday party. Charlotte's aunt had invited her to come and said she could bring a friend. Well, I was pretty excited to be invited. I had never travelled with a friend and the only place I had travelled was to my grandparent's farm in Oklahoma. Charlotte had everything planned. She said it was scheduled for the long holiday weekend and we would take the bus to Carroll. Her aunt would pick us up and we would stay at her house. It sounded wonderful and of course, I said I would love to go. Carroll is a small town with about 10,000 people, and it seemed to be a farming community. Charlotte's aunt was a jolly woman and she laughed a lot. Her house was clean and nice and I felt welcome there. She took us upstairs to a cozy bedroom and said we could put our things there. The following day, we went to the city park for a big birthday party. There were a lot of people celebrating her cousin's birthday. Charlotte's relatives were very nice people, and they made sure that Charlotte and I were comfortable during our stay. I remember how grown up I felt that weekend, travelling with my friend – just the two of us.

## Chapter 2
## A Wonderful Day in May

It was the last week of May 1953, and school was out for the summer. I had completed my junior year at Mount Carmel Academy, and was awaiting news of a possible summer job at Buck's Department Store in downtown Wichita. A few days after applying for a job, the personnel office called to say they had an opening in the handbag department. I was jumping up and down with joy. Yippee – I had my summer job! Buck's Department Store was known to be a classy place with beautiful things, and I was thrilled to work there. It was my first day on the job when I met my co-worker. She was nice and friendly and welcomed me to the store. The first thing she taught me was how to operate the cash register. Then she walked me through the vast display of handbags, describing the different brands and why some bags cost much more than others. I liked my new job right away. It was interesting and fun meeting the customers and helping them select a bag. Some were regular customers that I soon learned to call by name. Most days, I worked from nine to five, with time off for lunch. When payday rolled around, I couldn't resist the temptation to spend every penny on new clothes, and that's what I did.

One Saturday morning towards the end of May, I was hanging around the house with nothing to do when my sister, Mary, invited me to tag along with her and her boyfriend. She said her boyfriend was picking her up shortly and they were headed out for a drive around town. I had already met her boyfriend; his name was Don, and he seemed like a nice guy. I wasn't working that Saturday, and was thrilled at the opportunity to hang out with my big sister. I was sixteen years old at the time, and Mary would be nineteen the following week on June 5$^{th}$. Don was nineteen or twenty years old and he and my sister had been dating for a while. He was Catholic, and that made my dad happy. Daddy had the impression that Catholic's could do no wrong, and so, he always felt we were in good hands if we were in the company of a Catholic. I climbed into the back seat of Don's car and off we went cruising around Wichita. It was about one or one-thirty when we stopped for lunch at a drive-in burger place. Don parked his car in an open food ordering station. Each station had a menu post and ordering device. When the food was ready, a delivery person brought it to the car and hooked a tray onto the driver's open window. Drive-in restaurants were quite popular in those days, especially with the younger crowd.

After placing our order, we chatted back and forth while waiting for the food. Don looked up and noticed a friend of his parked two rows in front of us. "Hey, I know the guy parked over there. I think I'll go over to talk to him." Then he turned around and said to me, "Maybe I could set you up with a blind date this evening, if you're interested." That sounded fun, and I didn't have any plans until Sunday, so I said, "Sure, that sounds fun, but is he a nice guy?" Don said he has known him for a while, and he is a nice guy. My sister and I waited in the car, talking about how fun it would be to double-date. After a while, Don returned and said his friend was available, and he would like to go out with us that evening. The time was arranged, and just like that, I had a blind date. I was curious about my date and while we were eating our lunch, I asked Don about his friend. Don repeated that he's a nice guy, and went on to say he had taken his six-year-old nephew to a movie. "Awe, that sounds like something a nice guy would do." I said, but when Don went on to say, "He's twenty-one-years old" that made me a little nervous. I hadn't dated anyone that old and I felt uneasy about it. I should have asked more questions before agreeing to go. But I didn't want to be a wimp and back out – I had already agreed to go. It was just one evening, and besides, I would be with my sister – so why not?

After lunch, Don took us home and when he dropped us off, he said they were going to take us to a place where we could dance. Mary and I went inside and began making plans for the evening. Dancing sounded like a dress-up place and I asked Mary, "What do you think we should wear?" A nice dress with high heels seemed appropriate to her, so we opened the door to our closet and the two of us stood looking at our clothes. Mary worked at a nice downtown dress shop and she had some lovely dresses. I had just bought a new dress at Buck's, and it still had the price tag on it. We made our selection and took turns taking our baths, then we started fussing with our hair. We both felt pretty and were ready to go when Don picked us up that evening – we were on our way to pick up my blind date.

## An Enchanting Evening

When Dale Rieger climbed into the back seat of Don's car and sat down next to me, I felt a little nervous. After we were introduced, I could tell that he was different from the high school boys I knew. He was certainly much older looking and more sophisticated. Without being too obvious, I tried to study him out of the corner of my eye. I noticed that he wore very nice clothes, he was well-groomed, and he was wearing dress shoes – not tennis shoes. That was impressive! He wasn't a bit shy and our conversation got off to an easy start. I soon found my date to be quite engaging, but I also thought he was a bit cocky.

The guys took us to a place called The Cowboy Inn. It was a nightclub in Wichita, with live music and dancing. I had never been to a nightclub and didn't know what to expect. I knew one thing for sure, my dad would have a fit if he knew where I was, especially with a non-Catholic. After we arrived, we found a nice table waiting for us. The guys were such gentlemen and bought lovely corsages for Mary and me. I breathed in the lovely fragrance as I pinned it to my dress. Mary and I ordered a coke and some snacks; I'm not sure what the guys were drinking. The band was playing a western melody and as the music picked up its beat, Dale offered his hand and we stepped onto the dance floor. I didn't know how to dance and tried to hide my embarrassment by letting Dale guide me around the dance floor. The only dancing experience I'd had was at the high school prom. I'm sure I stepped all over Dale's shoes, but he didn't seem to mind. It was fun dancing with Dale, and after a while, I got into the swing of it. We exchanged partners a few times, and that was fun too. Later that evening, the nightclub photographer stopped at our table and asked if she could take our picture. My sister and I both nodded our heads and said, "Sure, that would be nice."

My blind date turned out to be lots of fun and I was glad I hadn't backed out. My sister and I were having a wonderful time, but the enchanting evening was drawing to a close. We were getting ready to leave when the photographer came by to deliver the photos. The picture turned out great and was presented in a souvenir photo frame. The guys had treated us to a lovely evening and Mary and I both felt special. We got up to leave and both of us had a souvenir photo to take home. As we were driving home, I was quite surprised when Dale asked if I would sing a few songs. Don must have told him that I liked to sing. Could that have been what enticed him to go on the blind date? At first, I was a little apprehensive but said, "Sure, I can do that." It didn't take long to decide on a couple of songs, being sure I knew all the lyrics. Earlier that year, a girlfriend and I performed a little skit to a small audience at Riverside Park in Wichita. My friend's name was Sylvia, and she was one of my best friends. Using a suitcase as our prop, we performed a duet on the open-air stage singing "Sentimental Journey." So, I decided on Sentimental Journey as one of the songs. My sister was probably thinking "Oh, dear me, do I have to hear this again?" But she sat patiently in the front seat with her boyfriend. The other song was a western melody entitled "Your Cheatin' Heart." I began singing and Dale sat quietly, drumming his fingers to the melody as he listened to me sing. I could feel him looking at me. When I finished, Dale said, "Wow, you sing really well!" But what else could he say? And then, all of a sudden, he started talking about a nightclub he was planning to open, and he seemed excited when he said, "You could be the lead singer!" Well, this was way beyond my sixteen years and I said, "Whoa, I don't think so!"

## A Day at Sandy Beach

The morning light peeked through the edge of the window shade. I rubbed my eyes as I crawled out of bed, hoping for a nice day. I held the shade away from the window to look out. The sky was glowing with sunshine and it was a perfect day for fun at Sandy Beach. Since I had the weekend off, I was excited to spend

Sunday at the beach with a few of my high school friends. But first, I had to go to church. We always attended Mass on Sunday morning. Mass was held at various times on Sunday, with one High Mass and a few Low Masses. I decided to attend the early Low Mass, which lasted about thirty minutes. Then I'd be ready when my friends came to pick me up at ten o'clock.

My sister was still sleeping, so I tried to be quiet as I tiptoed out of the room. No one was around; my younger siblings were still asleep. I went to the kitchen and fixed a bowl of cereal. As I sat quietly eating my breakfast, my thoughts drifted back to my blind date and the evening at the nightclub. I hadn't dated very much, and certainly had not gone out with anyone like Dale Rieger, and I had never been to a nightclub. The whole evening seemed like a fantasy or a dream. Dale asked for my phone number before we said goodbye, but I didn't expect to hear from him. I have to admit, I liked my date. But why would he be interested in someone my age? While we were dancing, he asked how old I was and I think he was surprised when I said "sixteen." Then I thought about the souvenir photo secretly hidden in my dresser.

I tip-toed quietly and went back into the bedroom. I stepped into my brand-new one-piece bathing suit I had bought at Buck's. Then I put on my pedal-pusher jeans and a white shirt to cover the bathing suit. I could go to church dressed as I was. My dad always got upset whenever he saw me in a pair of shorts, so I had to cover up and later remove the top layer. He would really freak out seeing me in a bathing suit. One time my dad saw me wearing a cute pair of shorts and he was so upset about it that he became angry and slapped me. He sent me to my room and told me to put some clothes on. After that, I learned what I had to do.

When my friends arrived, the house was alive with noise and I shouted to my mom, "I'm going to Sandy Beach." Then I

## Chapter 2

dashed out excitedly and got in the car with my friends. Sandy Beach was about thirty minutes from my house and when we arrived, there were high school kids everywhere. We were there to celebrate "school's out" and the arrival of summer. It was the end of May, and already hot. I got a little sun-burned that day, but it was great fun. We had burgers at the beach hut, and we splashed around in the water. Most of the kids were good swimmers and I was wishing I knew how. My mom feared Polio, and was afraid to let us kids go near a swimming pool for fear of contracting the crippling disease. But the reservoir water at Sandy Beach was different and my mom didn't seem concerned about that water. By late afternoon, my friends were ready to leave and they dropped me off at my house around five o'clock.

No sooner had I opened the front door when my mom said, "Some guy has been calling you all day!" I asked who it was and she said she didn't know. I headed to the kitchen for a glass of water when the phone rang. "That's probably him again." My mom shouted. I answered the phone and sure enough, it was that guy – it was Dale Rieger. He seemed a little anxious and said, "Where have you been?" I told him that I had spent the day at Sandy Beach with a group of friends. Dale said he would like to see me again, and wanted to know when we could get together. I was surprised by his phone call – and so soon. I told him I was scheduled to work at Buck's Department Store on Monday, but perhaps we could get together after I finished work. Dale liked that idea, and said he would like to take me out to eat Monday evening. I said, "That sounds nice." And just like that – I had accepted a date to go out with the guy I thought was too old for me! That evening, I pulled the souvenir photo out of the dresser drawer and looked at Dale's picture.

## Caught in a Whirlwind

My shift at Buck's was over at five o'clock and I went straight home to freshen up. My mom was home from work and I chatted with her in the living room while I waited for Dale to arrive. I told her that Dale was a good friend of Mary's boyfriend, and that he was taking me out to eat at a sit-down restaurant. I had only eaten at burger joints and my mom could tell that I was excited. She said that was a nice thing for him to do. When Dale's car pulled up in front of our house I was bowled over. It was the most amazing car in a gorgeous burgundy color with a black top. I have to admit, I was a bit overwhelmed. It wasn't just the car – there were chrome air horns mounted on each of the front fenders. They were quite impressive and I wondered if they were put there for a specific reason. Dale came to the door and I invited him in to meet my mom. It was a brief introduction, but he and my mom seemed to hit it off. We said goodbye, then left and walked down the porch steps and over to Dale's car. I'm sure my mom was watching from the window – I wonder what she was thinking? Like a gentleman, Dale opened the car door for me. As I stepped inside, the rich leather scent entered my nostrils and it reminded me of the expensive leather handbags at Buck's. I sat down in the cushy seat and I felt like a fairy princess. I complimented Dale on his beautiful car, but said nothing about the air horns.

Some girls fantasize about meeting their prince charming, falling in love, getting married in a beautiful gown, and living happily ever after – just like in the movies, right? Well, no, not exactly. My mind hadn't traveled in that direction – not yet. But I was suddenly caught up in a whole new world – Dale Rieger's world, and it was exciting! Dale was fun to be with and I found myself fascinated with his way of life. He spoke about his work at

## Chapter 2

the farm, and then he talked about a nightclub he wanted to open. He said he had built a scale model of what it would look like. He remarked about his plans to become a millionaire by the time he reached the age of twenty-five. Dale's life sounded interesting and fast-paced. I wasn't sure what to make of it.

In the ensuing weeks, Dale turned up rather often at my doorstep. Our courtship evolved quickly, and he kept me busy. In fact, between work and dating Dale, there wasn't much time left to do things with my girlfriends. Dale and I were seeing each other several times a week. We had many movie dates, we went out to eat at various restaurants, we listened to country western music, danced to romantic lyrics, and sometimes we just sat in his car and talked. One evening, we went to a drive-in movie theatre and I couldn't believe it when Dale went to sleep during the movie. I had to wake him when the movie was over! Between his farm work and dating me, I guess he was worn out!

One day, Dale told me he received his draft notice from Uncle Sam the prior year, but he had gotten a deferment. The reason for the deferment was because of a bad accident and Dale was still recovering when the draft notice arrived in the mail. Dale said he would most likely receive another draft notice but he didn't know when. And, very adamantly, he said he did not want to be in the military. The draft was common in the 1950's, and I didn't think much about it, but it was obvious that Dale didn't want to be part of it. Dale talked about the accident and said he was driving a truck loaded with a tractor on the bed when he fell asleep at the wheel. He hit a culvert and was thrown from the truck onto the pavement. He said he had several broken bones and he was unconscious. Dale's brother was driving the vehicle ahead of Dale, and he watched the whole thing through his rear-view mirror. Dale was taken to a small-town hospital where he had umpteen stitches to his face to repair cuts and a broken nose. I was amazed at his recovery because there were no telltale scars. Dale said he was lucky to be alive, and lucky to have had an excellent surgeon.

Growing up in the midwest, I was used to the Kansas wind but I never learned to like it, and during the summer months it was a hot wind. People used to say, "The wind makes the wheat grow." One time when I was out with Dale, he told me about the approaching harvest. He said it would be a very busy time for him. I was amazed that Dale had his own farming business. He owned a combine (the big machine to cut the wheat), he owned a two-ton truck and he owned the beautiful car he drove. He talked about taking his harvest equipment on the road to cut wheat for other farmers. That seemed like a huge task, and I was impressed with his abilities. I had never met anyone like Dale, and I was beginning to realize that he had me under his spell. As time went on, I felt more comfortable and our courtship seemed easy and natural. I loved sitting close to Dale, feeling his warmth when he put his arm around me. I remember his first kiss – so gentle and sweet. But when he asked if I would have sex with him, I shook my head and told him "No, I cannot do that." The Catholic religion taught me that having sex would make babies, and sex was only for married people. I was not going to have sex with him, and that was that! Dale was a gentleman. He accepted my response and treated me with tender respect.

It was around the middle of June, and we were only a few weeks into our courtship when Dale came by the house to pick me up. We had plans to go for a drive and I got in the car and scooted over to sit next to him. There were no seatbelts in those days and sitting close to your sweetie in the car is what we did. We were chatting about various things as Dale was driving, then, out of the blue, he said, "I think I'm falling in love with you, and I don't know what to do about it." I was surprised to hear him say that, and I wasn't sure how to respond. I just looked at him as a little smile spread across my face. He pulled over to the side of the road, stopped the car, and we kissed in a warm embrace. My head began to spin and I didn't know what was happening to me. Dale Rieger had swept me off my feet!

## Surprise in the Glove Compartment

When I left the store, I squinted as the late day sun caught my eyes. Then I spotted Dale's car parked at the end of the block. I was excited to see him and hopped in his car with a big smile. He started the car and pulled away from the curb. Right away, he said he wanted to talk to me about something, and he began by saying, "You know I have to leave soon for the wheat cutting job with my brother and crew." I turned my head to look at him and said, "Yes, I remember you talking about cutting wheat in Nebraska." Then, as he held the steering wheel with one hand, he reached over and opened the glove compartment. I could see a small jewelry box sitting inside. Dale pulled the car over to the side of the road and stopped. He reached for the little box and opened it. I was surprised to see a diamond ring and it looked like an engagement ring. I took a big swallow and said "Wow, that's beautiful!" I waited for Dale to speak, but he said nothing. After a few seconds, he closed the lid on the box and tossed it back into the glove compartment. I looked at him quizzically, wondering what he was thinking. Then a thought crossed my mind – perhaps the ring had belonged to someone else and he was going to tell me about it. But then he looked at me and said, "I'd like for you to go with me on this trip." I took another big gulp and replied, "That's a nice thought, but that's also impossible."

When Dale dropped me off at my house later that evening, my mind was filled with questions and wonder. I thought about the ring in his glove compartment and it seemed a little mysterious. Why was he driving around with a ring like that in his car? Was he planning to propose to me but then changed his mind? Why didn't I ask him why he showed it to me – what was his point? And why did he ask me to go with him on the wheat cutting job? I know he said he loves me – is he concerned that I might not be there for him when he gets back? I was confused and realized that I still had some things to learn about Dale Rieger.

Dale called the next day and wanted to get together. He talked more about his trip and once again, tried to entice me to go with him. He picked me up after work and after having a bite to eat, we sat in the car and talked. Lo and behold, he took the ring out of the glove compartment again but this time, he handed it to me. Then he said, "I really do want you to come with me and when you get there, this ring will be yours." I took this as a proposal and assumed it meant we would be getting married. Then Dale went on to explain how I could take a bus to Chappell, Nebraska, saying that would be the best way for me to travel. I looked at the ring I held in my hand and when I looked up at Dale, his eyes were filled with such emotion and I could feel his love. There seemed to be a pulling force drawing me closer to him. I closed the lid on the little box and put it back in the glove compartment. I told Dale I would think about it.

# Chapter 3

# Life Changing Events

Is it possible? Could I do this – should I do this? After mulling over Dale's offer, it made sense for me to take the bus – that is, if I decided to go. For one thing, I could understand how Dale's brother wouldn't allow a sixteen-year-old girl to travel with the crew. This was a business trip and they had been hired to do a job. He would not want me tagging along. I had a lot to think about and consider. My parents must not find out about Dale's offer. For one thing, my dad hadn't met Dale. He had been working the late shift at the hospital from three to eleven o'clock at night, and he hadn't been around all those weeks when Dale picked me up at the house. He had no knowledge of Dale, or even that I had a steady boyfriend. If Dad found out that I had been dating a non-Catholic, he would have a fit – he would forbid me from seeing Dale. It was bound to happen eventually, and then what? He might use his razor strap on me – he could lock me away and forbid me from going anywhere. If I decide to go away with Dale, it would be my secret. But how could I make it all work? Anticipation was building and my heart was pounding. I didn't have it all figured out but I had an intense feeling that if I went to Chappell, I would be with Dale forever.

While Dale hadn't said the word "marriage," he did say the ring would be mine when I got there. That was "sort-of" a proposal, wasn't it? That's when I made my decision – I wanted to be with Dale. I opened the dresser drawer and took out my souvenir photo. I traced the outline of Dale's face with my little finger, then I tucked it back into the drawer.

That night, I lay awake thinking as a gazillion thoughts danced around in my head. I had to create a plan. First of all, I would have to get my clothes packed and out of the house unnoticed. It would be tricky but I had an idea. I would need help doing this and I thought about a friend who might help me. My head was spinning with ideas but I finally dozed off. The next morning, I rushed to be first in the bathtub. After breakfast, I caught the bus and went to work. The store was having a big sale and was bustling with customers. When it was time for my break, I used the phone in the lunchroom to call my friend. I asked her if she could keep a secret. She promptly said, "Of course I can. What's going on?" I told her I was going to take a little trip and needed her help, but said, "You can't tell a soul – not your parents, not my parents, not your friends – no one!" She promised – crossed her heart promise, and I filled her in on the details.

After I got home from work that day, I closed the bedroom door and quietly began sorting through the things I would need to take. I didn't have a lot, but even so, I couldn't take everything. I would pack only my favorite things. I chose a few outfits in the closet and hung them at the end of the rack. Then I selected other essentials like underwear and pajamas and placed those things together in the dresser. There were two small suitcases stored in the cubby hole storage in my bedroom, but I had to stand on a chair to reach the opening. I would watch for my opportunity to retrieve those bags.

## Chapter 3

Time was drawing near. I had been waiting for the right opportunity to sneak my suitcases out of the house. If the next-door neighbor would let me, I could leave them on her porch; they would be out of sight and ready for my friend to pick up. Then, luck was with me – both of my parents were gone. I think my dad was at work, but I didn't know where my mom was or when she might be back. My sister, Mary, was at work. Paula and my little brothers must have gone to their friend's house because it was quiet at my house. I grabbed a kitchen chair and took it into the bedroom. I climbed up and pulled the suitcases out of the cubby hole. I sat them on the floor and closed the cubby hole door. Those old suitcases were the same ones my mom used when Mary and I were little girls visiting our grandparents. Well, they would do just fine. I returned the chair to the kitchen then rushed back to the bedroom and stuffed the suitcases full with the things I set aside. Then I tucked my souvenir photo inside one of the bags and snapped the lids closed.

I hurried over to our neighbor's house, hoping she was at home. Her name was Glenn, and she was a really nice lady. She lived there with her husband, Don. I knocked and Glenn opened the door with a smile. I asked if it would be okay to leave two small suitcases on her porch. I explained that I had to go to work and I didn't want to leave the bags on my porch because my little brothers wouldn't leave them alone. I went on to say that the bags belonged to a friend and she wanted to pick them up. Glenn said she didn't mind at all, then she laughed and said she understood about brothers. I thanked Glenn and told her I would bring them over. I hurried back to my house, grabbed the suitcases and went back to the neighbor's house. On my way, a sudden thought crossed my mind – What if one of my parents came walking up the sidewalk and saw me carrying those suitcases? My heart was beating so fast I thought it might jump out of my skin. But I made it back to Glenn's house and managed to tuck the bags in a corner on her porch. I casually walked back to my house and breathed a sigh of relief – Whew!

It was the day before my departure and I was working at Buck's that day. I was surprised when Dale walked in. He came over to my counter and said he wanted to talk to me. We weren't busy at the time and I asked my coworker if I could take a short break. She nodded and Dale and I went outside for a walk. Dale said he only had a few minutes as they were ready to load the harvest equipment on the trucks. He wanted to make sure I was ready to go. I told Dale that I had arranged for a girlfriend to pick up my suitcases at a neighbor's house. I went on to tell him that the bus was scheduled to leave Wichita at one o'clock in the morning and my friend would meet me at the bus depot with my bags. I sensed that Dale was relieved to hear this. Then he said, "When you get to Chappell, find a motel and check-in as Mrs. Dale Rieger. Chappell is a very small town, and I will find you." I couldn't believe my ears – check in as Mrs. Dale Rieger! I felt a slow rising smile spread to a broad grin and said, "Okay. I'll do that." Dale and I walked back to the store holding hands. Then Dale pulled out his wallet and handed me some travel money. We hugged each other and kissed goodbye.

Departure day: I worked all day at the store and was scheduled to work the following day, but I wouldn't be there. I left the store at five o'clock and went directly to the bus stop. The bus arrived on schedule and I got home at the usual time. When I walked in, my little brothers were tearing through the house, making enough noise to break an eardrum. This was normal, and as usual, Michael was screaming at the top of his lungs while James chased him. I was starving and went straight to the kitchen to fix a sandwich.

## Chapter 3

I had been thinking about what Dale said – "Check in as Mrs. Dale Rieger." I envisioned myself as Dale's wife, wearing the ring he promised to give me, and I wondered what his family was like. Dale lived at home with his parents, and he had his own private space in the upper level of the farm house. I hadn't met his parents or his brothers and sister. Well, that didn't matter. I would meet his family someday. The only thing I truly cared about and felt sure of – I would be with Dale. I finished my sandwich and went back into the living room. Ironically, just as I glanced out the front window, I saw my friend pull up in front of the neighbor's house. She was true to her word. I had wondered if my bags were still sitting on the neighbor's porch. I watched as she and her boyfriend loaded my suitcases into the car. When they pulled away from the curb, I was relieved and felt lucky to have such a nice friend. I don't think my young siblings noticed anything peculiar during all this – but of course, at their age, they didn't pay much attention to their big sisters. My brothers were seven and eight years old, and little sister, Paula, was ten. But, sharing a bedroom with my older sister was a different matter – she must have noticed the extra space in the closet – she must have suspected something, but she never said a word.

## No Goodbyes

It was around seven o'clock in the evening when I stepped out of the bedroom and went into the living room carrying my little overnight bag and my purse. My mom happened to be working the late shift that day, which was unusual. My little brothers were on the couch being boys, teasing and pushing each other with their bare feet. I don't know where my little sister was – probably downstairs reading in her quiet space. My dad was sitting in his chair reading the newspaper. Very casually, I said "Hi. I'm going to spend the night with a girlfriend, so I'll see you tomorrow." My dad seemed absorbed in his reading and he didn't look up, he didn't look my way, he just nodded his head and said, "Okay" and continued reading the paper. That would be the last word my dad would say to me for a very long time. About then, Mary came into the living room and said she would walk me to the bus stop. I was glad my dad hadn't asked who I was spending the night with. I opened the front door, walked out and never looked back. I was focused on being with Dale, and nothing else seemed to matter. I had no second thoughts about leaving, no thoughts about how my parents might feel when I didn't return home the following day. Those things never entered my sixteen-year-old mind.

My family had become somewhat dysfunctional. It was obvious my parents didn't like each other anymore. They had stopped talking to one another, and both of my parents seemed frustrated and unhappy. I remember the day when I realized that my dad no longer shared a bed with my mom. He was sleeping in the basement with my little brothers. My dad became quite grumpy and he took his frustration out on us kids. Going without sex probably caused his frustration, but it served him right. He didn't believe in birth control and would have kept making babies. But my mom was done – she didn't want any more kids! My dad was a strong Catholic, and he seemed to become even more devoted to the Catholic faith after Mom kicked him out of their bedroom. My mom had long since lost interest in the Catholic church and she stopped attending Mass. My dad used to say, "A family that prays together, stays together." Perhaps that's why he woke us kids up when he got home from work at eleven o'clock at night and made us say the Rosary with him. This happened after we moved to the bigger house. Kneeling down next to the bed, half asleep, whining, crying, we said those Hail Mary's with our dad. My

## Chapter 3

mother must have put a stop to it because after a few times, my dad stopped waking us to pray.

The evening air was warm when Mary walked with me to the corner bus stop. The sun had not yet set and was casting long shadows across the walkway. Mary and I shared casual conversation while waiting for the bus and I tried to act normal. I asked Mary why she broke up with her boyfriend and she said, "He tried to get fresh with me." The bus pulled up and came to a stop. I said goodbye to my sister, and boarded the bus. I found myself wondering why Mary didn't ask any questions – she surely knew that something was going on. Many years later, she told me she had a feeling that she would never see me again. When I arrived at the bus depot in downtown Wichita, I went straight to the ticket counter to buy my ticket for Chappell. All of a sudden it dawned on me – what if they are sold out? I hadn't thought about that possibility, but luckily, tickets were available. I paid the agent and he handed me a ticket. He said the bus wouldn't be leaving Wichita until one o'clock a.m. – indicating I had a long wait.

The waiting area in the bus depot was lined with wooden benches, similar to church pews. I looked around for a place to sit and spotted a vacant seat at the end of a row. I walked over to sit down and made myself comfortable. Then I reached into my purse for the friendship ring. It was a simple silver band and would pass for a wedding band. I slipped the ring on my left hand. Friendship rings were quite popular in those days when girlfriends exchanged rings with each other. About that time, I noticed my friend walk in with my suitcases. I waved to her and she came over with my bags. She was wonderful to help me out like that. I don't think I tipped her – what was I thinking? I know – friends do things for friends and never expect anything in return. I thanked her and gave her a hug. She wished me good luck and then she left with her boyfriend.

    I sat down and stared at the large clock on the wall. It would be several hours before my bus left Wichita. The bus depot was a busy place and I was surprised to find so many people there in the evening. I was curious about where everyone was going. After a while, I grew tired of watching people and wished I had a magazine to look at. The time passed slowly and I kept glancing at the clock. I wanted to get on the bus before something went wrong. The twilight sky had grown dark and most of the people had left the depot. I started to feel a little anxious. But then, finally, after waiting over four hours, I heard the announcer call out, "All aboard for Chappell, Nebraska." I looked at the clock again. The time was 12:58 a.m. I stood up, gathered my bags, slid my purse over my wrist and walked toward the Exit sign.

# Chapter 4

# Chappell & Julesburg

A feeling of calm swept over me as I watched the driver load my bags. I took a deep breath and boarded the bus. I glanced around for a seat and saw that many were already taken. But then I spotted an empty aisle seat and sat down next to an older man. He seemed old to me, but looking back, he was probably about forty-five. The bus driver took his seat and closed the door. Soon the bus merged onto the highway and I was on my way to Chappell. The man sitting next to me started a conversation by asking where I was headed. I casually replied that I was going to meet my husband in Nebraska – how easily I let those words slip off my lips – "my husband." Then I went on to say, "He's cutting wheat for some farmers in that area." I told him I preferred taking the bus, rather than riding in the truck with the combine crew. The man spoke to me as if I was an adult, and I remember feeling like an adult. But I didn't want him to ask more questions, so I laid my head back and closed my eyes. I soon started to relax and it wasn't long until I fell asleep.

The bus travelled all night and part of the next day, with many stops along the way. Early that morning, the bus pulled into a small town and stopped to let some passengers off, including the man sitting next to me. After he got off the bus, I scooted over to the window seat. The driver said he would be leaving in twenty minutes, and anyone needing a break could go inside for the restrooms. I placed my scarf on the seat to save it, and went into the bus depot. I was feeling hungry, and luckily, there was a snack bar inside. I bought some food and a bottle of soda to take on the bus. Soon the bus driver was ready to leave and we were on the highway again. I was glad to have the window seat and enjoyed looking at the countryside.

I was wide awake, excited, and full of anticipation. The bus ride to Chappell, Nebraska seemed to take a long time, and I was anxious to get there. We travelled several more hours and I glanced down at my watch and realized it was mid-afternoon. We should be there soon. Sure enough, it wasn't long until I heard the driver say, "Next stop, Chappell, Nebraska." The bus slowed to a stop and the driver opened the door. A few other people were standing in the aisle waiting to get off. I followed behind and stepped down from the bus. I looked for my bags then saw the driver set them on the pavement. The driver got back on the bus, and drove away from the curb. I glanced up and down the street, but there were no motels in sight. I suddenly felt very alone and wondered where to go, and how I would get there?

I turned around and squinted to shield my eyes from the late afternoon sun. I saw a small gray building behind me and I noticed someone had just gone inside. I assumed it's where people bought bus tickets and I decided to go inside to inquire about a motel and possible ride. About that time a nice couple walked up to me and asked if I needed a ride. They must have noticed the worried look on my face. I had no idea where they came from – perhaps they were the first passengers off the bus. I was very grateful and relieved to be offered a ride and said, "Oh, thank you so much!"

## Chapter 4

Then I asked if they knew of any nearby motels. I told them that my husband was travelling with a combine crew and that he would be arriving the following day. They were so kind and said they would be happy to take me to a motel. I followed them to their car, which was parked on the other side of the building. They loaded my bags, along with theirs, and drove me to a motel a few blocks away. I noticed the vacancy sign as we pulled up. I thanked them, and said I would be forever grateful. As I think back, it was rather miraculous that this couple was there and offered to help me. They were my angels!

After checking in as "Mrs. Dale Rieger," the clerk gave me a key and directed me to my room. The motel clerk didn't ask for any identification. Apparently, that wasn't unusual in those days, especially at a small-town motel, but I had not stayed in a motel or a hotel and didn't know what to expect. The motel was a simple brick building, with about twelve rooms on one level. I picked up my bags and as I walked to my room, I noticed a cute little diner on the other side of the highway. "That will be a good place for breakfast in the morning." I thought to myself. As it turned out, that little diner became my favorite place in Chappell. I unlocked the door to my room and went inside. I sat my bags on the floor and looked around. The room seemed to be clean and tidy. I noticed two glasses on the dresser and realized I was thirsty. It had been a long journey and I suddenly felt very tired. I couldn't wait to change my clothes and take a bath. I opened my suitcases and found my pajamas. After my bath, I opened the curtain and looked out. The sun was setting and it seemed too early to go to bed, but I was exhausted. I closed the curtain and crawled into the bed. I was soon fast asleep.

Suddenly, I was awakened by a loud noise. I jolted up in bed and realized that someone was pounding on my door. I got out of bed and went to the door. It was the motel clerk. I must have been in a deep sleep and didn't hear the initial knock. The clerk spoke in a rushed voice and said, "Ma'am, I've been trying to rouse you – someone is on the phone for you, and he said it's important. The phone is in the lobby." It was dark outside and I didn't know what time it was but, in my pajamas, I sleepily followed the man to the lobby. The phone was laying on the counter and when I picked it up and said "Hello," I was relieved to hear Dale's voice. He had found me! Dale said he was still on the road with the crew and they would arrive the next day. I asked him where he was but didn't recognize the town. Before we finished talking, Dale said, "And one more thing, when I get there tomorrow, I have something to ask you." I knew what that "something" was – Dale was going to (officially) propose to me! As I walked back to my room, a warm sense of comfort swept over me.

Dale arrived the following day with his brother and crew. They went directly to the harvest field in Chappell. After the equipment was unloaded and organized, Dale came to the motel carrying his clothes bag – and he had something else. "This is for you." He said as he handed me the ring. Dale stood looking at me with smiling eyes and said "Let's get married – that is, if you want to." My heart was doing flip flops and I could feel a smile spread across my face. I didn't have to think twice or ponder my answer. "Okay!! Yes – I want to marry you!" I said, and I slid the ring onto my finger. It fit perfectly! I stretched my hand out to admire it, then I looked back at Dale and felt his warm lips on mine. At that moment, I couldn't have been happier.

It would be one of the shortest engagements; we wanted to get married right away. Dale asked if I would like a Justice of the Peace or a Christian minister to marry us. I said I preferred a Christian minister; Dale was okay either way and began checking

## Chapter 4

into the details of getting married. He quickly discovered the minimum age to be married in Nebraska was twenty-one. That was not a problem for Dale, because he was twenty-one, but I was sixteen. I thought I looked a little older when I was dressed up, but it might be a stretch to pass for twenty-one. The area where Dale was cutting wheat was near the Nebraska-Colorado state line and we were told that in Colorado, the minimum age was eighteen. I was certain I could pass for eighteen. The following day, Dale skipped out of the harvest field and we drove to Julesburg, Colorado, which was about thirty minutes away. We went directly to the courthouse to apply for a marriage license. The clerk asked my age and I was relieved when she didn't ask for identification, however I did have my Social Security card. The clerk proceeded to issue the paperwork, then told us we would need blood tests. She directed us where to go and said it would take three days for the test results. That was disappointing and I didn't understand why they needed blood tests, but we went to the lab and had our blood drawn. I started to worry and hoped that nothing would go wrong – my parents might have sent the police looking for me. I told myself to be patient, trying to calm my nerves.

During our drive back to Chappell, Dale commented that we need to go shopping for wedding bands. Well now, that sounded fun and I wondered if Chappell had a jewelry story. Dale dropped me off at the motel and went back to the harvest field. He came back around lunch time and we drove into town. There it was – the one and only jewelry store in Chappell. Dale parked the car and we went inside. It was a cute little place, and we were greeted by a friendly sales clerk. After our hello's, we told the clerk that we needed two wedding bands. We browsed the glass case and I think we spotted them at the same time – two matching gold bands. The store clerk reached into the glass case and set the tray of rings on the counter for us to look at and try on. Both rings were a good fit, and the ladies wedding band was a nice compliment to my beautiful engagement ring. Dale paid the clerk for the rings and we left the store happy and smiling. Then Dale took me back to the motel but before leaving for the harvest field, he told me that he was going to tell his brother what was going on.

When Melvin heard what Dale had to say, he wasn't happy about the situation and he did not offer his congratulations. He wasn't prepared for this news. What was Dale thinking – had he lost his mind? They were in Chappell to work the harvest; they hadn't come for a wedding! He didn't want anything jeopardizing the wheat cutting job. Melvin was the oldest sibling, eight years older than Dale, and married with one child. He was quite upset and proceeded to call their parents in Wichita. He told them, "Dale's got a girl out here and he says he's going to marry her! Just thought I should let you know." When Dale came back to the motel that evening, he told me that his brother had called their parents. He said he wouldn't be surprised if his folks showed up in Chappell.

While I will never know all the details of what transpired after I left Wichita, I learned much later how my parents found out that I had gone missing. When I didn't show up for work that next day, my co-worker at Buck's Department Store called my house to see if I was sick. My mom was home and took the call. She said she didn't know because I had spent the night with a girlfriend and she assumed I had gone to work from there. The lady proceeded to tell my mom that my boyfriend had come by the store to see me the day before. Mom had met Dale, and she had seen him come by many times to pick me up, so she knew who my boyfriend was. However, my dad hadn't met Dale. He was working the three to eleven o'clock shift during those weeks of our courtship, and he

## Chapter 4

wasn't at home when Dale came to the house. I don't know what happened after that phone call or how much time lapsed before my folks realized they didn't know where I was.

My parents knew most of my girlfriends, but they didn't have their phone numbers. I'm guessing they soon came to realize that I hadn't spent the night with any of my girlfriends. Perhaps this is when they called the police. It may have been a few days before the pieces to the puzzle started coming together. Somehow, they found out that Dale had left Wichita with his combine equipment and that he was cutting wheat in Nebraska. They may have discovered this by getting in touch with Don, my sister's past boyfriend. Later on, I learned that Dale's parents and my parents got connected, and that Dale's parents went to my house to meet my parents. As the story goes, when Mary and John Rieger went to my parent's house, my little brothers answered the door and when they saw John dressed in full western attire with his cowboy boots, cowboy hat and western belt, eight-year-old James said, "Wow, a real cowboy!" That may have broken the ice a little bit. When John told this story much later, he laughed and laughed; he got such a kick out of my little brothers.

### Our Wedding Day

The three-day waiting period was over and our marriage license was ready. It was July 9, 1953 – our wedding day! I woke up happy as a lark that morning. I had already decided what to wear and had set it aside. I slipped into my prettiest and best outfit. It was a two-piece suit in a light speckled-gray fabric. It had a straight pencil skirt and cute jacket fitted at the waist. It fit my figure perfectly and I couldn't resist buying it at Buck's – little did I know it would become my wedding dress. Dale must have planned ahead because he brought dress-up clothes with him on the trip. He was dressed in a nice outfit and looked very handsome. Dale had already told his brother he was getting married that morning and he would be a little late getting to the field. I stepped into my high heels and we were on our way to Julesburg.

The morning air was fresh and there was a light breeze as we left for Julesburg. It was an easy drive and we went straight to the courthouse to pick up our marriage license. When we applied for the license, Dale asked the clerk if she could recommend a Christian minister. Luckily, the clerk knew one who lived nearby and she gave us his name and address. After leaving the courthouse that day, we went directly to the minister's house, hoping to find him at home. He was at home, as well as his wife. They were both older and I wondered if perhaps he was a retired minister. We introduced ourselves and told him that he had been recommended by the clerk at the courthouse. "Ah yes," he said. "I think I know who that is." We told him that we planned to get married in a few days and asked if he would be available to marry us. The minister was very cordial and said he would be delighted to perform our wedding ceremony. He scheduled an appointment for us and said he could marry us in his home.

The minister and his wife were waiting for us. They were so kind and welcomed us with warm smiles. When I stepped inside, I could smell the sweet aroma of fresh baked cookies. The minister made arrangements with the next-door neighbor to be our witness. They were the cutest couple, and appeared even older than the minister! Both couples seemed to have longevity in their married life. Dale handed the minister our marriage license and he directed us to stand in front of him. The minister began reading the wedding message from his prayer book as Dale and I stood side by side. Then he asked us to face each other. We turned towards one another and held hands as we said our vows, making

## Chapter 4

our solemn forever promise to each other . . . "In sickness and in health, till death do us part." We exchanged rings, and then the minister said, "I now pronounce you man and wife." He smiled as he said to Dale, "You may now kiss your bride."

Our wedding ceremony was as simple as it could be and we were as happy as we could be. I had no fantasies about getting married in a beautiful flowing gown and walking down the aisle of a grand cathedral. But I had just married my prince charming and I was the happiest girl alive! The marriage license was signed and Dale proceeded to pay the minister, while the minister's wife rushed to the kitchen. I could smell fresh coffee brewing as she returned with a tray of homemade cookies. They looked delicious and she was so gracious to invite us to stay. Dale said he was sorry we couldn't stay, that he was expected in the harvest field. The minister's wife said she understood but insisted on sending some cookies with us. We thanked them for inviting us into their home and for marrying us, and we thanked the couple that bore witness to our marriage. We left feeling very grateful for these lovely people. On the ride back to Chappell, I told Dale how proud I was to be his wife – to be Mrs. Dale Rieger. Dale said he was proud too. I sensed that he was feeling a bit rushed, knowing he was late getting to the harvest field. His brother might send the posse after him – just kidding! We went back to the motel and Dale changed into his work clothes. He gave me a kiss, and off he went to harvest more wheat. I slipped out of my high heels and changed my clothes, then I walked over to the little diner and ordered a BLT sandwich and a cup of coffee.

The sky had a soft glow of twilight when Dale arrived back at the motel. I noticed the colorful sky when Dale opened the door and I commented how pretty it was. We greeted each other with a kiss, then Dale asked if I had eaten. I nodded yes, and told him

I walked over to the diner. Dale said he had dinner (called supper back then) in the field with the crew, which seemed to be common practice. Dale had stopped at the liquor store to buy a bottle of sloe gin. He took it out of the bag and said, "It's time to celebrate!" Then he reached for the water glasses and poured a little gin in each glass. Then we made a "happy forever" toast. I took a sip but didn't like the taste. I wasn't accustomed to alcohol and I set my glass aside. It was our wedding night and I was nervous, but I trusted Dale. Those of you reading this probably won't believe that we did not have sex before this night.

## Meeting the Parents

After leaving the diner, I waited for an opening to safely cross the (not very busy) highway and went back to the motel. It was a nice sunny day and that made the farmers and the harvest crew very happy; their mutual goal was to harvest the wheat before the weather changed. I had no sooner stepped inside when I heard a knock at the door. Who in the world could that be? Dale wouldn't knock; he had a key and would come right in. I opened the door and there stood Mary and John Rieger, Dale's parents, and they were not smiling! His mother looked as though she had been crying because her eyes were red and swollen. I greeted them by saying, "Hello, I'm Barbara," and invited them to come in. I hadn't considered the possibility of meeting Dale's parents under these circumstances, but oh my gosh – there they were! They were obviously concerned about their son and what he might be getting himself into. They didn't know me and didn't even know that Dale had a steady girlfriend. However, I remember Dale telling me a few weeks ago that he told his mom he had met someone special.

Dale's mother started the conversation rather defensively by saying, "Dale isn't rich, if you think he has money. He drives a

## Chapter 4

nice car and all that but in fact, he owes us $2,500." I made a gesture with my hands and calmly said, "Well, the two of us will pay it back together." She said they had gone to my house to meet my parents and said they also met my little brothers. Dale's dad didn't say much; he just seemed to be more observative of me as he pondered the overall situation. I do think he appreciated my response about paying the debt together; I noticed his expression when I said it. But I could feel Dale's mother's angst, and I knew she didn't like me. I realized the concern they felt – that's why they drove to Nebraska. They didn't stay very long – thank goodness! After they left, I mulled over the meeting and hoped they felt better, having met me, and I hoped they would like me once they got to know me. I have to say, I was proud of myself, proud of my bravery – meeting Dale's parents like that, under those circumstances! And I was also thinking, "How could you do this to me – leave me there to meet your parents by myself?"

The following day, there was another knock on the door. "Could that possibly be Dale's parents coming back for another visit?" I was actually relieved to see the motel clerk standing at the door. "You have a long-distance phone call, Ma'am. There's a lady on the phone – said she wants to talk to you." I followed the clerk to the office. When I picked up the phone and heard the quiver in my mother's voice, I could tell that she was sad. "Why didn't you tell me?" my mother asked, and I softly replied, "I'm so sorry, Mom, but I just couldn't." The owner of the motel was standing close by, leaning against the counter. She was hanging on my every word, and she kept looking at me out of the corner of her eye. I wished she would go away and mind her own business. I wanted to talk more openly with my mother, but the phone was attached to the counter and I couldn't move away. My mother wanted to know when I was coming back to Wichita. She didn't yell at me, she didn't say any cross words to me, but I could feel the hurt and concern in her voice.

I began to wonder why my parents didn't pursue having our marriage annulled. I had heard about marriage annulments and I worried that might happen to us, me being a minor and all. But nothing happened; they made no effort to have it annulled. Later on, I learned that my dad had sought advice from the parish priest, asking what he should do. Apparently, the priest asked my dad if his daughter and boyfriend had been together for three days or more. He went on to tell my dad, "If they have, she is probably pregnant and you don't want that on your hands." Surprisingly, so the story goes, the priest advised my dad to leave it alone, so my parents decided to do nothing. I also heard later through the grapevine, that everyone (relatives, friends) all said, "This marriage will never last."

## Visiting the Harvest Field – The Woman from India

The aroma of freshly cut wheat filled the air in the small farming community. It was another sunny day in Chappell, and that morning, Dale asked if I would like to visit the harvest field. I had never been in a harvest field and was thrilled at the opportunity. Dale told me about their current job at a nearby farm, and said the owner had a visitor from India. He said they were celebrating their guest and she would most likely be in the field. Dale said the lady had travelled all the way from India to be there in time for harvest. When we arrived at the field it seemed like a busy place. The farm owners were there with the lady from India, and Dale's brother was there with the harvest crew. The lady from India seemed quite intrigued with the combine. Dale told me that she was familiar with grain farmers in India, and how they farmed wheat, maize and rice, and she was curious about the farming process in America. I was pleased to be introduced to this woman, and found her to be very friendly. She smiled and teased me about me being a new bride.

The lady was dressed in colorful Indian attire with a shawl draped over one shoulder. I noticed that she wore a red dot between her eyebrows. At the time, I didn't know what this meant, but later on, I learned the red dot is called a Bindi, and is worn by married Indian women as a commitment to long-life and the well-being of their husbands. I watched this woman climb up onto the combine, dressed as she was, and proceed to take a seat behind the wheel. She didn't seem a bit intimidated by the huge machine, and she held a big smile as she rode along. I was fascinated by this woman and wanted to know more about her culture. I watched and observed as the combine cut the wheat and dispensed the wheat kernels into the big truck. It was a very interesting day, and I was especially excited about meeting the lady from India.

# Chapter 5
# The New Bride Returns to Wichita

The wheat cutting job in Chappell had been accomplished and the harvest crew was ready to head back to Wichita. The farm owners were pleased with the hard work of the crew, and happy their wheat had been harvested before any weather disasters. But now, it was time to leave this sweet little town. I thought about all the things that happened during the two weeks we were there, and I found myself feeling a little sad about leaving. Chappell was beginning to feel like my new home, but of course, we couldn't stay in that motel forever, and Dale had work to do at the farm in Wichita. I found myself wondering if perhaps we might go back to visit Chappell and Julesburg someday in the future. I have to admit, I was not looking forward to going back to Wichita, or the prospect of facing Dale's parents, and my parents too, for that matter. Apparently, Dale had talked to his parents on the phone and it was decided that we would stay with them at the farm house in Wichita, until we found a place of our own. I was nervous about staying with his parents. After meeting them in such a strange way, I knew they didn't like me, and I didn't think I would be welcome there. But maybe Dale had told them a little bit about me on the phone, and perhaps after they got to know me, they would change their mind.

Riding in the big truck with my husband was a new adventure. The combine was loaded on Dale's truck, and the other equipment was being prepared for the journey back to Wichita. Dale told me they were considered a "wide load" with the 14-foot combine header tied securely to the top of the truck cab; the other part of the combine was loaded and secured on the truck bed. Seeing all this was rather daunting, and I tried to imagine how Dale got that big thing up there. When it was time to leave, I climbed up into that big truck and scooted over to the middle so I could sit close to Dale. I didn't have to buckle up because there were no seatbelts. I looked all around and felt excited to sit so high above the ground. Dale climbed in and turned the key in the ignition. Soon we were on our way, with the crew and other equipment following behind. Riding in the truck proved to be a bumpy experience. The seat moved up and down most of the time and I didn't realize that it was rubbing the skin off my skinny backbone. I ended up with a nasty sore, but it healed without any problems. It was a long slow journey and after many hours of travel, we finally arrived at the farm in Wichita.

The day was hot and windy – so typical that time of year. I was feeling anxious as I climbed down from the truck. I looked around and noticed several large outbuildings. "This is a big place." I remarked to Dale. Then I glanced at the farm house. It was a large two-story house painted white, with dark green trim around the windows. There were large trees surrounding the house, and I noticed a small detached garage near the house. Dale's dad, John, was standing in the doorway at the back of the house. He held the screen door open and welcomed us inside. Dale's mom was in the kitchen, and she had prepared food for us. I was surprised to see a

## Chapter 5

smile on her face as she had been so sad and upset when I met her. I wasn't sure what to expect, but she said, "Make yourself at home" and that made me feel better. I was quite impressed with this old farm house. It was lovely, and I noticed how clean and tidy it was. I would soon learn that this was normal at Mary Rieger's house; she would be a tough act to follow! The house had 4 bedrooms, one bathroom, a living room with a brick fireplace, a large dining room with built-in storage benches below the windows, and the kitchen had an adjacent breakfast room. There was also an unfinished basement. Dale opened the door leading upstairs to his bedroom. I climbed up the stairs and Dale followed with our bags. The room was quite spacious and open, and I noticed the floor was painted gray. I stood there looking around and admired the beautiful knotty-pine wood bar situated at one end of the room. Dale told me that he built the bar. I was amazed that he could do things like that. And then, there was Dale's bed – our temporary bed. I often wondered if Dale's parents could hear the bed squeak when we made love.

The next day, I used the phone at the farm house to call my mom. We had a nice conversation and she didn't seem to be mad at me. I told her about my experience riding in Dale's truck with the combine loaded on it. She was glad to know that I was back in Wichita, and said she wanted to see me whenever we could come over. After talking to my mom, I felt much better and I knew that everything would be alright. A few days after our return to Wichita, Dale mentioned that he wanted to buy a used trailer house for us to live in. In today's world, it's called a mobile home but back then, we called it a trailer house. He had talked to his dad about it and John said we could park it at the farm and hook onto their power. That sounded fine to me and I was anxious to have our own space. The search for a trailer house didn't take long and Dale made arrangements for delivery to the farm. The trailer was actually kind of cute; everything inside was small scale and built-in. The front room had a built-in sofa and chair. There was a tiny kitchen with a small stove, a little refrigerator and a small round table. It had an itsy-bitsy bathroom and a bedroom located at the back of the trailer. The bedroom had a full-size bed, a small chest, and there was barely enough space to walk sideways around the bed. I thought it would be fun living in a trailer house, at least for the time being. Dale was used to living on the farm and since that's where he worked, the trailer house seemed to make perfect sense. Thankfully, they parked it a good distance from the farm house. After the power and plumbing was connected, we moved in. I was very happy to have our own private space.

It was time to set up housekeeping and this new bride and groom were starting from scratch. We had no cooking utensils, no dishes, no bedding, nothing to set up housekeeping in this cute tiny place. Dale's mother offered to go with us for our first grocery shopping experience. She was a well-experienced homemaker and knew exactly what we would need. We grabbed a shopping cart and walked through the grocery store, aisle by aisle. Dale's mom made sure we had all the necessary basic staples to stock our kitchen. In addition to food, we bought an egg beater, a spatula, a can opener, various other utensils and some grocery store silverware. Our cart was full when we checked-out.

I knew very little about cooking, and I was eager to learn. I could fix scrambled eggs and toast, prepare hot Cream of Wheat, and I could open cans to heat on the stove, but my expertise was fixing butter-sugar bread to dunk in coffee – oh my, it was so good! After unloading the bags of food and staples, I placed the items neatly in the little kitchen. The next morning, I decided to fix eggs for Dale's first breakfast in our little trailer house. I retrieved

## Chapter 5

a pan from the cabinet and placed it on the stove. Dale's mom had donated a couple of pots and pans from her cookware collection. I was nervous, but I think the eggs turned out okay. Dale ate them but he was probably thinking, "It's not Mom's cooking, but she'll learn." In the early days, I opened a lot of canned foods but I soon realized that if I was going to learn how to cook, I would need a cookbook. It wasn't long until I had my very own Betty Crocker Cookbook.

After being around Dale's parents for a while, I started to relax. But I didn't know how to address Dale's mother – Mrs. Rieger sounded so formal. So, one day I asked her what she preferred to be called "Mary – Mrs. Rieger?" She waited a few seconds, then said, "Oh, just call me mom, like everyone else does." I thought it was nice of her to offer that to me, but it didn't sound natural and I didn't feel comfortable calling her mom, so for quite a while, I didn't address her by any name. It wasn't long until I met the rest of Dale's family. No doubt they were anxious to meet the girl Dale had married. Of course, I had already met Melvin, then later met his wife, Pauline, and their son Monty. Then I met Bud and his wife Imogene, and then Zelma and her husband, Hiram. Dale's siblings brought wedding gifts and they were very nice to me. I soon started to feel that I was part of the Rieger family.

One day, I was very surprised when Dale's mother invited my mom to come for lunch at the farm. This made me so very happy, and my mom was pleased to be invited. I think it sort-of broke the ice all the way around. It was comforting, seeing these two women together, getting to know each other. My mom was warm and loving toward Dale and me, and it was obvious she didn't want any hard feelings. I showed the house trailer to my mom and she thought it was very cute. Dale's mom prepared a lovely lunch, and we sat around the table in the breakfast nook enjoying each other's company. My mother brought us a wedding gift that day, and such a thoughtful gift. She knew that we didn't have an iron and that's what she gave us. My heart filled with joy, knowing that my mother wanted to give us a wedding gift. I knew she had forgiven me.

Not long after settling into the cozy little trailer house, I had a surprise visitor. I was home by myself when I heard a rap at the door. "Who could that be?" I wondered. The door to the trailer house opened to the outside and it swung open wide when I opened it. I was shocked to see one of the priests from St. Joseph's Catholic Church. He wasted no time and came up the step and into the trailer, without being invited in. He was aggressive and began his visit by questioning me. He wanted to know if I had been praying and saying the Rosary. I was embarrassed by his visit and felt intimidated. It seemed as though he was lecturing me and I wasn't sure how to respond, so I remained silent. Then he kneeled down and asked me to join him in prayer. I didn't kneel, and I didn't respond to him – I said nothing. After a bit, he appeared to be frustrated, shrugged his shoulders and left. His visit was upsetting, and I was certain my dad had put him up to it.

Lo and behold, the following week a different priest came to visit. I peeked out through the edge of the curtain and considered not answering the door. But I was prepared this time – I knew I had to put a stop to these visits. As I opened the door, the voice in my ear was telling me, "He's a priest – don't be disrespectful." So, very calmly and quietly, I simply said, "I'm really sorry, but I don't want you or any other priests visiting me in the future. I'm doing fine and I don't need your help or advice." I was relieved when he nodded his head and left without saying a word. He would no doubt tell my dad what I said, but so be it. My dad had withdrawn from me completely, and I came to realize that he was more upset

## Chapter 5

about my getting married outside the Catholic faith than leaving home as I did. Various times when Dale and I went to the house on Athenian to visit my family, my dad ignored us and went to the back bedroom and closed the door. He remained there until we left. It would be two years before my dad softened and began talking to us.

I was anxious to introduce Dale to my aunts, uncles and cousins. So, one day, I took Dale to meet Aunt Hermina and Uncle Russell (Hendricks). Hermina was my mother's sister, and a special aunt. She wanted to meet my husband and actually invited us to come to their home in west Wichita. They were so warm and welcoming to Dale, and made him feel like he was part of the family. Hermina and Russell had two adorable little girls. Donna was about three-years-old at the time, and Becky was a baby. We had a very nice visit with them and when we left, I felt encouraged and happy. Beulah and Ed (Kinsley) lived in Wichita, and they had three daughters (Dorothy, Betty and Elaine). Charlotte and George (Kinsley) also lived in Wichita, and they had three daughters (Maxine, Virginia and Janet). Frances and Gene (Kinsley), lived in California, and they had four boys (Larry, Donny, Bobby and Wesley). Ed, George and Gene were my mother's brothers. My mother had another sister and her name was Pauline. I didn't have a chance to meet her because she died during childbirth. When I was a little girl visiting my grandparents in Okeene, I saw a picture of a lady with a baby, both lying in a casket. They looked as though they were sleeping. I didn't understand and I asked my grandma who they were. Grandma told me the story about Pauline and the baby and how sad it was to lose them. She said Pauline was my mother's sister, and that made her my aunt. Harvey was Pauline's husband but I never met him. On my dad's side of the family, my dad had two sisters (Eleanor and Eva) and one brother (Julien). My Grandma Winter died before I was born. I rarely saw Grandpa Winter, and I barely knew him. I was ten-years-old when he died. As time went on, Dale got to meet and know my entire family.

After returning to Wichita, I had very little communication with my high school friends and I lost contact with them for a while. The summer had been a whirlwind – an exciting whirlwind, but so much had happened. School was starting that fall but I would not be part of the Senior class at Mount Carmel Academy. Marrying Dale had changed my life – things were different and I didn't feel that I was a part of that group anymore. Dale asked me about completing my senior year, but I didn't feel comfortable about it. I told Dale that I wouldn't fit in at Mount Carmel, as a married woman, and I wasn't sure that I would be accepted as a student, having married outside the Catholic faith. I didn't want to think about it. I will finish school later. So that was that – I was content and happy as things were.

## Uncle Sam Knocking on the Door

It was mid-August, 1953, when the notice from Uncle Sam arrived in the mail. Dale was being drafted into the United States Army and he was ordered to report for Basic Training at Fort Leonard Wood, Missouri on September 15th. He was being inducted for a period of two years, followed by several years in the Army Reserve. We knew this could happen, but when the draft papers arrived, we were not prepared for the overwhelming reality. Dale didn't want to be in the Army, and I didn't want him to go. I wasn't allowed to go with him and that left me feeling scared and concerned.

When we were dating, Dale told me he received his draft notice the prior year. However, when the notice arrived, Dale was

## Chapter 5

in the hospital. He had been seriously injured in a truck accident. Due to his injuries and the healing time frame, the US Army gave him a deferment. By the time we met, one-year later, Dale was completely healed of his injuries and his health had been restored. Dale was hopeful that he wouldn't have to go, since he was now a married man. After receiving the notice, he immediately contacted the Army to let them know. But when he spoke with the Army official, he was informed that it made no difference – married or not – the Army was drafting both. However, the official did say, "But if your wife is pregnant within the next month, we won't draft you." The Army had just enforced a new rule, whereby if the wife was pregnant, the husband would not be drafted, at least for the time being. Dale hung up the phone somewhat disappointed but hopeful that we would get pregnant within the next few weeks. But that didn't happen – it wasn't meant to be.

September 15th arrived all too soon. I swung my legs over the side of the bed and sat watching Dale. He was awake before me and I heard him shuffling about as he put his things in the duffle bag. I took a deep breath, let out a sigh and got up. This was a sad day for us. It seemed as though the joy had been sucked out of our lives. I fixed a quick breakfast then it was time to leave. Dale's parents drove us to the Bus Depot – the same place I sat waiting to leave for Chappell, Nebraska, just two short months ago. So much had happened since then, and it felt as though I had been with Dale a very long time. Dale's ticket was ready and waiting for him to pick up at the counter. His bus was parked nearby and I could hear the engine running as we walked toward it. I needed to be strong, but I felt down and helpless and thought I might cry. We hugged each other tight and kissed goodbye, then Dale boarded the bus. He took a window seat and sat looking at us. I will never forget the forlorn look on Dale's face. "Be brave – don't cry." I told myself. But when the bus pulled away from the curb, I could no longer hold back the tears. There was nothing I could do. I stood watching as I waved goodbye to my husband. Dale was gone and we would not see each other for six weeks.

Before Dale left, he talked to his folks about the house trailer and what should be done with it during his absence. Dale thought it was best to sell it, and his parents agreed; otherwise, it would sit idle and deteriorate. Dale would be in the Army two years and who knew what our needs would be after that. It was also decided that I would stay in the farm house with his parents until Dale finished Basic Training. And – another surprising thing, Dale traded his beautiful luxurious car for his dad's two-door 1951 Mercury. Cars weren't important to me at the time, and besides, I hadn't yet learned to drive. Army pay was quite modest for a new soldier, and Dale wouldn't have any income from his farming business; that was all put on hold. But I would be looking for a job and that would help.

## Life's Little Challenges

It felt strange, moving back into the farm house without Dale. For one thing, Dale's nephew, his sister's boy, was staying there too. But I gathered my things together, filled those two old suitcases and carried them over to the farm house and back upstairs to Dale's room. The first thing on my agenda was finding a job. I enjoyed working but knew that transportation could be challenging because the farm was located outside city limits. There was no bus service in the rural area, and the bus stop was way beyond walking distance. But Dale's dad, John Rieger, stepped up to the plate and didn't see this as a problem. He was a wonderful, thoughtful, kind man, and so good to me. He said he would be happy to drive me to the bus stop and pick

## Chapter 5

me up later when the bus brought me back. He made sure his son's wife was taken care of.

My first day looking for work, John took me to the bus stop and dropped me off. I rode the bus to downtown Wichita and spent the day walking, looking for work. One place I didn't dare apply was Buck's Department Store. I had burned my bridges at that place! I stopped along the way at various dress shops (now called boutiques), a drugstore, and any place that looked inviting. A few of the dress shops offered me an application to complete and leave with them – which I did. Then I began walking the side streets, and I got lucky. I went into Walker's Department Store, and learned that they had a job opening in the office. A lady had just quit and they needed someone to operate the payment processing machine. I had no office experience whatsoever, but the personnel lady said they would teach me. She said they needed someone immediately and asked if I could start the next day. She said the machine is easy to operate, and she was sure I could learn how to use it in one day. The pay was $136 per month - now remember, this was 1953. Actually, I was surprised that they hired me for that job without experience, and I was so very excited – I had landed my first office job! I couldn't wait to tell Dale.

I yawned, stretched my arms and climbed out of bed. I was excited to start my new job. I rushed downstairs to wash my face and noticed that Dale's mom had prepared a hot breakfast for me. I thought that was really nice and thanked her. She said it was no trouble because she was fixing it anyway. I dressed in one of the nice outfits I had bought at Buck's a few months ago, pulled on my nylon stockings and slipped into my high heels. I glanced in the mirror, giving myself approval, and went back downstairs. After breakfast, Dale's dad drove me to the bus stop and dropped me off. I had not ridden this particular route to downtown Wichita, and noticed different things along the way. When I got to Walker's, I went straight to the store office where I was introduced to the other employees. They were nice people and gave me a warm welcome. Then I was shown my work station. I stood looking at the intimidating machine and took a big gulp. Another employee, who would be my teacher, smiled and said, "Relax. It's much easier than it looks." I took a seat and she began showing me how to process the incoming checks and other paperwork. After a few hours of training, I started to get the hang of it and soon felt right at home. I remember thinking, "I like this job, and the lady was right – this is easy." Occasionally, my mom came to hang out with me on my lunch break and other times after work, I would be surprised to find her waiting for me at the bus stop. She stayed with me until my bus arrived. My mom wanted to be my friend; it was very special. But at the time, my head was filled with other things and I failed to recognize and appreciate it for what it was – until many years later.

That fall, Dale turned twenty-two and I was seventeen. Basic Training in the U.S. Army kept Pvt. Dale busy from dawn to dusk. The Army worked those guys endlessly with military training and physical fitness workouts. During that period of time, Dale and I were able to talk on the phone occasionally, but mostly we wrote letters to each other. One day, I slipped out the front door hoping to find a letter from Dale in the mailbox. There was nothing in the box but as I was heading back to the house, Dale's mother met me in the driveway and started a conversation. She began talking about Dale, when he was a little boy in first grade and he had a crush on a girl in his class. She went on to say how cute it was when Dale said the little girl had really pretty skin. At first, I didn't know where she was going with that conversation but then it dawned on me. My hormones

## Chapter 5

had kicked in causing a few pimples to appear on my face. I felt embarrassed and hated those pimples. My skin has always been nice and clear. I tried using Noxzema, but it didn't seem to help. I don't think Mary meant to hurt my feelings; it was just her way of telling me to do something about it before Dale came home from Basic Training. That evening, she gave me a towel and said it was just for me and she preferred that I use that towel. It took a while for the two of us to get to know each other, but eventually Mary and I did become friends.

Adjusting to my new way of life was sometimes difficult and stressful. In looking back, I realize it must have been a difficult time for Dale's parents too, having me in their home – someone they barely knew. In addition to that, his parents took care of their six-year-old grandson – Dale's nephew. That kid was a little brat and he wasted no time in letting me know that he didn't want me around. One day I was outside walking on the driveway when suddenly – WHACK! I felt a sharp sting across the back of my legs. I looked around and there was Dale's nephew lurking in the bushes, holding a piece of cut-off garden hose. He had intentionally hit me. I stood rubbing my legs and said, "Why did you do that?" He took off running. A couple of days later, I was going to the mailbox and it happened again – WHACK! This time he swung the hose even harder and it caused red welts on the back of my legs. I was stunned and upset. There he was, hiding in the bushes again. I turned around and said, "Listen, you little snot, if you ever do that to me again, I'm going to call your Uncle Dale and tell him what you did. You'll be in big trouble!" Later on, I learned a few things about this kid. His biological sailor father skipped out before he was born. His mother wasn't around very much, and she left him for his grandparents to raise. Dale was probably the only father figure he had ever known. Then, when

Dale left town shortly after I showed up, he most likely blamed me. And now I was living at his grandparent's house in his Uncle's bedroom. Obviously, this six-year-old kid was confused, resentful and angry. He missed his Uncle Dale, and he took it out on me.

    I loved getting Dale's letters and enjoyed curling up by myself to read them in private. A few times though, at the end of his letter he wrote a note saying "Let my folks read this too, because I don't have time to write to them right now." Honestly, I hated sharing my letters with his parents, but I always did whenever he asked. I realize that was selfish of me because sometimes Dale wrote about the things he was required to do in Basic Training. He wanted his parents to know, but he didn't want to write it twice. Dale didn't like being in the Army, and it was reflected in his letters. He too, was lonely, and I could tell from his letters that he hated being at Fort Leonard Wood. I used to worry that Dale might go AWOL (absent without leave), and then he would be Court Marshalled and put in military jail.

    Time seemed to drag by slowly and it felt like an eternity since I had been with Dale. But then, some good news – the soldiers in Basic Training were allowed to see their wives during one weekend. When Dale's brother, Bud, heard about it, he and his wife Imo, offered to drive me to Fort Leonard Wood to visit my husband. They said it would be a fun weekend. I was surprised and excited about their offer, and could hardly wait. At the same time, I was nervous – nervous about Dale seeing me with pimples on my face. My skin was smooth and clear when Dale left. What would he think when he saw me? Would he still love me?

    The morning air was crisp when the three of us left for Fort Leonard Wood, Missouri. I had my little overnight bag and made myself comfortable in the back seat. It took several hours to get there but I enjoyed visiting with Bud and Imogene. My excitement was building – I would soon be with my husband! It was Saturday afternoon when we arrived at the Army base. Bud told the gate soldier that we were there to visit Pvt. Dale Rieger, and that he was expecting us. The gate soldier checked his log, then authorized us to pass through the gate. I looked around and immediately spotted Dale waiting for us inside the gate. Bud parked the car and I got out. My heart fluttered as Dale walked toward me, and I remember thinking he looked different. The Army had cut off his hair, and he had a very short crew cut. But I must say, he looked quite handsome in his Army uniform. We rushed to each other and our bodies molded together in a tight embrace. Then I felt the warmth of his lips on mine. It was wonderful to be in Dale's arms and I wanted him to hold me like that forever. Dale greeted Bud and Imo, and the four of us got in Bud's car and we left the base in search of a nice place to eat. I don't recall what Bud and Imo did after that, but Dale and I had a beautiful, romantic night together. Dale said nothing about the pimples; it was as if he didn't notice.

After Dale finished Basic Training, he was allowed to leave the Army Base and travel out of state. That meant he could come home to Wichita on some weekends. Dale had expected to receive his transfer orders immediately after Basic Training, but the Army decided to keep him at Fort Leonard Wood for additional training. Once he completed the training, he would become part of the U. S. Army Corps of Engineers. This meant I would not be allowed to be with Dale as long as he was at Fort Leonard Wood. I was extremely disappointed. And the Army gave no timeline as to how long they would keep him there. I worried that Dale might be sent overseas, and I knew that I wouldn't get to go with him. Only officers were allowed that privilege. There was so much uncertainty about the future. Not knowing how long it would be until I could join Dale, his mother felt it would be best if I found an apartment close to a bus route. It made total sense – after all, his parents needed their privacy back and John shouldn't be burdened with the task of taking me to the bus stop every time I needed to go somewhere.

Winter seemed to arrive early and I buttoned up my jacket as I waited for the bus to arrive. It was the middle of November and I was feeling somewhat anxious that morning. Thinking about finding a place to live was a little scary. I didn't know where to start. One thing I knew for sure, I couldn't go back to my parent's house, nor did I want to. I had lost contact with my high school friends and I found myself feeling very lonely; I suddenly felt alone in the world. My bus arrived and came to a stop. A big gust of wind whipped around my skirt and I reached down to grab it as I climbed aboard. I took a seat next to a window, and tried to sort things out in my mind. While gazing out the window, I started thinking about my job. Then something popped into my head. I remember seeing a bulletin board in the lunchroom. Perhaps I would find some rentals posted there. I would check it out on my lunch break. Then I had another thought - I could look in the newspaper too. There was always a newspaper lying around in the lunchroom. We were nearing my stop and I pulled the stop-cord above the window to alert the driver. The bus came to a stop and I got off feeling somewhat encouraged – I had a plan.

I walked across the street to Walker's and the attendant released the door latch to let me in. My work day started one hour before the store opened. I rushed upstairs to the office, took off my jacket and hung it on the rack. I greeted the lady next to me, then sat down and began processing the paperwork stacked at my station. The morning flew by and soon it was time for lunch. I grabbed my bag and headed for the lunch room. Once inside, I went directly to the bulletin board. Just as I started looking it

## Chapter 5

over, one of the ladies in my department stopped to chat. It felt comforting having someone to talk to and I told her about my situation. Coincidentally, the lady said she and her husband live in a basement apartment and they had an extra bedroom. She said they had thought about renting it out, and asked if I might be interested in something like that. She went on to describe their apartment and said I could use their kitchen and share the bathroom. She also said that their apartment is close to a bus stop and within walking distance to a grocery store. She was nice and friendly, and I felt comfortable talking to her. I nodded my head enthusiastically and said, "It sounds like it could be workable." So, she called her husband to check with him and ask about the rental amount. Then she asked if I would like to go home with her after work to look at it. That seemed like a good idea and I thanked her and said I would love to.

When we arrived at the apartment, she introduced me to her husband and showed me around. The place was quite modest and I immediately noticed that it had no windows, except for tiny windows situated close to the ceiling. The extra bedroom had one tiny window, also close to the ceiling. I didn't like not being able to look out; however, the little window would allow light to come in. The bedroom was clean and tidy and had linens on a regular-size bed. There was a dresser with plenty of drawers to hold my things, plus the room had a closet and a small chair. The couple seemed like nice people, and I already knew the lady from work. The rent was very reasonable, and no doubt less than an apartment. I said I would take it and asked when I could move in. This was my lucky day!

Earlier in the day, I had called Dale's parents to let them know I would be on the late bus. John was waiting for me when I got off the bus that evening. I got in the car and told him I had found a place to live and planned to move my things that weekend. When we got to the farm house, Mary said she had kept my supper warm in the oven. That was really nice of her and I told her that I appreciated it very much. And then I told Mary the exciting news that I had found a place to live. I shared the details with her and she seemed glad that I knew the people I would be living with. After finishing my supper, I washed my dishes then went upstairs and began getting my things together.

I placed my suitcases on the bed in Dale's bedroom and packed them full. Those two old suitcases and my little train case were ready to go again but wouldn't be travelling very far this time. My new friend and her husband were so kind in offering to pick me up at the farm on Saturday morning. On the way to their apartment, they said they needed to stop at the grocery store for a few things. That worked out perfectly and gave me a chance to get a few things to put in their refrigerator. While I was there, I bought a new jar of Noxzema. My new friends helped me carry things into the apartment and I got settled in. This would be my home until Dale got his orders.

Thanksgiving Day arrived, and Christmas soon followed. The best part was Dale coming home for both holidays. I stayed at the farm house during those times when he came home. His mother prepared fabulous meals for each occasion, truly a feast! It was Christmas Eve morning when Dale's mother came to me and asked if I would play Santa that evening while the family was there for a gift exchange. She showed me the well-used Santa suit and said they stuff it with a pillow. I looked it over and remember thinking the head piece would destroy my hair, but I agreed to do it. She told me the six-year-old boys still believe in Santa. That evening, I got dressed in the funny looking Santa suit and stuffed the pillow inside the pants. A red Santa bag was waiting for me on

## Chapter 5

the front porch. I stomped up the stairs and pounded my feet on the porch, then I reached down to pick up the bag of toys. I shook the brass bell and pounded on the door with my fist, still stomping my feet. I tried making my voice sound deep and gruff as I sang, "Ho, Ho, Ho, Merry Christmas!" Dale's mom opened the door wide. The Rieger family filled the room. Dale's two brothers, their wives, his sister and her husband, his two nephews and Dale's parents were all gathered in the living room. I marched in the front door making a loud ruckus, shaking the bell and chanting "Ho, Ho, Ho" in my deepest voice. The grown-ups were laughing so hard, and I could tell they enjoyed the show I put on. Dale's two nephews looked up at me with startled expressions and their eyes grew big as dollars. I was laughing too, but since the mask covered my face, they couldn't see the merry twinkle in my eyes. I think I made a pretty good Santa.

The basement apartment was cozy and warm during the winter and I had grown accustomed to my new housing arrangement. The couple I lived with were genuine, good-hearted people, and I knew that I had made a good decision to move into their spare bedroom. They were wonderful to me. I think they were both in their thirties, and they seemed to treat me like a little sister. I confided in the lady that I was trying to clear up the pimples on my face and she knew that I was self-conscious about it. One evening, she told me about a treatment and offered to help. She wrote down what I needed to buy, and the next day I slipped out to the drug store during my lunch break. That evening, she applied the treatment to my face and we let it set until it was completely dry. It looked like, and felt like, a thin layer of pink plastic. After a while, the solution was dry and she peeled it off. Then she applied something else. The next day, my skin had a reddish tinge and this lasted a few days. Then a miracle happened! My pimples dried up and went away. There was no trace left behind and my skin was smooth and clear. I am forever grateful to this lady and her wonderful kindness.

The seasons went from summer through fall and it was now the middle of winter. The office manager at Walker's hung a new calendar – a reminder of time passing and still no transfer orders from the Army. It was the middle of January, 1954 – four months since Dale left for the Army. I was beginning to wonder if he would ever get his transfer orders. How long could it possibly take to prepare a soldier for the Corps of Engineers? I was a lonely bride missing her husband. My job at Walker's kept me busy during the weekdays, but the evenings and weekends were long. I didn't want to intrude on my landlord's privacy so I spent a great deal of the evening hours in my room. Most of the ladies at Walker's were considerably older than me and besides, they already had their circle of friends. I had nothing in common with my old high school pals. I needed a best friend; I began to feel discouraged.

Had I known that something wonderful was about to happen, I wouldn't have felt so lonely and sad. That weekend, Dale bummed a ride with an Army buddy and came home to Wichita with big news. He had received his orders! I was at the farm house, anxiously waiting for him to arrive. Dale wanted to surprise me and he walked in wearing a big smile. He looked at me and said, "How would you like to go to Washington, D.C.?" I could hardly believe my ears! Washington, D.C. – that sounded important! Of course, I would have gone anywhere to be with Dale. I jumped up, hugged him and said "Oh my gosh, I can't believe it – this is the best news!" He said he would be stationed at Fort Belvoir, Virginia, and the good news was – he would be allowed to live outside the Army base; we could have our own apartment! He went on to say that he had to live within certain miles from the

## Chapter 5

Army base, and because of that, we would live in Arlington or Alexandria, Virginia. Washington, D.C. was about thirty minutes away and too far from the base. Dale said this would all happen in mid-February – just a few short weeks away. This was the news I had been waiting for.

On Monday, I shared the news with my boss at Walker's Department Store. I wanted to give plenty of notice and perhaps have time to train the new employee. When Dale's brother, Bud, heard the news he wanted to help. Bud always loved road trips and said he wouldn't mind driving across the country. He told us that he and his wife, Imo, would take me to Virginia. He offered to drive our gray Mercury, then leave it there for us, and they would fly back to Wichita. What a wonderful, thoughtful idea! We were so appreciative that Bud and Imo would do this for us. At the time, I didn't know how to drive and therefore, couldn't drive our car to Virginia. This was such a great plan because Dale would need a car going back and forth to the Army base.

Anticipation of living on the east coast grew stronger with each new day. I tried to envision what it might be like. Washington, D. C. – our nation's Capitol, so magnificent! I thought about living in our very own apartment and I looked forward to making new friends with other Army couples. When I told my mom that we were going to move away to the east coast, she was sad but happy for me at the same time. She came downtown to see me as often as she could. We talked about my plans and that Dale's brother would drive me to Virginia. I think my excitement made the time pass more quickly because it wasn't long until I was packing our things in preparation for the trip to Virginia. On my last day of work at Walker's, my co-workers surprised me with a little goodbye party. It had been less than six months since I started working there and I was surprised they would do that for me. They showered me with well wishes, and gave me a going-away gift. It was a lovely turquoise jewelry box. I still have that little jewelry box, all these many years later. I bid them farewell and told them how much I loved my job, but especially how I loved working with them. As I left work that day, my heart was filled with pride and joy.

A few days before leaving Wichita, I moved my things out of the basement apartment and went back to the farm house to finalize packing. Then I rode the bus to my parent's house to say my goodbyes to Mom and my siblings. I told my mom she could come visit us. I said we would take her to Washington, D. C. to visit the Capitol and see all the sights. "I just might do that," she said. Then I hugged my mom goodbye and told her I would call when I got there. I noticed the sad look on her face when I left. I rode the bus back to North Broadway and John picked me up at the bus stop. This was the last time he had to do that, albeit he never seemed to mind. I finished packing the few things we had stored at the farm house – our red chenille bedspread, pillows, the yellow-green chartreuse tablecloth, our small supply of kitchen utensils, and our personal items. Then I put those two old suitcases on the bed and neatly packed my clothes inside. My little train case was filled to the brim and I was ready to go.

## Chapter 6

## Army Life in Virginia

The gas tank was full and everything Dale and I owned was loaded in that gray Mercury. I said goodbye to Dale's parents, and thanked them for putting up with me. I climbed in the car and made myself comfortable in the empty side of the back seat. Bud was chipper as usual and said he looked forward to the trip. He and Imo got in the car and we were on our way. We left early that morning and travelled for two days over many miles; each mile brought me closer to Dale. Bud loved to drive and still seemed energized when we got there, but Imogene was tired after the long journey. I was too excited to be tired. When we arrived at Fort Belvoir, we stopped at the gatehouse where the soldier granted us entry. Dale had given Bud instructions where to go once inside the Army base. We found each other and I was finally with my husband.

One of Dale's cousins lived nearby in Alexandria, Virginia. Dale hadn't seen his cousin in quite some time but when he learned that he was being stationed at Fort Belvoir, he called Richard to let him know. Richard was married to Joan, and they had one-year-old, Debbie. They were thrilled to get Dale's call and so happy to know that family would be moving to the area. Dale told Richard that he had gotten married seven months ago and that his wife would be joining him. Richard congratulated Dale on his recent marriage and said he looked forward to meeting me. Richard was a little older than Dale, but I think he and Bud were the same age. The evening we arrived, Bud and Imo, Richard and Joan, and Dale and I went out to enjoy a nice dinner together. I was thrilled to meet my new cousins and loved them right away. They were warm and welcoming and we connected so easily. During dinner, Richard said he had made plans to show us around and help us get acquainted with the area on Sunday afternoon. How great was that!

    The February air was pleasant and gave the promise of spring. It was Sunday morning with little traffic when we took Bud and Imo to the airport in D.C. We arrived in plenty of time to enjoy breakfast before their flight. I believe this may have been their first commercial airline flight as they seemed very excited about flying back to Wichita. I told them how much I appreciated their help in getting me moved to Virginia. Bud just laughed his great laugh and said "It was no trouble at all, and besides – I like driving." There were no airport restrictions back in the day, and non-ticketed people could accompany a passenger all the way to the plane. We shared hugs and wished Bud and Imo a safe flight. They climbed up the metal steps and into the waiting aircraft. We stood on the tarmac waving as the airplane sped down the runway and sailed up into the sky. Then we walked to our car and drove back to Alexandria to meet with Richard.

    We would have been lost without Richard's help. He drove us all around various areas in Alexandria and Arlington. Then he mentioned a place that he thought might be a good temporary rental. Since we had no furniture, we needed a furnished place and we needed it right away. He took us to a stately older house

## Chapter 6

in Alexandria. Richard parked across the street so we could look it over. It was a charming two-story brick house. I remember the lovely vines growing up the side, clinging to the brick. Richard had noticed an ad in the newspaper about this house. He had called the owner to ask if he could bring his cousin to look at the home. He told the owner we had just moved there from Kansas. The owner was offering to rent part of the house - mainly a large upstairs bedroom, plus use of the kitchen and use of the main living room. We were eager to find a place quickly and were excited to see the inside.

Richard knocked on the door and the owner seemed to be expecting him when she opened the door. Richard made the introduction and the owner invited inside. The owner's name was Mrs. Cadel. She was a charming lady in her 70's, and she seemed very nice. The house was just as charming on the inside as it was outside. It was clean and well-kept, and nicely furnished with Victorian style furniture. Mrs. Cadel said she was leaving for a trip and would be gone for two to three weeks. She hoped to have someone move in before she left. The rent was reasonable and it seemed like a good fit for us. We would have the place to ourselves for a while and that was intriguing. Dale and I stepped to the side and chatted about it for a minute then nodded our heads in agreement. We told Mrs. Cadel that we would love to live in her home and said we would like to move in the next day. Dale paid the first month's rent and Mrs. Cadel gave us a key.

Richard was pleased about finding a place for us to live. He and Joan were so helpful and kind. They made us feel welcome, and we took comfort in knowing they were close by. Monday morning, we unloaded the Mercury and carried our things into Mrs. Cadel's house. She seemed pleased to have us there – kind of like having house sitters. She left town the following day, leaving us to enjoy her lovely home. Our bedroom was a nice size and I loved the charming dormer windows. The only drawback – it was furnished with twin-beds. We stood there looking at the beds, then each other. Hey, no problem – we would shove the two beds together and pretend it was a king-size bed. While that sounded logical, we quickly realized it wouldn't work. When we climbed into bed that evening, the two beds separated and slid apart. Oh, my goodness, we hadn't thought about the beds being positioned on rollers. We started laughing because we almost landed on the floor. So, we got up and put one of the twin beds back where it was, and we slept together in one single twin-bed, and not just that night, but the rest of the time we lived in Mrs. Cadel's house. Actually, it was pretty nice in that small bed. We would have snuggled together anyway, no matter what size bed we were in. It remains a joke with us, and we laugh every time we think of those twin beds.

After a couple of days in Mrs. Cadel's house, we felt right at home. Of course, we had the place to ourselves and that was awesome. Dale was busy and spent his days at Fort Belvoir, while my time was spent pursuing a job. That first week, I rode the bus to D.C. every day looking for work. I soon learned that it wasn't easy for a military wife to find work. It seemed everywhere I went, they weren't interested in hiring a military wife. "Military wives get pregnant or their husbands get transferred." I heard this time after time, but that didn't deter me and I kept looking. I figured I could get a job in a five and dime store, but I didn't want that. I wanted an office job. I considered my job search and thought about where to go next.

I sat down at the kitchen table and opened the telephone book. The Pentagon – there it is. I had found the address. Those working at the Pentagon are military, and that would be a good thing.

## Chapter 6

Surely, they would need office clerks and wouldn't frown on my being married to a soldier. The Pentagon was located in Arlington County, Virginia – across the Potomac River from Washington, D.C. In checking the bus route, I saw that I would have a bus transfer midway. The following day, I caught the bus and went to the Pentagon. When I arrived, I told the person inside that I was there to apply for work and I was directed to the personnel office. There wasn't any big security in those days (1954) – much different from today, and I walked freely by myself. The clerk at the desk handed me an employment application. I took a seat and filled out the form. When I gave it back to the clerk, she said it would be reviewed and someone would be in touch with me. I was excited and left feeling encouraged; working at the Pentagon would be very cool. As I walked down the hallway towards the entrance, a friendly soldier spoke to me. He asked if I worked there, and I told him I had just filled out an application. The soldier winked at me and said, "I hope you get a job here." He obviously didn't see that I was wearing a wedding ring.

## A New Job in Washington, D. C.

Our cousins, Richard and Joan, kept in close contact with us. I talked to Joan quite often on the phone and we soon became good friends. I told her about my dilemma in looking for work but said I was hoping to hear from the personnel office at the Pentagon. Joan told me her mother worked at the Chesapeake & Potomac Telephone Company in downtown D.C. She said she would talk to her and perhaps she would be able to help me. She said her mom is pretty high up in the company. The next day I got a phone call from Joan's mother. She said there was a job opening in the lobby for a Teller position. Her mother had spoken to the personnel office and they said they would be happy for me to come in and fill out an application. I thanked her and said I would be there first thing in the morning. The next day I rode the bus to downtown D.C. The telephone company was a half mile from the bus stop – an easy walk. When I got there, I went directly to the personnel office and they seemed to be expecting me. After completing the application, the personnel lady looked it over and I was hired. This was my lucky day! We needed the money, and I knew Dale would be happy to hear that I had a job.

The trees had started to bud and spring was in the air. I enjoyed the fresh morning air while waiting for the bus to arrive. I was headed to work at the Chesapeake & Potomac Telephone Company! After a short wait, I boarded the bus. The trip from Alexandria to downtown Washington, D.C. took 45 minutes. I got off at the bus stop in D. C. and walked to the telephone company. The lobby at the phone company was a large open space. The payment counter was situated at one end of the room with four teller windows, similar to a bank. My first day on the job, I met a lot of people and tried to remember their names. The teller manager was a very nice mature lady and she put me at ease right away. That first day, I stood beside one of the experienced tellers for training, and after a couple of days I had my own window. The job was easy, and I enjoyed greeting the customers and accepting their payment. It was sort of like being a bank teller except that we didn't give money back to the customer. Some days were very busy and customers had to wait in line. Most customers mailed their payment to the telephone company; however, many people had to wait for their paycheck, then come in person to pay their bill.

Mrs. Cadel returned from her trip and we welcomed her back. However, we had gotten spoiled during her absence and now that she was back, our privacy was limited. While she was gone, I had a little accident with a refrigerator defrost tray. Before leaving on

## Chapter 6

her trip, Mrs. Cadel asked me to defrost the refrigerator and she showed me what I needed to do. The defrost process took a while for the ice to melt and drain into a large glass tray. After it finished draining, I carefully lifted the tray from the refrigerator and carried it to the sink to empty the water. As luck would have it, the heavy tray slipped from my hands, then a big splash as it fell into the sink and broke. Fortunately, this happened towards the end of Mrs. Cadel's absence, and I only had a few days to worry about it. I was a little nervous when I told her what happened. I knew she was disappointed, but she was nice and said she expects a certain amount of breakage. She said she would find a replacement tray. I wondered how she had managed to carry that heavy tray of water without spilling it or dropping it.

Our stay at Mrs. Cadel's turned out to be brief. After two months living in her charming home, we were ready to move on to a place of our own – we wanted our privacy. After checking the rental listings in the local newspaper, we quickly discovered that one-bedroom furnished apartments were not readily available. But then we saw a listing for a two-bedroom furnished apartment. We certainly didn't need two bedrooms, but the owner said we could rent it month-to-month and we decided to take until a one bedroom was available. The apartment was over crowded with too much heavy furniture and after moving in, we stood looking at all that furniture. We didn't like it and felt like we were being swallowed by furniture. But then an idea popped into our heads. We could move several pieces of furniture into the second bedroom, and that's what we did. The other bedroom had a bed and dresser, but we moved things around and crammed that room full. We closed the door and forgot about it.

Dale was promoted to Private First Class (PFC), and I thought it was pretty cool. However, I don't think it meant much to Dale.

His pay did increase a little, and we were glad for any extra money. Dale's job assignment placed him in the Army Corp of Engineers at Fort Belvoir. Then after several months, Dale took on the task of driving the Company Commander around the base. In addition to driving the Company Commander's jeep, Dale was assigned the task of taking soldiers to the Guard House (the military jail). When a soldier was being punished for wrongdoing, such as missing guard duty, missing kitchen duty, or something more serious like a Court Martial – which was very serious, the accused soldier was taken to the Guard House. I think Dale liked driving the Company Commander around the base, but he did not like being in the Army. When he was in Basic Training at Fort Leonard Wood, I worried that he would go AWOL. But after his transfer to Fort Belvoir, and we could live together, I think he settled into the Army routine and finally accepted things for what they were; although, he never stopped counting the days until he would receive his Honorable Discharge.

## Surprising Visit

Having our own apartment was a boost to our well-being. We didn't have to tiptoe around or be concerned about the landlady. I was learning to cook and enjoyed thumbing through the pages of my Betty Crocker Cookbook. One evening that summer, we were surprised when Dale's parents called to say they were planning a trip to visit us in Virginia. They said they would like to come the following weekend, if Dale was off duty. By coincidence, Dale wasn't scheduled for duty and he told his folks to schedule their flight and said we would pick them up at the airport in D. C. When Dale hung up the phone, we looked at each other and started laughing, thinking about the furniture we had stacked in the extra bedroom. Mary and John would need a place to sleep.

So, we rolled up our sleeves and moved all that stored furniture back into the living room. And, oh my gosh, I would have to bake a pie and prepare a meal for them. That's what you did in those days, right? Well, that's what Dale's mother would do for guests. I was very nervous about all this. I had never made a pie and I didn't know anything about baking. This would be my first try, and my mother-in-law would be my first guest!

As the weekend approached, it was time to make the pie. I decided on a cherry pie and when I got home from work, I began the process. I followed the pie crust directions on the flour bag and proceeded to roll out the dough with my newly acquired rolling pin. Carefully, I picked up the rolled-out dough and placed it on the pie plate. The dough was short on one side, so I stretched it with my hand to make it fit, being careful to not tear it. I drained the cherries through a tea strainer. Then I poured the cherries in a bowl, added some sugar, stirred it together, and poured it into the pie crust. As I rolled out the top crust, it seemed too thick in places and too thin otherwise. I picked up the piece of dough and it fell apart. At the time, I didn't know that folding the dough in half before picking it up would make it easier to handle. Well, I pieced it together and placed the torn dough on top of the cherries. Whew, that part was done! Now, all I had to do was put it in the oven and let it bake until the crust turned brown. Imagine this pitiful looking pie with its patched crust! Well, at least I made the effort, and I think Dale's mother was somewhat impressed because she said, "Barbara, it's not bad for your first pie." Thankfully, Dale's dad took us out to eat and I didn't have to cook any meals.

## New Apartment and New Friends

It wasn't long until we grew tired of the furnished apartment. First of all, we didn't need two bedrooms and it was foolish to pay for a furnished place filled with furniture we didn't like. Dale was familiar with the PX at the Army base and just discovered that they sold furniture for a reasonable price, and it was tax-free! We started looking for a one-bedroom apartment and by chance drove by the Shirley Duke Apartments. We liked the location and stopped at the manager's office. Luckily, they had a ground floor one-bedroom available. We walked over to take a look and it seemed perfectly suited to our needs. We said we would take it and signed a lease. Then Dale went to the PX to buy our furniture. He bought a sofa, two matching chairs, a coffee table and a Muntz TV for the living room. He also bought a kitchen table with four chairs, and a full-size bed and dresser – all brand new and all for $500. The furniture was contemporary fifties deco style with blonde wood. The kitchen table had chrome legs with a Formica top. Compared to the heavy furniture at the last place, we thought it was pretty cool. After settling in, we invited a few of Dale's Army buddies and their wives for a little get-together. It was fun making new friends and I was very happy with my new home.

One Saturday afternoon, shortly after moving into the Shirley Duke Apartment, Dale and I went out to buy some groceries. We had just returned home to the apartment when there was a knock at our door. We opened the door and there stood a guy with a friendly smile. He said he noticed a car in the parking lot with the Kansas license plate. He wanted to know if the car belonged to us. "Yes, our car does have a Kansas tag." Dale said. The guy got very excited and said, "I've been going door to door trying to find the owner." And then he introduced himself as Claude Robbins, and said he had recently moved there from Parsons, Kansas, and was excited to meet someone from that part of the country. Claude said he lived in the adjacent building with his wife, Pat, and their little girl. He said he worked for Montgomery Ward, and

## Chapter 6

the company had relocated him for the new manager position at the store in Arlington. Claude and Pat were warm, friendly, and seemed like genuine people. Dale and I liked them a lot and we soon became best friends.

Our first wedding anniversary was approaching. So much had happened that first year and it seemed we had been married much longer. Dale and I wanted to do something fun and special on July 9th. Dale asked me what I would like to have for an anniversary present and when I told him I wanted an electric mixer with two bowls, he didn't think that sounded very exciting and poo-pooed it. Oh well. That weekend, I was visiting with my new friend, Pat, and mentioned our upcoming first anniversary. I told her we wanted to go out and do something special. Pat said she had heard about a sunset cruise on the Potomac River. I had never been on a boat and that sounded romantic and fun. I told Dale about it and right away he said "Yes, I like that idea – let's do it." We decided to ask Pat and Claude to join us. They were thrilled to be invited and I called to make reservations.

The breeze was warm and gentle as the boat slowly left the shoreline. It was a picture-perfect evening that July 9th and we were celebrating. I spent most of the day getting ready and fussing with my hair. It had grown long and I wanted it styled just right. I set my hair in pin curls using bobby pins and let it dry thoroughly. When I ran the brush through my hair, it became a whimsical curly style and it looked great. I slipped into my beautiful two-piece white suit and high heels. Dale dressed in his white suit and I have to say, we made a handsome couple. We were in love and ready to celebrate our special day. Before we left, Dale surprised me with the mixer I wanted. The four of us drove to D.C. and went to the pier to board the boat. Once on board, I soon realized that we were over-dressed because most of the passengers were more casual. This was a new adventure for both of us and we were excited to be on the boat. Our friends, Pat and Claude were easy to be with and we enjoyed their company. As we cruised down the Potomac River the sun began shedding a glorious array of color across the western sky. The reflection on the water was spectacular! Dale and I stood next to the railing with our arms wrapped around each other as we watched the sun slide below the horizon. Our first anniversary was truly special and I felt like I was tasting life to the fullest.

## Happy News

Not long after our anniversary, I scheduled an appointment with an Obstetrics doctor in D.C. The Army Obstetrics Department at Fort Belvoir wouldn't schedule an appointment until I had missed two periods. I had missed one cycle, and when I thought I might be pregnant, I was anxious to find out. I didn't want to wait another month to see a doctor so I scheduled an appointment with a non-military doctor. After my examination, the doctor said, "It appears to me that you are pregnant." I was beyond excited – I was ecstatic and wanted to shout it to the world. On the bus ride home, I could hardly contain my joy. Dale knew I had a doctor appointment after work and he expected me to be late. When I got home, I was wearing a big grin and I'm sure Dale sensed what I was about to tell him. I walked over to him and said, "We're going to have a baby!"

During the 1950's, letter writing was the most common form of communication. In 1954, the U.S. The Postal Service charged .03 cents to mail a one-ounce letter. Mostly, people used light-weight onion skin paper and envelopes to save on postage. I wrote letters to my mom and dad every week. I never knew if my dad read my letters; I hoped he did, but I didn't ask. I wrote to my

## Chapter 6

Grandma and Grandpa Kinsley as well, and Grandma would always write back. But sometimes we called each other just to hear the voice of a loved one. Being pregnant was exciting news and I wanted to tell my mom in person, so I picked up the phone and called her. When she heard me say that we were going to have a baby I knew that made her happy, and she was thrilled about becoming a grandmother. She asked when the baby was due and how I was feeling. I told her the anticipated date was February 26th. My mom said she wanted to be there when the baby came and she would stay for two weeks to help us. She told me that she would schedule her vacation time around my due date. I was so pleased that she wanted to be there. My mom had been a nurse for many years and besides that, she had given birth to five babies – she would know exactly what to do.

Excitedly, I stood sideways in front of the mirror hoping to see the start of a baby bump. Day after day I looked and then slowly, ever so slowly, I could see a slight bulge in my tummy. I was anxious to wear maternity clothes but I needed a big tummy to fill the space of maternity wear. In today's world, women wear snug-fitting tops with baby bump on proud display. But in 1954, women wore wide maternity tops to cover the bump. When I told my friend, Pat, that I was pregnant, she was generous and gave me her maternity clothes. She said they were done, and she wouldn't need them anymore. Joan and Richard recently had their second baby – a little boy named Michael, and Joan loaned me her maternity things too. She also gave me her copy of Dr. Spock Baby and Child Care. These were such nice gifts and saved us from having to spend money on maternity clothes.

Being pregnant was an absolute delight, that is, until morning sickness started. This part wasn't fun, and it did cause some issues for me when trying to make it to the bus stop on time. During that period, I came close to missing my bus and many times I left the apartment in a rush, running two blocks to the bus stop. Thankfully, I never missed the bus and I was never late for work. I knew the importance of exercise during pregnancy, and those walks to and from the bus stops provided good exercise. Walking has always been a part of my life and these short walks were easy for me. After a few weeks, the morning sickness went away and it was all good again.

I couldn't delay any longer; it was time to let my boss know that I was expecting. That afternoon I asked my boss if I could talk to her for a few minutes during my break. She invited me to sit down at her desk and I got right to the point. "I'm very excited to share the news that I'm expecting." Perhaps she had noticed the pregnancy glow on my face because she didn't seem all that surprised. She offered her congratulations and asked when I was due. Then she proceeded to tell me about the pregnancy policy at the telephone company. I was surprised to learn that I would not be allowed to work past my sixth month. I frowned, expressing my disappointment, and told her that I had hoped to work until two weeks before my due date. My boss said this policy had been in place for a good while but it only applied to employees who worked among the public. This seemed odd and made no sense to me, but since I worked with customers every day, it applied to me. My, how things have changed since 1954!

The chill of winter arrived and the days grew shorter. We enjoyed Thanksgiving with our cousins, Richard and Joan, and it was special. Christmas was just around the corner and holiday decorations were popping up everywhere! Dale seemed enthused and said he had a fun idea. "How about flying to Wichita for Christmas? We have enough money to pay for airline tickets, and it would be nice to spend Christmas with family." Well, that did

## Chapter 6

sound fun and I said I would check with my doctor. According to the calendar, I would be about seven months pregnant at Christmas. I had never been in an airplane and I got excited just thinking about it. I called my doctor the next day and was pleased to hear him say it would be okay for me to fly. Dale called his folks to let them know, then he called the airline company to make our reservation. I quickly wrote a letter to my parents to let them know. This was something fun to look forward to.

It was an ordinary day – the morning bus ride to D. C. was normal – everything seemed normal, except, it was my last day at the Chesapeake & Potomac Telephone Company. I enjoyed working there and wanted to continue working a bit longer, but rules are rules. It still seemed silly to me, especially since the maternity top covered my baby bump. Fridays usually brought the same regular customers to pay their bill, and this Friday was no different. It was nearly time for my break when my boss called me into the employee lounge. That seemed strange, but perhaps she just wanted to talk to me since it was my last day. When I entered the lounge, I saw a long table decorated with pink and blue balloons. I noticed a pretty cake in the middle of the table, also decorated in pink and blue, and there were several gifts on the table. Then all of a sudden, I heard "Surprise!" and my co-workers came out from around the corner. I couldn't believe it – they were having a baby shower for me! I was so overcome with surprise and joy that it brought tears to my eyes. The gifts were thoughtful, lovely things and it was a wonderful party; it warmed my heart. My co-workers were such good people and I would miss them. When I left work that day, one of the gals I worked with offered to help me carry the gifts to the bus stop.

Dale got home before me that day and he was sitting on the sofa when I walked in. When he saw me carrying the large bag, he immediately thought I had gone shopping. I noticed the worried look on his face and said, "No, no – I didn't go shopping. My co-workers had a surprise baby shower for me, and wait 'till you see what they gave us." I sat the bag on the sofa and told Dale about the shower and how special it was. Then I took the gifts out of the bag and placed them on the sofa for Dale to see. He was amazed and surprised about the beautiful gifts. He picked up the adorable little comforter and baby pillow and took them into the bedroom. Joan loaned us her bassinet, and it was already in the bedroom next to the bed. We placed the comforter and little pillow in the bassinet and stood admiring it. It was the perfect size for a bassinet! Then we placed the other gifts in the dresser drawer – our baby's drawer.

When Monday rolled around, it seemed odd not going to work. I wondered what I would do all day. Dr. Spock Baby & Child Care book lay on the dresser – I now had plenty of time to read it. Joan was so sweet loaning it to me saying "It's the baby bible." I could enjoy daily walks in the neighborhood and looked forward to it. I would browse my cookbook for new recipes, and have dinner ready when Dale came home from the Army base. It's amazing but I managed to fill my time and after a few days, I didn't miss my job. Fort Belvoir offered classes for first-time mothers-to-be, and I attended several classes. The instructor used a doll to demonstrate how to hold an infant, how to bathe an infant, how to change diapers without poking the baby with a diaper pin, plus other hints on baby care. Later on, I attended a class regarding the labor process and birth of the baby. The class was interesting and provided good preparation, but you don't know what it's really like until you actually give birth.

Christmas was a couple days away and I was about to experience my first airline flight. My anticipation was bubbling

## Chapter 6

over as we boarded the plane in D. C. We found our seats and settled in. After a few minutes, the flight attendant announced that we were ready for departure and reminded us to buckle up. I looked at Dale with a grin as I fastened the safety belt under my baby tummy. Within a few minutes the aircraft was speeding down the runway. As we lifted off, I felt a big rush of adrenaline. I looked out the window and watched as we sped through a cluster of clouds, and then we were above the clouds. I found it fascinating to be able to look down on the clouds. After several hours, we arrived at the Wichita Airport, and I was quite surprised to see such a welcome. We expected Dale's parents to be there to pick us up, but when I saw Aunt Hermina and Uncle Russell – and my twelve-year-old sister, Paula, I was completely blown away. I think they were anxious to see "pregnant" Barbara! It was wonderful seeing them and it made me very happy. I had a short visit with Hermina and Russell, and I got to introduce them to my in-laws. I wondered how Paula had gotten to the airport. When Dale's dad realized Paula was there by herself, he invited her to join us for lunch. That was so nice of John, and Paula was excited to go with us. It was awesome seeing my little sister and having her sit next to me at lunch. Later on, Dale borrowed his dad's car and I got to see my mom too, and that was special. Christmas in Wichita was very nice but it was a short visit and we were soon on our way back to Virginia.

It was our first Valentine's Day together in our own apartment. The prior year, Dale was in the process of transferring to Fort Belvoir, while I was getting ready for the cross-country trip with Bud and Imo. But this year, we were happily settled in Virginia. I was in the kitchen fixing supper when Dale came home that day. I was very pregnant by then, and my tummy filled the space in the maternity top. I remember that Valentine's Day so well. I was standing in front of the sink peeling potatoes when Dale came into the kitchen. I turned around and was surprised to see him holding a present for me. After drying my hands, I sat down at the table and opened the package. Inside was a bottle of luxurious Chanel No. 5 Perfume. I wasn't feeling very sexy those days, but Dale had chosen the perfect gift. I dabbed a little perfume behind my ears and enjoyed the sensuous fragrance. Dale had made me feel special and I suddenly felt pretty. I still have the empty bottle of that Chanel No. 5.

## My Mother's Visit

My due date was drawing near and my mother would be arriving soon. This was a very exciting and happy time in my life. Doctor visits at Fort Belvoir Medical were now weekly and Dale had been granted permission for time off when my labor started and after the baby was born. Our sweet little apartment had only one bedroom but I planned ahead, making sure we had enough bedding for Mom's bed on the sofa. Mom would be staying with us for two weeks and I wanted her to be comfortable. I was grateful she could be there and hoped the baby would arrive on time.

Dale and I drove to the airport in D.C. to pick up my mom. When she got off the airplane, we spotted each other and waved. It was a long flight and I knew Mom would be tired but she was smiling; my mom wore such a pretty smile. This was a big trip for my mom and we were excited to see each other. Mom got settled-in at our apartment and we began the waiting game. She would be a young grandmother at forty-three. My due date came and went and each morning I asked myself, "Will today be the day?" In the meantime, we made good use of the time by taking Mom to see the sights in D. C. The cherry blossoms were in full bloom and absolutely gorgeous! The first weekend after Mom arrived,

## Chapter 6

we took her to Washington, D. C. The weather was a bit chilly that day. When we drove across the bridge, we were in awe at the beautiful cherry blossom trees on both sides of the Potomac River. There are many historic places in Washington, and it was hard to know where to start. But I specifically remember we visited the U.S. Capitol, the Lincoln Memorial for our 16th President, the Washington Monument, Jefferson Memorial, and the Tomb of the Unknown Soldier – arriving in time to watch the Changing of the Guards. Dale took a picture of my mother and me, standing on the steps of the Capitol building.

My mother's two-week visit ended all too soon. We hadn't talked about the possibility of my being late but that's what happened. It was mid-March – two weeks past my due date. Mom wanted to stay longer, but her vacation time was over and she was expected back at work. It was terribly disappointing but she had to return to Wichita. I couldn't believe this was happening. It was especially disappointing for my mom. She had looked forward to being there for the birth of her first grandchild. We took Mom to the airport and waited with her until it was time for her to get on the airplane. It was hard saying our goodbyes, but we hugged, and waved to each other as she boarded the plane. Tears filled my eyes as I stood there watching the plane lift up into the sky. But in spite of our disappointment, I realized that those two weeks had been a special bonding time for me and my mom.

### A Child is Born

The days came and went and still nothing happened. I continued to see the doctor each week and he always said the same thing, "You're not ready yet". But finally, one afternoon I started to feel something different. I had a strong pain, but then it stopped. Then in about fifteen minutes, there it was again. I got excited and called the doctor's office at Fort Belvoir. The nurse asked when my pains started, and how much time between each pain. I explained it to the nurse and she told me to wait until the pains were consistently ten minutes apart, "That's when you should come to the hospital" she said. It wasn't long after that and I could easily say that my pains were ten minutes apart. Dale and I were prepared and ready to go. Dale took my arm as we left the apartment. He helped me into the car and we went to the Army hospital. When we got there, the clerk at the front desk checked me in, and we were escorted to the maternity ward. Dale was told to wait in the husband's waiting area. The nurse went on to say that husbands were not allowed in the labor room or delivery room. I remember wishing my mother were still there to keep Dale company during the wait.

The labor room seemed to be a busy place. It was a large room with several beds already in use. I was a little startled to hear some of the women yelling and making a lot of noise. I remember thinking "they must be in a lot of pain." The nurse helped me undress, and then she handed me a hospital gown. I had taken the labor and birthing class but all of a sudden, I didn't know what to expect next. I think the nurse sensed my anxiety because she said, "Try to relax as it will be a while before anything starts to happen – especially since this is your first baby." Well, I laid there in bed and tried to relax like the nurse said, but it wasn't long until my pains were closer together and became more intense. It was a long night and was now the next morning. I remember asking the nurse, "How much longer?" Dr. Ream came to the labor room to check on me. He told me that since this was my first baby, it takes longer and he assured me I was doing fine. As time went on, I realized I was moaning and yelling like the other ladies. I don't know why I made all that noise because it didn't help the pain.

## Chapter 6

    The nurse examined me again and finally I heard her say, "It's time." I was wheeled to the delivery room where Dr. Ream was waiting for me. The nurses lifted me from the labor bed onto the delivery table. I noticed a large mirror positioned at the ceiling above. Dr. Ream said I could look up and watch the birth of my baby. Humm – I sure didn't feel like looking up. I could feel the baby coming and continued pushing as instructed. But then, there seemed to be some quick action by the doctor and nurses and they began pushing hard on my abdomen, pushing down with the side of their palms, just below my ribs. I didn't understand why they were doing that – was my baby stuck? The pain was so intense that my toes felt like they were splitting open. About that time, I glanced up at the mirror and saw something that looked like white skin protruding. It wasn't my baby's head – it was the butt. My baby had turned and was coming butt first. Then I heard the doctor say, "It's posterior!" I was somewhat naïve but knew enough to know this wasn't normal. The doctor and nurses were working hard, and oh my gosh, I was working hard doing everything they told me to do. Then finally, after 28 hours laboring, Dr. Ream said, "It's a girl." Our baby entered the world and took her first breath at 7:55 p.m. It was our daughter's BirthDay, March 30, 1955.

    I lifted my head and listened. Soon I heard her first little sound as she started to cry. I looked up at the ceiling mirror and watched through teary eyes as Dr. Ream cut and tied the cord. Then the nurse carried our baby to a nearby table. I turned my head and watched as she used a syringe to clean our baby's mouth and nose. Then she sponged her little body with warm water, dried her off and placed her on the scale. I heard the nurse say, "Weight is 7 pounds, 15 ounces!" After wrapping her in a blanket, the nurse handed my baby to me. I was completely overcome with joy – a baby girl! I couldn't believe the miracle that had just happened. She opened her big blue eyes and looked at me. I kissed her and snuggled her close to my body as more tears ran down my cheeks. About that time, Dale walked in to find me holding our beautiful baby. He kissed me and I gently lifted my arms and handed our baby to her daddy, and said "Isn't she beautiful!" Dale beamed with a broad smile and said, "Yes, she is." I could see how proud he was holding our newborn daughter for the very first time. He looked at her, and I heard him say, "Hello, Pamela." Months before, when Dale came home after two weeks of vigorous Bivouac training, he told me he thought of a name he really liked – "Pamela" he said "and what do you think about Jean for a middle name?" I loved the name too, and so it was – our baby girl became Pamela Jean.

It was late that evening when Dale left the hospital. It had been a long day-and-half for him. Other husbands came and went as Dale sat waiting in the small room. He called both of our parents that evening to let them know the wonderful news. The next morning, Dale was back at the hospital and he showered me with gifts. I don't know when he had time to go shopping, but he walked over to my bed carrying two large presents. I wasn't expecting anything, and was very surprised! Each beautifully wrapped gift contained a gorgeous outfit. We embraced each other and kissed. I loved the pretty new clothes Dale bought for me. I smiled at him and said, "I can't wait to get my figure back so I can wear my new clothes!" Then, it was so cute when Dale quietly asked me, "Did you look the baby over? Does she have all her fingers and toes?" I laughed and said, "She is perfect in every way." I thought to myself, "Does he think we would send her back if she is missing a finger or toe?" Of course, that is not what he meant. He just wondered if there was anything that needed the

## Chapter 6

doctor's attention. It was precious though, the way he said it, and I still smile when I think about it.

The hospital room at Fort Belvoir Army Hospital was somewhat different from civilian hospitals, and that is an understatement! The room was an Army barracks consisting of 24 beds, with 12 beds lined up on each side of the room. Most of the beds were filled with new mothers. Looking around, seeing all the mothers holding their babies and nursing them at the same time, myself included, was somewhat comical – there were a lot of boobs in that room! The second day after our baby was born, the attending doctor was making his daily rounds. When he stopped at my bed, he checked me over and asked how old I was. I answered softly saying I was eighteen. The other mothers seemed much older and I felt a little intimidated. When the doctor heard my age, he said to the nurse, "Let's keep her another day." If my mother could have stayed longer, I would have told him that I had wonderful help waiting at home. But my mother wasn't there, so I didn't mind another day at the hospital.

The early light of dawn filtered through the window at the far end of the barracks. I was wide awake and hadn't gotten much sleep. My baby needed to be fed several times during the night, and just when I dozed off, the nurse was waking me again. I anticipated going home that day and was pleased when the doctor stopped by to let me know he had authorized my release. I wasted no time getting out of bed and shedding the hospital gown; I was dressed and ready to go when Dale arrived. I bundled Pamela snugly in her baby blanket and picked her up. The nurse was standing by and she helped me get situated in the wheelchair and escorted us outside. Bright sunshine greeted us when the nurse opened the door and I quickly shielded my baby's eyes from the strong glare. During the ride home, I snuggled Pamela close to my body and talked to her. She was soon asleep. In the mid-1950's, there were no baby car seats, no seatbelts in cars, and no laws requiring a child be strapped-in. It was all very casual in those days, and no one thought anything about it. Thank goodness we have safe baby carriers today.

Baby Pamela was still sleeping when we arrived at our apartment. We went inside and I laid her on our bed. Dale and I stood there and just looked at her; she was a beautiful baby. Then we looked at each other, and smiled with heartfelt love and joy. We were a family now, and so grateful to be blessed with a healthy baby. She was so precious, and we were proud parents. Dale was anxious to get some movie pictures, and he reached up in the closet for his movie camera. The camera had a large light bar for use in low light areas. Dale placed the light bar on the dresser, off to the side, careful not to have any bright light on the baby's face. Dale pushed the start button and the movie began. I picked her up and took her over to the bassinet. I laid her on her back and covered her with the baby blanket. I remembered what my mother had said before she left. She told me that I should never lay an infant on its stomach. Baby Pamela slept for a while, until she was hungry. And she didn't hesitate to let me know that she was hungry. Fortunately, Dale was granted time off from Army duty and could stay home to help. I was grateful for that, especially since my mom wasn't there.

As new parents, Dale and I had a lot to learn about babies but we took it all in stride. Even though my mom wasn't there to help, I felt no stress and for the most part things came naturally. We just did what we needed to do, a day-at-a-time, and I had Dr. Spock's baby book handy for quick reference. Our cousin, Joan, was an experienced mom with two little ones, and she kindly offered her help. Knowing that she was close by was very comforting, and I

## Chapter 6

did call her from time to time. I was happy being home taking care of my baby girl. I was tasting life in a whole new way – I was a mother.

Our military friends had their babies. Millie and Dan Mauk had their baby girl before us, then the other two couples soon followed suit; all four couples became new parents within a matter of a few weeks apart. It was fun sharing baby stories with each other. When our babies fussed and seemed to have colic, we sought each other's advice – take the baby for a walk outdoors, rub the baby's tummy, take the baby for a ride in the car, give the baby a warm bath, and so on. We all seemed to muddle through and our baby's colic eventually went away.

Dale's active military duty would end in September; however, after that, he was required to remain in the Army Active Reserve four years, with an additional two years Inactive Reserve – a total of six more years of military commitment after his Honorable Discharge. Meanwhile, back in Wichita, harvest time was approaching. Dale's dad needed help with the harvest, so he wrote a letter to the Army authorities, along with a request form, asking that Dale be granted an early release from duty to help with the harvest. It wasn't long after that when Dale received official notice that he would be granted an early release. The official notice stated that Dale would be allowed to depart from his military assignment in June, 1955 – three months early. Dale was extremely happy to receive the news and he began making plans for our return trip to Wichita. As for me, I enjoyed living in Virginia. I had settled-in and was happy with our life as it was. We had wonderful friends, and I felt a little melancholy about leaving.

Mary, age 6, me, age 4, (in front) with parents at 422 West 26th Street, Wichita, Kansas

My First Holy Communion, 1942. Me in back row, 2nd from right.

Grandma & Grandpa Kinsley.

The house on Athenian.

The Winter family, 1949. Back row from left, Mary, Mom, Dad, me.
Front row from left, Michael, Paula, James.

Photo taken the day we met, May 1953. Barbara, age 16; Dale, 21.

The harvest field. Dale cutting wheat in Chappell, Nebraska, July 1953.

Dale in the Army. He was home for the weekend, 1953.

Barbie & Dale in Alexandria, Virginia, spring 1954.

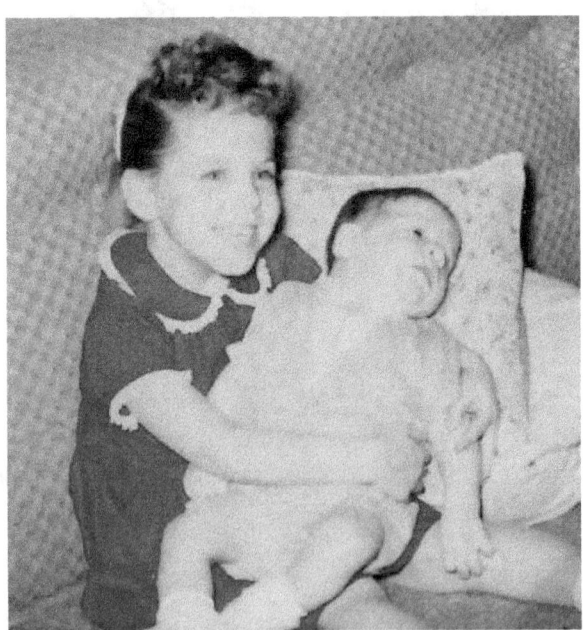

Pam holding baby brother, Randy, 1959.

Photos

Pam & Randy playing at the farm house, 1963.

Farm Equipment Auction, March, 1965.

Dale's parents, John & Mary Rieger.

The four of us in Hawaii, 1967.

Pam & Randy happy about standing in the Pacific Ocean, 1967.

Easter, 1968. Barbie with Randy & Pam. Pam made her pretty Easter dress!

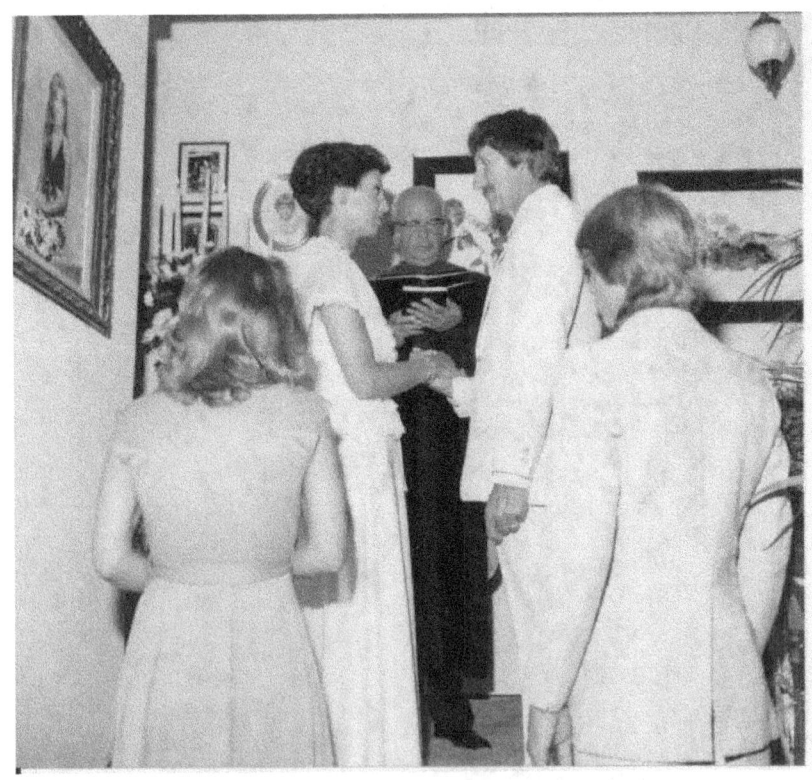
Renewing vows on 25th anniversary, July 9, 1978.

Family photo at 25th anniversary celebration.

Hot air balloon ride - a gift from our kids. July 1980.

Seymone with her puppies - spring, 1993.

Photos

Weekend trip to Durango, with friends Bev & Ed. (not pictured).
Then, we rode the train to Silverton. September, 1981.

Dale & Barbie in Marseille, France, 2006.

Santa's visit to Briarwood Drive, Christmas Eve, 1988
Pam holding Jason, Erin on Santa's lap, Tim on right.

Christmas Eve 1997. Back row, left to right, Pam, Tim, Barbie, Dale.
Front, Erin, Jason, Tyler, Cammille, Carrissa, Randy. Doggies: Seymone & Charnet.

Photos

All five siblings at niece's wedding, 1991.
Left to right: Barbie, Mike, Mary, Jim and Paula.

Alaskan cruise, July 2003. On top of Mendenhall Glacier.
Celebrating 50 years of marriage!

Winter family reunion at Waneka Lake Park, Lafayette. July 4, 2006.

Punting down the Avon River in Christchurch, New Zealand, January, 2008.

Photos

Visit to the Blue Mosque, Istanbul, Turkey, 2013.

Our great-grandson, Lewis, September, 2018.

Family celebrating Barbie's 80th birthday, 2016.
Standing, left to right: Blake, Erin, Tim, Tyler, Pam, Jason, Erin R, Randy.
Barbie & Dale on bench.

# Chapter 7

# Farewell to Army Life

The days went by swiftly as we prepared for the journey to Wichita. Travel by car from Virginia to Wichita would take at least two days and perhaps three, especially travelling with a baby. We needed a car bed for Pamela, something comfortable and a safe place for her to sleep. I had noticed some ads for baby car beds, so Dale and I went shopping to find one that would fit our car. Luckily, we found the perfect size and it came with a nicely padded mattress. The car bed had two large hooks that fit over the back of the front seat. When the baby needed her diaper changed, I positioned myself on my knees and leaned over the back of the front seat. Things seemed to be coming together as we prepared to leave Virginia. Just one more thing, and this was a biggie – we had to sell the furniture in our apartment before we left. We sure didn't want to tow a trailer. Dale put the word out at the Army base, and one of his Army buddies said he was interested in buying our furniture. We sold every piece of furniture for $500 – the same price we paid for it. The Army couple was happy with their purchase, and we were happy to pass it on to them.

After evaluating what we had and the things we needed to move, we wondered how we could fit everything in the car. We were now a family of three and our baby had her things too. Dale had a great idea and decided to buy a rack for the top of our Mercury. The rack would hold some of our belongings, and could be tied down and secured on top of the car. We filled a few boxes with kitchen items and bedding, and put our clothes in suitcases. The trunk of our car was fully loaded with our stuff and there wasn't an inch to spare. The back seat was filled with Pamela's travel bed, baby formula, bottles, diapers and her little clothing items. We found a special heater designed for baby bottles. The baby bottle fit into a round heating element that plugged into the car cigarette lighter. It was perfect for warming the baby's bottle. I called a few days ahead of our departure to arrange cancellation of our phone service and everything else had been taken care of. It was time to bid farewell to Virginia. Richard and Joan had us over for dinner before we left and we returned the bassinette. They were so kind and good to us and it was hard to find the right words of gratitude. As we hugged and said goodbye, they invited us to come back to visit. Claude and Pat had become good friends and it was sad telling them goodbye. After we left, we kept in touch with Claude and Pat for many years, but we never saw them again. We said goodbye to our Army friends and for many years we exchanged Christmas cards, but we never saw them again. Living in Virginia was a wonderful experience and while I felt somewhat sad about leaving, I looked forward to our new life ahead.

## New Beginnings in Wichita

The journey to Wichita stretched over hundreds of miles – around 1,300 to be exact. I remember hearing the birds chirping joyfully as we left our apartment that morning. I felt energized and ready to leave. I would always have warm memories of

## Chapter 7

our time in Virginia. We stopped at the office to drop off the apartment keys and we were on our way. After leaving the state of Virginia, our trip first took us into West Virginia, then into parts of Kentucky, Indiana, Illinois and Missouri. Pamela was 2-1/2 months old at the time. She was a good little traveler and enjoyed the slight movement of the car. Her colic seemed to be subsiding and that made things easier for her and for me. After the first day of travel, we stopped at a motel to spend the night. I was up and down a few times during the night to feed Pamela, but that was nothing unusual and I enjoyed snuggling her close while she ate. She always looked up at me with her big blue eyes when I talked to her. The next morning the three of us were up early and soon we were on the road again. We spent most of the second day in the car and stopped for lodging again that night.

The road trip continued to go smoothly and we finally crossed over the Kansas border. We arrived in Wichita the afternoon of the third day, and why was I not surprised when Dale went straight to the field? Dale's dad spotted us and came running over to the car. I was holding the baby on my lap when John opened the car door. He was on a mission, and that mission was to hold his baby granddaughter. He reached in for baby Pamela, and picked her up with his big hand and away he went to show her off. I could feel a frown settle on my forehead when John carried her away. But it wasn't long and he returned, holding his granddaughter gently in his arms. It was easy to see that John Rieger was a proud grandpa. Pamela was John and Mary's first granddaughter, and as time would prove, she was their only granddaughter.

After Dale and his dad chatted for a while, we left the field and went over to the farm house to find Dale's mom waiting for us. Mary couldn't wait to hold her granddaughter. A big smile spread across her face as she cradled Pamela in her arms. She walked around in the house with the baby, while Dale and I carried some of our things into the house. The first thing we did was bring in the baby's formula, her car bed and her diapers. We got the car bed situated upstairs in Dale's old bedroom. I mentioned to Dale that we need to buy a baby bed. He agreed and said we would do that when we found an apartment. The following day, Dale was up bright and early. He was anxious to start working the wheat harvest. John was happy to have his son back in town, and grateful for his help at the farm. I called my mother to let her know we had arrived. She was, of course, very anxious to meet her first grandchild. I had talked with Dale earlier about taking the baby to my parent's house, and told my mom we would come over to their house that evening.

    I didn't know what to expect when we got to my parent's house. My dad had been so upset with me, and I thought he might shut us out like he had done before. I dressed Pamela in her cute little dress and she looked adorable. I had just given her a bath and she smelled so sweet. How could anyone resist her? As it turned out, we were in for a nice surprise. My mom and dad were both waiting for us in the living room when we got there, along with my siblings. As we walked in, my dad had a calm smile on his face and that was a good sign. My mom had her usual pretty smile and she was overjoyed to meet her first grandchild. I handed Pamela over to my mom and her smile grew wide as she cooed and clicked her tongue making cute sounds for Pamela. After a while, I asked my dad if he would like to hold his granddaughter. His face lit up when Mom handed Pamela over to him. He smiled broadly as he rocked her back and forth in his arms. His first grandchild had warmed his heart. It had been two years since I last saw or spoke to my dad. I breathed a sigh of relief and took pleasure watching

## Chapter 7

my family play with baby Pamela. I knew that everything would be all right.

A hot summer breeze swept across my face as I gazed out across the wheat field. The summer winds helped ripen the wheat to its glistening golden color. We had arrived in time for harvest and Dale immediately resumed work at the farm. I, on the other hand, was anxious to find an apartment and began searching the newspaper ads. While my in-laws made us feel welcome and comfortable, I wanted to get settled into our own private space as soon as possible. In scrolling through the ads, I came across a two-bedroom furnished apartment and the ad said it was "near-new." Since we didn't have any furniture, it sounded perfect. I scheduled an appointment and we looked at it the same day. Dale and I both liked the place and it was available for immediate occupancy, so we decided to take it. Moving was easy, especially since most of our things were still packed in the trunk of our car.

I loved the apartment! It was such a nice place and still smelled like new. Dale was consumed with work at the farm and was gone most of the time. He was up early and out the door before sunrise, and most days he didn't get home until dark. After Dale got his early discharge from the Army, I think he felt a sense of freedom and he seemed happy to be working at the farm again. However, with Dale working such long days, I started to feel lonely. It was just the baby and me – home by ourselves. I didn't know anyone and I called my sister, Paula. Actually, Dale suggested that Paula might like to come stay with us and help me get settled. When I asked Paula if she would like to do that, she jumped at the chance. Paula was a big help and she seemed happy to be there. My little sister loved helping with the baby, and she was good company for me – I no longer felt lonely. Paula stayed with us for two weeks.

And then, we met our next-door neighbor, and it turned out to be the most wonderful friendship. The couple was about the same age as Dale and me, and they too had a baby girl. Their baby's name was Donna, and she was about the same age as Pamela. We first met outside on the walkway, each with our babies, and we introduced ourselves. We hit it off right away, and a few days later, we got together for a barbecue. This special couple, Edith and Larry Delanty, soon became our new best friends. Dale and I had started calling Pamela, "Pam." Our new friends called her "Pam or Pamie" and everyone else seemed to follow suit, and so, from then on, we called our baby girl "Pam."

Our stay in the apartment turned out to be short-lived. Dale decided he didn't like living there. He grew up living in a rural area with wide open spaces. So, one day, he mentioned buying a two-bedroom house trailer. He said we could park it at the farm, like we did before he was inducted into the Army. I, on the other hand, was content in the apartment, especially having met Edith and Larry. But, if Dale wanted to move into a house trailer and live at the farm, I was okay with that – although, I wasn't thrilled about living so close to his parents. We were renting the apartment on a month-to-month basis, so we weren't locked-in on a long lease. House trailers were not hard to find, and it didn't take long for Dale to locate one that he thought would work for us. Pam's new baby bed fit perfectly in the space next to the main bedroom, and that was the most important thing. So, we gave our notice to the landlord. After the house trailer was delivered and set up at the farm, we moved out of the apartment. The house trailer would be our home for eight months.

The two-bedroom house trailer was cute, but it was tight quarters compared to the apartment. I hadn't accumulated much kitchenware yet and managed to fit everything into the cabinet

## Chapter 7

space of the tiny kitchen. Pam would be crawling soon, and the small space would make it easy to keep an eye on her. I adjusted to the new place and it soon felt like home. Living at the farm was interesting and it seemed there was always something going on. Dale's dad, John, kept some animals at the farm. I especially remember the pretty horse named Simba. One day when Dale's brothers were at the farm, John and the brothers took turns riding Simba. They were excellent riders and sat proud in the saddle. It was fun watching those guys laugh and joke – and show off. They were having a good time riding that horse. John kept pigs at the farm, too, and the baby pigs were very cute. Pam was fascinated with the little piglets and loved watching them play.

Summer faded into fall and it was time to plant wheat seed for next year's harvest. Dale had already prepared the fields for planting and the land was groomed and ready. I was always amazed at Dale's farming skills and how he knew exactly which piece of equipment to use for this and that. There was the plow, the one-way, the tractor, the combine, and all sorts of other equipment. Dale's farm work kept him quite busy and he didn't seem to have much spare time. I was dependent on him taking me to buy groceries. I grew tired of that and told Dale "It's time I learn to drive a car." Dale agreed, and said he would teach me. The following Sunday, the three of us got into the gray Mercury, with me sitting in the driver's seat. Some might say "Wasn't it a bit risky, going for a driving lesson with a baby on board?" Well, yes it probably was, but that's what we did. Pam was in her baby seat (the kind that hooked over the back of the seat), and Dale sat attentively on edge as he told me what to do. Fortunately, we lived in a rural farming area with wide-open country roads. I had watched Dale's driving and was very observative, but still, I had plenty to learn – especially when it came to driving in traffic. The most difficult thing for me was synchronizing the clutch on the stick-shift car, but eventually, I got the hang of it. After several driving excursions and thoroughly studying the driver's manual, I was ready for the driving test. The day of my test, I was very nervous, but I managed to pass the driving test and the written exam. Two weeks later, my driver's license arrived in the mail. I tucked the license into my wallet and was happy to have my independence.

The holidays were especially fun that year. Pam was eight months old and it was her first Christmas. The whole Rieger clan was at the farm house and Pam didn't know what to make of all the presents and commotion. I think I may have played Santa again that year at the Rieger Christmas. We also celebrated Christmas at my parent's house, and everyone had fun playing with Pam. My mom prepared a nice meal for the family and we were all together. Winter seemed to hang on that year but eventually it warmed up and spring began to blossom. Pam loved being outside in the sunshine and I took her outdoors almost every day. As one might imagine, the house trailer was getting smaller by the day, especially with Pam's high chair, playpen and all the other baby things we had accumulated. I guess one could say, we were experiencing some growing pains. But then one day, we learned that the duplex located one-quarter mile from the farm house was going to be available to rent. The location was good for Dale's work. We were anxious to check it out and contacted the owner. He described the floor plan over the phone and it sounded like something that would work for us. The owner told us that the prior tenant had already moved out and the door would be unlocked. We jumped in the car and went over to take a look. When I walked in, I remember saying, "Wow, look at all this space!" Compared to our little house trailer, it was amazing. The duplex was an old structure, but it seemed to

## Chapter 7

have good bones. The main level consisted of a large living room-dining room combination and it had hardwood floors. The kitchen felt huge compared to the tiny kitchen in the house trailer. There were two bedrooms on the main level and that was just perfect. In addition to all this, there was a small upstairs bonus room, and the basement was perfect for hanging laundry during the winter months. This was our lucky day – the rent was reasonable, and we called the owner to let him know we would take it.

Every day seemed like an exciting new adventure – a new taste of life, so to speak. I was ecstatic about moving into the duplex. To me, it felt like a single-family house and there was so much space! Pam was already pulling herself up on things and she would be walking soon. No more cramped quarters – I was in heaven! We began making plans for our move. First on the agenda, we needed to buy some furniture. So, off we went furniture shopping! We took Pam with us everywhere we went. She loved riding in the car, and people always fussed over her. We shopped around and checked the ads in the newspaper, looking for the best value. After visiting several furniture stores in Wichita, we found what we needed – and we managed to keep it within budget.

After settling-in at the duplex, we invited Edith, Larry, and Donna, for a barbecue. We were anxious to show off our new place and when they arrived, we showed them around. But they too, had something exciting to share. They were expecting their second baby! Edith and Larry would eventually have four children: Donna, Debbie, Denise and Terry. They were such great friends, and we loved them. We shared many wonderful times together. Pam and Donna had play dates on a regular basis. And birthday parties were a must for every birthday, every year, for every one of the kids.

Being a farmer's wife kept me busy in the kitchen and I was always ready to set an extra plate for a hired hand. I didn't mind; my life was good and I was happy. For me, things were easy going in those days. There was no drama or stress and I lived my life one day at a time. Shortly after moving into the duplex, Dale mentioned that his hired hand needed a place to stay for a short time. I had already met Charlie, and remember thinking that he was a nice guy. The small room upstairs was not being used and it was fine with me if Charlie would like to stay there. Charlie was a hard worker and I knew that Dale depended on him. We put a cot in the upstairs room and Charlie was pleased to have a clean place to stay. He had a kind personality and he was a considerate guest. Charlie joined us for meals, and he seemed to enjoy my cooking. I had learned to cook by then – nothing gourmet, mostly meat and potatoes meals, and fried chicken was something I did well. I remember when I got an electric skillet and how thrilled I was. It became my favorite pan for frying chicken.

The hot summer lingered into September, but it started to cool down by the middle of the month. Dale begam to talk about taking a second job for income during the off-season winter months. After planting the wheat that fall, he accepted a job working for a finance company. The job involved travel within the state of Kansas, and some weeks Dale was away from home for several days. The job involved calling on customers who were behind on their car payment. In some cases, the car had to be repossessed and part of Dale's job involved making arrangements for the car to be towed. In some circumstances however, Dale towed the car himself. He said that was tough and he didn't like that part of the job. Pam missed her daddy when he was gone and, of course, I did too. One time, when Dale was gone for several days working in Hutchinson, Kansas, he came home with an

## Chapter 7

adorable teddy bear tucked under his arm. Pam loved that teddy bear to rags. She took it everywhere, and always to bed with her. When its feet became torn and tattered, I would say, "We will take him to the teddy bear doctor." Then I got out my sewing kit and repaired her teddy. Another winter, Dale worked for an insurance company in their sales department. Then another time, he worked for a contractor laying tile in homes. Another winter, he worked at Cessna Aircraft Company in Wichita. And, the following winter, Cessna called him back and trained him to be an inspector. Dale always seemed to find work during the off-season. The income was wonderful in sustaining us during those winter months when wheat farmers had no income.

Pam was talking and putting sentences together nicely. She loved telling me about everything she was doing, every minute of the day. We had fun little chit chats. Pam had been a healthy toddler, but when she was nineteen months old, she became very sick with a virus and had to be hospitalized. The virus spread rapidly, and the hospitals were filled with babies and young children. Our pediatrician left instructions at the hospital for Pam to be admitted, but when we arrived at St. Joseph's Hospital, we were told that all hospital rooms were filled. The hospital staff said they would put a hospital bed in the open hallway. It was temporary, they said, just until a room became available. I was upset about it but we had no choice. Pam was dehydrated and she had a high fever. She couldn't keep any food down, and she looked pale. The attending nurse put an intravenous needle in her leg, and started the flow of fluid into her body. We were worried parents and remained by her side.

Twenty-four hours had passed, and still, there were no hospital rooms – Pam remained in the hallway. Our doctor hadn't been there to see her, and the hospital care was minimal. By then, we were very frustrated with the situation at the hospital, and with our pediatrician. However, the IV fluid must have helped because Pam's color had returned to her face and she seemed to be feeling better. We decided to take her home – we would find another pediatrician. Well, that probably wasn't a smart decision, but we took our little girl home. Once we were home, I got Pam situated in her bed and I gave her a small amount of liquid. She seemed comforted being in her own bed, but she still had some temperature and I could tell that she felt weak. I sat in Pam's room until she went to sleep. She had tolerated the liquid and that was a good sign. But I remained worried and called our friend, Edith, hoping she could recommend a good pediatrician. She gave me the names of two doctors – the one they used, and another doctor a friend of theirs used. I called Edith's doctor right away and was able to get an appointment for the following day.

I went back to check on Pam and she was sleeping soundly. I decided to go downstairs and put some laundry in the washer. Worrisome thoughts crept into my mind. What if Pam got worse? I heard that some babies had died. That was frightening and I couldn't bear having those thoughts. I remember just standing there in the basement. My heart was pounding, and I began to pray. I pleaded with God, and asked Him to make our baby well. I took some deep breaths, and went back upstairs to check on Pam. She had been sleeping for several hours. I leaned in close, and listened to her breathing – it sounded normal. I touched her forehead gently – she no longer felt hot. That afternoon, when Pam woke up, she seemed much better. I checked her temperature and it was normal. My prayers had been answered! This was a blessing that I didn't take lightly. Pam continued to improve, and the next day, she was able to tolerate some light food, and she was hugging her teddy bear again!

## Chapter 8

## Life on The Farm

Gazing across a field of golden ripened wheat, and watching it sway gently in the wind is a sight to behold. We lived in the heart of wheat country. Kansas is the largest wheat producing state in the U.S. The year was 1957 – the wheat had been harvested and the wheat grain had been hauled to the elevator. Then came time to plow the fields and turn the soil. After the harvest that year, we were surprised when Dale's parents told us they wanted to move back to the farm they owned in Burlington, Oklahoma. Dale's dad said he was ready to retire from the farm in Wichita. John and Mary were leasing the farm house, along with 240 acres of land and outbuildings from some people by the name of Eyestone. John was offering Dale the opportunity to take over the entire farming operation in Wichita. John had confidence in his son and knew that he could handle the farm operation in a responsible manner. Dale was twenty-six years old at the time and I was twenty-one. This would be a huge responsibility for Dale, but he was excited about the challenge and considered it a good opportunity. John contacted Mr. Eyestone to discuss the change and so, it was all arranged. The annual cost of the lease would remain the same at fifty percent of the wheat crop from the 240 acres of land, and Dale would bear the expense of putting in the crop in addition to providing all the farm equipment needed. The plan was set in motion – we would move into the farmhouse at 3900 North Broadway, and Dale would work the land and manage the entire farm.

John and Mary's furniture was loaded on the truck. They were going back to the place where they raised their family, where Dale spent his boyhood years. Dale's brothers were helping with their move, and soon, they were on their way. I assumed they were happy about returning to Oklahoma, where so many memories still lingered. Meanwhile, we were in the process of getting our things ready to move into the house they had just moved out of. We had given notice to the owner of the duplex, and things were moving forward. When our moving day arrived, Dale's hired hand, Charlie, helped us move. The farm house looked different without Mary's furnishings, and I found it spotless. Mary had cleaned the floors, the kitchen cabinets, the bathroom – everything! The house was move-in condition! We got settled-in with our own things, and immediately felt at home.

It wasn't surprising that Dale was consumed with work – he was busier than ever. Managing that farm and tending to all the things that needed to be taken care of was a big job. In addition to the farm house, there were several large out-buildings, including two big silos. But all this would prove to be very useful for Dale. He had big plans and wasted no time in acquiring more land to lease and farm. Soon he was farming 450 acres. He bought more farm machinery which was needed to accommodate the additional farm land. And before I knew what was happening, Dale was in the cattle business too. He was a busy guy, full of energy and endless ambition!

## Chapter 8

Life on the farm was good – I loved the lifestyle, and loved being there. As a farmer's wife, I learned a lot about hard working farm families. Harvest time was especially busy for me when I cooked for the harvest crew. I learned to prepare good hearty meals, and most days during the harvest you could smell a pie baking in the oven. I didn't mind cooking for the farm hands; I just put on my apron and took it all in stride. Charlie was a regular at our table. Dale worked hard and barely took time to eat. Some days when he came in for lunch, he sat down at the table to eat and in less than five minutes, he was off again – always in a rush. I honestly don't think he knew what he was eating! During the busy harvest season, I took snacks out to the field for the guys. Supper was usually served early, around 4:30, and that meant a fourth meal of cherry pie, or some kind of desert in the evening.

Weekend get-togethers with friends is something I looked forward to. Most of our friends had children and we usually had cookouts at each other's house. We spent a lot of time with Edith and Larry, and many fun times with Evelyn and Keith Clark. Keith was a meat inspector and Evelyn was a housewife. They had three children. Linda was the oldest, and Kevin was about the same age as Pam. From time to time, Evelyn and I helped out at the elementary school, and I enjoyed being part of that. Another friend I remember is Johnny Girrands and his wife, Mim. Johnny always stood within two inches of a person's face to talk. I found myself always backing up. Johnny was a farmer, too, and we had that in common; however, they didn't have children. They enjoyed socializing as couples and invited us to dinner but we weren't comfortable leaving our little ones with a babysitter, so we didn't socialize with them very often. But we kept in touch and saw them quite often at the StockYards and various farm events.

I was yearning to have another baby – perhaps a little boy this time. It was 1958, and Pam was three years old; I wanted her to have a playmate, a sibling to grow up with. Dale and I had talked about it but hadn't made any specific plans. So, when I told Dale I was ready, he was on board right away. I was happy and hoping to get pregnant quickly, but it actually took several months. I was patient and finally the symptoms were there. Edith recommended her obstetrician, saying everything went well when he delivered Donna and Debbie; she liked him. That was good enough for me and I scheduled an appointment. When I met Dr. Anderson, I thought he had a kind face and a friendly smile, and he was easy to talk to. After the exam, Dr. Anderson confirmed that I was pregnant. According to his calculation, the baby's due date was October 2nd. I was over-the-moon excited and looked forward to being blessed with another healthy baby. When I got home, Dale knew by the happy look on my face and he was equally happy. I called my mom to let her know and it didn't take long for her to spread the word to the rest of the family. She was excited about having another grandchild.

## A Special House Guest

In spite of the summer heat, it was fairly comfortable inside the house. The large shade trees helped shield the house from the hot sun. Life was busy on the farm and most of my days were full. I was in my sixth month of a healthy pregnancy and I felt good. I loved being pregnant, and I was very happy. Dale had just completed another wheat harvest. Life was good. But then one day, we received a phone call from Dale's dad with some disappointing news. He called to tell us that Mary had some health problems and things were not going well at the farm in Oklahoma. John told us that Mary needed to be hospitalized for treatment in Wichita.

## Chapter 8

John would need a place to stay, and of course, we told him he would stay with us for as long as needed. John had done so much for us, and this was a chance to now help him. In preparing for his arrival, I explained to Pam that her grandpa would be staying with us for a while and he needed a place to sleep. I asked if it would be okay if he used her bedroom since it had a big bed. Pam shook her head "yes" and began picking up her dollies. We moved her things to the smaller bedroom with the twin bed. Pam was excited about her grandpa coming to stay with us.

John arranged things in advance for Mary's admittance to the hospital in Wichita. Upon their arrival, John and Mary were escorted to a nice private room. John stayed with Mary most of the day, then later on, he brought his things to the farm house. I adored Dale's dad and I tried to make him as comfortable as possible, but it was a tough time for John. He was very worried about his wife and was back and forth to the hospital every day; he was carrying a lot of stress. We were not only concerned about Mary's health, but John's as well. Most mornings when I got up, I found John sitting on the kitchen stool – a cup of coffee in one hand, and a cigarette in the other. In spite of it all, there was a bright spot in John's day and it was his granddaughter. Pam was adorable and would brighten anyone's day, and she certainly brightened John's. He loved his little granddaughter, and when he wasn't at the hospital, he enjoyed playing with her. Many times, if John was going out to run an errand, he took Pam with him – always with my blessing, of course. When the two of them came home they wore big smiles, and you can bet that Pam had a new toy.

One evening though, when John came home from the hospital, something seemed off – he wasn't himself. When he came into the house, we noticed he was out of sorts. He said he didn't feel well and he went straight to bed. That was so unlike John – not to sit and visit. We noticed that he had parked the car in a strange manner, and that was odd. John didn't drink alcohol, so we knew that wasn't the problem and we were concerned. The next morning, John was up early and when I asked if he felt better, he said he was okay. But when I noticed the torn sheets on his bed, I knew he had a fitful night. Many months later, we would come to realize that John had a heart attack that evening. John was with us for two months and after Mary's long struggle, her health improved and John started to relax. It wasn't long after that and Mary was released from the hospital. John was very relieved when he and Mary could return to their home in Oklahoma.

## A Blissful Event

Baby's due date was getting close. "I think it's a boy this time!" I exclaimed. I carried this baby much differently than my first pregnancy. Dale had already put the baby bed together and it was ready and waiting in our bedroom. We hadn't seen Dale's parents for a few weeks, and wanted to visit them before the baby arrived. Burlington was a two-hour drive from Wichita, and it would be an easy excursion for me. So, we left early that Sunday morning for the little road trip. I remember that day so well – the nice lunch, and nice visit we had with Mary and John. We were happy to see Mary doing well, and John seemed good too. During the ride back to Wichita, Pam was content playing with her toys in the back seat, and Dale and I both said how glad we were that we had taken the time to visit them.

October 2nd came and went and the baby was nearly two weeks late! But why was I surprised? I was really late with Pam. The day was October 14th, and I had an appointment to see Dr. Anderson that afternoon. When I woke up that morning, I was

## Chapter 8

filled with energy. I cleaned the house then did the laundry and hung the clothes outdoors to dry. Everything was in order and my hospital bag was packed. I had a strong feeling I would have the baby that very day. When I arrived at the doctor's office that afternoon, I was still full of energy. I told the nurse how energized I felt, and she said she hears that a lot when women are about to start labor. The nurse showed me to the exam room, and Dr. Anderson came in shortly. During the exam, I told my doctor about the energy I had all day, and said "I'm going to have this baby tonight!" But Dr. Anderson replied "Not tonight – You're not ready."

The laundry was flapping in the wind when I got home and I walked over to remove the clothes pins and brought everything inside. I enjoyed the fresh airy fragrance as I folded the clothes. My mind was focused on the baby as I fixed an early dinner. I continued to have the same feeling – this baby is ready! Well, by ten o'clock that evening, guess what – my water broke! The first labor pain gave me a little jab. "Told you so, Dr. Anderson!" I muttered to myself. I alerted Dale – "It's time!" Then I gently woke Pam, telling her "It's time for Mommy to go to the hospital." Pam rubbed her sleepy eyes as she climbed out of bed. I told her she could wear her pajamas to Edith's house. Our dear friend, Edith, was so kind in offering to take care of Pam. When I called Edith, she said she would stay up until we got there. I helped Pam slip into her little robe and slippers. She wasn't surprised about going to Edith's house because I had explained everything to her earlier. Her small bag was already packed and ready.

Dale turned on the bright yard light and we made our way out to the car. We went straight to the hospital. I wanted Pam to go with us to the hospital so she would know where her mommy was. A hospital attendant greeted us and motioned for me to sit in the wheelchair. Dale carried Pam, and walked along as I was taken to the admissions office. I hugged Pam and kissed her goodbye and told her "Very soon you'll have a baby brother or baby sister. Be a good girl for Edith. Mommy loves you!" Dale gave me a kiss and said he would be back soon. Then he and Pam left for Edith and Larry's house. After checking in, the nurse wheeled me to the obstetrics department. I hoped that Dr. Anderson would remember what I said.

I had heard that a second birth is much easier than the first. For me, that was absolutely true. By the time I got situated in the labor room, my pains had become much stronger and more consistent, but it wasn't anything I couldn't handle. The nurse handed me a hospital gown and I slipped it on. She helped me into the bed and I tried to make myself comfortable. I glanced at the wall clock and noticed it was already 11:30 p.m. I was twenty-three years old and I don't know if being older had anything to do with it, but I was more relaxed this time. I learned how to use the headboard rails to grip with my hands. I seemed to be able to work with the pain rather than fight it and it was definitely much easier this time. I noticed that Dr. Anderson had arrived. After a bit, he came over to say hello and I reminded him what I said about having the baby tonight. He obviously hadn't planned on being up all night. Time went on and I looked over at the wall clock – it was 1:30 A.M. My labor pains were quite intense by then, but I wasn't moaning and didn't feel the need for medication. But about that time, Dr. Anderson said he wanted to give me a "little something" to make it easier. I should have told my doctor that I didn't want anything, but I thought it's probably a little relaxant and the doctor knows what he's doing. But that "little something" knocked me out! Wasn't I supposed to be awake and able to push?

## Chapter 8

Our baby boy was born at 2:40 a.m., October 15, 1959. He weighed eight pounds, ten ounces! It was several hours before I knew these details. I was asleep when my baby was born and I was asleep when they wheeled me to my hospital room. I must have slept for a long time. When I woke up, I tried to get out of bed but I felt woozy and I remember feeling confused. I put my hand on my belly and could tell that I was no longer pregnant. I looked around and saw Dale sleeping in a chair. Still confused, I slid my legs out of the bed and I stood up. I felt something running down my legs. I looked down and realized it was blood. I wondered where my baby was? Dale must have heard me stirring because he woke suddenly and bolted out of the chair. He rushed over and helped me get back into bed. I think Dale could see that I was confused, but then I heard him say, "We have a boy!" My heart immediately filled with joy! "Oh, my goodness – a boy! Where is he?" Then Dale said "He's in the nursery."

Dale rang for the nurse and she came in promptly. She could see that I needed some attention and said she would come back to clean me up. Dale said he needed to go home to take care of things at the farm. He kissed me and said he would be back a little later. After Dale left, the nurse cleaned me and freshened up the bed linens. Then I asked her, "When can I see my baby?" and she replied, "Didn't they tell you about your baby?" I stared at her with questioning eyes. "Your baby is on oxygen and can't leave the nursery." Hearing this, I panicked. I became very upset and started to cry. "What's wrong with my baby?" I wanted to know. "Why does he need oxygen?" I was sobbing and shaking and I asked the nurse to call my doctor; I wanted to talk to my doctor! I became more upset by the minute. I wanted to see my baby – I wanted to hold him. The nurse tried to calm me and said she would go back to the desk and call my doctor. Did Dale know about this? I tried calling him at home but there was no answer.

Well, my doctor must have gotten the message because it wasn't long until Dr. Anderson walked into my room carrying my son. He smiled broadly as he handed him to me. I immediately noticed the plastic oxygen tubes in my baby's nose and saw the salve spread over the fine cuts on his little face. I snuggled him close to my breast and whispered "I love you little one." Then I kissed his forehead. He opened his blue eyes and looked at me. He was so precious and sweet and I began talking to him. I was still emotional with tears running down my cheeks, but this time, I was crying tears of joy. Dr. Anderson explained that my baby had done all his pushing with his face, and that is why he needed oxygen for a couple days. He went on to say that our baby was fine, and that we have a healthy boy. Hearing this, I felt a huge relief and my body started to relax. It no longer seemed important that I was asleep during the birth, and I didn't ask my doctor why he gave me that "little something."

I had chosen a boy's name long before my son was born and Dale liked the name. However, we just learned that some friends had their baby boy first, and they had chosen that same name. This was all quite silly, especially since we hardly knew these people, but we thought we should think about another name for our baby. When Dale came back to the hospital that day, we talked about it and Dale said he liked the name "Randy Dean." His brother, Bud, carried the middle name of Dean. And so, it was decided, we named our son Randy Dean Rieger. I completed the hospital paperwork for his birth certificate and gave it to the nurse. Dale and I were proud parents and we were overjoyed to have our baby boy. I called Edith and asked if I could speak to Pam. It was so

## Chapter 8

good hearing her sweet little voice. I told Pam about her baby brother and that she would get to hold him real soon.

After a couple days in the hospital, Randy and I were allowed to go home. I was very excited to introduce baby Randy to his big sister. Dale picked up Pam at Edith and Larry's, then came to the hospital and the four of us rode home together. Pam was anxious to hold her baby brother and when we got home, she climbed up on the sofa and made herself comfortable. I showed her how to hold baby Randy, and how to support his head. She held out her arms and I placed him on her lap. Pam cuddled him gently, then looked up at us with a big grin. She was a big sister and I knew she felt proud.

Everything seemed to be going well. We had been home from the hospital about one week when my Aunt Hermina called to ask if she and Grandma Kinsley could stop by. I was excited about their visit and pleased that they wanted to come. But then, around noon time, baby Randy began to fuss and cry. I figured he was hungry and I fed him. He took part of his milk and seemed finished. I burped him, changed his diaper, and laid him down in his bed. By the time Aunt Hermina and Grandma arrived, I could tell that something was bothering our baby. He was fussy and seemed uncomfortable. They came in and sat down, while I tried to soothe and comfort baby Randy. They had brought a gift for Randy, but unfortunately, their visit didn't go well because Randy began crying very hard and loud. Hermina wanted to hold him, to see if she might have the magic touch. Then, Grandma took Randy and held him close, but baby Randy continued to cry. I changed his diaper, and tried holding him in various positions, but he continued to cry. Hermina and Grandma decided it was best to leave. After a while, baby Randy calmed down and he went to sleep. I didn't know what had caused him to cry like that, and I hoped that everything was okay.

Things were not okay. The next morning, baby Randy woke with a terrible cold. He was sneezing and I thought it was unusual for an infant to have a cold. His nose was running and it was full of mucus. No one in the family was sick. He must have caught a germ in the hospital. Did it have anything to do with the oxygen he had been given and the tubes they put in his nose? I called our pediatrician's office immediately, and they said to bring him to their office. I bundled Randy in his blanket, and the four of us went to the doctor's office. I told the doctor how fussy Randy was the prior day and that he cried as though he was in pain. And I told the doctor that Randy was on oxygen the first two days after birth. After the doctor examined Randy, he asked that we take him to the hospital. He said he wanted to have him admitted for some tests and observation. He couldn't tell us what was wrong with our baby, but said he wanted to check for possible infection. The doctor phoned the hospital to let them know we were coming. It was heartbreaking, having to take our newborn to the hospital, but we left the doctor's office and went straight to the hospital. I stayed at the hospital with Randy, and Dale went home with Pam. After a few days in the hospital, the doctor said they didn't find anything wrong other than the cold. Our baby seemed better and he was released. We were so relieved and thankful that we could bring him home.

Those joyful moments were disrupted several days later when our baby was sick again. This time he had a significant fever, and it was obvious he didn't feel good. I called the doctor, and again, our baby was admitted to the hospital. Baby Randy would remain in the hospital for the next two weeks. His fever persisted, but it was up and down, and the pediatric doctors couldn't seem to

## Chapter 8

find anything seriously wrong, other than an ear infection. At one point during baby Randy's hospital stay, his temperature rose to 106 degrees! That was very frightening, and I was nearly sick with worry. Many tears were shed during that time, and I prayed a lot. Randy was given antibiotics and eventually his fever went down and he got better. The doctor told us that his fever must stay down a full twenty-four hours before they would allow him to go home. While I will never know what caused our baby to get sick, I felt that he was infected with a bad germ in the hospital, during or after his birth. Various things rolled around in my mind and I wondered if perhaps the oxygen tubes carried germs that traveled into his body. But now, Randy was well enough to go home.

Sunny skies gave warmth to a crisp fall morning. A fresh scent of baby powder filled the air as we walked into his room. I picked up Randy and snuggled him close, then I squatted down with him for Pam to take a peek at her baby brother. I wrapped Randy in his blanket and we were ready to go. The nurse handed me his discharge form and we left the hospital. Randy was nearly one month old. He had struggled the first few weeks of his life but he was a tough little guy. When we got home, he was wide-awake and his blue eyes looked around as if to say, "Where am I?" He held his head up and I could tell that he was strong. Pam was anxious to hold her baby brother again and she climbed up on the sofa and made herself ready. I remember how gentle she was with him. As I stood looking at the two of them, my heart was bursting with love. My children filled the house with sunshine.

Thanksgiving arrived and we certainly had many blessings to be thankful for. Randy grew stronger each day and he was a happy baby. In spite of a few allergies and a new formula of soy milk, he was doing well. The new year arrived swiftly and I hung the 1960 wall calendar in the kitchen by the telephone.

I felt the grip of winter that year, but finally, spring arrived and I welcomed the opportunity to be outdoors more often with Pam and Randy. On warm spring days, I put Randy in his stroller where he could sit in the sunshine and watch me hang the laundry on the clothesline. The kids were happy being outdoors, and Pam loved calling out to the barn cats; they always came running to her.

It seemed appropriate that we should have a horse, living on a farm and all. Dale started looking around and after checking various sources, he found a wonderful older mare that was calm and gentle around children. That's exactly what we wanted and Dale proceeded to buy that horse. Her name was Star, and so appropriately named because she had a beautiful white star on her nose. When Edith and Larry heard that we had a horse, they couldn't wait to bring their kids out to the farm. We usually had steaks in the freezer and were always ready to put some on the grill. I invited them to come on over and when they arrived, the kids were all giddy with excitement. We stood around watching as Dale put the saddle on Star. Larry climbed up onto the horse, then Dale lifted one of the kids up, and off they went in a slow trot. The kids were thrilled and expressed their excitement with big smiles. Pam loved riding Star with her daddy. She sat proudly in front of Dale, and smiled big when she got to help hold the reins. Then it was my turn to ride. After a failed first attempt, I got a grip on Star and placed my foot in the stirrup; I swung my leg over and positioned myself in the saddle and slowly guided Star around the farm yard. When baby Randy was old enough, he too, got to sit on Star with his daddy. Later on, Dale bought another horse – a half-Arabian, half-Quarter Horse colt. His name was High Noon. He was a gorgeous horse but not yet tame and the kids were not allowed to go near him. Breaking High Noon proved to be a challenging endeavor for Dale!

## Unexpected News

The morning began as usual and it was a perfectly calm day – no wind! I was going about my daily routine when we received a startling telephone call from Oklahoma. Dale answered the phone and I knew by the glum look on his face that something was wrong. Dale's brother, Melvin, was calling to let us know that John had a heart attack! "It's serious," he said, "and he's in the hospital." Melvin went on to say that his nephew had found John lying on the ground next to the tractor. Dale got in the car and left for Burlington. When Dale came home the following day, he said his dad was doing okay, but he had to take it easy. He went on to say that his dad was worried about the fields that needed to be plowed. I didn't understand why John hadn't hired someone to do the plowing; perhaps he couldn't find anyone. Dale told his dad not to worry, that he would send Charlie down to Burlington, to plow the fields and take care of what needed to be done. Charlie was soon on his way to Burlington. After a few days, John seemed to be doing much better, and the doctor felt it was safe to release him from the hospital. John went home with medicine, and strict orders from his doctor. Unfortunately, John's heart suffered damage from the heart attack, and the doctor told him that he needed to be careful. In today's world, John would have open heart surgery. But it was 1960. I often wondered, had John been treated at a large city hospital, would his treatment have been any different? We worried about him, and hoped he would follow the doctor's orders.

A light breeze drifted in through the kitchen window and it was a beautiful summer day. I was busy with morning chores while keeping an eye on Randy, as he crawled about on the kitchen floor. Pam was close by and occupied with her toys. I had just cleared the breakfast dishes from the table when the telephone rang. I picked up the phone and said "Hello." Then I heard Melvin's voice. "Barbara, Dad died this morning – tell Dale." That is all he said, and he hung up the phone – he was too emotional to talk. My hand went to my mouth, and my heart started pounding. It had been about one week since John was released from the hospital – what happened? I had to find Dale! He was plowing one of the fields, but I didn't know which one. I stood there thinking, trying to decide what to do. We had no cell phones back then. I decided to call Evelyn and Keith Clark, a neighbor and friend. They lived about two miles from us, and I thought Dale was plowing the field close to their house. They could look out their window and see Dale, if he was in that field. Keith answered the phone and I asked if he could look out and tell me if could see Dale's tractor. Keith came back to the phone and said he couldn't see the tractor. I told Keith that I need to find Dale, and if they do see him to please tell him to come home. Keith could tell that something was wrong, and he said they would scout around to find him. I thanked Keith, and hung up the phone. Pam was asking, "What's wrong, Mommy?" I thought for a second, then squatted down to Pam and said, "Something happened to Grandpa." I told her I would explain it to her after Daddy got home.

I was pacing about, anxiously waiting for a call back from the Clarks. It had been about fifteen or twenty minutes since I called them. I decided to put the kids in the car and drive around to the farm fields. I would leave a note for Dale, to let him know I was out looking for him – in case he came home from a different direction and we missed each other. But about then, I heard Dale's pickup in the driveway. I took a deep breath and tried to prepare myself. I rushed outside to meet Dale, and when I told him the sad news, he collapsed to the ground. He covered his face with his hands and began sobbing – he rolled back and forth on the ground. Dale's heart was broken – his beloved dad was gone. I tried to comfort him, but nothing could take away the anguish he felt. I was broken-hearted too; I loved Dale's dad. We had lost a wonderful man – a kind, good hearted soul. I knew I had to be strong for Dale, and I held back my tears. Dale was still rolling about on the ground when Keith and Evelyn pulled into our driveway. Later on, I learned that Keith went to the field that day, and finished the plowing Dale had started.

The loss of John Rieger was devastating. His family loved him so much; we all looked up to him. His life had suddenly been cut short; he was sixty years old. He died of coronary thrombosis on July 5, 1960. Pam and Randy would grow up without their Grandpa Rieger. Randy was just eight months old at the time; he would never know him. Pam was five years old and would miss her grandpa. During the time John stayed with us, Pam had fun with her grandpa. But being so young, how much would she remember? Our hearts mourned the loss of John, but we tried to heal and carry on with our daily lives.

## Raising My Family on The Farm

While a farmer's lifestyle can be busy and hectic at times, living on the farm provided a wonderful place to raise my children. Farm life instills a feeling for the culture of the land and raising crops. It teaches responsibility and builds character. It instills love and respect for animals and provides a wonderful atmosphere for children to romp and play. Our life on the farm was good, and I am grateful for the experience it gave Pam and Randy during their early years.

It was late August, and I could feel a hint of fall in the evening air. Soon it would be wheat planting time and long days for Dale. He was gearing up and getting the farm equipment ready. Late one night, we were sound asleep in bed when a large semi-trailer loaded with cattle arrived at the farm. We were expecting the delivery, but didn't know exactly when. The loud noise of the truck woke us and Dale climbed out of bed and got dressed. He went out to meet the driver and help unload the cattle. The cattle would stay at the farm a few days, perhaps one week, to feed and fatten-up, and then they would be delivered to the stockyards where they would be sold. The farm was located within a few miles of the stockyards and provided the perfect stop-over location for the cattle. It took a while for the guys to unload the cattle, weigh them, and get them confined to the feedlot. Dale had plenty of silage stored in the silos, and that's what the cattle would be fed.

Just when I thought things were merrily rolling along, a little hiccup came our way. Randy had been doing really well. He was healthy and happy and had not been sick since that first month – not even a cold. But one day when I was changing his diaper, I noticed a swelling in his groin area. He wasn't sick and he wasn't in any pain, but we took him to the pediatrician for an examination. The doctor knew right away what was wrong. "Ah, yes," he said. "Randy has a hernia hydrocele, common in little boys." He went on to say that about one to five percent of children will have a hernia or hydrocele, including newborns. The doctor explained how it would be easily repaired with a surgical procedure. Randy was only ten months old at the time and this news was unsettling, but we took some deep breaths and followed doctor's orders. Fortunately, the surgery went well and we were relieved to hear the doctor say that Randy would be fine with no lingering effects. Little did we know that before Randy turned two, he would have

## Chapter 8

another hydrocele on the other side! Randy was strong, and he recovered nicely from that operation too.

But Randy's health problems were far from over. When he was about two years old, he began having asthma attacks. The attacks came on suddenly and we had to rush him to the emergency room. Randy could inhale, but he couldn't exhale. His chest became inflated, and he had difficulty breathing. After arriving at the emergency room, the ER doctor gave Randy an injection. Then, we waited twenty minutes hoping his breathing would improve, and if it didn't, the doctor gave him another injection. It was extremely frightening watching my child struggle to breathe. One evening when I was home alone with the kids, Randy had an asthma attack. Ironically, Dale was in the hospital awaiting surgery to repair his double hernia. This attack was especially bad for Randy. I reached out to Dale's brother, Bud, and he took Randy and me to the ER that night while Imo stayed with Pam. On the way to the ER, Randy's breathing worsened and I worried we might not make it in time. I prayed silently as I held Randy in my arms. When we arrived at the ER, the doctor could see that my child was in distress and he immediately injected Randy with the medication. Thankfully, within a few minutes his breathing improved. Randy was a tough little guy and always hung in there. He never panicked, even at the worst times when he was in distress. Fortunately, as time went on, Randy's asthma attacks became farther apart and he outgrew the asthma by the time he was five years old. Dale's hernia surgery went well and I brought him home from the hospital a couple of days later.

Kitty Land was an amusement park in Wichita, designed for small children with the cutest animated rides. Pam and Randy loved going there and it was always a special treat. Sometimes we went there with our friends, the Delantys, and their kids. It was sure to put big smiles on those little kids' faces. Birthdays were always a special event and I had fun planning birthday parties for our kids and inviting all their friends. We had the perfect party room upstairs at the farm house where the kids could romp and play. Each year, I looked forward to making birthday cakes and planning fun games for the kids. One year, I made a train cake for Randy's birthday when he turned four. I used orange juice cans to bake the cake batter. I made an engine for the little train, and four train cars. Lifesavers worked perfectly for the wheels. Decorating the train was quite a process, but when it was all done, it was adorable. Pam's favorite cake has always been Angel Food but one year on her birthday, she had a pretty doll cake that looked like Cinderella. I think Edith may have made that one. Edith could make amazing cakes and eventually she turned it into a business.

During my adult years on the farm, I was very domesticated. In my spare time, I had fun with my brand-new Montgomery Ward electric sewing machine. I got creative and somewhat fashion conscious making little outfits for Pam's Barbie dolls. Pam and her little friends had fun playing with their Barbie Dolls and the doll house, sharing the array of cute Barbie doll clothes. Randy enjoyed playing with his GI Joe soldiers, but I didn't make clothes for GI Joe. The sewing machine was portable and I longed for a nice cabinet I could sit up to. One day, Dale surprised me and said he would build a cabinet for my sewing machine. When he had a break from his work, he built a cabinet complete with drawers and a hinged lid. The sewing machine lifted up out of the cabinet for use, then reclined down for storage. It was pretty cool. I had a few other domestic hobbies and sometimes on a quiet afternoon, one might find me sitting on the sofa with a crochet hook in my hand, making doilies, of all things! Or perhaps, you might see me with an embroidery needle, stitching a pretty design on a new pair of

## Chapter 8

pillow cases. Yes, I know – hard to believe! I was a young stay-at-home farm mom having fun raising my little ones.

School was about to start and my little girl was going to first grade. Kindergarten wasn't available at the school when Pam was five, so she went right into first grade when she was six years old. Pam was excited about going to school, but a little nervous at the same time. I talked to her about school, books, the teacher and all the many things she would learn, and we talked about making new friends. Pam loved books and she was already learning to read. I took her to visit the school on enrollment day and I remember how happy she was. The year was 1961, and children were required to be vaccinated before starting school. I was prepared and took Pam's vaccination card with me. We walked up and down the hallway and went into her classroom. Later on, I took her shopping to buy a few new dresses, and Pam couldn't wait to wear them. Riding the school bus was a new adventure for Pam. It was nice that the bus would pick Pam up and drop her off directly in front of the house. I took her the first day but after that, she rode the school bus. I will always remember the first time Pam rode the bus to school. Dale had the movie camera ready to capture the moment. She looked so little and sweet as she climbed up the steps of the bus, then she turned around and waved to us. Dale and I stood there waving to her as I blinked back tears. Where had the time gone – how was it possible that our little girl was in first grade? Pam loved school and she had so much to tell when she came home. She usually came home with a picture she had drawn and was excited to give it to me. I stored each and every one in a special drawer.

My children were happy kids and they loved spending time outdoors. The swing set was located near the house and the kids loved the swing; however, they loved exploring the farm even more. Randy was usually trailing after Pam wherever she went. Occasionally, Dale took the kids for a ride in the big two-ton truck and that was always a special treat for them. But one thing we taught our kids early – they were not allowed in the large outbuildings where farm equipment and supplies were stored – that is, unless their daddy was there with them. There were two tall silos at the farm and those were very important structures used for storing grain or fermented feed, known as silage. The tall windmill was an amazing landmark. I'm always a little fascinated by a windmill, especially in Kansas, where the wind keeps them spinning most of the time. We had a huge unheated water tank for the horses and cattle, but during the winter months and freezing temperatures the water would freeze. Dale had to chop through the ice to open up the water for the animals. A heated tank would have been nice. The buzz of a tractor was a familiar sound, especially during the spring, summer and fall. And the scent of freshly cut alfalfa hay is a memory I still have.

There were plenty of cats at the farm, and we had several dogs over the years. Pam and Randy's favorite cat was black with pretty white markings and they called her "Pitty Pat." One day I noticed Pitty Pat was getting a bit poochie and it wasn't long until she surprised us with a litter of kittens. Randy and Pam were fascinated, watching the tiny kittens snuggle up to Pitty Pat's tummy to eat. They named each kitten and spent many hours playing with them. Then, there was the duck named Casper, and the rabbit named Oscar. And then there was the stray dog that became part of our family. One day when Dale was plowing a field, that stray dog followed the tractor around the entire field all day long. When quitting time came, the dog whined and looked at Dale with sad eyes. Dale couldn't resist and when he opened the door to the pickup, the dog jumped in and came home with Dale. When Pam was a toddler, the first dog she

## Chapter 8

petted was called Max, and after that, she called every dog Max. So, when Dale came home with the stray dog, Pam petted it and right away she pointed and said "Max." The dog was a salt & pepper shaggy haired female Terrier mix, so sweet and gentle, and we fell in love with her. Of course, her name was Max. It wasn't long and Max was getting fat, and soon – you guessed it, she had a litter of puppies. The puppies looked like they were part Border Collie. My sister-in-law, Imo, wanted one of the pups; she chose a female and decided to call her "Tinsy."

Over the years, there were a few other dogs at the farm and some were rescued from the Humane Society. The last dog we had at the farm was called "Poncho." He was a shy little dog, a mixed-breed with long hair, and he was adorable. We found him at the Humane Society in Wichita. Poncho settled in and soon learned the sound of our car. Whenever we left in the car, I think he stood guard waiting for us to come back. He got excited when he heard our car coming home. I swear that dog could hear the sound of our car a mile away! He ran like a greyhound all around the farm yard and then he greeted us when we pulled into the driveway.

One summer, Dale and I decided to get a small pony for the kids. Pam was about six years old and Randy was a toddler. Dale began looking around and found a Shetland pony named Pepper. Shetlands are a Scottish breed of pony. They have short legs, and if gentle, they can be a nice size for children. When Pepper arrived at the farm, we put him in a small fenced-in area we felt would be safe for a test ride. Pam climbed on Pepper and we soon found out that Pepper was not gentle. The minute Pam climbed on, he took off running at a fast pace and nearly bucked her off! We were horrified as we saw what was happening, but then, Pam jumped off on her own and grabbed hold of the fence. Whew! Dale had a return agreement with the people and he took Pepper back to the owner. But he didn't give up and he set out searching for a different pony and it wasn't long until he found another Shetland. This pony's name was Shag. The owner assured us that he was very friendly and gentle. So, a few days later, Shag arrived, complete with a little cart. It was the cutest thing! Shag loved to trot around slowly with one of the kids in that cute little cart. We told Shag he could stay but as it turned out, he wasn't there very long. Shag was accustomed to pulling the cart but he didn't want anyone to ride on his back. We had concerns about the safety of the cart and decided it wasn't a good fit for our kids.

During the late 1950's and 60's, there was a popular kid's television show for the age group of four to six. It was broadcast weekday's on KAKE TV, Channel 10. The show was called "Romper Room" and Miss Beverly was the host teacher. Each show had six kids gathered at a round table, with Miss Beverly sitting in the middle. During the show, the children were served donuts and milk while Miss Beverly read stories to them. The children listened to the stories and afterwards they could ask questions, or perhaps tell a story of their own. It was so cute, and one never knew what the kids might say! Pam was first in our family to be a guest on Romper Room. The Delanty kids participated as well, and when Randy was old enough, he too was a guest on Romper Room. As parents, we were allowed to watch the live TV show through a plate glass window situated above the studio. The kids were absolutely adorable – so innocent and natural. Parents were not allowed to talk or make any noise, but we managed to contain our silent laughter.

## Road Trips in the New Car

A new car with an automatic transmission – Yippee! It was a gorgeous brand new 1961 Plymouth. When I learned to drive, we had the Mercury and it was a stick shift. And for a while, I drove

## Chapter 8

Dale's pickup and that clutch was challenging, so I was ecstatic about the automatic transmission. A few months after buying the new car, we decided to take a road trip to Georgia. Randy was three years old and Pam was seven. We hadn't seen Richard and Joan since we left Virginia. Richard had changed jobs, and they had since relocated to Georgia. They invited us to come for a visit and we were excited to see them. It was a long cross-country drive and the first big road trip with our kids. We planned on staying at a motel but when we arrived, Joan said she had already prepared guest rooms for us in the lower level and insisted we stay with them. Their children, Debbie and Michael, were a little older than our kids but the four of them got along well together. Michael played softball and we got to watch his game while we were there. It was hot and very humid that day, and the air felt heavy. I didn't care for the climate in Georgia, but the landscape was lush and beautiful. The journey was fun and the visit with our cousins was wonderful.

We seemed to be in travel mode and not long after our trip to Georgia, we were ready for another road trip. Today's kids have it made on road trips. To pass the time, they can watch movies or play games on their high-tech hand-held device. When our kids were young, they had the Etch-a-Sketch and a few other things I put together to help keep them occupied in the car. And I can still hear those famous words "Are we there yet?" This next road trip was much shorter than the trip to Georgia. We ventured over to Lake of the Ozarks. The scenery in that part of the country is absolutely beautiful. During this trip we also went to Kansas City. I made reservations for us to see a live stage play at the open-air Starlight Theatre. It was a gorgeous evening under a star lite sky when the four of us watched the performance. The play was wonderful and suitable for any age. We had not experienced anything like this, and I could tell that Pam and Randy enjoyed it. I remember thinking, "They would have fun telling their friends about it."

Another time, we went to Liberal, Kansas, to visit Dale's brother, Melvin, and his wife, Pauline. Pauline was a teacher at Liberal Elementary School. She had a warm loving demeanor and was a wonderful teacher. School was out for the summer and it was nice spending time with the two of them. Melvin was semi-retired and worked part-time at a western clothing store. One afternoon during our stay in Liberal, Melvin took us to the store. I knew he was up to something when I saw Melvin's smile and the twinkle in his eyes. He asked Randy to follow him to the boot department. We tagged along and watched as Melvin selected a pair of boots for Randy. Then he proceeded to grab a pair of tiny jeans and a western hat. Well, Randy got dressed in the clothes and boots Melvin selected. He was suddenly transformed into a little cowboy and he was adorable! Randy turned to look in the mirror and a big grin appeared on his face. He loved those boots and would have worn them to bed if I let him! The store didn't have clothes for little girls, so Pam left without boots but that didn't seem to matter. After visiting the store, we went back to Melvin and Pauline's house. Pauline took Pam aside and talked to her about school and things. Pauline was so loving and kind and she made Pam feel special.

It was a breezy Sunday afternoon in Wichita, and we decided to go out for a family drive with a stop at Dairy Queen. As we drove around, we happened to pass by a neighborhood church – the church sign read "Riverside Christian Church." Dale and I had been talking about joining a church, wanting our children to have that experience. We were married by a Christian minister and I thought it would be nice to belong to a Christian church.

## Chapter 8

The church was a nice brick building with stained glass windows and looked inviting. I made a mental note of the time for services and we decided to visit the church the following Sunday.

It had been many years since I had been inside a church and I wasn't sure what to expect. I assumed the Christian church would be less formal than a Catholic church – and it was. I dressed Pam and Randy in their Sunday best, and talked to them about going to church. I told them they would need to sit still for a while and be very quiet. When we arrived at Riverside Christian Church, we were warmly greeted at the door and welcomed inside. We settled into a pew about halfway down the aisle and made ourselves comfortable. My children were very patient throughout the service, and I remember how proud I was sitting in church with my family. We became members and attended church service nearly every Sunday. Many times, after the church service was over, we went to Brown's Grill for lunch. We each had our favorite entrée on the menu, except Randy – he always wanted cereal!

The farming lifestyle was special, but farming itself had its ups and downs. There were times when the crops had to be spray-treated for Green Bugs. Some years, those bugs were especially bad and if left untreated, they would strip a field clean. Another time on July Fourth, one of the wheat fields caught fire and the entire wheat crop, in that particular field, went up in flames. Apparently, the fire started as a result of someone being careless with firecrackers. Another year, after Dale planted the wheat, part of it was drowned out with high water flooding in the area. And each summer, we worried about the threat of hail. Operating the farm, maintaining the farm equipment and planting the crop was a big expense, and losing a crop was discouraging, but we always managed to pick ourselves up by the bootstraps and carry on with a positive attitude.

As time went on, I reconnected with my high school friends. They had long since graduated from Mount Carmel, and some were married with children. It seemed I could once again relate to them. The Mount Carmel Academy ten-year reunion was coming up and while I was a little apprehensive about it, I decided to attend. I was actually surprised to be included in the class of '54. I asked Dale if he would go with me and of course, he didn't want me to go alone and said he would like to go. It was a gala event held at the Cotillion BallRoom in Wichita. Charlotte was there and I was surprised that she had married someone other than Marvin. Marilee E was present and Jackie K, Nancy D, and many others I hadn't seen in a very long time. It was great visiting with everyone and I was glad that Dale got to meet my old high school pals.

The years seemed to pass quickly and another summer had faded away. It was September 1964, when Randy started Kindergarten. He was four years old when school started but he turned five in October, making him eligible for kindergarten. Randy wanted to go to school and I thought he was ready so I enrolled him. In hindsight, I would have held him back another year. During elementary school, age didn't seem to matter so much. However, as Randy moved up to higher grades most of the kids were a half-year older and taller, and Randy felt more comfortable hanging out with younger kids. But when Randy started kindergarten that fall, it was wonderful for him and I felt I had made the right decision. Randy loved going to school and each day after school he had cute stories to tell. One particular day, however, Randy had a little mishap and I received a scary phone call from the school principal. "Mrs. Rieger, you need to come over to the school right away. Randy had a little accident on the playground, and it looks like he needs some stitches." I was

## Chapter 8

startled but remained calm and said, "Oh, my goodness, I'll be right there." Dale was working in the round top building and I called out to him, motioning for him to come to the house. We got in the car and rushed over to the school which was about one mile from the farm house. Randy was in the principal's office when we arrived. He was sitting in a chair, holding a bloody towel on his head. I gently lifted the towel and saw the open gash on his forehead. The principal told us that Randy and another boy collided on the playground. The other boy wasn't hurt but Randy ended up with a nasty cut. I thanked the principal for his help and we rushed out with Randy and went to the emergency room. Randy was very brave and didn't cry when the doctor stitched the open wound. That same week, as luck would have it, the kindergarten kids had their school photos taken. Randy's picture bears the memory of that playground incident!

### Life's Surprising Changes

It had been eight years since we moved into the farm house. I had long since made my nest and felt as though I could stay there forever. But I sensed that Dale was becoming restless with farming. He worked very hard and he seemed somewhat burned out with the ups and downs of the business. There was the constant worry about the crop – would it be a good year, a mediocre crop, or perhaps a failed crop? The weather was unpredictable and always a threat. When a tractor broke down, I saw Dale's frustration. He usually did the repairs himself, and he seemed to be tiring of that too.

It shouldn't have come as any surprise when Dale told me he was tired of farming and he was going to make some changes. He said he wanted to sell out – sell the cattle at the stockyards, and auction the farm machinery. "I'll hire an auctioneer to conduct a sale." And he went on to say, "We'll buy a house and move to town. I'll find a new line of work, and you'll get a job – then we'll have two incomes and a nice life." It was obvious Dale had been mulling this over for a while; he seemed to have it all planned out. I tried to digest what he was saying but it sounded concerning and unsettling. I didn't want a new job. I already had a job, at home, taking care of our children and the household. I didn't say much at first and I tried to let it all soak in. But I had seen it coming – even so, it left me feeling sad. We had some wonderful years at the farm – such memorable history. But in spite of all that, I knew that Dale's ambition was pulling him in a different direction. Dale made the decisions in those days, and I was accustomed to that. Things had been good in the past, so why would I have doubts now? I told myself, "You need to support your husband." In spite of how much I loved my life on the farm, I had to remain positive and open to change. When we shared the news with Pam and Randy, they weren't sure about leaving the farm, but they were enthused about living in a neighborhood where they could walk down the street to a friend's house. Randy was five years old at the time, and Pam would soon be ten.

And so, plans were being made to vacate the farm. Dale needed to contact the owner to let him know that he wouldn't be there for the fall wheat planting. I remember so well the morning Dale made that call to Mr. Eyestone. It was a big decision and a hard phone call to make. Dale knew he was giving away something he had once considered a good opportunity. I listened as Dale told the owner how much he had enjoyed working the farm, that it had been a wonderful place for him and his family, and he appreciated the opportunity he had there; but now, he was ready to leave farming and move on to a new career. After Dale hung up the phone, I watched as he took a deep breath. I sensed his emotion as

## Chapter 8

he held it all in. But then, after a while, I could tell that Dale was relieved; he could now move forward with his plans. Later that day, Dale called Jack Bannon, the auctioneer.

It was February – several months until we would vacate the farm, but it was time to explore our housing options. First, we began talking about our housing needs. We wanted a house with at least three bedrooms, and we wanted a nice-sized backyard. And we thought it would be nice to have a brand-new house. We started driving around and happened upon a new housing development located in west Wichita. Herb Sparks was the developer and builder, and we arranged a meeting with him. He was a very nice man, and we liked him right away. Herb showed us the available lots, and then we looked at the floor plans he offered. We liked the tri-level design with three bedrooms upstairs, and it had two full bathrooms. This particular floor plan had a large living room plus a family room in the lower level along with a small bonus room. We considered the two-car garage a plus. The house didn't have a formal dining room but that wasn't important to us. We proceeded to choose a building site and signed the contract with Herb. He told us it would take four to six months to build the house, depending on the weather. The lot we chose had a large back yard, with plenty of space for the kids to play, and good space for our dog, Poncho. Our new address would be 4102 Bella Vista Drive. The price of the house was $20,300 and that included the electric fireplace log in the family room! Now remember, this was 1965!

It all began to feel very real and it was time for me to start thinking about a job. Secretarial skills would be important, and that's what I focused on. I enrolled in the Continuing Education Program at the Wichita Board of Education. They offered several classes suited for office work, such as typing and shorthand and I was soon back at school. Learning the skill of shorthand was fascinating. The abbreviated symbolic writing method was very clever and I was amazed at how quickly I could write an entire sentence. I still remember a few of the shorthand symbols, and occasionally use it to jot down a quick note to myself. After completing the Continuing Ed classes, I felt prepared to apply for work.

## The Big Auction

The prior fall, Dale planted wheat seed which would be ready to harvest in the summer. Since the combine would be sold at the auction, Dale hired a neighboring farmer to cut the wheat for us in July. The auction date had been scheduled for March 27, 1965. We had quite an array of farm equipment, and Dale was busy getting it ready for the big auction. We had a nearly-new Allis Chalmers tractor and plow, a 1962 Baldwin Combine, a 1963 Krause wheel disc, a 1959 two-ton truck with 15-1/2-foot grain bed and hoist, and a multitude of other farm items, horse saddles, etc. Hundreds of flyers were printed and posted in all the appropriate places. The flyer read, "Public Auction" with a complete list of all the farm machinery and equipment, plus a list of various other items to be sold at the auction. Our names and auction address were printed at the bottom of the flyer, "Mr. and Mrs. Dale Rieger" followed by "Jack Bannon, Auctioneer" along with his contact information. Everything was in place, and we were ready for the big day!

It was a chilly spring morning and I was up early. Dale was already outdoors checking on things. The auction was scheduled to begin at ten o'clock. Pam and Randy were getting dressed and I reminded them it was cold outside and to dress warm. Then I prepared a hearty breakfast for the four of us. The farm machinery, trucks, and equipment were nicely displayed in the large farm yard. Other smaller miscellaneous items were placed on long

## Chapter 8

tables. The auctioneer arrived ahead of time to set up his booth and get prepared. I glanced out the window and noticed that some people were arriving early, which was not unusual. Many came from out of town and had driven several hours to get there. Before long, the crowd grew and the farmyard was filled with a multitude of people. Pam was strolling about taking pictures with her little camera and Randy was trailing close behind.

The auctioneer stood tall above the crowd and began banging his gavel. It was time to start the auction. He began with the customary jibber-jabber, then he proceeded to call out each individual piece of machinery, describing it to the on-looking crowd. The auctioneer jibber continued and his head moved this way and that as he called for bids. It was fun to watch, as buyers nodded their heads and raised their hands with bids. The auctioneer's hand was waving back and forth, and his head was nodding too! Then, after the bidding went back and forth a few times, the auctioneer slammed his gavel and proclaimed "SOLD." The auction was a huge success – EVERYTHING SOLD!

In spite of the chilly weather, people lingered about after the auction was over. Some were paying for their purchase and were engaged with the auctioneer's bookkeeper; others just mingled and wanted to visit. Some were curious about our plans, and asked why we were leaving the farm. "A change of pace – moving to town; Dale's ready to try a new line of work." It had been an amazing whirlwind of a day – a memorable day! All of the farm machinery and equipment had been moved away within two days and the farm looked a little bare. The neighboring farmer Dale hired to cut the wheat that summer also took care of hauling the wheat to the local grain elevator where it was weighed and sold. It was our last wheat harvest.

## Chapter 9
## City Life - A New Home in Town

    Spring arrived with all its splendor and the daylight hours grew longer. There were glorious new blooms sprouting everywhere and the songbirds were building their nests. And a whole new lifestyle was sprouting for my family. Life on the farm was winding down and we would soon move on, leaving behind some of my happiest days. As I thought about the past eight years, I found myself feeling a little melancholy. I would miss so many things. I thought about the songbirds I had grown so accustomed to. There were no trees to attract the birds in our new neighborhood. But we would plant trees, I told myself as I tried to maintain a positive attitude. Our new house was well into construction and we could now walk throughout the house. The roof and windows had been installed and each time we visited the construction site, we discovered new additions. If everything was on schedule, we would be settled into the new house before school started in late August. One afternoon, we took Edith and Larry to see the house, then we went back to the farm and put some steaks on the grill. Edith and Larry said they would miss coming to the farm.

    It was enrollment week and I took Pam and Randy to visit their new school. They were excited but a little nervous too. Randy would start first grade that fall and Pam would be in fifth grade. Many families had already moved into the new neighborhood. As we drove up the street, we noticed a few kids playing outside in some of the yards – that made my children happy. They looked forward to having friends close by. The date for closing the VA loan on our new home was scheduled and things were moving along as planned. I had started packing some boxes in preparation for the move. It seemed we had accumulated a lot of things over the last few years. But of course, our family had grown since moving into the farm house.

Moving day arrived and the rental truck was headed to 4102 Bella Vista Drive. Pam, Randy and our dog, Poncho, rode in the car with me. When we got there, Poncho jumped out of the car and seemed to know this would be his new home. The four of us went to work getting things unloaded and began filling the space in our new house. I wanted to get the kitchen set up first and Pam helped me unwrap the dishes and arrange things in the cabinets. Randy was busy in his bedroom unloading boxes filled with his toys. We had been busy at the new house all day and had accomplished a lot. The only thing left at the farm was Poncho's dog house. Poncho was an outdoor dog and he was used to sleeping in his dog house at night. We wanted him to feel at home, so the four of us got in the car and went back to the farm to get the dog house.

Daylight faded away and it was dark by the time we got back to the new house. As we turned onto Bella Vista Drive, I suddenly had a frightening thought – like a premonition. I hadn't thought of it until that very moment; why hadn't I thought of this before? What if Poncho ran like a greyhound as he usually did when he heard our car? He was used to the farm, the country. We had moved to town, into a neighborhood

## Chapter 9

with other cars, and the fence had not yet been installed. As we turned into the driveway, I could see Poncho in the headlights; he was excited and running, his little ears flopping. Then I heard the screeching sound as the driver of the car slammed on the brakes. But it was too late – Poncho had gone into the path of an oncoming car – just as I feared only moments before. We jumped out of our car and rushed to the street to find our little Poncho lying motionless. The driver opened the car door; her startled eyes met my startled eyes. She was shaken and we were shaken. The lady said how sorry she was; she was about to cry. She said she lived on the block. Tears stung my eyes as I looked at Pam and Randy. I suddenly felt sick to my stomach that my children had witnessed this. We were all very saddened by what had just happened, but I told the lady it wasn't her fault. Dale picked up our little dog and carried him to the back yard. The next morning, he made a grave for Poncho.

Unexpected things happen – life happens, but we go on. The four of us were very sad about losing Poncho, and seeing his dog house in the backyard was a constant reminder. I talked to Randy and Pam about what happened, and hugged them often. I told them we would get another dog soon. I was glad to see them busy arranging their things; they were making their rooms their own. I suggested they think about what color they wanted to paint their walls. It didn't take long for Pam to decide on lavender. The next day, Pam and Randy got to meet some of the neighborhood kids. They were happy to have new friends and I was glad to see smiles on their faces. Dale made arrangements for the landscaping. The sod had to be laid, and a wood fence would be installed around the back yard. A few days after we moved in, Dale was busy helping place the sod in our yard and after that was done, he helped install the wood fence. Plans were made to complete the landscaping in the spring with trees and shrubs. And I was grateful to have grass in the yard, before the fall rain!

After being a stay-at-home mom for ten years, I went back to work when school started that fall in 1965. I was an office clerk at the Fourth National Bank in downtown Wichita. It just so happened that another girl in the department carried the same name – Barbara. When our name was spoken, both of us came alert and it was confusing. So, the head of the department asked if they could call me "Barbie." I didn't mind at all and so, I became "Barbie." That nickname soon caught on outside my work. Working full time was a difficult adjustment for me. I had a family to care for and I suddenly found myself feeling stressed. In the early morning I rushed around getting my children fed and ready for school, then I got myself ready for work. After the stress-free life I was used to at the farm, this was a big change for me. When I started my job, I couldn't seem to find a good balance between my family and working outside the home. It was nice to have a brand-new house, but I didn't have time to enjoy it. When I wasn't working at the bank, I was home cooking, cleaning, and doing laundry.

My job at the Fourth National Bank was boring and I soon changed jobs. I went to work at a different bank where I became a bank teller. I liked interacting with people and became a pro at counting money and balancing my register at the end of the day. As time went on, I adjusted to my daily routine and learned how to do a better job of balancing my life. Dale became interested in a real estate career and that seemed to be a good fit for him. Work time was somewhat flexible, allowing him to be home with the kids when they got home from school. However, during the summer months, we planned to hire a sitter to stay with our children, and that would be a "first." After Dale passed the real estate exam, he went to work for Womer Investment Company, selling new homes in Wichita. That summer, we hired my cousin Donna to stay with our kids. I felt comfortable having Donna stay at the house and that seemed to work out well. However, Pam and Randy didn't like having a sitter. Pam was eleven years old at the time, and she felt that she was old enough to take care of herself, and she probably was. However, Randy was seven and still too young to be left alone.

I had promised the kids another dog and browsed the newspaper ads. That's when this ad caught my eye. "Need loving home for my little doggie." I called the number to inquire, and a lady answered the phone. I told her I had noticed her ad, and asked if she could tell me about her dog. She described it as a male Dachshund breed, and said his name is "Schnapps." What a cute name, I thought, and I asked why she needed to find a home for the dog. She said she worked long hours and didn't have time for a pet. The lady said Schnapps was lonely. I told her about our family, and she invited us to come over to her house to meet the dog. The following day, we went to meet Schnapps. He was the cutest dog with short legs, a long body, and smooth shiny brown hair. Randy and Pam squatted down to pet him, and when he looked up at us with his warm brown eyes, we immediately fell in love with him. We took Schnapps home with us that very day. It wasn't long after that and we acquired a cat, too – a white cat named Sugar.

Pam joined Girl Scouts that year and Randy became a Cub Scout. Pam became the star of her Girl Scout troop when she sold more Girl Scout cookies than any of the other girls! She was a proud Girl Scout! And Randy liked wearing his Cub Scout outfit. I think it made him feel proud. I encouraged our kids to participate in things at school. When I was a kid, I had an interest in music and once in a while, I had an opportunity to tinker around with my friend's piano. I actually learned to play a song or two by ear. I thought it would be nice to have a piano in our home and checked the newspaper ads. I spotted an ad offering an upright at a good price. The owner said it had been tuned recently and they offered to have it delivered to our home. I think they really wanted to get rid of it! They were asking $50 and I thought I had scored a bargain, so we bought it. When the men arrived with the piano, they carried it downstairs to the bonus room. Pam was excited about learning to play the piano and I hired an instructor. But after taking lessons for a while, she lost interest and didn't want to practice. Later on, Pam told me that she didn't like practicing downstairs in that room by herself. I get that now. Had I chosen a smaller piano I could have put it in the living room and she would have enjoyed it. Randy may have taken an interest in piano too. Live and learn, as the old saying goes.

It was a beautiful morning in July. Our summer vacation would take us to Colorado. Dale and I were married in Julesburg, Colorado, but this trip would not take us in that direction. Instead, we were headed to the Boulder area. It was a ten-hour drive from Wichita to Boulder, and after being in the car for seven hours, we were tired and decided to stopover at a motel. The next morning, we were up early for breakfast and soon we were on the road again. Pam and Randy were especially excited to see the mountains. We had not seen mountains and this was a new experience for us. As we got closer to our destination, the mountains became more visible. I still remember the first time I saw the view. As we came upon the scenic overlook, it was so gorgeous and literally took my breath away. And there was Boulder, lying peacefully in the beautiful valley. The Foothills were amazing and the snow-capped back range mountains loomed large. "This place is spectacular!"

## Chapter 9

I exclaimed. "I want to live here someday!" I think each of us had the same feeling. We were swept away with the beauty and magnitude of the Rocky Mountains. And Boulder looked like a fairytale town.

We arrived in Boulder mid-day and checked in at the hotel. We spent the rest of the day tooling around Boulder and enjoying this beautiful place. The University of Colorado was in the center of town and most impressive. I noticed how clean and well-kept everything was. The following day we drove to Estes Park, and were amazed at this cute little town. It sat quietly in a valley surrounded by the Rocky Mountains with glorious views in every direction. From there, our journey continued into Rocky Mountain National Park. Trail Ridge Road quickly ascended as we wound our way up around the curves and finally reached Longs Peak, and an elevation of 14,259 feet! It was incredible seeing the vast Continental Divide. Everywhere we looked, the landscape and views were stunningly beautiful! The kids were excited to see chipmunks scamper about, and they were surprised to see patches of snow and reached down to touch it. It was the middle of summer and hard to imagine snow that time of year. And we noticed the change in temperature and marveled at how much cooler it was in the mountains. It was all quite amazing to us and we had a wonderful time on that vacation. After we got home, I thought about Boulder and wondered what it would be to live in a place like that.

I called my mom to tell her about our trip and how beautiful it is in Colorado. I told her about our exciting experience driving into the mountains. My mom hadn't travelled very much and she said it sounded fascinating. The following month, Mom invited us over for dinner. When we arrived at my parent's house, I was completely surprised and bowled over. My mother was having a birthday party for me – the first ever! She had prepared a birthday cake and a fabulous dinner. And she hung a "Happy Birthday" sign. Mom had invited the whole family to celebrate my birthday. It was all so special and I couldn't believe she had done this for me. Birthdays had never been a big deal when I was growing up, however, I do remember one time seeing my dad give my mom a birthday card. A year or so after I left home, I began sending birthday cards to my parents.

## Our First Really Big Vacation

Our lives had settled into a normal routine, and things were going well. It was 1967, and we had been in the Bella Vista house for two years. We were in the process of making plans for a "really big" family vacation – we were going to the Hawaiian Islands in the middle of the Pacific Ocean! A local travel agent helped us with our plans and made all the arrangements for us. We had never traveled that far from home, and we had not seen the Pacific Ocean. It would be Pam and Randy's first airline flight. The four of us were "over the moon" excited! First, we would stop over in Los Angeles to visit my Uncle Gene, Aunt Frances, and my four cousins. I hadn't seen those four boys since we were kids, and now they were adults with families of their own.

The house was quiet as I slid out of bed. I put on my robe and went to the kitchen to start the coffee. I peeked out and it looked like a beautiful day for travel. About then I noticed Dale was up and I decided to wake the kids. "Vacation time – rise and shine!" I didn't have to say it twice – Pam and Randy got out of bed with smiles on their faces. After breakfast, we took care of last-minute details and closed our suitcases. We dressed in our Sunday-best. Back in the day, people dressed up when travelling by air. I have to say, we looked quite nice – we were a beautiful family. Dale

## Chapter 9

loaded our bags in the car and we were on our way to the airport. We arrived early and were pleased to know that our flight was on schedule. We found a place to sit and waited for our flight to be announced. I looked at my children and enjoyed seeing the excitement in their eyes.

The announcer called our flight for Los Angeles, and said it was time to board. When we stepped inside the aircraft, Pam and Randy looked around in awe. I guided them down the aisle to our seats and we got settled in. Soon, the flight attendant announced a reminder to fasten our seat belts. As the plane lifted off the ground, I looked over at Pam and Randy and could read their excitement. They were feeling the sudden powerful surge as their body was snugly pulled to the back of their seat. I think they were awed by that sensation. After the plane reached its elevation, the captain came out of the cockpit and walked down the aisle. He spotted our adorable children and stopped to say hello. Randy and Pam told the captain that it was their first time on an airplane, and they were on their way to Hawaii. The captain smiled as he reached into his pocket. He gave each of them a wings pin, similar to the ones the flight attendant's wear. Pam and Randy were thrilled and broad smiles spread across their faces as they thanked the captain. It was a wonderful start to our big vacation!

Uncle Gene and Aunt Frances were waiting for us at the Los Angeles Airport. I spotted them right away and excitedly waved my hand. It was wonderful to see them. Gene and Frances were excited to meet our children. I loved the way they stooped down to hug Pam and Randy, and made them feel special. After retrieving our luggage, they led us to their car. They owned a double-wide house trailer and lived in a very nice trailer park in the suburbs of L.A. Gene and Frances were very gracious and insisted we stay with them while we were in L.A. The following day, they took the four of us to Disneyland. I was not expecting this, and needless to say, our children couldn't have been happier. We were amazed at the magnitude and splendor of Disneyland. Pam and Randy were in heaven as they went from ride to ride. It was truly an amazing adventure for them! We spent several hours at Disneyland, then Gene and Frances drove us around the area. They took us to the Naval Base and various other sites of interest. Later that evening, Dale and I went out to dinner with my four cousins – Larry, Bob, Don, Wes and their wives, while my aunt and uncle stayed with all the children. I will always remember this special time, but especially, the loving kindness of Aunt Frances and Uncle Gene.

The next morning, my aunt and uncle took us to the airport where we boarded the plane for Hawaii. The flight from L.A. to Honolulu was about five and a half hours and during that time, we watched a movie and enjoyed a lovely lunch served by the flight attendants. Pam and Randy thought it was cool being served lunch on the plane. When we arrived at the airport in Honolulu, we were greeted by a pretty Hawaiian lady. She placed a beautiful lei over each of our heads and welcomed us to the island. The flowers were gorgeous and the fragrance was unforgettable. A taxi was waiting and took us to our hotel. Our kids were anxious to play in the ocean, so we made that a "first" on our list of things to do. During our stay in Honolulu, we visited the historical Pearl Harbor Memorial site and many other places, and we enjoyed lots of time at the beach, watching Pam and Randy play in the ocean. After our stay in Honolulu, we boarded a small commuter plane and visited other islands, including the Big Island where we saw the famous Kilauea Volcano in Volcanoes National Park. Sadly, fifty-one years later in 2018, the small resort town near the volcano was destroyed when the volcano erupted, spewing vigorous lava and belching hazardous gases in and around the area.

The memory of our first "really big" family vacation will always be special. Hawaii is one of the most beautiful places on this earth. If I close my eyes and dream a little, I can feel the warm gentle breeze on my face. The trip was expensive at the time but worth every penny, and we actually had fifty dollars left of our travel money when we got back to Wichita – one $50 traveler's check. I proclaimed that we would use the left-over money to buy a little poodle. We had lost our sweet Schnapps a while back and missed having a pet. One morning, I found Schnapps paralyzed in his hind quarters, and he was unable to move. We rushed him to the vet but nothing could be done to save him. We missed Schnapps, and the kids wanted to get another dog. Dale wasn't sure about a poodle, but after some begging, the kids and I won and he went along with it.

After settling back into the real world, I called our veterinarian to ask if he could recommend a reliable poodle breeder. He did know of one and gave me the contact information. I called the woman and learned that her female dog just had a litter, but the puppies wouldn't be old enough to leave the mother until they were at least ten weeks old. I understood the importance of that but Pam and Randy were anxious and I hoped to find a puppy sooner. So, I started checking the newspaper and found an ad for poodle puppies that were ready to leave the mother. They were AKC registered and the breeder sounded reliable, so I made an appointment and the four of us went to look at the puppies that week. Pam and Randy were beaming with excitement and it didn't take long to choose the female puppy that would go home with us. We took turns holding the tiny white puppy and fell in love with her. I think that puppy fell in love with us too. I brought along a blanket, just in case, and it was laying in the back seat of the car. Dale paid the woman and we left with our new puppy. That little puppy knew the blanket was for her and she snuggled up and fell asleep during the ride home. I had thought about a French name such as "Cherise" and tossed it out there. The kids liked the name and Dale thought it sounded okay, so "Cherise" it was. She would be part of our family for many years to come.

Cherise was absolutely adorable. She was all white with black eyes and she looked like a little fluff ball. The first few weeks after we got her, we had to be careful to not step on her. She was so tiny and always under foot. It was fun having a puppy and she brought such joy to my family. Cherise had a wonderful personality and she loved everyone. When she was old enough, we thought it would be fun for her to have puppies. I had heard about a family that lived nearby who had a male poodle. I contacted these folks and asked about their dog's breeding and background. They said he was AKC registered and came from excellent breeding. They were happy to bring their poodle to our house to meet Cherise – when the time was right. And so, the two poodles met and got acquainted in our backyard. Time went on, and soon it was obvious that Cherise was getting a tummy. We took her to our veterinarian for an examination and he confirmed that she was healthy and doing well, and he could hear the little hearts beating. This was exciting news.

## Christmas Puppies

Christmas was approaching and Cherise's due date was a few days after Christmas. We had plans to celebrate Christmas with Dale's mother on Christmas Eve. Cherise was doing fine and I thought it would be okay to leave her for the day, so we left for Burlington. Dale's mom prepared a delicious array of food, and

## Chapter 9

the kids had fun opening presents. I began feeling a little anxious about Cherise, and we didn't stay late. When we returned home that evening, I thought it strange that Cherise didn't come to the door to greet us. Instead, she was quiet in her bed. I took her outside for a bit and when we came in, she went back to her bed. I wondered if perhaps she was getting ready for her puppies. It had been a long day, so the four of us got ready for bed. The next morning – Christmas Day, we were up early. Randy and Pam were anxious to open their presents. But my first thought was Cherise; she hadn't jumped on the bed asking to go out. I went downstairs and boy, was I surprised! There was Cherise – wide awake with five tiny little puppies snuggled up to her! I was bowled over – five puppies – that seemed unusual for such a small dog. I shouted to Dale and the kids to come see what I found. The kids dashed down the stairs and were very excited and surprised. Cherise looked up at us as if to say, "Merry Christmas!" We didn't have a white Christmas that year, but we did have five little snowballs!

The following day, I was surprised when Cherise picked up one of the puppies with her mouth, and carried it to the living room. She dropped it behind a chair and left it there. Then, she went back to her bed, picked up another puppy with her mouth, and carried it away too. After that, she seemed satisfied and she went back to her bed and curled up with the remaining three puppies. Well, that didn't seem right – why had she done that? I gently picked up the two helpless puppies and took them back to Cherise and placed them next to her. I squatted down to pet Cherise, and said, "These puppies need to stay with you." But Cherise didn't want those two puppies, and she wouldn't let them nurse; Cherise continued to move those two puppies away; she wouldn't accept them. Pam had a little bottle with a tiny nipple from her doll collection, so we warmed some regular milk and tried feeding the two abandoned puppies. That didn't seem to work very well, so I decided to take Cherise and the five puppies to the vet. The doctor examined the puppies and Cherise, but he couldn't find anything wrong. He said it could be that Cherise sensed something was wrong with the two puppies, or perhaps she felt she couldn't take care of that many pups. We continued trying to care for the abandoned puppies but they didn't take to the bottle and after two days, the two puppies died. Cherise was a good mother to the remaining three puppies. She cleaned them constantly and looked after them. I registered the puppies with the AKC. The owner of the male sire got to choose a puppy, and when they were old enough, they chose one of the females; the other two – a male and female went to good families. We called the male puppy "Pierre" and I was very tempted to keep him.

The job description stated, "Executive Assistant to the President of the Company. Skilled dictation, shorthand and speedy typing required." The job sounded interesting and it was time to put my secretarial skills to work. I decided to apply for the job and called to schedule an appointment. The company offering the job was a large shelving company with a manufacturing facility. After my interview with the personnel manager, he said he would get back to me in a few days. As promised, he called but said he would like to meet with me again. After a brief meeting the following day, the personnel manager introduced me to the president of the company – my future boss. I was hired that day and started my new job the following Monday.

The shelving company was a large thriving business and I was excited about the job.. The facility housed offices plus a large space where the shelving was manufactured. Thankfully, the offices were separated from the noise of manufacturing. The company had a big government contract for large shelving

## Chapter 9

orders, and they had their regular day-to-day customers. My boss was a big tall guy. I had only met him briefly and hoped he would be nice to work with. Being president of the company, he was a busy man and I soon learned he was very particular. Well, I was particular too and thought we should get along fine. It was common practice for my boss to dictate several letters a day. When he buzzed me to come to his office, I went prepared with my shorthand notepad. He usually had his head down, working on something at his desk when I walked in. If he wanted to dictate a letter, he motioned for me to take a seat in front of his desk. My boss looked at his notes and I could tell he was gathering his thoughts, then he started talking. As his words came forth, I began my abbreviated writing method of shorthand. There were times when he dictated several letters at a time. When he finished, I went back to my desk and typed each letter quickly, and neatly on the IBM typewriter. Then I placed the letters in his to-do box for signing.

One day, I made a big bobo and my boss got very upset with me. I was somewhat startled when he bolted out of his office and slammed one of the letters onto my desk. The letter was addressed to a Lieutenant Colonel. I had written everything down in shorthand, exactly as dictated to me. However, when I typed the letter, I used an incorrect greeting – "Dear Lieutenant." It should have read, "Dear Colonel" followed by the colonel's last name. Big, big bobo! My boss said it was an egregious mistake! Had the letter gone out, it would have been embarrassing for my boss. I tried to keep my voice steady as I apologized and said I would correct it immediately. I felt really bad about making that mistake. I thought my boss might fire me, but he didn't. I considered it one of life's many learning experiences. And I learned something else that day – my boss had a temper.

One Saturday afternoon, we decided to stop by my parent's house for a visit. While we were there, my dad gave Pam and Randy a Rosary – one for each of them. They didn't understand the purpose of the Rosary, but were happy to receive a gift from their Grandpa Winter. It was sweet seeing my dad close up with his grandchildren. After visiting a while, I found out that my dad hadn't been feeling well. He had recently retired from the Veteran's Administrative Hospital, where he worked for twenty-five years. My dad had a small pension and seemed to be enjoying his retirement. It was four years since Dad had kidney cancer surgery when one of his kidneys was removed. He recovered nicely from the surgery and he didn't seem to have any lingering problems. But then later on, after our visit that day, my mom told me the bad news – Dad had bone cancer. Right away, my mom hired a professional photographer to take a picture of two of them together. It's a beautiful photo of my parents. That year for Christmas, my siblings and I each received this lovely gift.

It wasn't long after that when my dad's health declined rapidly. I visited him at the hospital whenever I could and that year on Father's Day, I took a little gift for him. But it seemed the only thing of importance to my dad was the Catholic religion. He continually asked me to come back to the Catholic faith. I didn't want to hear that; I simply wanted some quality time with my dad and pleasant conversations. I tried changing the subject, focusing on him, or tried talking about his grandchildren, but he seemed preoccupied. I always left feeling disappointed. Looking back, I think my dad would have been a good priest. As Dad's cancer progressed, he became quite ill and it wasn't long until he was a permanent patient at St. Francis Hospital. He spent the better part of the last year of his life in the hospital. There was no Hospice care for the terminally ill in the 1960's.

## Chapter 9

 The smell of death entered my nostrils as I walked into his room. The inside of my dad's body must have started to decay. It was Sunday afternoon. My dad lay motionless in a coma; he did not know I was there. I was alone and stood by his bedside. I noticed his hand dangling outside the bed railing. I lifted his hand and placed it back into his bed, but it flopped back to the same position. I spoke to my dad – "Hi, Daddy – it's your daughter, Barbara." He did not respond. "Can you hear me, Daddy?" About that time, a nurse walked into the room. She gave me a sad look, and then she hugged me. She asked me to stop at the desk before I left. I stood there looking at my dad for a long while, then gently, I touched his cheek with my hand. I knew the end was near and whispered "Goodbye Daddy" then I turned and walked out of his room.

 When I got home from work on Tuesday, Dale handed me a note with a phone number. He said the hospital had called asking for me. I knew what it meant and I picked up the phone and dialed the number. My dad was gone and my mother was a widow. Allen Joseph Winter left this earth on July 23, 1968. He was seventy years old. Dale and I drove over to my parent's house to pick up my mom. This would be a difficult time for her. While my mother knew this day was near, I think she was in a state of shock. We went to St. Francis Hospital, and directly to my dad's room. The strong odor of death was present and I had the urge to pinch my nose, but didn't. I noticed my mom shaking as we entered his room. She stood looking at her husband – the father of her children. There must have been a thousand thoughts swirling through her head. About then, the head nurse came in and greeted us. I could tell that my mom was trying to gather her thoughts, while at the same time controlling her emotions. My mother gave instructions to the head nurse regarding the mortuary where my dad's body was to be taken. Then we collected Dad's personal things and took my mom back to her house.

My mother arranged a very nice funeral for Dad. It was held at St. Joseph's Catholic Church, and food was served after the service and burial. But the craziest thing happened – and this is a funny story. My dad had a tendency to be late for things. When I was a young girl, I recall many times hearing my mom kiddingly say to my dad, "Hurry up, it's time to go – you'll be late for your own funeral!" Well, sure enough – that's exactly what happened – my dad was late to his own funeral. The hearse broke down on the way to the church and my dad's body arrived forty-five minutes late! Yes, it's true. My siblings and I have joked and laughed about it many times over.

Summer gradually slipped into fall and before I knew it, the year was over and I was hanging the 1969 calendar. I was still working at the shelving company, but Dale left Womer Investment and went to work for Gene Miles Real Estate. Dale was intrigued by the neighborhood landing strip for small airplanes, and the upscale homes this company offered for sale. But as the year progressed, we began talking about moving out of state to someplace beautiful, with a good quality of life for our family. We reminisced about some of our travels and the beautiful places we had been. We talked about Boulder, and how much we loved that place. One evening, we were sitting around chatting with the kids about moving and Dale said he would like to move to Hawaii. Well, that idea was quickly pooh-poohed when the kids and I said it was too far away, and I said I did not want to live on an island. So then, Dale said how about Bel Air, California? Well, the kids and I pooh-poohed that too. Then, I mentioned Boulder again. "It's gorgeous there" I said, "so peaceful, and the wind doesn't blow there! Remember how we all loved it when

## Chapter 9

we were there a few years ago?" I was also thinking about the University of Colorado, and how it was situated in the heart of Boulder. Our kids could go to college in Boulder! Then, Pam and Randy chimed in and said they love Boulder, too! We continued talking about pulling up roots, leaving Wichita and starting a new life elsewhere. It wasn't long until we became quite serious about relocating to Boulder, and we started making plans.

We had lived in our house on Bella Vista about four years. Pam and Randy were settled in and happy. They had special friends in the neighborhood, and at school. I knew it would be hard for them to leave their friends, but if we were going to relocate, this would be a good time – before they got any older. Pam had just turned fourteen and Randy was nine years old. Dale was thirty-seven at the time, and I was thirty-two. We were young and filled with ambitious plans. But just as I had expected, when reality set in, Pam and Randy were very sad about leaving their dear friends. I tried encouraging them by talking about all the fun things we would do together in Colorado – such as, skiing, snowmobiling, trips to the mountains, the Royal Gorge in Colorado Springs. There were endless fun things to do, and they would make new friends there too. I told Pam and Randy that their Wichita friends could come to Colorado to visit them, and I think that provided a little bit of comfort. And I promised we would not leave Wichita until school was out. But I knew in my heart, when it was time to leave, it would be sad for my children and sentimental for all of us.

While I was excited about moving to Boulder, it was somewhat difficult telling my mom. I could hear the disappointment in her voice when I told her. My dear sister, Mary, had already left town, and was living in Aurora, Colorado. Paula, Jim and Mike were married adults in their twenties and who knew where their lives might lead them. I called Edith to tell her we were going to move to Colorado. I knew I would miss our special friends. When our kids told their friends that they were going to move away, word soon got out that we were going to sell our house. One day, a lady came to our house and knocked at the door. She introduced herself and said she was interested in our house, and said she heard it's for sale. "Yes, that's true." I said, "But we don't plan to move until the end of the school year." The lady said that sounded fine and asked if she could see it. So, I invited her inside and showed her around. I could tell that she liked our house and after I told her the price, she asked if she could bring her husband to look at it. Two days later, she came back with her husband. He liked the house too and said they would like to buy it. A few days later, we agreed on a closing date and the contract was prepared and signed. We had sold our house – how easy was that! It was meant to be.

We were the Winter clan – me, my sisters, Mary and Paula, and my brothers, Jim and Mike. We all made it to adulthood and managed to move on from our humble beginnings. My youngest brother Mike, and baby of the family, brought magic to a room with his great laugh and goofy jokes. He delighted me with his visits to the farm and later at our house on Bella Vista. After serving in the Army, he married and had a daughter named Julie. One day when Mike was visiting us on Bella Vista, he and Dale made a trade. Mike traded his motorcycle for Dale's video camera. That seemed like an unusual trade, but they both seemed happy with the deal. Mike divorced and later moved to Texas with Julie, and that's where he met Bonnie. They married and had two children, Michael and Beth. Julie was sixteen at the time and as her life evolved, she married and had a baby named Kayla. Julie divorced and Kayla was raised by her grandparents, Mike and Bonnie. Then there's my other brother, Jim, who never met a stranger. Many times, I saw Jim put his arm around someone he had just met, and it was like they were old friends. He was amazing that way. Jim liked trying new things and at one time, he competed in horse polo. Jim and his wife, Sarah, had two children – Susan and Jimmy. Jim and Sarah divorced, then Jim left Wichita and moved to Colorado. Jim became very successful in Colorado, where he owned and operated several Pizza Hut stores. Later on, Jim met Mary Snyder. They married and had two children – David and Sam. After my older sister, Mary, moved to Colorado, she met John. They married and had six children – Veronica, Patrick, Teresa, Suzie, Judy and Karen. I always admired how well they raised those six children. My baby sister, Paula, married Delbert Gegen, and they had two boys – Greg and Steve. Paula and Delbert divorced, then Paula married Dick Kunkle. Amazingly, Paula and Delbert remained friends. That can be challenging and I applaud them for that. Paula has a loving personality and cheerful smile, and I love her great sense of humor. She was the only sibling to remain in Wichita.

## Leaving Wichita

Moving on! Relocating to Colorado just got easier – we sold all of our furniture and that was our goal. But we did keep our TV, our dishes, pots and pans, our linens and personal things. Dale bought a small trailer to haul these items and he installed a trailer hitch on the car he would be driving to Colorado. Moving date was drawing near and we had to find a place to live in Boulder. We decided to rent the first year and get familiar with real estate in the Boulder area. Dale got busy on the phone searching for a three-bedroom furnished apartment. Luckily, he found what seemed to be the perfect place, located just outside the city limits of Boulder. Dale leased it sight unseen. It was a third-floor apartment modestly furnished with the basics. It was much different than what we were used to but would suit our needs temporarily. The apartment was located on Williams Fork Trail.

The move to Colorado was my ninth move in sixteen years. First was the cross-country move to and from Virginia, plus the time I left Wichita by myself, and a few other moves within Wichita. We lived in the farm house for eight years and that was the longest time spent in one place. Leaving the farm and moving to town was a big lifestyle change for the four of us. However, relocating to Colorado with two young children was a really big endeavor. We had no jobs waiting for us in Colorado, and some might say we were crazy. But we were young, optimistic, and filled with energy; we knew we could make it work. The closing on our Wichita house went well, and the new owner was happy with their purchase. The small trailer was loaded with our personal belongings and securely hitched to Dale's car, and both car trunks were stuffed full. I cleaned the house for the new owner and made sure it was pristine. We were ready to explore the next new chapter in our lives.

The alarm buzzed at 4:45 a.m. I switched it off and got up. The night sky clung to the early morning and it was still somewhat dark outside. Our beds had been moved away so we slept on the floor. I slipped into my jeans then woke Pam and Randy. Dale was already up and ready to go. I rolled up the bedding and went out to stuff it into the remaining spot in the trunk of the car. I had prepared a breakfast snack for us to take along. We were ready for our journey and I silently said goodbye to the house on Bella Vista. Dale and Randy climbed into the car with the trailer attached while Pam and I got into the purple Pontiac with our doggie, Cherise. As we began our drive up the street, I couldn't believe what I was seeing. The neighborhood kids had gotten up early and were standing curbside in front of their houses, waving

## Chapter 9

as we drove away. It was a sight to behold – Bless their hearts! My children were sad and cried as they waved goodbye to their friends. They didn't want to go and wondered why we were leaving. It broke my heart to see my children so sad.

That first day on the road, Pam and Randy wore unhappy faces. Dale and Randy were in the lead car and the purple Pontiac followed close behind. We stopped several times along the way and when we arrived in Pueblo, we decided to stop for lodging. Our little poodle was a good traveler. She didn't seem to mind being confined to the car, but once we got inside the motel room she happily roamed about. Dale and the kids went out to pick up dinner while I stayed at the motel and took Cherise out for a little stroll. As our children climbed into bed that night, they were still sad. I sat on the edge of the bed holding their hands, then I hugged and kissed them goodnight telling them they would feel better tomorrow; Dale was next to me with more hugs.

## Chapter 10

## A New Life Unfolds in Boulder

The early morning sun spread its soft rays across the Colorado landscape. It was a pretty day and we were well on our way to our new home. After checking out of the motel we stopped to pick up breakfast at a nearby restaurant. While eating our breakfast in the car, I talked to Pam and Randy about Colorado, telling them we would soon see the mountains; I hoped that would cheer them up. We left Pueblo, and were back on the highway. When we arrived in Colorado Springs, the mountains loomed large and the kids perked up immediately. I felt relieved. The drive through town was picturesque and I admired the beauty surrounding us. We passed by the impressive United States Airforce Academy. After two more hours on the road, we came upon the scenic overlook and there was Boulder, beautifully nestled in the valley below. This is the place we would call home! We continued on Highway 36 into Boulder, then once in town, I noticed it was also 28th Street. Dale and Randy were directly in front of us as we drove into town. And then, Pam and I spotted the most beautiful church with tall stained-glass windows that came to a peak, as if reaching up to the sky. We both got excited when we saw the sign, "First Christian

Church." We were members of a Christian church in Wichita. This would be our new church home in Boulder.

We drove through town, keeping on 28th Street, then we turned east and drove a few miles to the apartments on Williams Fork Trail. We stopped at the office and Dale went inside to pick up the keys. The attendant gave directions and we proceeded to our new home. We parked our cars, and each of us loaded our arms with a few items. I hooked the leash to Cherise's collar, and we went up the stairs to the third floor. She was such a good little dog and she had behaved perfectly the entire trip. We found our apartment and went inside. Dale and I stood there looking around at the modestly furnished apartment. Pam and Randy were already exploring and had chosen their bedrooms. "This apartment is only temporary." I told myself. I placed the doggie bed in the living room for Cherise. She sniffed around and seemed to understand that this was her new home. After several trips, all of our belongings were in the apartment. I began unpacking the boxes marked "kitchen."

I was up early the next morning and took Cherise out for a little walk. It felt good to stretch my legs and Cherise seemed to be smiling and enjoying the walk. We were strolling along, taking our time, and as I was going back towards the apartment, a lady on the walkway stopped to say "Hello." Then she reached down to pet Cherise, and said, "You're a cutie." The lady told me that she lived in one of the apartments with her husband and they had two children. I told her we had arrived the day before and that we had two children as well. After chatting a bit, the lady cautioned me about having my dog outside. She said the apartment complex was not dog friendly; she said cats were allowed, but not dogs. My hand went to my mouth and I said, "Oh, dear, I wasn't aware of a pet policy." Not knowing this lady, I could only hope that she

## Chapter 10

wouldn't report us to management. I thanked her for letting me know and I picked up Cherise.

I carried Cherise up the stairs and rushed to our apartment. I told Dale about my encounter with the lady and asked if he checked with management about pet restrictions. Oh, my goodness, Dale had completely forgotten to ask about a pet policy. I felt embarrassed but we were there now and we made a plan. We set out to buy a piece of sod for the balcony; it would work just fine for Cherise. I told Pam and Randy about the pet policy and said we had to make sure Cherise didn't bark. They stayed with her while Dale and I went looking for sod. Luckily, we found some at a local garden center and the grass was pre-cut to a perfect three-foot square. We wrapped the sod in a blanket and put it in the trunk of the car. When we got to the apartment, we carried the sod upstairs and placed it on the balcony. I'm sure we looked silly carrying the heavy piece of sod wrapped in the blanket, but I don't think anyone noticed us. As it turned out, the lady was a lovely person and she had no intention of reporting us. We met her family and soon became friends.

Pam was lonesome but felt better after writing a few letters to her friends. She had already mailed two letters and I knew she would be checking the mailbox daily, hoping for letters from her special friends. Randy kept himself busy with his toys and didn't appear to be bored. Actually, I think he kind of liked the close quarters of the apartment. Fortunately, there was a swimming pool at the apartment complex. The pool had just opened for the summer season and our kids couldn't wait to jump in the pool. I felt confident they would make some new friends at the pool. It would certainly help keep them occupied until school started that fall. A few weeks after arriving in Boulder, we had visitors. Dale's sister, Zelma, called to let us know that she and her husband,

Hiram, and their little boy, Barry Alan, would be in town for one day. They were on their way to Cheyenne Frontier Days, and the big rodeo. It was a nice surprise and we were delighted to see Dale's Oklahoma family.

Within a few days I interviewed for a secretarial job in Boulder, and began working right away. Dale was busy pursuing his real estate career and after passing the Colorado exam, he began working for Garret Bromfield Real Estate. We were careful to keep our little dog confined to the apartment but after living there for two months, it was obvious that we could no longer keep her hidden. It wasn't fair to Cherise – she needed her outdoor walks. We started looking around and found a nice apartment that was closer to the schools, and small dogs were allowed! The apartment was a nice corner unit and it felt homey with a lovely wood burning fireplace and a huge balcony. The landlord at Williams Fork was kind enough to let us out of our lease and we moved the following weekend. Our new address was 500 Manhattan Drive. Cherise was happy going for walks again and she loved being in the fresh outdoor air.

The new apartment was located within the city limits of Boulder, and I liked the fact that it was closer to shopping and things. I had been searching for a good hairdresser since we arrived in Boulder. Then one day when I was on my way to the grocery store, I noticed a hair salon close by. I decided to stop in and that's when I met Sandy. She was so sweet and friendly, and I liked her right away. I scheduled an appointment, and she became my hairdresser. Sandy was several years younger than me but that didn't seem to matter and we became good friends. Then as time went on, Sandy moved away to be with her military husband. In spite of the distance, we kept in touch with letter writing and maintained our friendship. And one time, I flew to Whidbey

## Chapter 10

Island to spend the weekend with Sandy. I was excited and felt so liberated flying there by myself. My flight took me to Seattle, and from there I flew to Whidbey Island in a small aircraft. Sandy's husband was stationed at the Marine base on the island. Whidbey is a small island located off Puget Sound. Sandy showed me all around the island and I found it to be very charming. I especially remember all the pretty flowers planted throughout the island. It was a wonderful visit, and Sandy and I continued to stay in touch with letters back and forth. As Sandy's life evolved, her marriage fell apart and she returned to Boulder with her two children. Sandy and I have remained dear lifelong friends.

Winter arrived early in 1969, and old man winter let us know he was serious! The snow began falling on October 4th – Dale's birthday! By the end of October, Boulder had received forty-nine inches of snow! The following March, we encountered sixty-five inches of snow! Skiing was amazing that year, and the kids were loving it! Oh, and by the way, I must mention the chinook winds and there's a little story that goes along with it. Before we moved to Boulder, I used to say "The wind doesn't blow in Boulder." I had grown accustomed to wind in Kansas, where it was common for the wind to blow almost every day. I never liked the wind, and when we visited Boulder, I noticed right away how calm it was – there wasn't any wind! I loved not having to fuss with my hair blowing around. However, we had not heard about the chinook winds and that it was common for the chinooks to visit the area during the fall and winter months. Well, that fall, our first year in Boulder, we quickly learned about the Chinook winds. One evening, while living at the apartment on Manhattan, a strong sudden burst of wind hit the building. The howling sound was loud and fierce. The wind quickly escalated to about one hundred miles per hour. It was scary! And then, all of a sudden, I noticed the curtains in the kid's bedroom moving significantly, but the windows were closed! I was frightened and concerned that the windows might blow in. So that night, I made beds on the floor in the hallway for Pam and Randy. The wind continued to howl all night and there was no sleep to be had. By the next morning, the wind started to calm down and the temperature dropped significantly, then it started to snow. "This is crazy weather!" I remember saying.

Being the new kid on the block and going to a new school can make any child nervous. But my kids were actually happy about going to school. I think they were starving for new friendships. Randy was in fifth grade at Burke Elementary that year, and Pam was in the ninth grade at Burbank Middle School. It didn't take long for them to settle into their new routines and make new friends. That fall, Pam had a nice surprise when she received a letter from Wichita. It was from her dear friend, Nancy Stiles. In the letter, Nancy wrote that she would like to come to Boulder to visit Pam over Thanksgiving weekend. Pam could hardly contain her excitement and we began making some fun plans for Thanksgiving. Nancy's parents escorted her to the airport in Wichita, and we picked her up at the Denver Airport. The girls were so happy to see each other; they had a lot of catching up to do and they didn't stop talking. That weekend, the four of us took Nancy to the mountains where we rented snowmobiles at Eldora. Those two girls had a ball in the beautiful Colorado snow. You don't see snow like that in Wichita, and this proved to be the perfect Colorado experience for Nancy – actually, for all of us as we had never been snowmobiling. Randy rode in the snowmobile with Dale, and he loved getting to guide the machine. It was all great fun, and I was happy and proud to live in a beautiful place with so many outdoor adventures.

# Chapter 10

## The Seventies

It didn't take long to tire of the cramped quarters in the apartment. The kids needed more space and we needed a yard for our dog. It was 1970 and houses in Boulder were more expensive, compared to Wichita. But we managed to adjust and bought our first house in Boulder. The house was located in the most enchanting neighborhood in southwest Boulder. It was called Devils Thumb, and was situated at the base of Boulder's Foothills. The house was new, but imagine this – it had six inches of water in the basement. When Dale took me to see the house and I saw the water, I looked at him and frowned. But Dale said "No worries." The builder agreed to drain the water and install a French drain fifteen feet below the surface, all around the perimeter of the foundation. We ended up with the driest basement ever. Our new address was 2489 Briarwood Drive.

The house had the perfect floor plan designed for main floor living. This adorable ranch style home had three bedrooms, two bathrooms, a formal living room, dining room, nice kitchen and family room plus a full unfinished basement and a two-car garage. I loved that house. Randy changed schools and became a student at Mesa Elementary, the neighborhood school, and Pam attended the brand-new Fairview High School. Both schools were within walking distance from our house. Our kids adjusted well and they loved their new schools; they were happy kids. After Randy got his new skateboard, he soon learned to do handstands on the board, down the curvy neighborhood streets! The first time I saw him do that, it made me shudder. I talked to Randy about it and reminded him how dangerous it was on the street. I made him promise to only stand on the board with his feet. He promised, and I hoped he would keep that promise.

My current job was unfulfilling and I was planning to make a change. Dale had progressed nicely in real estate, working with builders and land development, and he encouraged me to go to real estate school. I was considering it but about that time, I was offered a job at the National Center for Atmospheric Research (NCAR). The thought of working at such a remarkable place was enticing and I accepted a job in the Contracts Department. I enjoyed a nice private office and my days were busy with purposeful work. Dedicated scientists are among the people that work there and I was impressed by that. NCAR was founded in 1960, and is funded by the National Science Foundation. I recall the year when NCAR acquired their new Cray Computer. It was a big event! This was a huge powerful computer system, housed in a large temperature-controlled environment. NCAR is an amazing facility, designed by I. M. Pei, and perched high on the mesa above Boulder. My office was located off campus at the Marine Street facility. I enjoyed my time working at NCAR, and I'm proud to say I worked there.

The following year, Dale and I booked a fabulous trip to Asia. Our journey explored many intriguing places, such as, Bangkok, Thailand, Singapore, Malaysia, Hong Kong, Tokyo, Kyoto, and Osaka. This was our first trip outside the United States, and I remember how excited I was when our passports arrived in the mail. We hired a young couple with a baby to stay at our house with Randy and Pam. They came highly recommended by some people who lived in our neighborhood and we felt comfortable leaving them with our children. Randy was thirteen that October, and Pam was seventeen. While Pam was old enough to be left alone, we didn't want to leave her with the responsibility of keeping tabs on her brother. We

## Chapter 10

missed our son's birthday that year – only by two days, but this was a first! I'm not sure Randy ever forgave us for missing his birthday, and if I had it to do over – I wouldn't have gone at that time. We left a nice gift for Randy, with instructions for the couple to give it to him on his birthday. And I did manage to place a long-distance call to Randy on his birthday, but I was wishing I was there in person.

The Asian tour began the last week in September, 1972, and we returned home on October 17th. It was a long journey but an exciting adventure starting in Tokyo, where we connected with the tour group. From Tokyo, we toured up into the mountains to view Japan's Mt. Fuji Volcano. Riding the Bullet Train in Japan was an exciting new experience for us! Malaysia was a charming place filled with beautiful friendly people. That's the place where Dale held a live snake! I thought he was brave and a little crazy at the same time. We met some interesting people in our tour group. Two couples in particular helped make our tour more enjoyable. They were travelling together and appeared to be good friends. One couple was from Philadelphia, and the other from Dallas. They were a little older than us and we seemed to connect; it felt as if they took us under their wing. During our free evening time, these kind people invited us to join them for dinner several times. They had researched the best places to eat, and we eagerly accepted their invitation. My taste buds experienced many delicious flavors, with enticing choices of beautifully prepared entrees. I experienced Escargot and Cherries Jubilee for the first time. During our stay in Hong Kong, Dale and I had dinner at a fascinating revolving restaurant overlooking the harbor. Our trip to Asia was an incredible adventure, but I missed my children and I was so happy to come home to them.

## A Hole in One

Sandy always came up with fun ideas for things to do in our spare time. One time, she mentioned golf and asked if I was interested. I thought that was a great idea. Neither of us had played golf and we decided to take lessons together. Flatirons Golf Course offered a six-week course on Saturday mornings. We eagerly signed up and began our lessons. Our goal was to know everything there is to know about golf by the end of six weeks. . .Ha, Ha! We had private lessons, so it was just Sandy and me. Our instructor provided the golf clubs so we didn't have to invest in clubs before knowing if we liked the game. But after a couple of lessons, I knew I was hooked. I enjoyed the challenge and it was wonderful being outdoors in the fresh air. After a few weeks, I decided to invest in a set of clubs. Occasionally after work, I stopped by the golf course to practice with a bucket of balls. Many times, Sandy joined me and we played a round of golf whenever we had time.

The Ladies Nine-Hole Golf Club at Flatirons had an opening for a new member and I quickly filled the spot. I was the youngest member of this group, and the least experienced, but that didn't seem to matter. As time went on, my game improved and I became a pretty good golfer. Then one day, lo and behold, something amazing happened – I made a Hole-in-One! Albeit, the fairway to that green was shorter than the other fairways, but still, a hole-in-one! My ball went straight into that hole – WOW! I was so excited I ignored golf etiquette and raised my arms in the air shouting "Woo-hoo!" I invited Dale to play golf with me but he didn't have much interest; however, on occasion, he did play just to pacify me. One time in particular when we spent the weekend in Vail, Dale played nine holes with me. The view from the golf course was beautiful and it was an awesome

## Chapter 10

experience. My putting was the best ever that day and I sunk a forty-foot putt!

Construction had begun on a new house in Devils Thumb, and Dale had just listed it for sale. He told me about it and said it might be a good opportunity to have a great location in the neighborhood. It was only one block from our current home and the location was fabulous because the lot backed to open space with a gorgeous mountain view. The house was much larger than our current home and I quickly thought about how nice that would be when we had guests. And our kids would remain in the same schools. We walked over to look at the construction site and decided to buy that house. While we didn't have a big budget for upgrades, I had fun selecting the finishes. The home had an interesting design with four levels – lots of stairs, but we were young and stairs didn't bother us. The main living area was very open, with tall vaulted ceilings. It was a lovely space and great for entertaining. The three decks were especially nice for casual outdoor get-togethers. And I liked having four bedrooms upstairs. We moved into this amazing house in August, 1973. The address was 2407 Briarwood Drive. This was our home for nineteen wonderful years.

Southwest Boulder was a fabulous place to live and raise a family. We had wonderful friends in the Devils Thumb neighborhood, and enjoyed entertaining on a regular basis. The neighborhood pool had been completed, and there were six tennis courts within the neighborhood. Randy was a member of the Fairview Tennis Team and he spent a lot of time on the neighborhood courts. We met the Bensons in the 1970's and have been close friends ever since. Lorraine and Dick had four children – two boys and two girls. The ladies around Boulder were excited when Lorraine opened a small boutique in her basement. It was called "The Cellar". Lorraine had quite an eye for fashion and she carried the best-ever selection of designer clothes – things you would never find in the local stores. Lorraine was known for "dressing the gals in Boulder." This enchanting neighborhood was so cool. Every year on the Fourth of July, the fire department in south Boulder brought their fire truck to the neighborhood to lead the kid's bicycle parade. The firemen turned on the siren to start the parade, and the kids followed behind on their decorated bikes. It was so cute and a fun event for the little tots. Then every year in March, we enjoyed the incredible Progressive Dinner Party. These wonderful traditions continue today. During a period of time when the neighborhood was still developing, Randy and all of his buddies had great fun riding their motorcycles in the yet-to-be developed open land in the outer-lying area of Devils Thumb. Randy wasn't old enough to ride on the street at that time, and this open land proved to be the perfect place for the kids to ride their motorcycles. It was far enough away from existing homes, and I don't think it caused a noise problem – at least I didn't get any complaints.

Pam graduated from Fairview High School in May 1973. I believe she may have been the first or second graduating class at this new school, and we celebrated with a party at our house. That fall, Randy was a freshman at Fairview. And that same fall, Pam entered her first year of college at the University of Colorado. She was interested in a sorority and became a proud member of the Tri Delta Sorority. She was privileged to live in the sorority house for one semester. Pam was happy as a lark living in the sorority house with those amazing young women. And when Tri Delta hosted a Mom's Weekend, I was invited to attend. Those sorority sisters set up quite a party for us moms and I felt honored to be there. I had such fun and almost felt like a college student myself!

## Chapter 10

During 1975, our vacation took us to Europe. We booked an American Express tour, and travelled across Europe in a Mercedes bus. Our first stop was Paris – Oh, my goodness – Paris! It was our first time in Paris and I remember so well standing in the heart of Paris with Dale as we looked up at the Eiffel Tower! I was so excited to be in this romantic city! However, we were there only one day and we tried to make the most of it. That evening, we went to the Moulin Rouge and stayed up late partying, ignoring the fact that we had to be up early to begin our European tour.

Sleepy-eyed, I climbed out of bed the next morning feeling the effects of staying up until two a.m. I rushed through breakfast knowing the bus was waiting for us outside the hotel. Dale and I climbed aboard the bus and took our seats. Perhaps the Mercedes bus was too comfortable because we both fell asleep. The first three days of the tour, we had difficulty staying awake on that bus. The seats were soft luxurious leather and the motion of the bus seemed to rock us to sleep. But we finally recovered from jet lag and felt refreshed. We toured across France, Italy, Switzerland, Germany, Austria, Luxembourg, Liechtenstein, and England. Upon arriving in London, we were surprised to learn that there had been a bombing at the hotel across the street from our hotel. The Irish Republic Army (IRA) was rebelling and causing problems. This was our first experience being near any sort of terrorism. It was a little unsettling when armed guards searched our belongings upon entry to our hotel. London was our last stop and after a three-day visit, we flew home.

Our kids were growing up and I knew we wouldn't have many more opportunities for family vacations. It was a little sad coming to that realization. That's when we decided to book a week-long trip to Disney World in Orlando. The kids were excited to go and we scheduled it to coincide with spring break in 1976. It was an amazing vacation for the four of us and we had a fabulous time together. Disney World was filled with adventure and we explored it all. After our stay in Orlando, we put Pam and Randy on a flight back to Colorado, then Dale and I boarded a commuter flight to the Bahamas, where we spent a few days before returning to Colorado.

## Real Estate World by Rieger

After returning home to Boulder, we began talking about the possibility of Dale starting his own real estate company. Dale was the exclusive marketing agent for the Devils Thumb neighborhood, and the timing seemed right for opening his own real estate company. Late that summer, Dale gave his resignation notice to the manager at Garret Bromfield, and proceeded to move forward with plans. When the secretary at the Boulder office heard about it, she told Dale that she would like to work for him. Her name was Jo. She was a hard worker and Dale was happy to hire this woman. Plans were moving forward and we needed a name for the company. We had several ideas to ponder and after serious thought and consideration, a decision was made. Dale filed the name application with the Colorado Secretary of State, and soon we received notice that the name applied for had been approved. That's when "Real Estate World by Rieger" was born! We were excited and proud to open the new real estate company in Boulder. We needed office space and Dale began looking for just the right space in a good location. Next, office furniture needed to be purchased. We had been working on the company logo, and after the design was implemented and professionally drawn, letterhead was ordered. Then, custom real estate signs with our logo were ordered. We felt lucky to find office space available in a beautiful new office building. It was located at 3393 Iris Avenue. Real Estate World by Rieger opened its doors in November, 1976.

## Chapter 10

That year, I met a wonderful person who would become a dear life-long friend. That person is Gloria. Dale and I met Gloria and her husband as a result of a real estate transaction. After the transaction closed, they invited us to go out for dinner with them. We were delighted at their offer and enjoyed a fabulous evening together. We laughed and shared stories and felt comfortable in each other's company. From then on, our relationship blossomed and we became dear friends.

We celebrated Thanksgiving and Christmas as usual that year and enjoyed being together as a family. It was New Year's Day, and I stayed in bed later than usual. When I got up, I slipped on my robe and went downstairs. The sky was bright with sunshine but as I stepped out to get the newspaper, I felt the bite of winter in the air. It was a new year and I was optimistic about the future. I removed the well-used calendar and hung the new 1977 calendar. I thought about the year ahead and how busy and full our lives had become. I was still working at NCAR, and Dale was consumed with real estate. He had hired several agents and the company was doing well. Real Estate World by Rieger soon became a well-known name in Boulder real estate. Dale worked hard and at times, he seemed exhausted; I think he pushed himself too hard. It was around the middle of February when one evening a scary thought entered my mind. I was cleaning up in the kitchen and glanced over at Dale as he was resting in the lazy recliner. For some reason, I walked over and stood looking at him. I didn't think he looked well; he looked thin and seemed to be losing weight. I had a sudden feeling that Dale was sick. The next morning, I asked him how he was feeling, saying he looked a little tired. Dale said he was actually thinking about seeing his doctor and promised me he would schedule an appointment. Surprisingly, he made an appointment and he did see the doctor. After the examination, the doctor ran a few tests and told Dale he would call with results.

## Remarkable Resilience

A few days went by and Dale seemed to be doing fine; he actually said he thought he was feeling better. I don't recall why I was home that day, and not at work. Perhaps it was Saturday, because Randy was home too. That morning, Dale went to the office in the neighborhood where new townhomes were being built. He came home around noon, and I will always remember how he was dressed that day. He was wearing his three-piece navy-blue suit and he looked like a model out of Gentlemen's Quarterly! But Dale's glum expression told me he had bad news. He stood there and looked at me, then he said, "Well, the doctor called, and he said it's cancer." My heart sunk – I didn't want to hear that damning word. How could someone so vibrant have cancer? His work was too much, too stressful. Stress – yes, he had too much stress. Stress causes illness! Dale stood there, and after a pause, he went on to say that he had been referred to an oncologist and he had an appointment to see that doctor. I was trembling as we hugged each other. I remember asking, "What does this mean?" And he said we would find out when we meet with the oncologist. Then he went back to the office where a customer was waiting. I know he felt like the wind had just been knocked out of his sails. Hearing the news, I was shaken to my core. It felt like our life was suddenly turning upside down. And poor Randy – hearing his dad say "cancer" was very scary for him. I wanted to talk to him and comfort him, but he left the house quickly.

My head started spinning and I suddenly felt light-headed. I needed to do something, but I didn't know what to do. Dale had rectal cancer and I knew that probably meant surgery, but I

## Chapter 10

didn't know how involved it would be. I paced the floor, back and forth, and then I called Pam. Pam lived in her own apartment but she was working that day. I didn't want to break the news to her over the phone. When Pam answered the phone, I tried to hold a steady voice. I asked if she could take a break and come to the house. I said it was important and that I needed her. Without hesitation Pam left work and arrived shortly. When I told her the sad news, she was shocked and said, "Oh, no!" and I saw the tears welling in her eyes. We stood there and hugged each other. Pam stayed with me the rest of the afternoon.

The March wind was gusty as we left for the doctor's office. My boss at NCAR was understanding about time off for a doctor appointment; he assumed the appointment was for me. Dale and I arrived at the oncology office and met with the doctor he had been referred to. The doctor said he had reviewed Dale's tests and as he explained things to us, he was very blunt. He spoke about the surgery and the necessity for a colostomy. He was just being honest, but I didn't like his demeanor; a little compassion would have been nice. When we left the doctor's office, Dale and I agreed that we should get another opinion. I said I would start making some phone calls. I would find the best cancer treatment facility and the best surgeon for Dale. In those days, we didn't have the internet at our fingertips. Research meant making phone calls and asking questions. Dale saw two more doctors and both offered the same analysis – Dale needed surgery, and he would need a colostomy!

Dale made me promise that I wouldn't tell anyone about his problem. He was concerned about the business. I understood Dale's concern, but it was hard not saying anything when I felt so troubled. When I got back to my office at NCAR, I tried to maintain my cheerful attitude but I think my co-workers could tell that something was wrong. After a few phone calls, I learned about the Sloan Kettering Cancer Center, and also a well-known cancer facility in Texas. Both of those were miles and miles away, and too far to drive – we would need to fly there. My mind was full as I continued to ponder the options. That afternoon, I closed the door to my office and called my doctor. I would tell him about my husband's problem; he would keep it confidential. My doctor listened as I told him about Dale's cancer and the surgery that had been recommended. Without hesitation, my doctor knew who to recommend. He gave me the name of a surgeon in Denver, and his contact information. He said this surgeon was well-known for the type of surgery Dale needed, and he came highly recommended throughout the country. He was the Professor of Surgery at the University of Colorado Medical Center in Denver. I immediately felt a sense of direction and was glad to have this information for Dale.

After finishing my work at NCAR that day, I headed home. Dale was already there and I told him what I had learned. He was glad to know about the doctor in Denver, and especially that he specialized in the surgery needed. He asked me to arrange an appointment. The next morning, I called and spoke with the receptionist, explaining the urgency of Dale's illness. It wasn't long and I received a call back. The surgeon knew my doctor and he was happy to fit us into his busy schedule – he could see Dale that afternoon. We drove to Denver and were introduced to Dr. Waddell. He examined Dale and reviewed the tests that had already been done, then he explained the surgery to us in detail. He took his time and was very thorough; he told us there would be two surgical teams. Dr. Waddell said he wanted to run new tests and his nurse would assist us in scheduling. Dale and I left feeling comfortable with this doctor. I liked his demeanor and I

## Chapter 10

had confidence that he would make my husband well. Surgery was scheduled for March 18, 1977.

I could no longer keep Dale's illness a secret from my boss. When I told him, he was very supportive and said he surmised that something was going on. By this time, our friends knew about it too and of course, I told the family about it when we first found out. Dale's surgery was scheduled for eight o'clock a.m. and his two brothers, Melvin and Bud, arrived from Wichita ahead of time. My brother, Jim, came to the hospital that morning too, and he stayed the entire day with me and the kids. A couple of friends stopped by as well. It was comforting having such wonderful support. The surgery lasted several hours and when it was over, Dr. Waddell came to see us in the waiting room. He said that Dale held up well during the surgery, and that he would have the colostomy for the rest of his life. He told us that the very last lymph nodes he removed had cancer in them. He went on to say that Dale would be monitored on a regular basis, and they would soon determine if he needed Chemotherapy treatment. After a while, the nurse came in and said Dale was in recovery; he was not fully awake, but we could see him. The three of us walked quietly into the recovery room. It was a shock seeing Dale. There were tubes everywhere, and he looked very pale and gray. I regret not having prepared my children. Seeing their dad in that condition was hard for them and they began to cry. Dale's two brothers stayed at a hotel in Denver that night, and they were at the hospital early the next morning; they were surprised to see Dale awake and alert.

The recovery period was rough for Dale, but he was tough and got through it. He eventually learned to deal with his new situation. It wasn't long and Dale's positive attitude returned. I remember him saying, "This is not going to slow me down! I'm still going to travel and do the things I want to do." Hearing him say that was very encouraging. And you know what, Dale did continue to travel. In fact, two months after his surgery, he scheduled a weekend getaway to Las Vegas.

## My Children – The Graduates

Spring was in full bloom and time was moving on. Our kids were growing up all too quickly! But I was a proud mama watching their accomplishments along the way. Pam was already living in her own apartment and she would soon be graduating from college. Randy graduated from Fairview High School that May in 1977. The weekend of Randy's graduation, my mother boarded a plane and came to Colorado to enjoy the celebration. Randy was a handsome young man dressed in Fairview's bright red cap and gown. My camera was ready to roll, and I snapped many pictures that weekend. I enjoyed planning parties for our kids and loved celebrating their achievements. Randy had a job at the grocery store in the Table Mesa Shopping Center. He was well aware that he had to earn enough money to pay the expense of maintaining his car. He worked steadily that summer, but still managed to find time to drive around town and hang-out with his friends.

Randy wasn't sure about going to college in the fall and thought perhaps he would sit out one year and continue working. His buddies were still in high school and I knew that bothered him. I had concerns about Randy's plan and I encouraged him to complete the CU application. When I talked to Dale about it, he thought it would be a good idea to meet with the Dean of Admissions at the university and he scheduled an appointment. Then Dale and Randy went to CU to talk with the Dean. The meeting went well and afterwards, Randy seemed encouraged and

## Chapter 10

he proceeded to fill out the admission application. It wasn't long until he received his acceptance letter from CU. We were all very excited and proud – Randy would attend college at the University of Colorado!

That August, Pam graduated from the University of Colorado! Pam was not only the first woman in our family to attend college, she was the first member of our family to graduate from college! This was a milestone in our family and a huge accomplishment. Pam was dedicated and worked hard to achieve her college degree, while at the same time, she worked part-time at a department store in Boulder's Crossroads Mall. She enjoyed her job and appreciated having her own spending money. When graduation day arrived, it was an exciting time for the Rieger family. Pam looked beautiful in her cap and gown as she walked across the stage to receive her degree in Journalism. I watched the expression on her face as she was handed her college diploma and could see her pride, joy and gratification. I couldn't have been any prouder of my daughter.

### An Aspiring New Career

During the summer of 1977, I made a big decision. After Dale's health issues and major surgery that spring, I realized that he needed my help with the business. I had been giving it a lot of thought and decided to ask for time off at NCAR. I would use my vacation time to attend real estate school. I had some good years at NCAR, but I was ready to move on. I was ready for the challenge of real estate. When I told Dale about my plans, he said "Well, it's about time!" I registered at the Colorado Real Estate Institute in Denver. It was, without a doubt, one of the best decisions of my life.

The alarm clock buzzed loudly and I jumped out of bed. My real estate class started promptly at eight o'clock a.m. I had to get myself in gear; I didn't want to be late, especially on the very first day of class. In those days, Denver traffic wasn't any big deal; it was an easy commute from Boulder to the Colorado Real Estate Institute. The first day of class was interesting and I was anxious to learn everything there was to know about real estate. That evening, I locked myself in the lower level at home, away from the noise of the television. I told Dale and Randy "You're on your own for dinner" and I focused on my studies. Every evening, I studied hard in preparation for the next day's class. I hadn't been in a classroom for a very long time and I had to train myself to concentrate and focus. "This is hard" I remember thinking. The weeks zipped by and I completed the class. Then it was time to sit for the real estate exam. I was very nervous as I entered the exam room and took my seat. I found the questions to be tricky – tricky the way the questions were presented. I had studied hard and could only hope that I had chosen the correct answers.

The following Monday, I returned to work at NCAR. When I walked into my office, I immediately saw the stack of work sitting on my desk. Had no one filled-in for me while I was gone? I picked up the top file and began working. It was a busy office, and that is one of the things I liked about working at NCAR. I dug in and before long, I worked through that entire stack of files. But then, someone walked into my office with another load of work. I tried to put real estate out of my mind but I kept thinking about it and hoped I would receive my test results soon.

Two weeks had passed since I sat for the real estate exam. It was Saturday, and the mail carrier had just delivered our mail. I rushed down the front steps to the mailbox. I recognized the envelope laying on top of the stack of mail. I took a deep breath and my heart was racing as I hurried back inside. I held the

## Chapter 10

letter in my hands and looked at it. Someone had told me that if you receive a thin envelope, that means you passed. But if the envelope was fat, you probably failed and the envelope contained a registration form for the next exam. The envelope in my hand felt thin! I grabbed the letter opener and quickly zipped it open. My heart was still pounding and my eyes grew wide as I read the word "Passed" and I began jumping up and down as I waved the letter in the air chanting "I passed – I passed!" Dale was standing nearby and he congratulated me. As I read the letter again, it went on to say that my exam results had been forwarded to the Department of Regulatory Agencies, and that I could now apply for my real estate license and pay the required licensing fee. I will give my exit notice to NCAR on Monday.

I often wondered if my boss already knew that I was going into real estate – me asking for time off as I did, and Dale with his cancer surgery earlier that year. My boss's name was Landis. When I told him my plans, he was very nice and congratulated me. I remember him saying that I would do well in real estate. Landis was a nice man and so very kind to me when Dale was sick. I needed time off from work to be with Dale, and he was very understanding and supportive. It was a pleasure working at NCAR, with that great group of people. I couldn't know at the time, but some of the people I worked with would later become real estate clients. On my last day, they hosted a little reception for me. It truly warmed my heart, and I left NCAR with a happy feeling about my future.

And so, I was a real estate agent – now what? It was my first day on the job and my assignment was to take care of incoming calls and show the townhomes to walk-in buyers. New townhomes were being built at the north end of Devils Thumb, and Real Estate World by Rieger had an office in the show home.

I was on floor duty. I was there by myself and a little nervous. I actually hoped the phone wouldn't ring! I worried that I wouldn't know the answer to a question. "I'll just sit in the comfy chair" I thought to myself "and enjoy my coffee and muffin." I had no sooner sat down in that comfy chair when the phone jolted me to reality. A potential customer was calling to ask the hours we were open. And shortly after that, a young couple walked in and wanted to look at the townhome floor plans. My adrenalin started pumping and I no longer felt nervous – I became excited. After I finished showing the townhomes, they asked about the completion date, and luckily, I had that information. They said they would talk it over and come back later. After they left, I thought about how much I enjoyed showing the townhomes to the couple and I was enthused. That was the beginning of my amazing real estate career.

## The Chinook Winds

One cannot imagine that something awful is about to happen, when it happens so quickly. It was around nine o'clock Saturday morning, the Saturday after Thanksgiving in 1977. The chinook winds had been howling at a fierce pace throughout the night and the sound kept me from sleeping. As the night sky faded to daylight, the wind became even more intense and I could hear the velocity. I later learned that the wind was clocked at 143 miles per hour that morning at the NCAR building situated atop the mesa above our neighborhood. I was in our bedroom that morning, doing my stretching exercises, and Dale was pacing, pacing, pacing, like a cat. Then he stopped pacing and stood looking out the window. He was concerned about the pile of unsecured construction materials. The house next door to us was under construction and the contractor had been requested to secure the materials left outdoors; the contractor ignored the request and the materials remained unsecured.

All of a sudden, the force of the wind whipped those materials, piece by piece, up and under the large overhang of our roof, causing a huge section of roof to be ripped from our house! Dale began screaming "Oh my God, there goes our roof – our roof just blew off!" The bedroom door was closed and Dale rushed to open it and we went into the hallway. Debris was flying around inside our home. There was a white powdery substance swirling about, like a fog. It was drywall breaking into pieces as it fell from the ceiling. I looked up and could see the sky! The chinook wind had carried our roof up, up, and away, in the air, over our yard and across the street, then made a crash landing into our neighbor's garage!

Randy was still in bed and I rushed to his room to wake him. How could he still be asleep? I worried the whole house might fall apart – we had to evacuate immediately! My heart was pounding as I told Randy to get up and get dressed. "Our house is blowing apart!" I shouted. "We have to get out!" Then I asked Randy to call the fire department. "Tell them we just lost our roof!" I was amazed at how calm Randy was as he placed the call and gave our address. I picked up our dog and Dale grabbed the bird cage. We left our house and ran out into the fierce wind. We were in the middle of the street, looking around, we didn't know where to go. The wind was blowing us sideways and we could barely walk or stand up. It was dangerous to be outdoors; we could be hit by flying debris. Then I looked up and saw a neighbor in the corner house watching from their window. They motioned for us to go around to the back of their house. Their front door faced west and was bolted for safety. Carol and Jim opened the back door and welcomed us inside. I was shaking and distraught and may have been in a bit of shock.

Once inside, we stood looking out our neighbor's window watching for the fire truck to arrive. I'm not sure what the firemen did when they got there; perhaps they checked for gas leaks and things like that. After an hour or so, the chinook winds began to subside and we decided to go back to our house. We thanked Carol and Jim for their kindness, then Dale picked up the bird cage and Randy carried our dog; we headed back across the street to our house. About that time, a few neighbors started showing up with planks of wood, ladders and wood two-by-fours. I don't know where they got these materials but there they were, ready to help. The men placed two-by-fours inside our house to support the wall in the great room. They hammered and secured the wood to the floor. Randy told me later that Mr. Ross was the first to arrive; his son, Roger, is Randy's best friend. Other neighbors were on the roof, attaching big sheets of plastic to cover the huge hole in our house. That's when it started to snow!

Dale and I began assessing the damage to our home. Our great room had been ripped apart. The window treatments were torn and hanging loose from the wall. The back frame of our sofa was broken when a heavy beam fell from the roof (thank God no one was sitting there at the time); the new carpet was covered with debris and the room was a big mess. But when I saw my beautiful grandfather clock that Dale had given me, still standing and unharmed, I took a deep breath and was grateful. But most of all, I was grateful that we were safe and no one had gotten hurt! I picked up the phone and called Chuck, our insurance guy at State Farm. Then, I got my camera and started taking pictures.

Light snow continued to fall for several hours, but thanks to those who helped us, the big open hole was temporarily secured from moisture. There seemed to be a steady stream of cars going by our house that day. People were in awe at what had happened.

## Chapter 10

Still feeling a little uneasy, we decided to stay in a hotel that night. When we returned home the next day, we met with Chuck. He made a list of damages and took photos for his file. After a few days, roofing contractors came and began replacing the roof over our great room, making sure to secure it with hurricane clips. It took some time for the insurance claim to be settled, but eventually the damage was repaired and we were back to normal.

The townhomes sold out quickly and it was time to vacate our office in the show home. My desk was moved to our office on Iris Avenue, and I quickly settled into the office next to Dale's. Real Estate World by Rieger was a busy place and I found the hustle bustle exciting. During those first few months, I quickly realized that I enjoyed the challenge of real estate. With each new transaction I acquired more knowledge and gained confidence in my abilities. That fall, I became a member of the Colorado Association of Realtors, the Boulder Area Realtor Association, and the National Association of Realtors (NAR). When I became a member of NAR, I pledged myself to abide by the Code of Ethics and with that pledge, I received the Realtor pin. Prior to that, I was a real estate "agent." I took great pride in becoming a "Realtor" and holding membership in these wonderful organizations.

Our office manager surprised us one day when she said she wanted to move into real estate sales. Jo was a valued employee and had been such an asset to Dale when he opened the company. But we were happy to have her as an agent in our office and welcomed her aboard. We needed someone to fill Jo's position and the first person I thought of was our daughter, Pam. Pam had a degree in Journalism and I felt she would be perfect for the job. I think Pam was somewhat surprised when I called her and told her we had a job opening. I asked her if she was interested in coming to the office to talk about it. Pam stopped by later that day and

I explained what the job would entail. Managing the front desk, among other duties, was a big job and I expressed the responsibility involved. I'm not sure how Pam felt about working for her parents, but she accepted the job. Dale and I were absolutely delighted for Pam to be part of Real Estate World.

Pam jumped in with both feet and quickly adapted to the job. I was so proud of my daughter and very impressed at how well-organized and dedicated she was. Pam enjoyed using her creative skills in preparing design layouts for the company's print advertising and she was soon appointed Advertising Director. And it wasn't long until she also assisted her dad with his work and she became his right arm. She was amazing! But later on, Pam became interested in real estate sales and she pursued getting her real estate license. I knew it would be hard to replace Pam, but we interviewed a few prospects and hired a lady named Debbie. Debbie was with us for several years but she didn't assume the same responsibilities as Pam. It's interesting that Randy acquired his real estate license the same year as Pam, and for a while I thought my whole family would be working in real estate. But as it turned out, Randy didn't care for real estate and soon decided to pursue other opportunities.

New Year's Eve was great fun at Paolino's Restaurant in Boulder. I enjoyed getting all fancied-up and going out to celebrate with friends. On New Year's Day, Dale and I spent a quiet day relaxing at home while watching a parade and some football on TV. Our future looked bright as I hung the 1978 calendar. I thought about my real estate work and the year ahead. I was getting busier in real estate and found myself enjoying it more and more as time went on. I had managed to make connections with several large companies in the area, working with the out of state new-hire prospects. As a Realtor, I provided relocation tours

## Chapter 10

around Boulder County and beyond, helping the prospect get acquainted with the area and the housing market. If the prospect accepted a job offer, I was privileged to have the opportunity to help them with their real estate needs. Working with out of state clients was always interesting. Each client had different housing requirements and I enjoyed the challenge of finding the perfect home for each new client. My work was very fulfilling and I soon realized that I had found my niche in real estate. And I realized something else – I had my own identity. I no longer walked in the shadow of my husband.

### A Special Celebration

Oh, my gosh – twenty-five years of marriage, our silver anniversary! That called for a celebration and Dale and I wanted to commemorate it by doing something special. We tossed around a few ideas and decided to renew our wedding vows – that would be special! A little ceremony in our home followed by a champagne party would be lovely. I ordered nice invitations and invited our entire family and all of our friends. And to make it even more special, we scheduled a trip to Paris and Monte Carlo. I hired a photographer by the name of Hans, and I hired a good friend of Pam's by the name of Sally, to sing and play the guitar. Then, I hired the minister of our church to officiate our little ceremony. A travel agent took care of scheduling our trip and all I had to do was pack my bag.

It was a beautiful sunny day on July 9, 1978. When I woke up that morning, I was excited and happy, just as I felt twenty-five years ago. Everything was in place and the house was ready for guests. I stood admiring the dining room table, elegantly draped with a lace tablecloth. It was the perfect place to display the pedestal cake and the floral arrangement. The cake would be arriving shortly. Champagne was chilling in the cooler and sat waiting to be served. I slipped into the lovely floor-length dress I had bought for the occasion. Dale wore his nice summer suit and I have to say, we looked like we could have been newlyweds. Pam arrived in her beautiful mauve dress, and Randy, so handsome in his suit. Family arrived from near and far, and most of our friends had accepted our invitation.

The minister arrived early, as did the server and photographer, then Sally walked in with her guitar. It wasn't long until other guests arrived and soon the great room was filled with family and friends. Sally was seated with her guitar and her beautiful voice filled the air. The stairs leading to the upper level of our home provided the perfect spot for the ceremony. Dale and I took our places and our children stood next to us as our witness. The minister took his place on the landing in front of us. Dale and I began by saying in harmony, "I am I, and you are you, individually we share our lives together." Then the minister took over, prompting us as we once again promised to love and cherish each other forever. The little ceremony was lovely, and having our family and friends present made it even more special.

The following morning, Pam drove us to the airport. We retrieved our bags from the trunk of the car and hugged Pam as we said our goodbyes. I think we literally did feel a little bit like newlyweds going on a honeymoon. Celebrating with family and friends was memorable; it was the party we didn't have when we got married. Our flight to Paris was on time and the attendant announced they were ready for boarding. We found our seats and settled in for the long journey. As the aircraft lifted off the ground, I looked at Dale and we squeezed each other's hands. We were excited and ready for adventure. After many hours in the air, we finally arrived at Charles de Gaulle Airport in Paris. We breezed

## Chapter 10

through customs and found plenty of taxis waiting curbside. We were soon on our way to the Hotel Ritz. It almost seemed like a fairy tale that we were staying at that hotel.

The Hotel Ritz is located in central Paris, overlooking the Place Vendome. We were welcomed in grand style and were escorted to a lovely spacious room. I was in awe as I stepped inside the room. I looked around then walked over to the window and noticed a pretty little flower garden. There was a small table with four chairs at one side of the garden – the perfect spot for afternoon tea. I marveled at our room and how luxurious and ornate it was. The bath room was interesting with its long and "quite skinny" bathtub encased in marble. The hotel was very old, yet gracefully maintained and meticulous. That first night in Paris, we were too excited to sleep and our days and nights were somewhat turned around with the time difference. At 2:30 a.m., we sat up in bed, placed the small travel-size backgammon board in front of us, and ordered ice cream! It was such fun, and I remember the two of us laughing as we ate ice cream and played backgammon. During our week in Paris, we enjoyed many charming sidewalk cafes. We took in all the sights and dined at La Tour D'Argent, overlooking the Seine and Notre Dame Cathedral – it was fabulous! I feared my tastebuds were forever spoiled. It was a "once in a lifetime" experience.

But more adventure was waiting for us and we boarded a flight to Nice, France – the place where that famous artist, Matisse, once lived. From Nice, we travelled via private car to Monte Carlo-Monaco. Monaco is truly an enchanting place, with gorgeous views overlooking the French Riviera. It is one of the oldest countries in Europe, bordered by France on three sides while the other side borders the Mediterranean Sea. We rented a car in Monaco and drove north, up around a narrow winding road toward the Italian Riviera. The view was breathtaking but the road was a little scary, and after driving a short distance, we decided to turn around. First of all, Dale wasn't accustomed to driving on the opposite side. And the thin curvy road with fast moving cars, driven by crazy drivers around the cliffs, was somewhat frightening. I was glad we turned around and felt a huge sense of relief to be off that road.

That evening, we had dinner with some special friends. By sheer coincidence, Bob and Ray Ola Key were in Monaco the same time we were there, and we made arrangements to rendezvous with them. We met for dinner at the Hotel de Paris Restaurant. We were so excited to see each other and shared our joy with a warm embrace. After being seated at our table, I noticed faces on the outside looking in – their faces were pressed against the glass. I later learned they were looking for celebrities who might be in the restaurant, hoping to get their autograph when they left. I thought that was pretty funny. But there we were, such a long way from home and the four of us together in Monaco! We drank a toast to that special moment in time. Bob and Ray insisted on treating us to dinner that evening in honor of our anniversary – so kind of them and such a wonderful treat! Dinner was fabulous – the evening was fabulous and it's a memory I will always hold dear.

The exciting adventure was coming to an end but my heart was glowing and my mind was filled with an abundance of joyful memories. While I love the adventures, I always look forward to coming home and seeing my family. When we arrived at the Denver Airport, Pam greeted us with open arms and big hugs. There were no security restrictions in 1978, and Pam met us at the gate. Pam seemed especially happy and excited and I immediately noticed a gleam in her eyes. I first thought she was really happy to see us, but then Pam told us that she had met someone special.

## Chapter 10

My initial reaction was, "Well now, I think I've heard that before." Pam said, "No Mom – this is different. His name is Tim, and I can't wait for you and Dad to meet him." Dale retrieved our luggage and motioned for us to come over to help. Pam continued talking about this guy named Tim. She said that she had met Tim on a blind date. She said he was an engineer and that he was superintendent for Wyatt Construction, and that he built the building our office was in. Pam went on to say that Tim was five years older than her. All that sounded impressive and I'm thinking, "Humm – he's mature, he has a good job, maybe this guy named Tim is someone special." Then I told Pam "I look forward to meeting Tim."

### Wonderful Happenings

Not long after we got home from the trip, Pam invited us to her apartment for dinner. She wanted us to meet Tim. When we arrived, Tim was already there working in the kitchen. He was preparing his special chili recipe for us, and I'm thinking, "And he can cook too?" It didn't take long for me to see why Pam was so excited about this guy. I loved Tim right away, and Dale did too. Our conversation was easy and natural and Tim seemed like a genuine person. Watching Pam and Tim together, I could tell that they were smitten with each other and something special was happening. And, by the way, Tim's chili was delicious!

During the next couple of months, Pam brought Tim to the house many times to visit, and each time we got to know him better. Dale and I enjoyed having Tim around and we looked forward to his visits. Then one evening, Pam called to make sure we were home and said they wanted to stop by. When Pam and Tim got to our house, they bolted up the stairs with broad smiles and they were totting a bottle of Champagne. They were very excited and couldn't wait to tell us that they were engaged! Oh, my goodness – Dale and I were so happy for the two of them and absolutely thrilled to have Tim for a son-in-law. My heart swelled with joy as I hugged Tim and said, "Welcome to the family." Then the four of us hugged. Dale opened the cabinet and reached for the champagne glasses. This was cause for celebration!

A sense of anticipation and excitement swept over me as I thought about planning my daughter's wedding. I didn't know where to start, but I did know that I wanted it to be special. I had noticed a magazine advertisement for a Wedding Planner booklet and immediately ordered it. I talked to Pam about what she and Tim wanted their wedding to be and said I would plan accordingly. I would do the legwork, make the phone calls, and Pam and I would have fun planning it together. Tim's mother, Phyllis, had saved her engagement ring for Tim, and Pam was very proud to wear it. Tim's family lived in Illinois. He had two brothers, Mike and Brian, and one sister, Kitty. I could tell that they were a close-knit family and I looked forward to meeting them. Pam and I had great fun shopping for her wedding gown. We spent the day in Denver, and visited several wedding shops. Pam was beautiful in every gown she tried on, but when she slipped into the gown with French Alencon lace and a chapel length train, she knew it was hers. Pam looked gorgeous in that gown and her face glowed as she stood in front of the mirror! The store attendant fitted the gown perfectly to Pam's body and made arrangements for the alterations to be done.

"Marriage is the golden ring in a chain whose beginning is a glance and whose ending is Eternity." This quote, by Kahlil Gibran, was on the cover of Pam and Tim's wedding invitation. The date was March 3, 1979, and the wedding was held at First Christian Church in Boulder. The ceremony began at 11:00 a.m.

## Chapter 10

Out of town guests arrived the day before and it was nice to have family there for the rehearsal dinner. Charlie Kane hosted a lovely dinner at the Greenbriar Restaurant Friday evening. Grandma Winter's flight was delayed due to weather, and she didn't arrive until 11:30 p.m. She missed out on the rehearsal dinner and spent the night with Mary and John. Light snow began to fall that night.

The sun peeked through morning clouds and a light layer of snow glittered in the sunlight. It was a joyful, emotional time – It was my daughter's wedding day! Dale and I were at the church early, making sure last-minute details were in place. The florist arrived and arranged the flowers, while Hans, the photographer, was busy setting up his equipment. One week before the wedding I learned that Pam had lost five pounds! Her wedding gown needed last minute adjustments but, no worries, I got that taken care of and her gown was perfect. I was busy assisting Pam in the dressing room at church. I fussed with her hair a little then helped her slip into that gorgeous gown. I buttoned up the back, then placed the veil on her head. She looked stunning – she was a beautiful bride! When her dad walked into the dressing room and saw his daughter in her wedding gown, he was spellbound and took a step back. I will never forget the look on his face. Her beauty literally took his breath away. But he regained his composure and managed to place the lace garter on his daughter's leg. Pam was ready for her wedding and it was time for me to be seated in the church. As I left the dressing room I glanced back at my daughter. I felt a stir of emotion and thought I might cry.

Organ music played softly as Randy escorted me down the aisle. I took my seat and turned to see my mother and Dale's mother in the pew behind. I smiled and reached back to squeeze their hands. I was thinking how nice it was that Grandma Rieger and Grandma Winter could be there for their granddaughter's wedding. Tim's family was gathered together on the other side of the aisle. Our little ring bearer, Jimmy, and flower girl, Susan, were adorable as they walked down the aisle. They took their time and Susan had to nudge her little brother to keep him moving toward the altar. The organ music suddenly became louder and everyone stood. I choked back tears as Dale escorted our daughter down the aisle. Then I heard Reverend Ford ask, "Who gives this woman to this man?" Dale answered, "Her mother and I." Dale nodded to Tim, then turned and walked over to me. Reverend Ford began the ceremony by saying a few words, then Pam and Tim began reciting the vows they had written. Beautiful music and lyrics carried throughout the church as Pam and Tim proceeded to light their wedding candle. The wedding was absolutely beautiful!

After the ceremony, guests were offered a small bag of bird seed as they gathered outside in front of the church. The family and wedding party remained inside for a few photos. And then, the bride and groom appeared with glowing smiles. They were greeted with cheers and showered with bird seed. A delightful lunch-reception was held at the Flagstaff House Restaurant. Guests proceeded to their cars for a scenic drive on Flagstaff Road. The Flagstaff House is situated in the Foothills overlooking Boulder, and enjoys gorgeous panoramic views. Don Monette, the owner of the restaurant took special care to make sure that everything was perfect – and perfect it was! An array of beautifully prepared food was waiting for our guests. The lovely tiered wedding cake was displayed on pedestals, above a champagne fountain. When it came time for Pam to toss her bridal bouquet, my sister, Paula, stood anxiously in front of the younger girls. She was acting silly and got down on her knees in a praying position, then she stood up. Pam tossed her bouquet up over her head and it landed directly in Paula's outstretched hands! Paula was thrilled and expressed her

## Chapter 10

delight with a big grin. The wedding reception was wonderful, and it was obvious that everyone was having a fabulous good time. Dale and I were pleased at how well everything turned out. After the reception, the family gathered at our house to relax while watching Pam and Tim open their gifts. I had baked pies in advance and later that day, pie and coffee was served.

The morning air was cool but such a lovely day for a flight to Acapulco, Mexico. The newlyweds were leaving for their honeymoon. Our travel agent provided a nice brochure describing the Las Brisas Resort as "Set high on a hillside overlooking Acapulco Bay." After all the wonderful events, Pam and Tim were ready for a little relaxation. When I drove them to the airport, I sensed that they were a little tired – quite understandable. But they were all smiles when I dropped them off and I knew they were filled with anticipation and excited about spending a week in Mexico.

# Chapter 11

# The Eighties

The spring real estate market was blossoming and I was busy preparing for a potential client who was coming to Boulder for a job interview at a local company. The wife was the prospective new hire and when I spoke with her on the phone, she told me that her husband would be accompanying her on the trip. She provided me with details about their housing needs and I made arrangements to pick them up at their hotel at 10:00 a.m. the following Saturday. When meeting a new out-of-state client, I found it helpful to sit in the hotel lobby for a few minutes to meet, get acquainted, and tell the client my plan for the day so they knew what to expect. And, in most cases, I provided a packet of information about the area. I always liked to begin with a nice clean car, and I generally gave a tour around Boulder and the surrounding area, depending on the client's needs. Along the way, I would show a few houses in different neighborhoods. Many times, the tour involved taking a break for lunch. During the time spent with my clients, I got to know them pretty well.

When I was invited to serve on the Board of Directors for the YMCA in Boulder, I considered it an honor and a privilege.

The board was comprised of wonderful, caring men and women who were dedicated individuals, and a pleasure to work with. There were always important issues to discuss at the meetings, and each year, there were fund raisers of various kinds. One year, the board decided to hold a luncheon and fashion show. My friend, Lorraine, offered to help with the fashion show and she provided fashions from her boutique, The Cellar. Lorraine and Sharon were commentators for the event. The theme was "Phantom of The Opera." It was a gala event and I was surprised and honored when asked to be one of the models. The event was sold out and it was a huge success! Proceeds from the fund raiser contributed nicely to the special needs at The Y. I had great fun modeling the pretty clothes and found it gratifying to be involved in such a worthy cause.

An exciting adventure was on the horizon, but I had no idea what it was. Dale and I were given orders to be ready at five o'clock a.m. It was the first week in July, 1981, when Pam, Tim, and Randy told us we would be picked up at our house. We were told that we were going for a ride and would soon know the surprise. My anticipation was about to get the best of me. I was dying to know what was going on – what was the big surprise? We were ready as instructed and climbed into the car with Pam, Tim, and Randy. We were on the road for quite a while and my curiosity was bubbling over. The three of them were smiling at each other and said we would find out soon. As I recall, we were on Highway 52 when eventually, I noticed a sign that said Ft. Lupton. We were well into farm country when we approached an open field. There seemed to be a lot of people and they were assembling hot air balloons. Ah, yes – now I knew the surprise. Pam, Tim and Randy had arranged for us to celebrate our 28th anniversary in a

## Chapter 11

hot air balloon. "Yippee! Oh, my goodness!" I shouted. This was an incredible surprise, and the most amazing gift!

Tim parked the car and we walked over to meet the owners of the balloon. There were many balloons lying flat in the field that day, preparing for excursions. We shook hands with the owners of the balloon. They were a very nice couple, and gave us a warm welcome. The husband was getting the balloon ready for lift-off when suddenly, the wind started blowing. Weather conditions have to be perfect for balloonists, so the balloon ride had to be cancelled that day due to the wind. But, "No worries" the owner said, and one week later, we were back.

It couldn't have been a more perfect day for a hot air balloon ride. When we arrived, the owner of the balloon greeted us with a surprise. "Before you get in the balloon basket, you have to be initiated." Then the lady popped open a bottle of champagne and she asked us to kneel down. We followed her orders thinking that she would treat us to a glass of champagne, but instead, she started pouring that perfectly wonderful champagne on our heads. "Hey, wait" I said. "We'd rather drink the champagne!" But the lady kept pouring it on our heads and said, "Don't worry, we have another bottle to enjoy." It was all in good fun. Dale and I were good sports and we were initiated. The lady gave us a towel to wipe ourselves off, then she opened the other bottle. After a glass of bubbly, we climbed into the balloon basket. Once inside the basket, it seemed bigger than I imagined. The lady's husband took control of the balloon and he ignited the heater. It made a loud whooshing sound as the hot air was pumped into the big balloon. Soon we lifted off and waved goodbye. We went up, up, up and away, sailing high above the ground. It was an amazing experience! I was tasting life in a whole new realm of excitement!

## Special Times with Friends and Family

September is perhaps my favorite month of the year, not just because it's my birthday month, but the sky's the bluest blue and the weather is just about perfect. It was early fall in September 1981, when our friends, Bev and Ed Graeter, invited us to travel with them to Durango. Bev told me about the narrow-gauge train to Silverton, and said we would board the train in Durango. She told me about the beautiful San Juan Mountains we would fly over in-route to Durango. Our friends owned a small single-engine four-seat airplane. I was intrigued by small aircraft and, at one time, I had aspirations of learning to fly. On the other hand, Dale doesn't like small aircraft and he had some concern about the trip, but seeing me jump up and down he agreed and I told our friends we would love to go – but only if we could pay for the fuel.

It was a picture-perfect day on September 27th. The sky was clear, the air was calm, and the sun had just risen above the horizon when we arrived at the Vance Brand Airport in Longmont. Before boarding the small aircraft, I quickly snapped a few pictures. Ed was busy talking to the control tower while Bev, Dale and I got settled in and fastened our seat belts. Soon we were taxiing down the runway and lifted off. I was very excited but when I glanced over at Dale, I could tell that he was a little nervous. Flying over the San Juan Mountains was a sight to behold. The jagged snow-capped peaks were incredibly beautiful. Ed was a good pilot and we arrived safely at the Durango Airport. After the airplane was checked-in, we proceeded to the train station. Bev and I couldn't resist stopping at the Rocky Mountain Fudge Factory, where we bought one pound of fudge to take along. The historic steam engine train took us forty-five miles up through the canyons and curvy mountains. The fall colors were in their full glory and

## Chapter 11

the scenery was spectacular! Bev and I were singing songs along the way and the guys joined in – "She'll be coming 'round the mountain as she comes." We were having a good time. Eventually we reached the little town of Silverton, Colorado. There was just enough time for lunch in this tiny rustic place, but after eating all that fudge, we weren't hungry and skipped lunch. When it was time to head back to Durango, the engineer sounded the horn letting us know it was time to board the train. The scenery on the return trip was just as beautiful. That evening, we enjoyed a nice dinner with Bev and Ed. The next morning, we were up early. It was a perfect day for flying and Ed brought us home safely.

We enjoyed spending time with our friends at every opportunity. One Saturday, Dale and I went to Lake Dillon with our dear friend, Gloria and her husband (husband at that time). Their outboard motor boat was anchored at the lake and they invited us to join them. Having an opportunity to go boating was rare and we graciously accepted their offer. I packed a picnic lunch to share and enjoyed a picture-perfect day on the lake with our friends. There were many sailboats at Lake Dillon, and as the late afternoon sun gave way to a colorful sky, it made a beautiful backdrop for the boats as they sailed back to shore. But all good things must come to an end and it was time to secure the boat and head for home.

The drive back to Boulder was easy – no backup traffic on I-70 in those days! When we got to our house, Gloria's husband noticed my real estate sign in the yard across the street. I had just listed the property For Sale. He asked about the details of the home and the price, and said they had been thinking about moving from their townhouse to a single-family house; he wanted to look at it. I was happy to show it to them and scheduled an appointment. After walking through the house and pointing out some of the special features, I was surprised when they said they wanted to buy it. I thought that was just dandy and we proceeded to my office where I prepared the contract. After presenting the offer to the owner and reviewing dates and details, the offer was accepted. The owner was happy about the quick sale and I was happy too, but mostly, I was happy that Gloria would soon be my neighbor! Ironically, this is the same house our roof crashed into during the Chinook wind storm in 1977. Gloria knew about the event and the house had been repaired, so as buyers, they were not concerned. The inspection and closing went well, and Gloria and her husband moved in. Over the years, the friendship with Gloria continued to grow and blossom.

Eventually, Gloria and her husband moved to Florida, and I remember feeling sad when my friend moved away. But we kept in touch and visited them in Florida, and they visited us in Colorado. And one weekend, I flew to Florida by myself for a girl's weekend. Gloria and I went shopping, we went out to lunch, we walked on the beach – it was awesome! Gloria's life was changing though, and I could see what was coming. Then, one day, she just left that man. It took a lot of courage on her part, and I was proud of my friend; she deserved better. As time went on, Gloria met a wonderful man named Donald. Gloria wanted us to meet him, so she and Donald came to visit us in Boulder. Dale and I liked him immediately. He was a kind caring person and it was easy to see that he loved Gloria. The two of them married, and it didn't take long for Donald to become our friend. In time, the two of them moved to a charming place called Bigfork, Montana. We visit them in Bigfork, and they visit us in Colorado. Over the years, we have traveled many places together and always enjoy each other's company. One time we went to Banff, a resort town in the province of Alberta, located within Banff National Park in

## Chapter 11

Canada. We splurged and stayed one night at the old historic hotel in Banff. From there we traveled to Lake Louise, which I found to be one of the most beautiful places on this earth.

My life was going full-circle. Watching my children's lives evolve gave me great joy. Pam was happily married and she and Tim had bought a house in South Creek. They both had good jobs and lived a happy life. Randy was doing well as marketing representative for Rocky Mountain Sports of Boulder. He had been seeing a young woman for a while and one day, he announced that he was going to ask her to marry him. I can't say I was surprised – I just hadn't expected it so soon. Randy was 22 years old at the time, and perhaps a bit young for marriage – but who was I to speak about age when I was only 16 when I got married. But Dale and I trusted his decision and we gave our blessing.

I wanted to be helpful with wedding plans but as the mother of the groom, there wasn't much for me to do. However, I did assume the responsibility of the rehearsal dinner and secured reservations at Yocom Studio, a popular restaurant in Boulder. Then I made plans to invite the entire family to our home for brunch the morning after the wedding. That was August 29, 1982. It was a large group to serve and I have to say, my brunch was delightful. It was a beautiful day and guests were outside on the decks chatting with each other, laughing, and having fun. My mother and Dale's mother came for the event and it was very special having both grandmothers with us. Dale's brother, Melvin and wife Pauline, drove their car and brought Dale's mother with them. One morning during her visit, she was sitting in the family room watching me scurry about in the kitchen. Then, out of the blue, I was very surprised when Mary said to me, "Barbara, you made a good wife for Dale." That was the nicest compliment I ever received from my mother-in-law.

Fall arrived in all its glory with a beautiful display of color. It was just the right time of year for a drive up the Peak-to-Peak Highway to view the golden aspen trees. I grabbed my camera and Dale and I went for a drive. The array of color we saw that day was beyond my expectation and I was able to capture a glorious panoramic view. Blue skies provided the perfect background for the aspens, and I came home with my camera full of color. But of course, the golden aspen colors start to fade with the first frost and winter soon follows bringing cooler temperatures and snow. And that's another beautiful season in Colorado's sunny climate.

The month of January became my favorite time to slip away for a winter escape to the warm country. During the eighties and nineties, our travels took us to Mexico many times and we slipped in a few visits to Hawaii as well. Our favorite place in Mexico was Las Hadas in Manzanillo. This beautiful resort was built with adobe style structures in brilliant white color, casting its reflection upon the crystal blue bay. Dale and I spent many relaxing hours strolling amid the lush bougainvillea-lined grounds. I always felt like I was in Paradise at Las Hadas. During our many trips to Mexico, we also enjoyed Puerto Vallarta, Cancun, Playa del Carmen, Mazatlan, Cabo San Lucas, Ixtapa Zihuatanejo, and Acapulco. The Mexican people always welcomed us with a warm and friendly attitude. One of our trips to Puerto Vallarta was especially fun and memorable because we were there with our dear friends, Lorraine and Dick Benson. They invited us to join them at their lovely condo. We explored all the special places to eat and enjoyed way too many margaritas!

## Becoming Grandy

When I picked up the phone, I heard Pam's cheerful voice. Her first words were, "I have some exciting news – I'm pregnant!"

## Chapter 11

I was overjoyed to hear the news! "Oh, my goodness," I said. "That's wonderful! Congratulations!! I'm so happy for you and Tim." I was going to be a grandmother! I was "over the moon" excited! After Pam and I chatted for a while, I rushed downstairs to share the news with Dale. "Hey there – are you ready to be grandpa? Pam and Tim are expecting!" Dale was equally excited and expressed it with a broad smile and said "That's wonderful!" I began humming to myself. Then I thought about a name I had reserved in my mind for "someday" – that someday when I would be a grandmother. I once read a novel where the grandmother in the story was called "Grandy." I loved the grandmother character and remember thinking to myself that someday, I would love to be called "Grandy." I made the decision right then and there – my grandchildren would call me "Grandy." I wanted to make some phone calls and spread the news! I called Randy to tell him he was going to be an uncle. I called my mom, my siblings, and I called my friends.

Pam and Tim were in the process of building a new home on vacant land they had purchased in Boulder's foothills. Tim was building the house of course, and it was no small task because he worked full time at Wyatt Construction Company, and was their head superintendent. Tim's goal was to have the house ready for move-in before the baby arrived. In the meantime, their home in south Boulder was under contract and scheduled to close. They had to move out but the new house wasn't ready. So, they rented a small RV and parked it on the lot where the house was being built and they moved into the little trailer. Tim worked long hours. After his day job he worked evenings building the new house. One night, he stayed up the entire night working on the house. Baby's due date was drawing near when good news arrived. Tim received the Certificate of Occupancy and they could move into their new home. Tim accomplished his goal! They began moving and were nicely settled two weeks before the baby arrived. I had fun helping Pam unpack her kitchen items. Pam directed me by pointing her finger here and there as I went about filling the shelves in her beautiful new kitchen.

Christmas is a special time and I looked forward to our Christmas traditions and celebrating with family. It was Christmas Eve morning and the house smelled of cookie dough and pine scent. Garland was hung on the stairway railing and nicely wrapped gifts lay ready beneath the tall tree. The house looked very festive and ready for our Christmas celebration. The family would be arriving for a buffet dinner and gift exchange that evening. I had just removed a tray of cookies from the oven when Pam called to tell me that she was having some labor pains. She said the pains were sporadic and not very strong, but she wasn't sure what to expect later in the day. The baby wasn't due for another week but perhaps the baby had other plans. I asked Pam to keep me posted and suggested we bump up our get-together time. Pam thought that was a good idea so I called Randy and his wife and asked if they could come early. Randy said "No problem – we'll definitely be there early."

In recent years, it had become a Christmas tradition that I prepare dinner for Mary and John, and their six children on Christmas Day. They would be at our house the following afternoon. The turkey was ready to put in the oven and I had everything else organized for easy preparation. I enjoyed doing this for my sister's wonderful family. It was a special treat for them and I knew they looked forward to. I would be up early Christmas morning to put the turkey in the oven and set the dining room table. But what if Pam is having the baby tomorrow – I didn't want to miss the birth of my first grandchild. I never

## Chapter 11

once thought that I might not be able to fix dinner for Mary's family on Christmas Day. I tried to sort it out in my mind – how could I make it all work?

Our favorite Christmas songs played on the turntable and Christmas cheer filled the air. Randy arrived with his wife, and Pam and Tim were right behind. We were all pretty excited, but more so about the baby than Christmas. We shared Christmas greetings and hugs then started milling around the array of yummy food displayed on the dining room table. However, Pam wasn't in the mood for food and I could tell that she was focused on her baby and the progressing labor. The rest of us wasted no time filling our plates. It was all very casual and after dinner we exchanged Christmas gifts, but all eyes kept darting back to Pam. By then, her labor had gotten stronger and her pains were more consistent. It wasn't long until she said it was time to head for the hospital. Pam brought her hospital tote with her and it was waiting in the car. I hugged Pam and Tim as they left for Boulder Community Hospital. Randy and his wife left shortly thereafter and I promised to keep them posted. Then Dale and I cleared the food from the table and tidied up the kitchen. I was fidgety and anxious and couldn't get it done fast enough! Pam and Tim had invited us to be present for the birth. I was so happy about that and felt so honored. Pam wanted some discrete photos of the birth and I was the designated photographer. I was beyond excited and thankfully, I remembered to grab my camera before leaving for the hospital.

By the time Dale and I arrived at the hospital that evening, it was around ten-thirty. Pam was well situated in the labor room and she was being attended by the nurse. Seeing the look on Pam's face, I surmised that her labor had become more intense. But then I saw Tim. He didn't look good and I soon realized that he was sick. Pam was obviously worried about her husband. At first, I thought Tim might be suffering from nerves and anxiety, but he said he felt like he had the stomach flu and I wondered if he ate something that didn't agree with him. By midnight, Tim was much worse and the nurse prepared a bed for him in the labor room. Poor guy – he had been under so much stress working and now he was sick. He wasn't able to stand by his wife's bedside or be her labor coach. Then the nurse asked me if I would be my daughter's labor coach. She didn't have to ask me twice. I was happy to be involved, but I felt sorry for Tim.

The nurse showed me what to do and the breathing method to use. Pam and Tim had attended Lamaze classes and Pam knew about the breathing technique. But she needed coaching, especially being her first baby. My job was to coach and encourage Pam to breathe, and we performed the breathing exercises together – over and over, again and again. But then, the nurse decided that Pam needed to get up and walk to stimulate the labor process and speed things along. And that's what we did. I helped Pam get up and helped her with her robe, and we began walking. Pam put her arm through mine and we walked and walked, and walked, and walked, up and around the hallways. Why hadn't I changed into my walking shoes before we left the house? I was still wearing my high heels!

I glanced over at the clock on the wall and realized it was the next day. It was the middle of the night, but it was Christmas. My first grandchild would be born on Christmas Day! I stood next to my daughter's bed while thinking how brave she was. Then it was time for more breathing exercise. I began and Pam followed in rhythm. We did the breathing routine again, and again, and again. My son-in-law was in misery as he lay sick on the cot next to the wall. Dale found a lounge chair, but he was up and down

## Chapter 11

checking on Tim. I had asked the nurse if she could give Tim something to make him feel better, but she said she didn't have any authorization for that.

Dr. Clayton Evans was on-call and he arrived at the hospital around six o'clock Christmas morning. I recognized his voice when he asked the nurse for a fresh cup of coffee. The hospital was short-staffed because of the holiday and he was the only obstetrics doctor on duty. I knew there was at least one other woman in labor, and I hoped that she and Pam were not on the same timeclock. Dr. Evans came to check Pam, then informed her that the baby wasn't ready yet. I asked him if he could give Tim something to make him feel better, and thankfully, he did. Soon it was daylight and I could see the morning light streaming in through the window. Then, all of a sudden, it dawned on me – Christmas dinner! How could I possibly fix dinner for Mary and her family? Well, it just wasn't possible. I called Mary and told her that Pam was in labor and I was at the hospital. I told her we would need to postpone Christmas dinner a few days. I felt bad cancelling at the last minute but my sister said she understood and she was happy about the wonderful blessing on Christmas Day.

Pam was nearing exhaustion as the morning hours passed. But then finally, the nurse said, "It's time." I felt a stir of excitement as Pam was wheeled into the delivery room. The nurse invited me to go along and she handed me a green paper gown, paper hat to cover my hair, and green booties to cover my shoes. She said I would need to wear these things for admittance to the delivery room. No worries! I dressed quickly in the paper attire, and felt honored and proud as I entered the delivery room with my camera. I was ready to capture the moment of my grandchild's birth. Tim was given a mask to wear and while he wasn't feeling well, he managed to stand outside the delivery room where he and Dale watched through the plate glass window. I glanced over at Tim and felt bad that he wasn't in the delivery room with his wife.

A surge of adrenaline rushed through my body. I was about to witness the most incredible miracle – the birth of my first grandchild! I looked at Pam and saw how exhausted she was. But she remained strong and brave as Dr. Evans tended to her. The baby was coming! I stood off to the side and began taking pictures. But when I saw the baby's head emerge, I stopped for a moment and stood completely still, watching in awe as Erin was born. In that moment – that once in a lifetime moment, I witnessed a beautiful miracle! I raised my camera and began clicking. "It's a girl!" the nurse said. I was spellbound as I saw her take her first breath, and make her first little sound, and then I heard her cry. My eyes met Pam's and we both started to cry tears of joy. Tim and Dale stood looking through the glass, very proud – they were both smiling. I could hardly contain my excitement but I managed to continue taking pictures.

The nurse carried baby Erin to a bathing table and cleaned her little body. She wrapped a blanket around her, then carried her over to her mother's open arms. The nurse asked Tim to come meet his daughter. After Pam and Tim had a few minutes with their baby, the nurse said she needed to take her to the nursery to perform a few tasks. She asked if I would like to carry the baby to the nursery. Well, I didn't have to think twice about that! I felt so proud and happy holding my precious granddaughter. I held her close and whispered, "Welcome to the world little one." When we got to the nursery, I helped measure her height. How many grandmothers get to do that?! I held her adorable little feet in position while the nurse stretched out her tape measure.

## Chapter 11

The nurse proceeded to dress baby Erin, then she slid her in the cutest red and white Christmas stocking and put a little hat on her head. Baby Erin was ready to go back to her mother. Erin Marie Kane was born at Noon on December 25, 1984. She was the best Christmas present ever!

Becoming Grandy was one of the greatest joys of my life. I was a young grandmother at forty-eight and Dale and I would forever be "Grandy and Pappy." Randy and his wife were anxious to see the baby and they came to visit. After two days in the hospital, Pam and baby Erin went home to their brand-new house. Thankfully, Tim was feeling better by then. That morning, I went to the hospital to assist Tim in getting mother and baby settled into the car and baby secured in the baby seat. Then I snapped a few "going home" photos. I was ready to help when they got home. My recipes were in tow and meals were planned. Tim was busy at his job during the day and I was at the house with Pam and Erin, to do laundry, fix meals or whatever was needed. Two weeks later, Tim's mother, Phyllis, came to take over and help out. I'm happy that Phyllis could be there to enjoy that special time with the new grandbaby. I think she brought her recipes too.

Being a grandparent continues to amaze me. Just when I feel like my heart is filled with so much love it might burst, there's always more space to tuck in more love. I am truly blessed as my life continues to go full-circle. The seasons come and go and sometimes pass too quickly. We had just celebrated Erin's first birthday on Christmas Day. But before Christmas, the family was given strict instructions from Pam – "Anybody who wraps Erin's birthday present in Christmas wrap will be in big trouble." Well, I was going to make sure I never did that – and I don't think I ever have.

## South America Journey

That January, plans were in place for a lovely vacation in Brazil. Dale made arrangements with our travel agent for a ten-day trip to South America. The thought of visiting another Continent was exciting for me. From Denver, we flew to Miami, then changed planes. The flight across the water to Rio de Janeiro was about nine and one-half hours. I packed my bag ahead of time in case I had last minute work to take care of. The date was January 19, 1986. The trip was long and tiresome but when we arrived in Rio, we were greeted with nice warm weather. After a night of good rest, we felt refreshed and ready for a fun day. Looking out from our hotel room, we could see all the way up and down the Copacabana and Ipanema beaches; we could see where the two beaches came together. Sun-bathers were already gathering on the sandy beaches. Our travel guide was waiting for us in the hotel lobby and we were ready to see all the special places in Rio. Our guide was a pretty young woman in her late twenties – very friendly and nice, and she spoke fluent English.

The day was warm and sunny as we set out to explore this huge seaside city in Brazil. In the distance, I could see the famed Christ the Redeemer statue atop Mount Corcovado. I found it interesting that Rio and Boulder have something in common. Each city has a mountain called "Sugarloaf Mountain." This mountain in Rio is a granite peak with cable cars to its summit. The cable ride provides an enchanting journey high above Rio with gorgeous views. Rio is also known for its shanty towns and its raucous Carnival festival featuring parade floats, flamboyant costumes and samba dancers. Fortunately, we were not in Rio during the crazy festival time. Our guide was wonderful in providing an amazing tour while explaining important details about the city and its surroundings.

## Chapter 11

Dale and I were having fun exploring this interesting place where people love to party.

We had been in Rio for about one week and things were going as planned. But then, things got a little topsy-turvy when Dale said he wasn't feeling well. At first, he thought it was indigestion. Dale always carries Alka Seltzer when he travels – his old standby. He dropped a couple tablets in a glass of water and after a bit, he started to feel better. We left the hotel to go out for a stroll but while we were out walking, Dale's stomach ache returned. By the time we got back to the hotel, his pain had intensified. That's when I decided to call for the hotel doctor.

We hung out in our room waiting for the doctor and after a while there was a knock on the door. I welcomed the doctor in and hoped she would be able to give Dale something to make him feel better. She gave Dale a brief examination and in her Rio accent, she said, "You no sick, no sick. Go outside, enjoy – you feel better then." I looked at the so-called doctor with a question mark on my face as she walked out of the room. Dale and I both looked at each other and shrugged our shoulders. Well, Dale did get out of bed and we went down to the lobby and then we went outside. Dale decided to take another dose of Alka Seltzer, and we went back up to our room. His pain did not go away and by the next morning he was doubled over in pain. I was worried and knew that something was seriously wrong with Dale. I was concerned that he had a bowel obstruction like he had before, which required surgery. I knew I needed to get Dale home to the United States. It was a nine-hour flight back to Miami. The plane would leave that evening.

Prior to checking in at the airport in Rio de Janeiro, I told Dale that he had to pretend he wasn't sick. If the airline knew he was sick, they wouldn't let us board the plane. We found an out-of-the-way place to sit and wait for boarding. Dale felt terrible but managed to hang on, and finally it was time to board the 747 aircraft. I breathed a sigh of relief when the plane lifted off the runway. Fortunately, the flight was not full and I spotted a few rows of empty seats at the back of the airplane. I spoke with the flight attendant and got permission for Dale to stretch out across the five middle seats in one of the empty rows. I pushed the arm rests up and padded the seats with airline blankets. It was a long nine-hours across the water. We arrived in Miami the following morning, January 28, 1986. It was 28 degrees and freezing cold (coincidentally, the same temperature as the date). How could it be this cold in Miami? I later learned that the Space Shuttle Challenger had broken apart after liftoff that very morning, and that all crew aboard had perished. I felt saddened to hear this tragic news.

 Cold air stung my cheeks as I walked out of the Miami airport with my sick husband towing our luggage. I knew that I had to get Dale to a hospital as soon as possible. He was very ill and in terrible pain. I don't know how, but Dale managed to walk off that airplane and we made it through customs. When the taxi pulled up at the curb, I asked the driver to please take us to the nearest hospital. It wasn't long until we arrived at the Pan American Hospital Emergency Department. Once inside, I quickly realized that no one spoke English – it was a Cuban hospital! Oh, my goodness – what should I do? It seemed like we were in a foreign country. I motioned with my hands as I spoke, but it was difficult to communicate. But the ER doctors did seem to understand that Dale's stomach was hurting, and they could see that his abdomen was very tight and distended. They proceeded to take X-rays and other tests. After considerable time and frustration in the ER, Dale was given pain medication and placed in a hospital room

## Chapter 11

with another patient. Not long after that, a nice lady from the administrative office came to the room. She spoke a little English, and I was able to converse with her. She told us that a doctor, a specialist, would be coming to see Dale.

Later that day, the specialist doctor came to Dale's hospital room and introduced himself. And thank goodness, this doctor spoke fluent English! He told us he is a surgeon and that his main practice was at Cedars Medical Center in Miami, but today was his day to volunteer at Pan Am Hospital. The doctor told Dale that he had spoken with the ER doctor and had reviewed all the tests. He said that Dale has an obstruction, and that he needed surgery to repair the blockage. The doctor went on to say that he would make arrangements for Dale to be transferred to Cedars, where the surgery would be done. I felt somewhat relieved just knowing what was wrong with Dale, however, I already suspected that was the problem. I was grateful for this surgeon and the fact that he was at Pan Am Hospital on that particular day. I was wishing we were home in Colorado, but Dale was too sick to travel any farther.

After the doctor left, I called my kids in Colorado. Pam was home with baby Erin when I called. I tried to hold a steady voice but I don't think I succeeded. Pam wanted to come to Miami. She said she would bring Erin with her. That, of course, was not a good idea and I told her that Miami was not a safe place. I said I would stay in close contact by phone. Randy was working at Rocky Mountain Sports, and as I searched for his work number, my thoughts drifted back to the time I visited Randy at his office. I could still picture him on the phone when I walked in and he motioned for me to have a seat. I sat down and listened as he finished his call. He was so professional on the phone and I remembered how proud I was of my son. Randy was sitting at his desk wearing a tank top and cutoffs but the person at the other end of the phone line would never know. When Randy picked up my call and realized it was his mom on the phone, he thought I was calling about the Shuttle disaster. I said that I had heard about the tragedy, and how awful it was, but I was actually calling to tell him we were in Miami and his dad was in the hospital.

Dale was transported via ambulance to Cedars Medical Center, and I followed behind in a taxi. The hospital had been alerted that Dale was on his way, and thankfully, the check-in was quick and easy. Dale was placed on a hospital cart and wheeled directly to a room on the surgical floor. The admittance nurse told me that Cedars had an entire wing in the hospital reserved for family members. She was a kind lady and arranged for me to stay in one of those rooms. We would be in Miami for two weeks, perhaps longer, depending on Dale's recovery. The hospital staff at Cedars said it was not safe to be out in Miami by yourself after dark. I was grateful to be able to stay at the hospital and Dale was very relieved to know that I would be safe. That was one less thing for him to worry about.

Dale appeared anxious as he was prepped for surgery and the nurse gave him something to help him relax. We kissed each other, and I stood watching as he was wheeled away. After seemingly a long wait, the surgeon came to the family waiting area to let me know that my husband's surgery had gone well. He said that he removed a section of Dale's intestine where the blockage was located. I breathed a big sigh of relief and thanked the doctor for letting me know. Dale slept most of that day until the strong pain medication started to wear off. He was doing well until the following night. I had just gone to bed in my room when the phone rang. When I heard Dale's voice, I knew something was wrong. He was talking weirdly and I knew he was hallucinating.

## Chapter 11

I put on my robe and slippers and rushed to the elevator. When I got to Dale's room, I climbed in bed with him and snuggled close. I spoke softly to him and told him everything was okay. I could feel his body start to relax and within a few minutes, he was fast asleep. I slipped out of his bed and went to the nurse's station to let them know that Dale was hallucinating. The nurse was very prompt in contacting the night doctor and Dale's pain medication was changed immediately.

A few days after the surgery, my brother, Jim called to say he was going to fly to Miami to see us. Bless his kind, thoughtful heart! Jim took time out of his busy schedule to fly across the country to be with us. He came to the hospital to visit Dale, but I think more so to give me some moral support. That evening, Jim took me out for a nice relaxing dinner. Boy, did I need that! I felt like a ball of string wound tight and I needed to relax. I will always remember that evening and the one-on-one time with my brother. When we got back to the hospital, Jim was given permission to stay the night as a guest. He flew back to his work the following day. Jim was an amazing brother – always there for his family.

Dale tired of the hospital quickly – no surprise there! I'm not sure how he did it, but he managed to convince his surgeon to release him and allow him to finish his recovery at the Fontainebleau Hotel. The doctor said he could remove the surgical staples later at his office before we left for Colorado. We checked-in at this luxurious place, and I must say, I was somewhat embarrassed because my husband looked so bad. In any event, we got settled in our room, then proceeded to go out to the pool area where I found the perfect shady spot for Dale. I helped him get settled in a comfy chair with a cool drink, where he could relax and watch the pretty sunbathers. On our way to the pool, I noticed the cute boutiques within the hotel and I wanted to go shopping. I left Dale at the pool and told him to stay there; I said I would come back to get him in about an hour.

I rushed back to the hotel shops. I was ready to do some serious shopping. I was having fun trying things on as fast as I could, and believe me, I can do a lot of shopping in one hour, no problem there. It had been forty minutes since I left Dale at the pool and I assumed he was napping. Well, not really, and here's where my little shopping excursion gets pretty funny, however, I didn't think it was funny at the time. Imagine if you will – me, standing in front of the full-length mirror admiring the cute outfit I had just put on, when suddenly, who do I see in the reflection of the mirror? It was my husband! OMG, there he stood with his hands on each side of his face and pressed to the glass, his eyes peering into the store. His face was moving back and forth as he searched for me. "Oh, my God!" I said to the clerk. "That's my husband! I have to go." I was so embarrassed! He was standing there with his shirt wide open, his long row of surgical staples exposed. My poor husband – he looked pitiful. I wanted to wrap a towel around him and cover him up. I rushed out to Dale and told him I needed to change my clothes and I would be back in a minute. I took off that cute outfit and left it at the store. Luckily, I had time to purchase a couple of things before Dale showed up. I grabbed my shopping bag and went back to Dale. I asked him why he didn't stay at the pool and wait for me. He said that he didn't want to be there by himself. He seemed tired, so we got on the elevator and went back upstairs to the room where he could lie down on the comfy bed.

Two weeks after Dale's surgery we were at the doctor's office for his follow-up visit. The surgeon commented about how pleased he was with Dale's recovery. He proceeded to remove all of those staples and said Dale could travel. Yippee! We were going home! I

## Chapter 11

thanked Dale's doctor, and told him I was grateful that he was on duty that day at Pan Am Hospital. After leaving the doctor's office, I confirmed our flight and we checked out of the magnificent Fontainebleau Hotel. That afternoon we flew back to Denver. It had been nearly one month since we left for the trip and, my oh my, I was happy to be back in the comforts of home.

The approaching spring offered new energy and a promise of good things ahead. It was early March when I noticed a few buds starting to form on the trees. I was ready to get back in stride with more time outdoors and brisk morning walks. The spring real estate market had already kicked in and I had some catching up to do. Towards the end of the prior year, several past clients had been in touch, letting me know that they hoped to transition from their present home into something new and different in the spring. I was excited about making contact with these folks and looked forward to working with them again.

When I first obtained my Colorado real estate license, I was issued the salesperson license. In order to acquire a Broker's license, one had to be a licensed real estate salesperson for two-years consecutively. I wanted the Broker's license and after two years I decided to attend a few classes to help me prepare for the Broker exam. Dale knew I was nervous about it and the day of the exam he was so thoughtful and drove me to Denver so I wouldn't have to worry about parking. He dropped me off at the building where the exam was being held and said he would be back in four hours. During my last class, the instructor said he was sure the closing statement portion of the exam would be a "New Loan" Closing Document. I had studied well for it. I was given an exam folder when I entered the room. I took my seat and opened the folder. I flipped through the pages to the last portion of the exam to check the closing document portion. When I saw the words "Loan

Assumption," I almost said "Oh no!" I hadn't studied enough for the loan assumption. I shouldn't have sneaked a peek at the last portion of the exam. That was a mistake and I had to gather my thoughts and focus – focus – focus! The exam was lengthy and I kept plugging away, answering the multiple-choice questions one by one, sometimes skipping a question that required too much thought, then going back to it later. That seemed to work well, because when I went back later to a difficult question, the answer was more obvious. When I got to the last section of the exam and the Loan Assumption closing statement, I tried to focus my mind on common sense answers. I was tense, wishing I had studied more about the assumption portion. I didn't know why that was on the exam in the first place because the mortgage company prepares the loan documents, not the Realtor. I completed the exam and turned in my folder.

I felt stressed when I walked out of the exam room, but there was Dale, standing across the hall waiting for me. I burst into tears and rushed into the restroom feeling certain that I had failed the exam. After a couple minutes, I blew my nose and went out to Dale. I told him about the exam and that I feared I had blown the last portion. I tried to put it out of my mind and told myself "If I failed the exam, I would take it again." Ten days later, the letter arrived in the mail. I was prepared for bad news and told myself, "Suck it up – it's no problem." I heard that most don't pass the Broker exam at first try. I slid open the official envelope and removed the folded letter. The first thing that caught my eye was the word "Congratulations." I passed my Broker exam!

## Embarrassing Real Estate Moments

Someone once asked me, "What was your most embarrassing real estate experience?" While this story I'm about to tell was

## Chapter 11

somewhat embarrassing, it's also rather comical. It was a hot summer afternoon in Boulder when I was showing property in the Foothills. I was working with a nice middle-aged couple and we were looking at homes in the Pine Brook Hills neighborhood. I had scheduled my appointments the prior day and received showing confirmations. I was all set and ready when my clients arrived at my office. They were eager to get started and climbed in my car. I gave them a list of the homes we would see that day along with information about each home and, I handed each a bottle of cold water. Off we went, talking about various things along the way. When we arrived at the third house on our schedule, my clients commented on how hot it was and said they hoped the house had air conditioning. I rang the doorbell and waited a bit, then rang the bell again. No one came to the door so I assumed there was no one at home. I proceeded to turn the dial on the lockbox, entering the combination. I removed the key and opened the door. The three of us stepped inside and I called out "Hello – Hello." The house was quiet and I proceeded to show the couple through the home.

After touring the main living area, we proceeded to the bedroom wing. I noticed a closed door at the end of the hallway. When we approached the closed door, I tapped lightly, thinking there might be a pet inside, then I opened the door. I was surprised to find a man and woman in bed. There was a fan blowing and apparently, they didn't hear us come in. In that brief moment, I saw that they were naked. My hand was still on the doorknob as I turned to leave quietly. But then, the man stirred, grabbed the sheet and quickly sat up in bed. "Oh – it's alright, it's alright" he said. "We forgot you were coming." I was embarrassed and said I was sorry to disturb them, but again he said "It's no problem." About then, the wife sat up and covered herself. I said we would come back another time and guided my clients to the front door. But then, all of a sudden, I was surprised when the man came rushing after us while tying his robe. "Really, it's fine, no problem," he said. "Me and the wife were just taking a little siesta and we overslept. Don't rush off." Then the wife appeared in her robe and insisted that we stay for a cool glass of iced tea.

The man followed us out to the front porch and he insisted that we stay for tea. He said, "Please sit and relax. We have tea already prepared." By this time, my clients could hardly contain themselves. They thought it was all pretty funny and were grinning from ear to ear while nodding their heads "yes" – accepting the offer of cold iced tea. So, we sat down on the shady porch and within a few minutes the couple came out carrying a full pitcher of iced tea and a tray with glasses. The iced tea was very refreshing and tasted wonderful. Dressed in their robes, the owners of the property showed no embarrassment whatsoever, and we proceeded to have a lovely conversation with them. If you're wondering how old the couple was, I'd guess they were in their sixties. Perhaps at that point in their life they were beyond being embarrassed. We finished the iced tea and everyone was relaxed. The couple asked if we wanted to see the master bedroom, but we were late for our next appointment and I said we would have to come back another day. We thanked them for the tea and went on our way. When we got back in the car, my clients were laughing out loud and making jokes and I said, "Some days are full of surprises."

## A Time to Rejoice

I discovered that during one's lifetime, life can go full-circle many times – the circle just gets bigger. The birth of my second grandchild was drawing near. Pappy was invited to go to the hospital to film the event, while I stayed home with Erin. I made

## Chapter 11

sure to have plenty of toys and fun things lined up to keep her occupied and happy. Pam and Tim brought Erin to our house before heading to the hospital. I picked her up and held her as she waved goodbye to her mommy and daddy. Erin understood that something special was happening. We had fun playing together and I loved the one-on-one time with my two-year-old granddaughter. As evening approached, I could tell that Erin was getting a little tired but I hadn't put her to bed yet, hoping the phone would ring. And sure enough, Erin was still up when Pam called to share the wonderful news. Jason Daniel Kane made his grand entrance into the world on May 28, 1987. I told Erin her mommy had something to tell her and I handed her the phone. I watched Erin's expression as a big smile spread across her pretty little face. When I tucked Erin in bed that evening, my heart swelled with love and joy. We talked about her new baby brother and that she was a "big sister." I told her that Pappy and I would take her to the hospital the next day to meet her baby brother. Then I read a story to Erin, and soon she was fast asleep.

Erin was awake bright and early the next morning and she was excited about her baby brother. When it was time to go to the hospital, Pappy carried the giant Teddy Bear out to the car. I helped Erin climb into her car seat and I strapped her in. She giggled when she saw big Teddy sitting next to her in the back seat. I told Erin that we were taking Teddy to the hospital for her baby brother. She continued to giggle and she was so excited. We parked the car at the hospital and I helped Erin climb out of her car seat. Dale picked up Teddy and away we went to meet baby Jason. When we walked into the hospital room, Erin ran to her mommy and daddy. Baby Jason was in mommy's arms and I watched in awe as Erin looked at her baby brother for the first time. Then she got to hold him – I felt blessed to be there to witness this moment in time. I snapped a few pictures of the happy family, and then Pappy and I took turns holding baby Jason. Being a grandparent is one of the greatest joys in life.

When it came time to leave and take Erin back to our house, she seemed fine and was eager to push the elevator button. However, when we got outside and were walking towards our car, things changed. All of a sudden, Erin had an unhappy look on her face. I think it had just sunk-in that she was leaving, while her mommy and daddy, and the baby, and big Teddy were staying at the hospital. Erin didn't like that arrangement; she wanted to stay at the hospital, and she started to cry. I picked her up and hugged her, talking to her and trying to comfort her. I got her situated in her car seat but she was upset and cried all the way home. Once we pulled into the driveway, she seemed to feel better but she was still sniffling. I took her inside and told her I had a surprise for her. We went to the toy wagon and I told her to dig down deep to find her surprise. Erin giggled as she searched in the wagon to find an adorable stuffed animal to cuddle up with. We talked some more, and I promised her that her mommy, daddy and baby brother would only be at the hospital for a little while, and then they would all be together. I treated her to a cookie and some ice cream and Erin was happy again.

A couple of days passed and it was time for baby Jason to go home. Pam called that morning and I was surprised to learn that Jason's oxygen level was slightly low for an infant. Pam said the baby was fine but the doctor recommended that he not go home to the higher elevation in the mountains. The doctor went on to say that the baby could leave the hospital as long as he could stay at a location in town for a few days before going to the higher elevation. Yes, you guessed it, the baby and parents came home to our house in town and that's where they stayed for a few days.

## Chapter 11

I became even more excited having the little family with us. The guest room was ready in the lower level, giving them plenty of privacy. Baby Jason's oxygen level soon became normal and Pam was happy to be back in her own house. I went up to their house later to help. "Have recipes – will travel!"

The summer months flew by and my real estate business kept me busy, but I managed to sneak away every chance I got and head up the mountain to spend time with Pam and the little tots. That fall, Dale and I were able to get away for a few days and we booked a trip to the beautiful Las Hadas Resort in Manzanillo, Mexico. We had previously vacationed there in 1980 and 1981. I loved that place and looked forward to our return visit. It was the perfect time of year to go as the weather had turned cold in Colorado. And I was fortunate in that I had a good agent to cover my real estate business while I was away – a good piece of mind allowed for good relaxation. We arrived at Las Hadas the second week in November to find sunny blue skies and a warm gentle breeze. After taking our bags to the room and slipping into my bathing suit, we headed out to the pool to relax with a margarita. It was wonderful, like being in paradise!

We arrived home from Mexico shortly before Thanksgiving. Pam and Tim offered to host Thanksgiving again at their house. Not long after Pam and Tim were married, they offered to take over the task of preparing Thanksgiving dinner. While I had always enjoyed preparing the big feast, I was happy for them to take over. My new task would be baking pies and preparing the cranberry salad – how perfect is that? And of course, I help Pam in her kitchen with the last-minute things like preparing the stuffing and gravy. Going to the Kane household in the mountains above Boulder is always special, but on Thanksgiving Day, it's even more special. We are greeted by the yummy aroma of roasting turkey. A warm fire is aglow in the living room fireplace, the dining room table is beautifully set, and relaxing music plays in the background. And when the whole family is there, well, it doesn't get much better than that! Randy always loved Thanksgiving at his sister's house, but occasionally – back in the day, he had to attend a second dinner and that became challenging. That's when he started alternating years. After my nephew, Steve, moved to Colorado, he too joined us for Thanksgiving. Another memorable time, our good friend Ardis was in town from Canada, and she joined us for Thanksgiving dinner. There's always room for another plate at the table.

## Santa's Visit on Christmas Eve

The neighborhood newsletter had just arrived in the mail. My eye immediately went to the highlighted box on the cover page: "Santa's Visit on Christmas Eve!" Bless Phil Smith's heart, our dear neighborhood Santa! I wasted no time scheduling Santa's visit to our home on Christmas Eve. I got tickled just thinking about our little darlings and how surprised they would be when Santa showed up at Grandy and Pappy's house. "This will be a fun Christmas" I thought to myself. Time passed quickly and soon we needed to shop for a Christmas tree. The air was crisp that day but the sky was filled with sunshine. We found a beautiful twelve-foot tree, just perfect for our vaulted ceiling great room, and we made arrangements for delivery. Dale set up the tree and stabilized it, then he brought the ornaments up from the basement. The two of us had fun decorating the tree together and with each ornament we hung, it brought back memories of Christmas' past.

Christmas Eve arrived and I was filled with excitement getting the house ready for the evening. Baby Jason was seven months old and such a sweet baby. Erin would be three years old on Christmas

## Chapter 11

Day! Those little ones filled our house with sunshine. I had set aside the gifts Santa would bring for the grandkids. Later in the day, I put the gifts in a plastic bag and hid them behind a bush near the front door; they were ready for Santa to bring inside. I had heard that Santa liked a little "nip" now and then, so I left a surprise for Santa too. I gave instructions to Santa, and he knew exactly where to find the gifts.

There was a blustering wind blowing when Randy arrived that evening. But it was nice and warm in the house and he rubbed his hands together as he stepped inside. Pam and Tim arrived with the kids shortly thereafter. I decided to serve dinner buffet-style and arranged the food on the dining room table. After getting the kids situated at the table, the rest of us filled our plates and sat wherever we wanted. Santa was scheduled to arrive at eight o'clock. I kept watching the clock, then all of a sudden, I heard a stomping sound and a bell ringing. Erin's eyes widened as she looked around wondering who was at the door. I said I would find out and when I opened the door, there stood Santa Clause! I welcomed Santa inside and he came stomping up the stairs with his pack over his shoulder. I offered Santa a chair and he sat down. Erin's eyes grew bigger and bigger as she looked at Santa. Jason didn't know what to make of it. Santa held out his hands and asked Erin if she would like to sit on his lap. Erin nodded her head "Yes" and she climbed up onto Santa's lap. Santa began talking to her as he reached into his bag and handed her a gift. Then Santa said, "Oops, I've got something in there for your little brother too." It was so sweet and fun to watch. Santa stayed for a while and I could tell that he was having fun too! When Santa got up to leave, he waved his hand while saying "Merry Christmas to all." This was the merriest Christmas! But lo and behold – Santa decided to visit Grandy and Pappy's house again the following Christmas.

## Sponsoring Miss Colorado

Exciting things were happening at Real Estate World by Rieger. We were the proud sponsor for Carol Jansen, a contestant at the Miss Colorado Pageant. We knew Carol's parents and one day, her mother approached Dale asking if our company would consider sponsoring her daughter in the pageant. Carol had studied music her entire life and she was an amazing pianist! At the time, she was an aspiring music student at Julliard School in New York City. Carol was a beautiful young woman with a warm, sincere personality. She was a caring person with a glowing inner-beauty. Carol handily won Miss Colorado 1986, and that September, she went on to compete at the Miss America Pageant in Atlantic City, New Jersey. Carol needed a sponsor for the Miss America Pageant, and we were honored to sponsor her for that pageant as well.

Dale and I thought it would be fun to attend the Miss America Pageant, so we reserved our seats for the event and booked a flight to Atlantic City. The weather was beautiful that weekend in Atlantic City, and we enjoyed walking up and down the famed Boardwalk. For years, I had enjoyed watching the pageant on TV, but seeing these young women in person was remarkable. And this year, Dale and I were in the audience, watching this spectacular event as it was broadcast live on TV. Carol's performance on the grand piano was spectacular! She won First Place in the talent contest and she received a very nice scholarship. We were proud to be her sponsor! The following year, Real Estate World was again asked to sponsor one of the girls. LaTonya Hall was a gorgeous black woman with an incredible singing voice. She was a wonderful person with a glowing personality and we were very proud and happy to sponsor her. LaTonya became Miss Colorado, 1987, and she went on to be First Runner Up at the Miss America Pageant!

## Chapter 11

### If only . . .

There was a hint of fall in the air when Dale drove me to the airport. My flight was on time and within an hour the plane landed at the Wichita Airport. As I walked off the ramp, I could see my sister in the distance. Excitedly, Paula and I waved to each other. It was our mother's 77th birthday – September 12, 1988. Unfortunately, our mom's health had been failing and she was not well. She was having little strokes, called TIAs. It all started five years earlier when she suffered a massive stroke at the base of her brain stem. It was a sobering day when my brother, Jim called to tell me what had happened to our mother. A lump swelled in my throat when I heard Jim say, "It's serious!" I quickly scheduled a flight to Wichita, and Dale and I left the next day. Sadly, by the time we got to the hospital, my mom had lapsed into a coma. All five siblings were by her side, Mary, Jim, Mike, Paula and me. Due to the severity of the stroke, the doctor didn't offer any hope for a reasonable recovery. In fact, he recommended that we remove the life support from our mother. He told us that if she came out of the coma, she would be in a vegetated state. I looked around the room at my brothers and sisters and each of us, one by one, shook our heads saying, "No, can't do that – we want to give our mom more time; let's wait and see what happens." The doctor respected our wishes. After sitting by my mom's bedside for one week, Dale and I decided to go home to Colorado.

Mom remained comatose for a total of three weeks but then, miraculously, she woke from the coma. After a while, my mother was able to comprehend what had happened to her. She had a strong will to live and she struggled through a long courageous recovery battle. Paula played a big role in our mother's recovery. Fortunately, Paula lived in Wichita, and she was able to visit our mom every day during her recovery. At first, Mom wasn't able to speak but she did seem to understand when she was spoken to. Our mom had to learn how to walk again; she would learn how to do the things she used to consider simple tasks. Paula went to the rehab facility on a regular basis. With our mom's will, Paula's help, and the amazing medical rehab staff, she endured the challenge. Mom's quality of life never returned to what it was, but her mind was good and I think she was glad to be alive.

Five years later, Paula and I walked arm in arm, happy to see each other. I climbed in Paula's car and we went directly to the assisted living facility where our mother lived. My mom didn't know I was coming and when I walked into her room, she was quite surprised. Then when she heard me say, "Happy Birthday, Mom!" her face brightened with a beautiful smile. I sat down next to her on the bed and hugged her, then I handed her a little gift. My mom always loved getting presents, but I quickly realized that she had no interest in "things." She needed help opening the small gift and once it was open, the gift was set aside. I could tell that my mom was glad to see me because she wanted me to sit close to her; she wanted to touch me and hold my hand – I was her birthday present.

While I was there visiting, Mom frequently drifted in and out of sleep and her conversation timespan was brief. I stayed for a few days, spending the daytime hours with my mother and the nights at Paula's house. When the time came for me to leave, my mom was sleeping. I didn't want to wake her, so I quietly left her room and Paula drove me to the airport. What was I thinking – I didn't say goodbye to my mother. I must have been in denial, not allowing myself to accept the fact that this was the last time I would see my mother alive. "If only" I had gently touched her arm to wake her, to tell her goodbye and give her that last hug.

## Chapter 11

She passed away two weeks later on September 30, 1988. She was seventy-seven years old.

My brother, Jim was excited about a new endeavor – he was building a cabin near Breckenridge! Jim always seemed to have a new adventure on the horizon. I remember the time when he owned several Polo horses, and for a while he actually participated in Polo hockey. But more recently, Jim had commented that he would like to have a mountain getaway – a log cabin. So, when he found a wonderful building site with ten acres near Breckenridge, he hired a builder to build his cabin. During the construction phase, Jim took a few pictures. I was blown away when I saw the photos and exclaimed, "Holy smoke, Jim, this is no cabin – this is a house!" The following year, Jim hosted a family reunion and everyone came – nieces, nephews, all the children – the entire Winter family was there. Granted, it was a big house, but I found myself wondering, "Where will all these people sleep?" But no worries, Jim had that figured out and he pre-assigned a room or a place on the floor for everyone. His new log home was amazing! It had a big wrap-around deck, and the setting was like a private retreat filled with splendor. Some of us went out for hikes, and some went fishing and came back to the cabin with beautiful trout. The next morning, Jim cooked the trout for breakfast. Jim was a good cook and the fresh trout was delicious! There are many great memories from that weekend at Jim's cabin.

## Chapter 12

## The Nineties

A new decade arrived and with it came a recession in 1990. During the eighties, the real estate market saw unprecedented interest rates skyrocket up over eighteen percent for a fixed rate mortgage. However, adjustable-rate mortgages (ARM's) were around thirteen percent and most buyers opted for an ARM. The excessive interest rates made buying a home difficult, and mortgage lenders looked for creative financing options. But it was what it was, and I remained optimistic. I thought about past economic downturns and how the real estate market in the Boulder area seemed to sustain itself better than other parts of the country. This recession ended during the spring of 1991. It felt good to move forward on a positive note.

And then, a beautiful thing happened to brighten our world. Dale and I were blessed with our third grandchild! Carrissa was born on April 11, 1990. We were invited to be present for the birth, and of course, I was toting my camera. We stood off to the side waiting, watching, as the moment drew near. Then the miracle happened and Carrissa entered the world. Her loud cry was a beautiful sound as she said hello to the world. My camera was clicking away and I managed to get some nice discrete photos.

Dale and I took turns holding our granddaughter and once again, we felt the joys of being grandparents. A few days later, the photos were processed and I arranged them nicely in a keepsake album. This was a blessed, joyful time as our family circle continued to blossom and grow.

It was the perfect day for a drive to Loveland. My birthday was approaching and I was surprised when Dale asked me if I would be interested in getting a puppy for my birthday. "Oh, my goodness." I replied. "That would make me so happy!" It had been seven years since we lost our precious Cherise. Cherise was the smartest dog, and so sweet. We spoiled her rotten and let her sleep with us. One night after climbing into bed, I was amazed when Cherise grabbed hold of the blanket with her teeth and pulled the blanket over her body. From then on, she always covered herself on chilly nights. How many dogs do that? Cherise was part of our family for sixteen years. I was excited about getting a puppy and after checking around, found a breeder in Loveland. I placed a call and spoke with a lady named Pat. She told me she was a breeder and that she also owned the grooming salon at her home in Loveland. Pat said that she had one female puppy and it was ten weeks old. She had first planned to keep it but had since changed her mind. She invited us to come meet the puppy and I scheduled an appointment for the following day.

The next morning, Dale and I enjoyed a pleasant drive to Loveland. When we arrived at Pat's house, she introduced us to the cutest little white poodle with black eyes. This sweet little puppy was prancing around. She was very friendly and when I squatted down, she came to me right away and let me pick her up. That very moment, I fell in love with her. She snuggled up to me, almost as if she was waiting for me to take her home. Had there been a full litter to choose from, I would have chosen this puppy.

## Chapter 12

I told Dale that I was not leaving without her. Dale didn't argue and I could tell that he loved the puppy too. Excitedly, we paid Pat her fee and headed back to Boulder. That precious puppy laid on my lap and snuggled close all the way home. I decided to call her "Seymone." As it turned out, whenever Seymone needed to be groomed, we took her to Loveland. Pat was our dog groomer for several years.

It was almost noon when we got home with our new puppy. Seymone pranced about exploring the house. She was happy and settled right in. I filled a water dish for her and she didn't hesitate to take a drink. Pat gave us a bag of her favorite dog food and I poured a little in a dish. I still had our old doggie bed and brought it upstairs from the basement. I put a new cover on the cushion and patted it with my hand, inviting Seymone to her bed. I looked around and realized I wasn't prepared to leave a new puppy alone in the house. I had a few business things to take care of that day, including a board meeting at the YMCA. I had served on the board for several years, and this was an important meeting. I went downstairs to the basement and looked around for a large box. I found the perfect box filled with stuff. I emptied the contents and carried the box upstairs. I covered the bottom of the box with newspaper and put a small blanket in the box, along with a dish of water. Seymone would be safe and secure until I got back – so I thought. I'm embarrassed to tell this, but I picked up my puppy and placed her in the box, telling her that I would be back soon. I assumed she would lay down and sleep until I returned. What was I thinking? No animal wants to be cooped up in a box, even for a short time.

The YMCA meeting lasted about one hour and I decided to rush home and check on Seymone before going to the office. It's a good thing I did because when I walked in, I heard a whining sound. Seymone had managed to tip the box over and she was running through the house howling pitifully. I called her name and rushed to her. I picked her up and snuggled her and told her I was sorry that I left her there alone. I held her in my arms and petted her gently and soon she was calm and happy again. I would not leave her by herself again until she adjusted to her new home. I was glad when Dale showed up. I told him what happened and asked if he could stay with the puppy while I went to the office to take care of business. When I finished my work, I stopped by the pet store to pick up a crate and a few other things for the new member of our family.

I was having such fun with my new puppy. I took her with me in the car whenever I could. While I didn't take her to the office, she went with me when I ran errands and even to the department store and Starbucks. Boulder has always been a pet-friendly city, and it was never a problem when I walked into a store with Seymone in my arms or on a leash. She was an adorable little white fluff ball and everybody loved her. Our grandkids loved Seymone, and Seymone loved our grandkids and she didn't hesitate to express her excitement whenever they came to visit.

## A Blessed Event

One afternoon, Erin and Jason came to stay at Grandy and Pappy's house while their mommy and daddy went to Denver for a test. Their mommy was pregnant, and the amazing test would tell if the baby was a boy or girl. Erin and Jason waved goodbye to their parents and then went straight to the toy basket. I had accumulated a large basket of toys for the kids, and invariably I found myself adding something new and different at every opportunity. The grandkids looked forward to spending time at Grandy and Pappy's house, and it was our greatest joy to spend

## Chapter 12

time with them. The afternoon seemed to go by quickly and Pam and Tim returned with exciting news. They walked in with smiling faces and Pam patted her tummy as she told Erin and Jason, "You're going to have a baby brother!" This was wonderful news! I placed my hands across my heart to express my joy.

Another grandbaby to love and nurture – how special is that! Pam's third pregnancy went well and her due date arrived. Jason's birthday was the following week and for a while, we thought the baby might be sharing a birthday with Jason. But the baby brother was ready and there was no chance of that now. Pappy was standing by to video the birth and I stayed with Jason and Erin. When Pam and Tim left for the hospital, I put my arms around them as they waved goodbye. The kids were very well-behaved and so cute. I talked to them about the new baby and told them their mommy might need some help when she brought the baby home from the hospital. At four and seven years old, Jason and Erin did a good job entertaining themselves. When they were toddlers, I couldn't take my eyes off them for a second. Children are so fascinating and I'm always amazed at their creative imagination.

The blessed event happened on May 21, 1991, and once again I am "over the moon" excited. Dale and I were blessed with another grandson. His parents named him "Tyler James Kane." Pam was anxious to share the news with Jason and Erin, and she called as soon as she was able. They were happy to hear their mommy's voice and very excited to have a baby brother. Pam and Tim were thrilled to welcome their new son into the world. When I talked to Pam, she told me how adorable the baby is and how grateful she is to have another healthy baby. I remember when I first held Tyler, how my heart swelled with love. He was so cute and sweet and I snuggled him close. After a while, I let Pappy have his turn. I felt very fortunate to live near my family, and that we could see each on a regular basis. Being able to watch our grandchildren grow and mature over the years is one of the greatest joys a grandparent can have.

## Turn of Events

Sometimes when life happens it calls for difficult decisions. Real Estate World by Rieger was closing. Owning our own company was exciting but it also proved to be a challenging endeavor. Dale gave so much of himself to the company, making it a well-respected name in Boulder real estate. It was a tough decision but seemed the best thing to do. Dale had worked in real estate for twenty-six years and the timing was such that he was ready to retire. His health issues were interfering with his work and he didn't feel that he could continue in real estate. Once the decision was made, I began looking at other possibilities to continue my career with another company. I scheduled meetings with managing brokers at several real estate firms in Boulder. After interviews and touring offices, I took a couple of days to consider my options. Moore and Company seemed to be the best fit for me. They were an independent Colorado company with offices in Boulder and the Denver metropolitan area. I felt positive about my decision and signed their company agreement. I was well-received by the other Realtors in the company and made to feel welcome.

A few days after making arrangements to transfer my real estate license, a neighbor in our cul-de-sac called and wanted to list their home for sale. The husband had accepted a new job and they were relocating to Arizona. I had to tell them that we had just closed the company and I had transferred my license to another real estate firm. They seemed disappointed and said they were looking forward to having the "Real Estate World by

## Chapter 12

Rieger" sign in their yard. I assured them that they would have the same wonderful service because I would be managing the entire transaction. We were long-time friends and many years ago, we rendezvoused with them in Monte Carlo. Their Boulder home was lovely, nestled on a beautiful lot at the end of the cul-de-sac. It wasn't long after I planted the sign in their yard that I received an offer. Our friends looked forward to living in Tucson, and said they were happy about moving to a place where it doesn't snow! They didn't seem to have any remorse about leaving the Devils Thumb neighborhood.

My real estate career began fifteen years ago at Real Estate World by Rieger. That was 1977, and I was so proud to join my husband in the real estate business. Transferring my license to another real estate company was a big change and it took some getting used to. I settled in at my new office and placed a sticky note on my phone "Barbie Rieger at Moore & Company" and I underlined Moore & Company to remind myself when I answered the phone. But this was a big transition for Dale too. After we closed the company, Dale took over the task of managing the household, which included grocery shopping, and I was not sorry to let go of that job! Dale and I had a complete role-reversal that year, but it allowed me to focus on my real estate work. That's when I became the sole breadwinner.

Over the years, I sold many homes in the Devils Thumb neighborhood. Sometimes when an owner became emotional about leaving the neighborhood, I would say to them, "Change is sometimes hard, but a new adventure awaits and there is life after Devils Thumb." It was 1992, and that was the year Dale and I made another change. After nineteen wonderful years in that amazing house, we decided to sell it. We were empty-nesters; our children were grown with children of their own. When we moved into this house it was new and we made it ours. It's the place where Randy spent his teenage years. During those years, the neighborhood was still developing and Randy and his pals had fun riding their motorcycles on the undeveloped land. Pam was in college when we moved in, but she was still living at home that first year. She too had spent her teenage years in the neighborhood and celebrated many special events such as high school prom and graduation parties. But it was only the two of us living in that big house – the place we called home for so many years. While I would carry the memories with me, I would leave a lot of history behind and I had to remind myself, "There is life after Devils Thumb."

Some might say that a realtor shouldn't list their own home because of the personal element involved. But that's exactly what I did. I completed the listing contract to sell our home and submitted the paperwork to the office for processing. Our house was ready to show and I gave the okay for my administrative assistant to input the listing information to the MLS. I loved that house and the location but, being a multi-level home, I thought it could take a while to sell. However, the house backed up to open space and boasted a gorgeous view of the mountains! The interior was bright and open with vaulted ceilings, and the space was quite nice and very inviting. Well, our house did sell. A Realtor from another office showed our home to an out-of-state buyer. They bought the house and proceeded to live there for twenty-eight years. A few years after purchasing the home, they completely remodeled it. They even changed the exterior façade, transforming that house from wonderful to spectacular!

Selling our home of nineteen years was another big transition for us. We accumulated a lot of stuff over the years and had filled that big house. Before moving out, we held a garage sale and sold

## Chapter 12

some furniture and other miscellaneous items. Dale and I decided to rent for a while and take our time discovering our next house. Dale looked around for available rentals and he found a charming place in the Frasier Meadows neighborhood in Boulder. It was a tri-level design and well-suited to our needs. The owner was out of the country, and they were happy to know that their agent knew Dale and me. Fortunately, they loved animals and didn't mind that we had a dog. The house was much smaller than our home in Devils Thumb, but it had plenty of space in the lower level for guests to stay when they came to visit. The house on Kiowa Street would be our home for eighteen months.

It was fall 1992, when Dale's brother, Melvin, came to Colorado for a visit. Melvin lived in Liberal, Kansas, and it was an easy six-hour drive to Boulder. His wife, Pauline, had passed away a while back and we missed her dearly. Pauline taught third grade students for many years at the elementary school in Liberal. Pauline's sister, Doris, was also a teacher, and she was best friends with their family. After Pauline passed, Doris took it upon herself to look after Melvin. Melvin didn't want to drive alone so he brought Doris with him. The two extra bedrooms at the Kiowa house worked perfectly for our guests. After Melvin and Doris arrived, I prepared a nice dinner for the four of us that evening. After dinner, we sat around the table visiting and when Melvin spoke of his wife, he became melancholy. I knew he was sad and lonely and hoped our plans for the following day would cheer him up.

I was up early the next morning and smiled to myself when I saw the sunshine. It would be a nice day for our guests. After a casual breakfast at home, Dale and I took Melvin and Doris out for a drive to show them around town, including a visit to the Pearl Street Mall. Then we enjoyed a lovely lunch at the Boulder Dushanbe Tea House. It was fun describing this ornate landmark, and how it was shipped piece by piece from Dushanbe, Tajikistan, and later rebuilt in Boulder. I had not heard of Dushanbe until the teahouse became news, and that's when I learned that Dushanbe is located in the heart of central Asia. I explained to Melvin and Doris how the intricately constructed Persian tea house was a gift to the City of Boulder, from the Mayor of Dushanbe, Maksud Ikramov, and that Dushanbe had become a sister city to Boulder. I told them how all of the pieces of the teahouse sat stored in large boxes for about ten years, until Boulder found the perfect spot to reconstruct it next to Boulder Creek. Melvin and Doris were fascinated with the story and impressed with the unique style of the teahouse. The following day, we treated the two of them to a delightful brunch at Nancy's Restaurant on Walnut Street in downtown Boulder. They left that afternoon for the six-hour drive back to Liberal. I think they thoroughly enjoyed their visit, and we certainly enjoyed having them. I thought it was wonderful that Dale and Melvin could have some quality time together. A few years later, Melvin and Doris came back for another visit and somewhere in-between, we visited them in Liberal.

Morning sunlight glistened across the fresh layer of snow. It was a gorgeous winter day when my granddaughter, Carrissa came to spend the day with me. It was a very special time because Carrissa's sister was born that day. The date was February 4, 1993, when Cammille Chandler Deane Rieger was born! Our family circle was growing again as Dale and I were blessed with another granddaughter! Randy was at the hospital with his wife when he called with the exciting news. Carrissa was two-years old and we had such fun together that day. The fresh snow provided perfect conditions for building a snowman. Carrissa and I stepped into our snow boots and went outside. I showed Carrissa how to roll the snow and the two of us rolled and rolled the snow into the

## Chapter 12

biggest snowball. Then we rolled it to the perfect spot, left it there and rolled more snow for the next big ball. But we weren't done yet, we needed another big snow ball and it had to be the perfect size for the snowman's head. We made the most amazing snowman. He stood proudly in the back yard of that house on Kiowa Street. The following day, Pappy and I got to meet our new granddaughter. Cammille was a beautiful, precious baby. She was warm and cuddly and I fell in love with her as I held her close. I looked at her adorable face and commented that she had so much hair! My heart got bigger that day, and my family circle grew larger. Being Grandy is one of the greatest joys of my life.

"Yes, I'd love for Seymone to have a litter of puppies." I don't recall if this was Dale's idea or mine. In any event, by doing a little research, I found a breeder that we were comfortable with and we took our little poodle to visit the breeder's stud. Both dogs were about the same size – around six pounds. The lady put the two dogs together and it was like a match made in heaven. Seymone and the male dog hit it off right away, and after a few minutes, the lady said she was sure that our little poodle would have puppies in about two months. On the way home I told Seymone that she was going to be a mommy, but she didn't seem to care one little bit and she laid down in the car and took a nap – obviously tired from her little encounter! I thought about the grandkids, and how exciting this would be for them. And we had the perfect space for puppies in the sunroom adjacent to the kitchen. The room was ideal because it had a vinyl floor that could easily be kept clean. All I needed was a baby gate.

My real estate business was doing well and I was grateful when past clients called me back and I could work with them again. I continued working with relocation clients and I was listing properties as well. Most of my weekends were booked with tours and showing houses to prospects. I always appreciated the opportunity, even though there was never a guarantee that the prospect would become a buyer. But it seemed to average itself out and was never a problem. In spite of my busy schedule, I attended additional real estate classes to achieve my certification as a Certified Residential Specialist (CRS). To become a CRS, a realtor must provide evidence of experience by having completed a certain number of transactions and dollar volume, in addition to completing thirty hours of Residential Real Estate Council (RRC) training. I have always been proud to carry the CRS designation.

Tuesday morning rolled around and I was up earlier than usual to attend the weekly sales meeting. Just as I was about to leave for the meeting, I noticed Seymone was acting a little odd. According to the calendar, her due date was a couple days away but it could happen any time. I had already prepared a box for her to use when she had the puppies and it was ready in the sunroom. When I showed the box to Seymone, she sniffed it and walked around to check it out. I secured Seymone in the sunroom and left for the office. The meeting lasted about thirty minutes and when it was over, I grabbed a few files to take home. Thinking about Seymone, I decided to work at home that day. I had been gone for about one hour and when I returned to the house, I couldn't believe what was happening. Seymone was laboring in the box and she had already given birth to one puppy. Oh, my goodness, I hadn't expected it to happen so quickly! Dale was at home, and the two of us stood close by without disturbing her, but she knew we were there. I was excited but also on edge, hoping that everything would be okay. I kept Dr. Woods' phone number handy, just in case. It wasn't long until the second pup emerged. Seymone did a good job cleaning and looking after each puppy. I was amazed by her instinct in knowing what to do. She continued to labor as she

## Chapter 12

stretched her body. I sensed that she was feeling pain and I had the urge to pet her, but decided that wasn't a good idea. Another thirty minutes passed and the third puppy was born. Seymone fussed with the puppies, making sure they were snuggled close and could nurse. She took care of the after-birth and then she seemed to relax. That's when I spoke to her and said, "Good job, Seymone!" I waited a while then checked the pups; we had three females! I gave each puppy a name – Charnet, Tara and Monet. Later that week, I registered the puppies with the American Kennel Club (AKC).

The grandkids were excited when they came to visit the new puppies. Before they came, I explained that the puppies were too tiny to hold, but said "When the puppies grow a little bit, and their eyes open up, you can hold them very gently." When the pups were a few days old, Dale and I took the little family to visit the veterinarian doctor. Dale carried the box with the puppies and I carried Seymone. After an examination, Dr. Woods said, "Mother and pups are all in good health." Then he patted Seymone and said, "You did a good job, Seymone!" Then Dr. Woods bobbed their tails. Watching him snip those little tails made me cringe, but apparently it didn't bother the puppies because they didn't wince. Feeling relieved, we gathered the little family and went home.

### Little Bump in The Road

Awe, spring – such a beautiful time of year! Flowers were in full bloom and I enjoyed listening to song birds in the early morning hours while having coffee on the south deck. But this particular morning, I wouldn't be having coffee on the deck. It was Friday, and after getting up that morning, I knew something was wrong. I had been feeling very tired and I visited my doctor six months ago when he sent me to the lab for some blood work. The test indicated that I was a little anemic and my doctor prescribed iron tablets saying the iron would help build up my blood and should make me feel better. I took the iron tablets faithfully as my doctor recommended, but continued to feel tired and I made a note in my Day-Timer to call my doctor to let him know. But after seeing a plentiful amount of blood in my urine that Friday morning, I was prompted to call my doctor. The office opened at eight-thirty and I spoke with the receptionist. I told her what was going on and she said they could work me in at ten o'clock.

Instead of going to my office that morning, I went directly to the doctor's office. Dale dropped me off and said he would join me shortly. I checked-in at the reception desk then took a seat and waited for my name to be called. After about ten minutes, the nurse escorted me to the exam room where I waited another ten minutes. My doctor came in and we chatted a bit, then after the exam, he said he would like for me to have an ultrasound and he sent me to the imaging department. The technician helped me get situated on the table then she started the ultrasound. She gently slid the monitor across my abdomen and I thought it was odd when she kept asking me if she was hurting me. I shook my head and said, "No, it doesn't hurt at all." But apparently the tech could see my problem. I got dressed and went back to the reception area to find Dale waiting for me.

After Dale dropped me off earlier, he went to meet Pam at the veterinary clinic to help with the kids and their dog, Rosie. Rosie was a beautiful Golden Retriever and she was sick. Pam had three little tots to manage in the car, plus the dog, and when Dale offered to meet up with Pam and help, she was grateful and took him up on his offer. The veterinary clinic wasn't far from the doctor's office and when Dale finished, he came back to the doctor's office. The timing was perfect as I had just finished the test.

## Chapter 12

I sat down next to Dale, telling him about the test and said the doctor would see us after getting the results. It wasn't long and the nurse said the doctor could see me. She escorted us down the long hallway to the doctor's office. Dr. Pearlman was sitting at his desk looking very professional and he motioned for us to sit down. He didn't mince any words and got right to the point. I was not prepared for what he was about to say. "I'm afraid I have some bad news." Dr. Pearlman said. "You have a tumor in your left kidney and most likely, it's cancer. I'm going to refer you to a Urologist." He proceeded to write the doctor's name on a piece of paper and handed it to me. He said that he would be in touch with the Urologist, and that I should contact that office right away. I looked at the paper and saw the name Dr. James Clark, along with a phone number and address. I was shocked by the news and didn't know what to say. I took a deep breath and replied, "Whew! I wasn't expecting this." I glanced at the piece of paper again and said, "I'll call the doctor today." Then it dawned on me – of course, this is why I have felt so tired. That tumor has been growing inside me all these months! I got up to leave and my head started to spin.

Walking out of the doctor's office, I suddenly felt shaky and tried to maintain my balance. Dale took hold of my arm and I don't know if he did that to steady me, or to steady himself. Dale and I looked at each other but said nothing. We got in the car and I was the first to speak. "Well, that was a jolt to digest!" Dale started the car, then he reached over and squeezed my shoulder as he struggled for words. I could tell that he was concerned and scared. He must have felt the same way I had felt all those years ago when he told me he had cancer. After we got home, I sat down and tried to steady my thoughts. I knew this probably meant surgery and time off from work. I was concerned about my clients and my work. I still couldn't believe what was happening but I picked up the phone and called the urology office. When I gave my name to the receptionist, she knew who I was and the office seemed well-prepared for my call. Several tests were already scheduled for Monday, including a test that would measure the exact size of the tumor. After finishing the call, I told Dale I was going to my office – I had work to do. As I was leaving the house, I could hear Dale on the phone. His voice was emotional as he called our children.

Monday was a busy day. The first thing on the agenda was visiting the imaging department for the scheduled tests, then meeting with the Urologist. Dr. Clark was a surgeon, specializing in Urology. He was very professional and he explained everything to me in great detail. I liked his demeanor and I appreciated how he made me feel comfortable. Dr. Clark had a large imaging screen on the wall in his office to view PET/CT scans, MRI's, etc. I looked at the screen in awe as I saw my kidney on display, and there lay the tumor resting inside my left kidney. It looked large per scale, then I noticed the precise measurement in centimeters. Dr. Clark told me that the surgery would take several hours, and that he would be removing my entire left kidney. He said that most likely the cancer is contained within my kidney, but he would know for sure once he got in there. Dr. Clark was reassuring when he said, "You should be able to live a normal life and do just fine with one kidney." That was comforting to hear. Then he followed up to say that I would need a few weeks after the surgery to lay low and recover.

As I tried to digest everything, my thoughts drifted back to my dad. How ironic this is – my dad had the same thing when he was 65 years old and one of his kidneys was removed. Then four years later, he was diagnosed with bone cancer. I pushed that

## Chapter 12

thought out of my mind and tried to maintain a positive attitude. Before leaving Dr. Clark's office, I told him about my dad and he said that was quite the coincidence. As I left the doctor's office, I told myself "This is just a little bump in the road. I will get through this!"

Surgery was scheduled for the following week and I was relieved to know that I had a few days to prepare and attend to getting my work in order. My colleagues were wonderful and offered to help with my clients. I had several clients scheduled for house hunting trips. In addition to that, I had six clients under contract and those closings were scheduled for June. I delegated my client files to the agent best suited for each particular client. Then I proceeded to contact my clients to let them know that I would be having a little surgery and I needed to take some time off from work. I assured each of them that they would be in excellent hands and well taken care of. They were all very understanding and offered me their best wishes for a speedy recovery.

Knowing that my business would be taken care of, I could focus on taking care of myself. I came to terms with my problem and accepted what had to be done. I called my sister in Wichita to let her know what was happening. Paula was shocked to hear the news and immediately said she wanted to be there for my surgery. I told her that wasn't necessary – I just wanted her to know what was going on. But she insisted and said she wouldn't have it any other way. Paula said she would call the other siblings to let them know. Within a very short period of time, I received phone calls from Jim, Mike and Mary. They too said they wanted to come for the surgery. I felt their love, concern and support and it touched my heart.

The puppies were growing and they were adorable! I was having such fun with them, and Dale and I both said we were glad that we let Seymone have puppies. Our grandkids came often to visit, and they were excited when the puppies were old enough to hold. Dale and I decided to keep one of the pups, and we chose to keep Charnet. I was surprised when Paula said she might be interested in one of the pups. Since she was coming to Boulder, she could take one home with her on the plane. The pups were already AKC registered, but we had no interest in selling them. We just wanted them to have a good home – perhaps someone we knew would like to have a poodle puppy. As I began thinking about some of our friends, I thought about Ardis Monarchi – maybe she would like a puppy. Her husband Joe had passed away a while back and she now lived alone. I would call her.

In the meantime, there I was, dressed in a hospital gown, sitting up in bed at Boulder Community Hospital. I was awaiting surgery to remove my left kidney. That kidney had been with me for fifty-seven years and I was kind of attached to it but since it had gone bad, I didn't mind saying "adios." Earlier that morning I wrote a note on a small piece of paper and taped it to the left side of my abdomen. The note read, "It's my LEFT kidney." I had heard stories of the wrong knee, hip or whatever, being operated on, so I would remind the surgical team. If nothing else, it might give the doctors a good laugh. Dale, Pam and Randy were there with me, and believe me – I needed the moral support! I was feeling emotional that morning. The nurse came in earlier to give me some Valium – to help me relax, she said. I told the nurse I didn't need anything but she said they give it to all patients prior to surgery. Well, I took the Valium and perhaps that's what caused me to be emotional.

My four siblings walked in and I couldn't believe how they were dressed. Mike and Jim wore a coat and tie; Mary and Paula were dressed in their best. I opened my arms to them and they

## Chapter 12

came over to the bed for hugs. "Wow - you all look so nice!" I said "but really, you didn't have to get all dressed up for me." Then Jim replied jokingly, "Hell, we didn't dress up for you. We got dressed up to impress your doctor!" My family stood around cracking jokes to cheer me up and then Mike said, "You know, Sis, there are eight kidneys right here so if your other kidney ever poops out on you, we've got you covered." He was serious and didn't say that as a joke and the other siblings were shaking their heads "yes." My family gave me tremendous support and it was very comforting, not just for me, but for Dale too, and I was glad he wouldn't be in the waiting room by himself. It wasn't long until the hospital attendant came in and said, "I think they're ready for you, Miss Barbie." As I was wheeled out of the room and down the hall, my emotions took over and I began to cry. I was so grateful for my wonderful family.

Someone was calling my name. It sounded far away and faded in and out. I felt groggy and confused and didn't know where I was. I squinted my eyes open but couldn't focus. Someone was standing next to me but looked blurry. I turned my head and then I saw Dale, but his face was fuzzy and I thought I was dreaming. Dale seemed to be smiling and then I heard him say, "Good news! Dr. Clark said the cancer was contained in your kidney. He removed your kidney and he said you are going to be just fine." I think I must have gone back to sleep because I don't remember anything else that day. The following day, I do remember feeling very weak and I didn't seem to have enough strength to talk above a whisper. The doctor ordered a blood transfusion and within hours I felt new energy. I later learned that my cancer was called "Renal Cell Carcinoma." My siblings left for home, except Paula – she stayed on for a few days and I was glad to have her there. Then, the flowers started to arrive – one after one, after one! I couldn't believe it – I was showered with so many gorgeous bouquets! Some came from family, some from friends, and some were from clients. Soon, there wasn't enough space in the room for any more flowers, and Dale had to take some of them home. The loving care and support I received warmed my heart in such a special way!

Paula decided to accept a puppy and she chose Tara. This made me so happy. While I was in the hospital, Dale helped Paula acquire the paperwork needed to take the puppy on the plane with her. And she also needed a small carrier to fit under the seat on the airplane, so Paula and Dale went shopping to find the perfect size carrier for Tara. Paula was all set and ready to fly back to Wichita. She came to the hospital to tell me goodbye, but our goodbyes were always hard. We hugged and promised to see each other soon. After nearly one week in the hospital, I went home to the house on Kiowa. It was wonderful to be home, and I knew that I would be back to normal very soon. During my recovery period, Ardis came to visit. She immediately fell in love with Monet, and Monet loved her back with puppy kisses. Ardis already had a cat but she said she would love to have Monet, if her cat would allow it. As it turned out, Monet and the cat became best pals. Monet lived a long life and she travelled with Ardis and the cat when they moved back to Canada.

My recovery from surgery went well and I felt good. It was the summer of 1993, and that July was our 40th anniversary. Dale and I wanted to celebrate the event, and my recovery, by doing something a little different. We talked about the possibility of a cruise but Dale had a tendency to get seasick on small boats if the water was wavy, and he had some concerns about that. We talked to our travel agent and she told us that large cruise ships are built with stability features and we wouldn't feel any movement

## Chapter 12

on a large cruise ship. She also said that Dale could wear a small medical patch specifically for motion sickness. After hearing all that, we decided to book a short four-day cruise from Los Angeles, crossing the sea border into Mexico. We would give it a try and test the waters – so to speak.

There were a few puffy clouds floating about in the sky, but it was mostly sunny and quite warm when we boarded the plane for Los Angeles. I was extremely excited and ready for the big adventure – our first cruise! It was an easy flight from Denver to Los Angeles, and we flagged a taxi at the L.A. Airport. By the time we arrived at the harbor it was mid-afternoon and we were allowed to board the ship. Looking at our ship from the ground up, it was ginormous! As we climbed up the gangway and stepped inside the ship, I was filled with eager anticipation. The steward greeted us warmly as we handed him our identification. Then he gave us an envelope with our names perfectly inscribed, and told us the keys to our stateroom were tucked inside. He followed up saying that our luggage would be promptly delivered to our stateroom. I looked around in awe at the magnitude of the interior of the ship. We found the elevator which took us up to the deck where our stateroom was located. When Dale opened the door, I was surprised to find our luggage already inside. Our stateroom had its own private veranda and I thought that was very cool. We walked over to check it out and discovered two chairs and a small table.

We were anxious to explore the ship and wasted no time in doing just that. The ship was huge and it was a destination in itself. There were restaurants and shops, a hair salon and spa, a theatre, a casino, and much more. That evening, the ship left the harbor and we were on our way to San Diego. And to our surprise, we could not tell that the ship was moving. Dale and I had a lovely dinner at one of the restaurants and later enjoyed a live musical performance at the theatre. I slept like a baby that night and when I woke the next morning, the ship was already docked at the San Diego Harbor. After a leisurely breakfast in our stateroom, we ventured off the ship. We had several hours to stroll along the beach, shop, and enjoy lunch at one of the cute cafes. The ship remained docked at San Diego Harbor until evening, then cruised during the night. Our next stop was Catalina Island. Dale and I loved exploring this island and we hope to go back there someday. As we continued our adventure, the cruise was very smooth and neither of us felt any ill effects of being on the ship. The following day, the ship took us across the sea border into Mexico, then docked at Ensenada. Ensenada is truly Mexico, and we enjoyed getting to see it. Our 40th anniversary was a wonderful experience, and you guessed it – we love cruising! This was the first of many more cruises to come.

Time seemed to pass all too swiftly and our eighteen-month lease would soon expire. I liked the house on Kiowa Street. The style was warm and inviting, and it had been well-cared for. And I appreciated the fact that it was much smaller than our prior home on Briarwood Drive. I found it easy to care for, and I thought it was the perfect size for the two of us. I had settled-in and was feeling comfortable and I wasn't ready to move again so soon. We talked about buying this home, but when we mentioned it to the owner's agent, he said the owner had plans to move back into the house themselves. So, we wouldn't be buying the house on Kiowa. I was busy with work, so Dale took on the task of looking for another place we could rent temporarily. He found a cute patio home in Louisville, in the Coal Creek neighborhood. I wasn't sure about leaving Boulder, but we ended up renting the patio home and we moved out of Boulder. I knew we should be buying another house in Boulder to keep up with housing prices

## Chapter 12

but we continued to rent for a while longer. If we bought a small house in Boulder, it would be an older home. But if we chose to build a new house, it would most likely be located east of Boulder, and we would need a place to live while the house was being built, or so the logic goes.

The best part about that house on Fairfield Lane, was the master bedroom closet. It was ginormous! This closet was the size of a bedroom with enough space to hang all the seasons of my wardrobe! After unpacking the necessary items, we still had many boxes to unpack but I decided to leave them stored in the garage for the time being. It didn't take long to get settled-in with our doggies, Seymone and Charnet. They were happy sniffing every nook and cranny and made themselves right at home. I soon discovered a nice trail not far from the house and it was perfect for walking our dogs. They needed exercise and I did too.

The real estate market was tight with limited inventory and I had a hard time finding the right home for an out of state buyer who wanted to live in the western part of Boulder. After a full day showing property to the couple, nothing seemed to click with them. When I dropped them off at their hotel, I sensed that they were discouraged. I asked if they would be willing to look at homes in other parts of town. They were hesitant at first, but said it can't hurt to look. I said I had some things in mind and would also pull a new search for the area they preferred. I told them the market was a little tight but assured them that I would find a home they would love. That seemed to lift their spirits and they left saying they looked forward to getting started at ten o'clock the next morning.

While driving home, I thought about other possibilities for my clients. I was almost home when the unexpected happened. I was turning left onto McCaslin Boulevard when suddenly, there was a hard jolt and a loud noise as the Jeep crashed into me. I went flying out of my seat into the passenger side of the car. Then I was jolted back into the driver seat. I was stunned and momentarily, I felt frozen in time. What had just happened? In the split second before the crash, I saw the Jeep out of the corner of my eye. The driver jumped out of the jeep and stood outside my car saying he was sorry, that he was fiddling with his radio and didn't realize the light was red. I later learned that he was sixteen years old. Others rushed over and said they saw what happened. Someone must have called the police because within a few minutes I heard sirens blaring.

I was covered in glass – shattered glass was everywhere! I reached up and touched my face. I felt tiny splinters, like stickers, embedded into my skin. I wanted to get out of the car but the door was pushed in and it wouldn't open. Was I okay? I could move and I could feel – I must be okay. Then I thought about my clients. "Thank God, they were not in the car! They could have been hurt – or killed." About that time, a kind lady came to my car and asked if she could help. My car phone wouldn't work and I asked if she would call my husband. I gave her the number, then said, "His name is Dale. Please tell him I'm okay." About that time the EMT guys arrived. They came rushing over and tried to open the car door, but it was smashed. They struggled with it but had no luck. Then they decided to help me out through the passenger side. I scooted my body up over the center console into the passenger seat. That's when my stomach started to feel strange and I could tell that something was wrong. The EMT guys helped me get out of the car and they secured me to a board and lifted me up into the ambulance.

Dale arrived at the scene just in time to see the EMT personnel working to get me out of the car. He looked at me with

## Chapter 12

sad eyes and said, "Oh, Baby Doll!" I was taken to the hospital in Louisville, and after being examined, I was wheeled to Imaging for an MRI. It was determined that my spleen had been damaged and I had internal bleeding. The ER doctor called for a surgeon and he arrived promptly, prepared to operate. I asked the doctor if there was any way to avoid surgery. I told him I just had a kidney removed the year before and the prior year I had emergency surgery to remove my gallbladder. I didn't want more surgery. The surgeon said he understood and would hold off for a bit, but he said I would need to be monitored carefully and he ordered that I be placed in the ICU. The doctor told me that I would be confined to bed and he said if I could lay perfectly still for twenty-four hours and give the spleen time, the bleeding might stop; but if the bleeding continued or worsened, he said I would need surgery.

I followed the doctor's orders and laid perfectly still, but my thoughts went back to my clients. They were expecting me to pick them up at ten o'clock in the morning. I called Ted, one of my colleagues, and told him about the accident. I ask if he might be able to help out. Without hesitation, he came to my rescue. I gave him the details with contact info, and told him about the homes we had already looked at and offered suggestions of other possibilities. Ted was wonderful and took over. Dale was with me in the ICU, but it was getting late and he went home to take care of our doggies. Later that evening, one of the ICU nurses went to work cleaning the glass splinters from my face. Very gently and carefully, she removed tiny splinters of glass. She did the best she could, but some were left behind and it took some time before all of the glass fragments were gone.

Fortunately, my spleen stopped bleeding by the end of the following day and I was relieved to know that I didn't have to endure surgery. After a couple days in the hospital, the doctor said

I could go home but he said I needed to take it easy. Dale came to the hospital to pick me up and when I got in the car, I was suddenly terrified. I didn't want to be in the car. The accident had shaken me to my core and I was afraid to ride in the car. I was on edge and began shaking. I feared that someone would run into us. I realized that I had been traumatized by the accident. My nerves were shattered and I wasn't able to work for several weeks.

I wanted to get back to work and tried to get a grip on myself. I was troubled about not being able to take clients in my car. After a week or so, I started to feel better and thought I was ready to drive. I began working at home to gently ease into my work routine. I was referred to a young couple from Texas, and made arrangements to pick them up at their hotel in Westminster. But when that day arrived, I became terrified at the last minute and realized I wasn't ready to drive with clients in my car. I told Dale, "I can't do this." Dale hadn't shown any real estate in quite a while, but his license was still active and he said he would pick up my clients and show them the homes I had selected. Dale had worked primarily in Boulder, and he wasn't familiar with the area where these houses were located. Remember now, this was 1994, before navigation systems or pocket cell phones to guide the way. I jotted down the directions for Dale, but it was a challenging day for him. After that, I forced myself to get in the car and drive around. My car had been totaled in the crash and I leased a new Cadillac. I grabbed a jacket, went out to the garage and climbed in my new car. I took it slow and easy and drove around the side streets. The next day, I ventured into traffic. The following day I did the same thing, but this time I drove to the office and parked. I went inside and sat down at my desk. It felt good to be back and I had good vibes – a positive attitude. Some of my colleagues stopped by to say hello and welcome me back. I

## Chapter 12

turned the corner that day and I was back on track; I had taken charge of my life again.

### Time to Build a New House

As Dale and I talked more about where we might purchase our next home, our thoughts kept going back to the idea of building a new home. I focused my search on new home subdivisions and we started visiting show homes. We looked at floor plans, we talked to builders, and I started comparing prices, lot sizes and neighborhoods. I had sold a few custom homes in the Indian Peaks neighborhood and I liked the location. It was a beautiful new area in Lafayette, and still in the early development stages. The Indian Peaks Golf Course had just been completed, and it was nicely located within the neighborhood. There were many pocket neighborhoods in this master planned community. Some of the homes were quite large with over 6,000 square feet and of course, those were much too large for us. At the time, Starlight Ridge was the newest neighborhood within Indian Peaks. I loved this area and Dale loved it too. The lots were nicely sized and we liked the curvy streets. After considerable looking, we decided to have a new home built in Starlight Ridge. We chose a lot and hoped it would accommodate the house and floor plan that we liked. We met with the builder, Pat Murphy, and he confirmed that the house we liked would fit nicely on the lot we wanted. Our new address would be 2324 Rimrock Circle.

Building our new home was slow getting started. It took much longer than either of us anticipated. But finally, ground was broken and it wasn't long until the basement concrete was poured. Then there was another waiting period, waiting for the concrete to cure. In the meantime, it was fun choosing our colors and finishes, and we had an opportunity to make a few changes, such as adding windows, skylights, etc. We hoped the house would be completed around the same time our lease was set to expire at the rental on Fairfield Lane; if not, we would ask for a short lease extension. But as it turned out, the owner was hesitant and decided not to grant an extension because that would leave her with a vacant house for rent during the winter months.

Having been denied a lease extension, I placed an ad in the local newspaper "Executive couple needs short-term rental." Within a couple days, I was pleased to receive a call from the wife of a local builder. She told me about a new home her husband had built in Lafayette. She said it had been on the market but hadn't sold and they would consider renting it short term. They were interested in meeting us. When I told her that we have two little toy poodles, she said they would like to meet them as well. We scheduled an appointment and took our doggies to meet Penny and David. They were very kind and entrusted us to rent this lovely new home for a few months. I promised to wipe the doggie's feet after they went outside, and we left the plastic runners in place within the home. I didn't use the oven or the master bathtub during the time we lived in the home and we were careful to keep the house as new as possible for them. As it turned out, they asked me to list this beautiful new house on Lake Meadow Drive and I ended up selling it to the most wonderful couple, who I'll tell you about later.

After waiting patiently, our new home on Rimrock Circle was complete and we were scheduled to close that November in 1995. We moved in the Saturday after Thanksgiving, and Pam came to help me unpack the kitchen and get things organized in the cabinets. Over the years, during my many moves, I found that having the kitchen organized was top priority. If the kitchen was ready for use and the bedroom was set up for sleeping, the

## Chapter 12

household would function. Gradually, everything was unpacked and we got settled-in. When I unpacked all the stored boxes, it was like Christmas. I found things I'd forgotten I had. We loved our new house on Rimrock Circle, and we loved our new neighborhood. This would be our home for many years to come.

The December issue of Where to Live magazine had been distributed to newsstands and offices. I thumbed through the magazine and was excited to see my full-color ad for the home on Lake Meadow Drive – the home Dale and I rented for four months. The house presented itself beautifully and I was enthused about marketing the home and getting it sold. We had moved out a few weeks before and showing activity had been pretty good, however, it was the holiday season and I expected things to slow down. But I was about to meet a very special couple who were interested in the property. This couple saw my ad in the magazine and they called me to schedule an appointment to look at the house. It was Christmas week when I met Lynne and Howard Brown at the property. I showed them around the house, and the yard, and I proceeded to tell them that my husband and I had lived in the house for a few months, awaiting the completion of our new home. I think they were surprised that it looked like a brand-new house. After the showing, we visited awhile and I told them about the neighborhood and how much I had grown to love it during the short time I lived there. I liked Lynne and Howard right away and I felt we had bonded that very day.

Lynne and Howard thought about the house for a few days, then called to say they would like to look at it again. They were so gracious and considerate and I looked forward to seeing them. I believe it was Christmas Eve when we went back for a second look. As we walked through the house again, I could tell that they loved it and that's when they decided to buy it. After the showing, as Lynne and Howard were leaving, I pointed to the house across the street and told them about the fun-loving couple that lives there – Marcia and Alan. I said that my husband and I had gotten to know Marcia and Alan, and we really liked them and had become friends – and still such good friends as I write this. I remember saying to Lynne and Howard, "You will love this couple!" During the time I spent with Lynne and Howard for the real estate transaction, we became friends. And when I introduced them to Dale, they hit it off right away and we have remained friends all these many years. I feel truly blessed to have such a special friendship with these amazing people.

Spring arrived and I was excited about getting the landscaping done at our new home. Dale and I talked about a landscaping plan and tossed around some ideas. We wanted our yard to be beautiful – a place where we could relax and enjoy time with our family and friends. Dale sketched a design for the front walkway and also for the rear patio. Then he contacted a landscaper and scheduled an appointment. When the landscaper came to look at our yard, Dale gave him copies of the sketches he made and asked if they could be incorporated into the overall design. The landscaper appreciated having our input and was happy to do that. After a week or so, he came back with his design. We were pleased with his landscape plan and Dale hired the company to landscape our yard. But before moving forward, we needed approval of the Architectural Control Committee (ACC). We submitted the drawing to the ACC and after our design was approved, the work began. The concrete was poured for the front walkway, the rear patio concrete was poured, large evergreen trees and deciduous trees were planted, the irrigation system was installed, sod was laid, and decorative bushes were planted. The progress went smoothly and every evening when I got home

## Chapter 12

from work, there was something new in our yard. It was exciting to watch the transformation, and when it was all done, we had a beautiful yard.

I was completely surprised but delighted when Pam called one day to say that she would like to work part-time as my assistant. Pam had been busy raising her children (my grandchildren), but all three kids were now in school and she was available. I didn't have an assistant at the time, and Pam knew how busy I was and that I could use some help. And she may have heard me mention that I was planning to hire a personal assistant. My real estate business had increased significantly and I was joyfully busy. Pam was experienced in real estate, and she became a tremendous help to me. Of course, we knew each other like a book and we made a good team. It wasn't long and Pam was working more and more hours. She was an incredible asset to me and my business. Pam was my assistant from 1996 to 2005. Those were some of my best years in real estate!

Sometimes things happen in life that you have nothing to do with, but it turns your world upside down. I knew that my son's marriage was struggling. Randy shared with me the abuse and stress he endured. He said his marriage was beyond repair and he wanted out. The marriage of thirteen years had brought two beautiful children into our family. This was a painfully difficult time in Randy's life and it became a dark period in my life. I stood by feeling helpless, but there was nothing I could do. After the divorce, Dale and I were allowed to see our granddaughters. I remember the time we were given permission to take them to the Denver Zoo. It was a magical day for the girls and a special day for us. But things changed and visits with the girls became limited and I saw them about once a year – usually around Christmas. Then one day when I called and asked to speak with the girls, their mother told me that I could no longer visit them and she asked me to discontinue phone calls. This was around the time when The Supreme Court ruled that grandparents had no rights with regard to having time with grandchildren. Those two little girls slid away from us and out of our lives. My heart filled with sorrow and I grieved the loss of two precious granddaughters. I learned to accept what I cannot change, but the pain lingers. Thankfully though, throughout the struggles of that dark time, I didn't lose sight of the love and joy I have with my other grandchildren and my amazing family. They are the core of my being. And I am grateful that my son found a new direction and managed to build a new life for himself.

Paula and I were giddy with excitement. She was coming to Colorado for a visit and she would stay with me for one whole week! I picked her up at the Denver Airport and brought her to our new house on Rimrock. This was Paula's first visit to our new home. I was glad that our landscaping was installed and was anxious for her to see it. Our basement wasn't finished yet, but we had plenty of space upstairs with extra bedrooms. I scheduled some time off from my real estate work and planned several fun things for us girls to do. But a couple of work-related things came up, requiring some time at the office. Paula didn't seem to mind and she went with me. I think she enjoyed sitting there listening to me when I was on the phone. She was very patient and when I finished my work, we got back to having fun.

After Paula got settled-in, I invited the family over for a barbecue. Our grandkids, Erin, Jason and Tyler were there and that added to the fun. Paula was glad to get to know them a little better. Then later on, Pam and Tim invited all of us for dinner at their house in the mountains and that was a special treat. Paula loved going into the mountains when she came to Colorado.

## Chapter 12

Another day during her visit, we had a family picnic at a small park in Louisville. Mary's family came, including Mary's grandkids, Jim and Mary were there, Randy came, Pam and Tim and our grandkids were there – the whole clan! It just so happened that my birthday was the same day as the picnic. I turned sixty that September 1st – 1996. I hadn't chosen the date for the picnic and I didn't think anyone realized it was my birthday, but I was quite surprised when someone showed up with a wonderful birthday cake and balloons!

It was a glorious day and a beautiful drive to Estes Park. Paula and I spent the entire day browsing the touristy gift shops. We didn't miss a beat and walked up one side to explore the shops then crossed the street to browse the shops on the other side, and we stopped for lunch along the way. The two of us have done this more than once! I remember one year when Paula came to Colorado, the three sisters, Mary, Paula and I went to Estes Park, and Pam joined us. The four of us girls had a fun lunch at the Stanley Hotel – a special time to be sure! But this vacation was over and Paula had to go home. The week went by all too quickly, and I didn't want her to leave. I took her to the airport and when it was time to say goodbye, we both cried and said we had to start planning for the next time.

When the Editor of Women's Magazine called me to request an interview, I was very surprised. She said that she would like to do a cover story about me. I remember my response so well. "Deborah, I am very flattered that you thought of me, but what in the world would be interesting enough about me for a story in your magazine?" Deborah Rosenberger gave a little laugh and replied, "I'm sure we'll find plenty to talk about. Just let me do the interview." Well, I was curious and we scheduled an appointment for her to come to my office. Deborah was well-known in the

Boulder area and I had met her before at various functions. I was still curious when she arrived, wondering how a conversation could create a story for her magazine. We made ourselves comfortable in my office and Deborah turned on her recorder. She had a warm friendly demeanor and she knew exactly how to gently lead her subject into talking about themselves, and before I knew it, she had me talking and answering questions. And whenever she sensed a lull in the conversation, she was ready with her next perfect question. She was amazing! After the interview, Deborah asked if I had time to meet with her photographer.

A few weeks went by and I hadn't given much thought to the upcoming article in the magazine. I was busy working in my office when the receptionist buzzed me to let me know that Deborah Rosenberger was there to see me. She had stopped by to personally deliver a copy of the April, 1997 edition of Women's Magazine. She wanted me to be the first to see the publication. I wasn't sure what to expect or how she managed to turn the interview into a story, and I was bowled over when I saw it. There I was on the cover! She delivered the magazine to me in a nice folder tied with a ribbon. I thanked her for choosing me for her article, and said I would read it right away. After she left, I sat down at my desk and began to read. Deborah has a gifted writing style, and I was pleased at how beautifully she had constructed the article. Very thoughtfully, she articulated my real estate career. She wrote about my personal life, letting the reader know what I was all about. She had made me feel proud.

## Life is Full of Surprises

When I signed on with Moore & Company Real Estate, I was under the impression that the owner would never sell the company to a national real estate company. Well, surprise, surprise – that's

## Chapter 12

exactly what happened. I enjoyed working at Moore & Company, and I had confidence in the ownership and management. Bill Moore was the owner of the company and he was a terrific individual with a charismatic personality. He had the amazing ability to remember everyone's name and when he saw you, he could immediately greet you by your name. When it was announced that the company had been sold to Coldwell Banker (CB), Mr. Moore promised it would be a seamless transition and I have to say, overall, it was fairly easy. As it turned out, the office manager at the Boulder Moore office was hired to manage the new CB Boulder office. Fortunately, I didn't have to move out of my office because CB took over the office lease and we remained in the same location. I got busy and ordered new business cards and I sent letters to my clients to let them know about the change. I would miss Moore & Company, but CB offered some nice perks. Every year they treated their top producers to a fabulous three-day getaway, all expenses paid! I was thrilled to learn that I was among those invited. Dale got to go with me on those trips and it was always a fun time.

I'm always amazed at my children and grandchildren and take great pride in watching them grow in their own light. My son, Randy, worked at Rocky Mountain Sports of Boulder for many years, but he was ready to move on to a different line of work. I could hear the excitement in his voice when he told me he was seeking a new opportunity. I have always known the importance of loving what you do and feeling good about yourself in doing it. Randy's new job was still in marketing and sales but involved a lot of travel, and he soon became a regular passenger on Frontier Airlines. My son's personal life was evolving too. He had been dating a special woman for a couple of years. Her name was Erin, and she had an adorable little boy named Connor. Ironically, Erin carries the same name as my oldest grandchild. Erin's beaming smile and a warm, bubbly personality captured my heart and we clicked right away. Erin is Canadian born, and she came to the United States with her mother and sister many years ago when she was a child. After Randy had been dating Erin for a while, he learned that she hadn't seen her father since she was a small child, and she had no idea where he was. Randy, being the compassionate person that he is, set out to find her father. After much research, the mission was accomplished – her father was living in Canada. Randy arranged for Erin to fly to Canada to meet this stranger – her biological father. Erin stayed in Canada a few weeks, hoping to reconnect with him, but that was the last time she saw her father. Randy was anxious for Erin's return, and after she got back to Colorado, Randy asked her to marry him.

The sky carried heavy clouds and threatened rain all week but when Saturday arrived, I woke to find blue skies and a few puffy clouds. It was a gorgeous day on June 14, 1997 – It was Randy and Erin's wedding day! The small outdoor wedding was held that afternoon in the foothills above Boulder, in Pam and Tim's yard. It was the perfect setting for this special event. A few of Randy and Erin's close friends were invited to attend, including Randy's best friend, Roger Ross. Roger lived in California, and it was questionable whether he could be there. But at the very last minute, Roger managed to schedule a flight and he came with his fiancé. And of course, the immediate family was there plus a few of our friends. Erin's sister, Kate, was the maid of honor, and a friend of Randy's was best man. And little Connor was the cutest ring bearer! Erin was beautiful in her white dress, and Randy was handsomely dressed to compliment his bride. As we all gathered 'round in preparation for the ceremony, I took special notice of the aspen trees as their leaves danced and glistened in the sunlight. Soft music played in the background as the Rev. Janice Deville

## Chapter 12

spoke the most wonderful, inspiring words. As Randy and Erin stood together and said their vows to each other, one could easily see the love radiating between the two of them. And then, upon rejoicing in one another with a kiss, Rev. Deville proclaimed – "May I present to you, Mr. and Mrs. Randy Rieger." The wedding was lovely and so very special! After the ceremony, we enjoyed a lovely champagne reception with an array of yummy appetizers. The gorgeous wedding cake was lovingly prepared by Erin's mother, Jan. The cake was not only gorgeous – it was delicious!

A rendezvous with Gloria and Donald in Jackson Hole, Wyoming. Dale and I were celebrating our forty-fifth anniversary that July, 1998, and we planned to celebrate with a trip to Jackson Hole, then on to Glacier National Park and Yellowstone National Park. When I told Gloria about our travel plans, I asked if she and Donald would be interested in joining us in Jackson Hole. Gloria thought it was a great idea and the perfect opportunity to see each other. Jackson Hole isn't far from Montana, and Gloria said she and Donald would do a roadie and meet us there. I had always heard about Jackson Hole and how charming and beautiful it is, and I was excited about the adventure. Dale and I flew from Denver, then rented a car at the Jackson Hole Airport. My, oh my, I couldn't believe the traffic in that small place. We soon found ourselves caught in the worst traffic jam ever! There were so many tourists in Jackson Hole, one literally couldn't drive through town. We found our hotel and met up with Gloria and Donald. We parked our cars and walked around town. Us girls had fun browsing the cute boutiques along the way. That night we had a wonderful dinner together.

The next morning, we enjoyed breakfast with Gloria and Donald, then we said our goodbyes and they headed back to Montana. Then Dale and I ventured out onto the water for a float trip up and down the river. This was my first experience on a float trip and I loved the new adventure. Thankfully, it was very gentle and we could enjoy the scenery without worrying about falling out of the rubber raft. The next day, we ventured into Glacier National Park, where the scenery was absolutely breathtaking! I held my camera steady, ready to click away at every opportunity. I became even more excited to see herds of buffalo roaming about freely. We explored the incredible Grand Tetons, and from there we visited Yellowstone National Park. I stood spellbound watching the magnificent Old Faithful geyser erupt in all its glory! Witnessing this amazing wilderness and the vast beauty of nature was an amazing experience!

## An Essay for My Sister

One fall morning while getting ready for work, I had the radio tuned to KOA. I liked to catch the early morning news and weather. The announcer was talking and I was only partially listening, but something he said caught my attention. The radio station was offering a nice prize for writing an essay with details describing someone's hardship, expressing why that person should be worthy of such a prize. A round-trip airplane ride on a small aircraft from anywhere in the United States was the prize. My thoughts immediately went to my sister, Paula. Paula's home in Wichita had been flooded out three times, with the most recent flood the worst of all. Paula and her husband, Dick, lost many belongings when flood waters gushed into their home. Their home sustained severe damage, and they could no longer drink the well water because of pollution that had seeped into the well. Paula suffered emotionally, causing stress to her health. That very day, I sat down to compose an essay. I first described the terrible flood in detail. Then I wrote about the sadness and hardship my sister

## Chapter 12

and her husband were still enduring because of the floods. A getaway to Colorado would give them a boost and perhaps a few rays of sunshine in their lives. I folded my essay neatly, placed it in an envelope and mailed it to KOA Radio

A few weeks passed and I hadn't given much more thought about my essay. But then, lo and behold, I received a phone call from KOA Radio informing me that my story had been selected. The representative at KOA said the essay I wrote about my sister was so heartfelt, and they were happy for her to have the prize. The lady at KOA Radio told me that a pilot by the name of Mike Chaput would be calling me with the details and he would need the contact info for my sister. I was jumping up and down excited, and I couldn't wait to call Paula. It would be a short visit, just a long weekend, but so special to have that time together. When I spoke with the pilot, he told me the aircraft was a six-place Cessna 210, and that my sister and husband would board the aircraft at an airport in the Wichita area. I was glad for the opportunity to thank Mr. Chaput for his kindness and generosity. I called Paula and she could hardly believe it when I told her the exciting news. She checked her calendar and selected a date that coordinated with the pilot's schedule. I gave Paula the name of the pilot and told her that he would be calling her.

It was the month of January, 1999, and yippee – the day arrived! My sister and her husband would arrive sometime that morning. The winter air was crisp and I zipped up my jacket as I left for the office. The Boulder Airport was less than ten minutes away – I could do a little work while I waited for the call. I didn't know the flight time from Wichita to Boulder in a small aircraft, but I knew it would take longer than a large commercial jet. It was mid-morning when I got the call; the pilot said they were on the ground. I jumped in my car and off I went to pick up Paula and Dick. When I pulled into the parking lot, I spotted Paula standing by the hanger. I waved and she came walking over to meet me. As we hugged, she said Dick would be along shortly. After a minute or two, I saw a man walking towards us but it wasn't Dick – OMG, it was my brother, Mike! I was bowled over with surprise. Mike had driven from Texas to Paula's house in Wichita, and Paula's husband stayed home to let Mike take his seat on the airplane. Wow! Now I was the one getting a big surprise! I was overjoyed to see my brother and sister.

It's amazing how things came together that weekend. As it turned out, our other brother, Jim, was in town. That evening, the rest of my Colorado family came for dinner at our house on Rimrock Circle, and all five siblings were together. During Paula and Mike's visit, we drove to Fort Collins to see Jim's new Pizza Hut. He had just opened another new store and he was proud to show it off. Jim treated us to some yummy pizza. The weekend slipped away all too quickly and the pilot called to let me know he would be leaving from the airport in Broomfield, and not the Boulder Airport. The morning of departure, I was glad to have the opportunity to meet the pilot and thank him again. The three of us hugged each other and said goodbye, then Paula and Mike boarded the plane. I stood watching and waved to them as they lifted up into the air.

## Fun in Bigfork

During the summer of 1999, Dale and I travelled to Bigfork, Montana to visit Gloria and Donald. Bigfork is a charming little town located in the Flathead Valley. The town has many great restaurants to enjoy, some with a view of Flathead Lake. And one can walk down to the lake for a swim or take a boat trip during the summer months. We always try to see our friends every other year or so – us there in Montana or them with us in Colorado, but occasionally we had to skip a year. One thing's for

## Chapter 12

sure, it's a good time whenever we do get together. Gloria had everything mapped out before we arrived, with something fun scheduled for each day. One day she arranged to take Dale and me on a three-hour trail ride. "Horseback riding – what fun!" I thought. I hadn't been on a horse since we left the farm in 1965, and back then I had only ridden our horse Star, in the farmyard. When we arrived at the trailhead, the horses were ready and waiting for us. Gloria pointed to my horse and told me it was a gentle mare, and indeed it was.

Dale gave me a lift up and I managed to swing my leg over the saddle and secure my boots in the stirrups. I grabbed hold of the saddle horn and made myself comfortable. Once we were all set and ready to go, we followed our guide up the mountain trail. The trail was laden with trees and beautiful scenery and the guide knew just the right places to take us. It was a wonderful experience and great fun. Gloria was an experienced rider and a cowgirl at heart with two horses of her own. She rode on a regular basis with her saddle pals. As for me, I looked just dandy dressed in my western attire and I felt like a cowgirl, but three hours on a horse was a long time for a girl like me and the next day my inner thigh muscles were quite sore. I didn't want Gloria to know and after a couple Tylenol, I was fine. Dale had grown up with horses and he had no problem whatsoever.

Another time during our many trips to Bigfork, Donald took us out on his boat to cruise around Flathead Lake. The day was warm and sunny, just perfect to be out on the lake. We cruised over to the small town of Polson, where Donald could secure his boat at the restaurant dock. We went up the walkway to the restaurant and the hostess seated us at the perfect table overlooking the beautiful Flathead Lake. After a relaxing lunch, Donald's boat was waiting for us and we cruised back to Bigfork. This is another wonderful memory of a fun time with dear friends in Bigfork, Montana.

## Chapter 13
## Turn of the Century
## 2000

A time to celebrate – not just the new year, it was also the turn of the century! And along with it came the Y2K dilemma. It was also referred to as the Millennium Bug. Would our computers survive? We didn't know for sure what would happen at midnight, December 31, 1999. Would computer calendars fail to move forward to 2000 – would they suddenly stop working? Well, we all know that nothing bad happened. The computer clock changed to 2000, computers continued to function and the world continued to go 'round. However, as a result of the Y2K scare, computer manufacturing flourished as consumers rushed out to buy new computers before the end of 1999.

When I began my real estate career, I worked primarily with relocation and out of state buyers. As time went on, those buyers became sellers. Many times, when they were ready to sell their home, they called me to list it. I was steadily listing properties and soon realized how much I enjoyed working directly with the owner of the property. I still worked with buyers of course, but I thrived on the challenges involved with listing and marketing homes. I wanted to use the best approach in getting the property sold. I looked for creating marketing strategies tailored to fit each particular property. A successful timely sale made my clients happy and consequently, I was happy. You've probably heard the old saying "If you love what you do, you never work a day in your life." Well, that's not exactly true because I did work, but I had a passion for my work. Perhaps that's what this old saying means.

The alarm buzzed earlier than usual on Tuesday morning and I jumped out of bed to shower and get myself ready for the day. Our weekly sales meeting was always held on Tuesday, and it began at 8:30 sharp. I turned on the radio to catch the morning news while applying my makeup and getting dressed. One last glance in the mirror and I was ready to go. I grabbed my jacket and briefcase and was on my way. The drive from Lafayette to Boulder took about fifteen minutes, giving me time to enjoy the gorgeous panoramic view of the back range, and be grateful for where I lived. The management team at my office was wonderful and always provided a buffet breakfast for their agents to enjoy during the sales meeting. I arrived early and helped myself to coffee and food and found a seat in the front row. The meeting began as usual but then the manager said he had an announcement to make. The corporate office had decided to close the Pearl Street office. The lease was expiring and they had plans to relocate the Realtors to the CB office in north Boulder. I could hear a sudden buzz among the Realtors in the room; they were not happy about this announcement.

The office building on Pearl Street was very nice and it was conveniently located. The work environment was comfortable and I had a nice private office. Things were going well for me and I wasn't thrilled about moving to an older building in north Boulder. It wasn't long after the meeting that I heard rumble among some of the agents that they were not going to continue with CB. And

## Chapter 13

then I learned that the manager of our office had decided to join WK Real Estate, and that he was buying into that company. I was extremely busy at the time and didn't have time for all this fuss. If I had to move my office to north Boulder, I would just do it. I was grateful that Pam was working as my assistant; I knew I could count on her to help me get settled at the new address. Within a few days, I was getting phone calls from the WK management, trying to entice me to join their firm. Apparently, many of my colleagues had decided to move their business to WK. After a couple of weeks, most of the agents at the Pearl Street office had already moved out and had moved on.

I was completely absorbed with my work and may have been the only Realtor still working at the Pearl Street office. Plans were in place to move my office to north Boulder. I hadn't even considered the possibility of moving my business to another real estate firm. But, the WK management team had been calling and then one day, a dozen gorgeous yellow roses arrived. Those people were making every effort to get me to join their firm. I was also receiving phone calls from my colleagues begging me to join them at WK. "What's going on?" I asked myself. "Perhaps I should take some time to focus on the big picture and evaluate my options – perhaps I'm missing an opportunity." I sat in my office pondering things. I thought about the fact that WK was a successful family-owned company – similar to Moore & Company, not a franchise like CB, and that was something to consider. I returned the phone call and spoke with the owner of WK Real Estate.

The following day, I met with Lew and the management team. I was impressed with their business model, and I could see that they were miles ahead of the curve on technology. And I got the impression that WK truly cared about the Realtors. This was a big decision and as I thought about it, I reminded myself about the importance of being in a happy work environment. I liked the people at WK and I liked their friendly, personal attitude. After thinking it over and giving careful consideration to all the details, I made the decision to join WK Real Estate. I proceeded to contact the CB manager to let him know. I transferred my license to WK on March 1, 2000. My wonderful daughter was such an asset to me and my work. She knew exactly how I liked things done, and I felt lucky and blessed to have such an amazing assistant. Pam was a tremendous help in getting both of us situated in our new work environment. It turned out to be a pleasant transition, and I have never regretted my decision to join WK Real Estate.

It was late afternoon when Dale called me at the office. "Hey, I just listened to a message on our voice mail but I couldn't understand who it is or what the person is saying." I told Dale I would call our home number and listen to the message. I immediately dialed our number and pressed the button to retrieve messages. I recognized my sister-in-law's voice. "Will one of you call me as soon as possible." I could tell that something was wrong and I hurried to dial Mary's number. When she answered, I heard these four words "Jim has passed away." I let out a whine as my hand went to my chest. I could feel my heart start to pound, but I tried to keep my voice calm when I said, "I'm so sorry, Mary. What happened?" She told me the highway patrol had come to their house in Basalt that afternoon. She said when they showed up at the door, she thought Jim had been in an accident, but the officer told her that he had died of a sudden heart attack that morning at their Fort Collins house. The housekeeper found Jim sitting in his office chair when she arrived to clean the house; that was at eleven o'clock. Mary said that Jim had returned to Fort Collins from a business trip the night before.

## Chapter 13

It was Halloween, October 31, 2002. Jim had planned to drive to Basalt that day and take the two boys out "trick or treating" that evening. But instead, my brother's body was lying in the morgue. Hearing this news was heartbreaking. I was alone in my office and I needed a shoulder to cry on. I had just lost my brother. I knew that my sister-in-law's heart was broken too. She had just lost her husband. I felt the need to comfort her. When I spoke with Mary, she said she would drive down with the children in the morning and would be at the Fort Collins house by nine o'clock. I told Mary that I would meet her there at nine. When I hung up the phone and sat still in my chair. I felt completely numb as the reality of what Mary told me began to sink in. I was trembling but I held myself together. I knew I had to stay strong – Mary needed my help and support. Jim would want me to help her. I picked up the phone and called Dale to let him know what happened, then I proceeded to call the family.

Sleep was hard to come by that night and I tossed and turned. I was up early the next morning and drove to Fort Collins to meet my sister-in-law at her house. She brought her nanny with her from Basalt, to help with the little boys. Mary and Jim's children were so very young – David had just turned three and Sam was only eight months old. When Mary opened the garage door, David saw his daddy's car and he ran into the house calling "Papa, Papa" but his Papa wasn't there. I held back tears as I thought about these precious little boys who no longer had their daddy. My brother had been married before, and had two grown children with his first wife. His adult children, Susan and Jimmy, both lived in Kansas. Jim left us way too early and sadly, he would not know the two children that Jimmy and his wife, Tammy, would have later or the child that Susan would have later – his grandchildren.

I could feel Jim's presence in the house. There was so much of him there – his jacket hanging over a chair, his dress pants laying on the bed, the remnants of a fried chicken dinner – his last dinner, and the skillet still sitting on the stove. I asked Mary what I could do that would help her the most and she asked if I would compose an obituary for Jim. I sat down at my brother's desk, in the very chair where he sat the prior morning – the place where he took his last breath. I opened Jim's laptop and tried to gather my thoughts. I felt sad and stunned, finding it hard to believe that my younger brother was gone. Jim was such a charismatic person – so full of life – so kind and caring. He was eight years younger than me, but after we both became adults, Jim was more like a big brother. He had been there for me so many times. I knew that Mary's head was spinning, and she needed help. I tried to keep my composure and remain strong for my brother's wife. The last thing she needed was to see me sobbing. I would be her crutch; I would help Mary at this difficult time. I sat there thinking about Jim's life, and I started typing as things came into my mind. "James Edward Winter passed away suddenly on October 31, 2002, at his home in Colorado. He was 58 years old." After typing a draft obituary, I told Mary that I was sure she would have more details to add – there was so much to say about Jim.

My son, Randy, arrived at the Fort Collins house later that morning. I was so glad he was available and could be there to give his support. Jim's body had been taken to the morgue, which was located at the local hospital. We were scheduled to view his body at one o'clock. The nanny stayed at the house with the little boys while Mary, Randy and I went to the morgue. After a short wait, an attendant came to the waiting area and escorted the three of us to the room where Jim's body had been placed. The attendant opened the door then graciously excused himself

## Chapter 13

to give us privacy. Jim's lifeless body lay still on a gurney. He was fully dressed and his shoes were still on his feet. He looked as if he might be sleeping. But in that moment, the realization sunk deeper – my brother was gone. Randy and I stood by as Mary went to her husband. We could barely contain our own emotions as we watched Mary kiss her husband. I watched as she gently kissed his eyes, his lips, and she kissed his ears. She was crying and her tears fell like rain upon my brother's body. My eyes welled with tears and I felt shaky. I needed to let go and just cry, but I bit my lip and stiffened my body and held it all in. Why did this happen? Why was my brother taken from us?

The Pizza Hut jet sat waiting for Mary and her immediate family. We climbed aboard and took our seats. Normally, a trip in this private jet would be exciting, but we were travelling to my brother's funeral and we were a somber group. Jim's body had already been taken to the mortuary in Wichita. Jim and Mary's close friend met us at the airport in Wichita. I had not met this kind woman named Chloe. She and her husband were so gracious to invite Jim's family into their home where they prepared a wonderful meal for us. A Catholic funeral Mass was held for my brother. Six hundred people came to pay their respects and there wasn't a vacant seat in the cathedral. I was tense and on the verge of tears the entire day. I needed to cry but I held back my tears and grieved silently for the loss of my brother. I had to remain strong for Mary. On the way to the burial site, I rode in the vehicle following the hearse. Mary was seated next to me. It was a chilly fall day but she wasn't wearing a coat. I noticed that she seemed cold and I took off my jacket and put it around her shoulders. Then my thoughts trailed back several years to a spring day in May, when Mary and Jim were married at their home in Basalt. The evening before the wedding, the family went out for dinner at a nice restaurant in Aspen. Mary was wearing a lovely sleeveless dress and she looked so beautiful. I was sitting next to her in the car and noticed she was hugging her arms and I could tell that she was cold. I took off my coat and gave it to her. It's ironic that I gave my coat to Mary at her wedding and again at her husband's funeral.

The last time I saw Jim alive was on Easter Sunday that year. Jim and Mary had a new baby – baby Sam; he was only one month old. His big brother, David, was two at the time. Earlier in the week, I had called Mary to invite them to come for Easter brunch. She was thrilled and said that they would love to come. It was a beautiful day, and I remember Jim walking around outside with David, searching for the plastic Easter eggs I had hidden. My mind still carries the vision of my brother, holding the hand of his two-year old son as they searched for those eggs. I am so grateful for that day, grateful that Jim and his young family could be there with us. I hold onto the memory of that special Easter Sunday, the fun we had, and how very happy we all were that day – just being together.

Days came and went and time moved on. I was happy to be busy. It was a big year for Dale and me as we were celebrating our 50th wedding anniversary! So fortunate we were to have had so many years together. I was excited about the big trip we were planning – an Alaskan cruise! I tried to schedule my work so as to not have any conflicts with the trip. Once again, my wonderful daughter – my assistant, would take care of many details during my absence and I also had an agent standing by. One day, when I came home from work, Dale greeted me at the door and said he had met Pam for lunch and she gave him an envelope to take home, and she had given him strict instructions "not to open it until Mom got home." Dale handed me the envelope and I looked

## Chapter 13

at him with surprise. "Humm, what's this all about?" Dale just shrugged his shoulders. I opened the envelope and slid the card out. I was bowled over with surprise. The envelope contained a beautiful invitation. Our children were planning a brunch at the Boulderado Hotel, to honor us on our golden wedding anniversary, July 9, 2003! Dale and I were completely surprised and overcome with joy. It warmed our hearts to know that our children wanted to do this for us. I later learned that our granddaughter, Erin, had designed the beautiful invitation. That evening, I called my kids. All they needed was a guest list.

There was positive energy in the air, fueled by my own excitement and anticipation. It was a gorgeous summer day and Dale and I were dressed in our best and ready for the event. We arrived at the Boulderado Hotel and were greeted by a lovely sign set on an easel at the foot of the grand staircase. Our names were printed on the sign, welcoming our guests to the party. We proceeded up the gorgeous ancient staircase to the Mezzanine where the brunch was being held. Jody Price and her string quartet could be heard softly in the background. Pam and Randy welcomed us with big hugs. Then they presented me with a lovely corsage for my dress, and a white rose for Dale's jacket. We looked around in awe, taking it all in. I noticed the amazing array of food, so beautifully presented. In the center of the large open mezzanine was a table displaying a gorgeous three-layer tiered cake, decorated with lovely flowers delicately placed on each layer. Then I spotted the crystal champagne glasses, a gorgeous floral arrangement and a few photos of years past, including the photo of Dale and I taken the night we met. The guest dining tables were perfectly set with white linens. It was all so elegant and special. My children had planned and put all this together – I was impressed! Then I spotted our grandchildren – Erin, Jason, Tyler and Connor. My heart was overflowing with love and joy. It was a special day! The guests started to arrive and it was such fun seeing them and greeting them. Many members of our family and many dear friends were there to join in the celebration. In some ways, it felt like the wedding party we didn't have all those years ago. Dale and I were so honored and very proud.

Paula sat on the bed watching as I packed for the Alaskan adventure. She had come from Wichita to attend our 50th wedding anniversary party. It was a nice hot day in July, and I couldn't imagine, even in Alaska, that one might need a warm hat in July. I looked at Paula as I held the hat; we both shook our heads "No – don't think so" and I tossed the hat aside. Boy, would I be sorry later that I hadn't packed that hat! The big adventure started the following week when Dale and I flew to Anchorage. We spent two nights at a hotel in Anchorage and while there, we rented a car and drove to Talkeetna, with hopes of viewing the amazing Mt. McKinley, since renamed Denali. Unfortunately, heavy clouds moved in the night before and hung low, covering the beautiful mountain. But in spite of that, we enjoyed a delightful lunch at the amazing Talkeetna Lodge.

The following day, Dale and I boarded the Grandview Train in Anchorage. The four-hour train ride took us to Seward. The train had a glass dome enabling us to enjoy the beautiful scenic journey. During that train ride, we shared table seating with a charming couple from London – Nigel and Lisa Hess. It's interesting that Nigel was celebrating his 50th birthday and we were celebrating our 50th wedding anniversary! We were thrilled to meet such a delightful fun-loving couple. During those four hours on the train, we bonded with them and quickly became friends. After arriving in Seward, we were escorted to the harbor and the Seven Seas Cruise Ship. During the Alaskan cruise, we shared some

## Chapter 13

fun times with Lisa and Nigel, and we have maintained a lasting friendship with them. On our travels to Europe, we rendezvoused with them a couple of times – once on the French Riviera in Saint-Tropez, and another time in London when Nigel and Lisa gave us a tour around London. Nigel is a music composer and he shared with us his experience when he was commissioned to compose a beautiful piece of music for Queen Elizabeth. Nigel's music is beautiful. I have several of his CD's, and never tire of listening to his music.

Of all our travels, the Alaskan cruise was one of my favorites and I must say, meeting Nigel and Lisa contributed to the fun. During the cruise, Dale and I took advantage of the many adventurous excursions offered – most of which were things I had never done before. The helicopter flight from Juneau to the Mendenhall Glacier was thrilling in itself. But the real thrill was landing on the Glacier, then walking on the Glacier. That's when I wished I had packed that warm hat – it was icy cold and windy up there on the glacier! Walking on the glacier can be very dangerous and deadly. In fact, I had to be careful to not slip and fall into a crevasse. As I inched closer, I peeked down into the bottomless icy blue crevasse. I was glad to be wearing crampons with steel spikes attached to the bottom of my boots. Carefully, I moved away from the crevasse opening. As I slowly turned around, I was spellbound to see the magnificent 360 degrees view; I felt as if I were on top of the world! Another highlight for me was flying in a sea plane and landing on water in the Misty Fjords. It rained steadily that day and seemed to make Dale a bit nervous, but I was ready for the adventure. The pilot carefully landed the plane and it sat idling on the water. A surge of adrenalin filled me with excitement as I stepped out onto the wing of the small plane. My poor husband, however, who doesn't like small planes in the first place, was concerned about the fifty-year old aircraft. The pilot assured Dale that the engine was new, but that didn't alleviate Dale's anxiety and he declined going outside to stand on the wing. Alaska is filled with so much adventure – its diverse wildlife, the unique geography, its indigenous crafts and rich artistic heritage. From whales to bears, glaciers to totem poles, there are unlimited things to explore.

The Alaskan cruise was our second cruise and by the time it was over, I knew I was hooked and I wanted to do more cruising. Luckily, Dale felt the same. Our ship docked in Vancouver, and we planned things so that we could stay an extra day in this beautiful city. While there, we visited Stanley Park and enjoyed seeing the amazing totem poles in the park. I do love Vancouver! During our stop over, we had an opportunity to visit with our long-time friend, Ardis Monarchi. We enjoyed a fabulous dinner with her at the famed Five Sails Restaurant on the Waterfront. While having dinner, we saw our ship leave the harbor and sail away. Seeing Ardis was a wonderful finale to an amazing journey!

I had just been elected to serve on the Board of Directors for Boulder Area Realtor Association. I considered it an honor and a privilege to be associated with this dedicated group of realtors. It seemed the busier I got, the more efficient I was and the more successful I became. My Real Estate business had grown tremendously and I felt blessed to be consistently ranked in the top-five category. 2004 was an incredible year for me when I was honored to be the Number One Producer at WK in both the Listing category and Sales category, and Number One in Outgoing Referrals. And in 2005, I was again honored as the Number One Producer in Sales. I considered myself fortunate and always appreciated the opportunity to work with such wonderful people – my clients. They are the ones who made it all possible.

## Chapter 13

Mike was the youngest in our family and he always had a funny joke to tell. I recognized his number when I picked up the phone. "Hey sis – how ya doin'?" Mike called to talk about organizing a family reunion in Colorado. I thought that was a great idea and replied, "That sounds like a wonderful plan, Mike – maybe this summer?" We talked a while and looked at the 2006 calendar and penciled in July 4th. I told Mike I would make some calls to other family members regarding the date, then I would start making plans. After we hung up, I circled in a big happy face in my Day-Timer on July 4th and wrote "Winter Family Reunion." Then I proceeded to call the family and soon confirmed the date.

My sister, Mary, lived nearby in Westminster, and she and I talked about the best place to hold the reunion and decided on Waneka Lake Park in Lafayette. It's a beautiful park with lots of fun things for the little tots. The large array of colorful play equipment was up-to-date and the kids would love the adorable animal paddle boats. I promptly reserved one of the picnic Pavilions for July 4th. The hard part for me was figuring out how much BBQ to order. I contacted the BBQ place telling them I would need to serve about 30 people including some children. In addition to the meat, this place could provide the buns, beans, coleslaw and brownies. The catering manager figured out how much meat we would need and she made it all so easy. All I had to do was pick it up. The family chipped in on the cost and provided their own beverage. We were all set to have a good time.

July 4th rolled around and it was a perfect summer day. Mike arrived ahead of time with his grown daughter, Beth. Paula came from Wichita, and Susan and Kurt also came from Wichita with their little boy, Charley. Teresa and Frank came with their two children, Suzie was there with her five children, Sarah and Jack came, Mary of course, and Judy, Karen and Veronica were all there. Connor came with Randy and Erin, Steve was there with his dog, and Pam and Tim came with Tyler, Jason and Erin. The little kids loved the paddle boats and each one of them got to go out for a ride with an adult. There were a total of 33 who came to the Winter Family Reunion of 2006. Paula, Mike and Beth stayed at our house in Lafayette, and I enjoyed the extra time with them. I'm so glad that Mike got the ball rolling for a family reunion. The kids had fun, the adults were happy and it was a wonderful celebration!

## Close Call in Barcelona

Late summer, 2006, Dale and I travelled to Portugal, France and Spain. We enjoyed a leisurely cruise with Oceania Cruises. One of the ports along the way was Oporto, Portugal. It just so happened that we were there on September 1st – my birthday! Oporto is known for its stately bridges and port wine production. It's a charming place with narrow cobbled streets and cute little cafes. I had a delightful birthday in Oporto. The cruise was wonderful and we saw many enchanting places. Our last port was Barcelona, Spain – home of the famed La Sagrada Familia. The giant Basilica is one of Antoni Gaudi's most famous works in Barcelona. It has been under construction since 1882.

It was a beautiful Sunday morning in Barcelona, very quiet, and it seemed that Dale and I were the only ones out walking. We were on our way to visit the Basilica, which was an easy walk from our hotel. We were casually strolling along, very relaxed and enjoying our walk when suddenly I felt a light thump on my back, then Dale felt the same thing. It felt wet. Bewildered, we looked at each other then looked at each other's back and saw brown goo splattered on the back of our clothing. We couldn't figure out where it came from. I looked up towards the sky thinking

## Chapter 13

it might have been a bird, however, the splatters were quite wide spread for a bird. About that time, a young man appeared from behind and he approached us. He offered to help and handed us a small package of tissue. He didn't speak English, and I assumed he was a native. He motioned for us to follow him and said, "I help – get water." We thought he was kind in offering to clean the mess from our clothing. I thanked him as we followed him to his apartment building a few feet away – so naïve we were! The young man invited us in through the iron gate and motioned for us to wait while he went for water. He came back with a squirt bottle filled with water. He offered to help Dale and motioned for him to remove his watch as he was squirting him with his water bottle. But then he tried pulling the watch off Dale, scraping Dale's wrist and causing it to bleed. The young man's actions were strange and we suddenly realized that we were about to be robbed. Dale's eyes met mine and we both knew what was happening. We dashed for the iron gate leading out, and thank God it wasn't locked. We ran out and rushed to the curb. I stretched out my arm and hailed an oncoming taxi.

After arriving back at our hotel, we went up to our room to change clothes. We were both shaking, realizing how foolish we had been. Later that day, we bumped into some people who were on the same cruise and we told them what happened. One of the ladies said, "Oh, yes, the infamous Bird Pooh trick. I read about that in the Miami paper before we left for the trip." And she went on to say, "They squirt you with a coffee solution from the window above and people think a bird splashed them, then they pretend to help you but they rob you." We soon came to the realization that the young man is the very person who sprayed us with the brown goo, and we realized how vulnerable we were. After thinking about it, we figured the guy who attacked us was just learning; perhaps we were his first victim because he could easily have hit us over the head and robbed us, or maybe killed us. We fell prey to the scheme. The young man was of slight build and I feel certain that Dale could have overtaken him. But what if he had a gun or a knife and had threatened us – what would we have done then? My nice white shirt was ruined by the brown goo, but we had been lucky and we were safe. And we did see the Basilica later that day, but we took a taxi!

This is a cute little story I want to share. That October, our friends, the Cipriani's, held another fun Halloween costume party. This was an annual event and let me tell you, Marcia and Alan know how to throw a party! It was fun dressing up silly and that particular Halloween, Dale dressed as Superman and I wore a sassy kitten outfit complete with tail. Marcia and Alan set up a Room of Horror in their garage. I never thought anything like that would frighten me – I'm an adult, right? Well, when I walked through the maze, I have to say, it was scary! Marcia and Alan have a collection of Halloween decorations like none other! Inside and outside their home, Halloween is on display – there are decorations everywhere! Once you visit their home on Halloween, you soon learn to be cautious when approaching the front door – something scary is sure to get your attention. And once inside, you never know when something silly may jump out and say, "Boo!" It's always fun at Marcia and Alan's, no matter what the occasion.

A big red circle was prominent on my December calendar. The date was December 16, 2006, when Dale and I attended our granddaughter's college graduation. Erin graduated with honors from Truman State University in Kirksville, Missouri. Erin was always at the head of her class and Dale and I were so proud and happy to convey our congratulations on her many achievements. The Kane grandparents, uncles, aunt, Pam and Tim, and Erin's

## Chapter 13

brothers were there as well. That evening, the whole family gathered together for dinner. It was such a pleasure to have the opportunity to visit with everyone. But Erin wasn't done with school yet – she would soon be off to study Veterinary Medicine at Kansas State University.

I looked out and could see it was a winter wonderland. Snow fell steadily all day and by the next morning the storm was labeled "The Blizzard of 2006." The snow storm dumped three feet of snow in Lafayette! It was Christmastime and that year I decorated the house in grand style. I strung garland up and down the stairway on both sides with small red bows between each swag. Poinsettia plants were here and there, and the live ten-foot tree glowed with lights and Christmas ornaments. Dale decorated the outdoor bushes with colored lights but they were now covered with snow. That morning, after it had stopped snowing, Dale stood looking out from the front door; he wasn't sure where to start clearing the snow. Three feet is a lot of snow! Dale scurried around in an effort to clear the walkway and little by little, he made a path from our porch out to the street. When the family came to celebrate Christmas, we treated them to dinner at Via Toscana Restaurant in Louisville. Then after a relaxing dinner, everyone came to our house on Rimrock Circle for gift exchange. Christmas has always been a very special time for our family and I relish the times when we are all together.

I heard singing in the distance and wondered who would be outdoors on such a cold night. Then I bent my ear to listen more intently – the sound became louder. Lo and behold, the big snow and bitter cold temperatures didn't stop the Starlight Ridge carolers. It was dark outside and I turned on the big porch light. Soon the carolers were on our porch. I opened the door to the beautiful voices as they sang in harmony. There was Don, dressed in a Santa suit and Grace stood by his side looking so cute. Then I saw Diane, Toni, Sandy and Al, Bobbi and Bob, and Karla. Did I miss anyone? They were each wearing a red and white Santa hat. I quickly grabbed my camera to snap a picture. After they finished singing, they gave a wave and were on their way. This was so special and it reminded me of Christmases past. Here's a little jingle I thought of after they left: "They walked in the snow on a frosty cold night bringing holiday cheer to our home, then they strolled along, singing their song, spreading joy to the entire neighborhood."

2008 was an amazing travel year. Dale and I travelled halfway around the world to another continent. We visited Australia, and from there, New Zealand. The trip took place during the month of January – their summertime, and the perfect time of year for me to get away, work-wise. Travelling to Australia from Colorado involved many hours, so we planned a stop-over in Hawaii. After two relaxing days in Hawaii, we were energized and ready to travel. The flight to Sydney was long but very nice and we arrived on schedule. The Four Seasons Hotel in Sydney was fabulous, and our room had a stunning view of the Sydney Opera House! During our stay in Sydney, we were lucky to have the opportunity to see a play at the Opera House. "The Age We're In" was playing at the time. While it wasn't my favorite play, I was totally excited about the experience of being there. It was hot and sunny, and walking along the shoreline was delightful. After two days in Sydney, we boarded Oceania Cruise Line and sailed off into the sunset for an amazing journey! The ship was an adventure in itself. It was fun to explore and the crew couldn't have been more accommodating – we were treated like royalty! Our ship docked at several places in Australia, and each day was a new adventure. Animals are a big attraction for me and I loved

## Chapter 13

seeing the kangaroos with their babies in the pouch. I learned that kangaroos are of cultural and spiritual significance to Aboriginal people across Australia.

We said goodbye to Australia, and sailed away during the evening hours in the direction of New Zealand. The Oceania Cruise ship would take us to the South and North islands. The ship cruised during the nighttime hours while the guests were sleeping. After a yummy breakfast, we were ready to disembark for amazing pre-arranged excursions in every port. One of the ports in the South Island was Dunedin. After getting off the ship there, we went to the Taieri Gorge Railway where we boarded the train and enjoyed a scenic ride to the Taieri Gorge. The train took us into the spectacular Central Otago Hinterland and up the rugged Otago Coast, north of Dunedin. The scenery was amazingly beautiful!

Another special memory is the day we spent in Christchurch, New Zealand, where we went punting on the Avon River. It was a chilly day in Christchurch, but the sunshine provided warmth and we were quite comfortable. The punt was similar to a gondola and our punter was an interesting fellow. As we glided on the river, we meandered through the city center, where I noticed lovely cycling paths on the river banks. We slowly passed by the green expanse of Hagley Park and Christchurch Botanic Gardens. There were children feeding ducks on the river banks and graceful swans floating here and there. This simple little excursion was such fun and I thoroughly enjoyed it.

The cruise ship entered its last port in New Zealand's North Island. It was time to bid farewell to the crew who had worked so hard to make things wonderful for us. While in Auckland, we visited the iconic Sky Tower and enjoyed panoramic views of Viaduct Harbor, which is full of superyachts and lined with cafes and bars. We enjoyed lunch at the top of the Sky Tower and it seemed like we could see forever. We watched bungee jumpers sail by the window at 62 miles per hour! The trip to Australia and New Zealand was truly an amazing journey. I took a gazillion photos and captured a lot of memories with my camera. It was a long trip home and we decided to break-up the trip by stopping over again in Hawaii. It was nice to get off the plane and enjoy another Hawaiian sunset. But I missed our little doggies and was anxious to be home. My sister, Mary, was house sitting and tending to Seymone and Charnet. It gave me great comfort and peace of mind knowing she was there. She was a sweetheart to do that for us.

After being home a few days, my internal clock was in tune with Colorado time. I settled in and let my mind drift back to real estate. I soon had several new listings to market and sell and I looked forward to an active spring market. I was happy being back at work and busy scheduling appointments. Having just gotten home from a trip, the farthest thing from my mind was travel, but Dale was planning and it seemed we were not quite finished with travel that year. But the trip wouldn't come about until September, and that was six months away, so I let Dale plan while I focused on my work.

The spring and summer months were a very busy time for me and when September rolled around, I was ready for a little break. We hadn't taken a road trip for quite some time, mainly because Dale doesn't like to drive long distances. But he had planned a trip to Moab, Utah, and the logical thing to do was drive. Dale agreed and that's what we did. Moab is only 354 miles from Denver, and it took about five and a half hours to drive there. It was late afternoon when we arrived and we spent the rest of the day relaxing. Our adventure began the next day at Arches National Park, then on to CanyonLands. Both are magical places, but we spent most of the

## Chapter 13

time at Arches. I was in awe at all the stunningly beautiful rock formations at Arches! Each stone formation had a name, and the one that is most significant in my mind is "The Three Sisters." I think that's because I am one of three sisters. I learned that there are over 2,000 stone arches in the park, however there is one particular free-standing arch that has become famous. It is called Delicate Arch. As Dale and I stood in the open arch, a nice young couple was kind enough to take our picture. And we, of course, returned the favor. The trip went well and we both enjoyed it very much, however, Dale still isn't convinced about road trips.

The morning air was fragrant as I stepped out onto the patio. It was springtime in the Rockies, but already the temperature felt warm. I decided to rush summer a bit and wear shorts. Normally, Pam organizes a family gathering for Mother's Day, but this year my son, Randy and his wife, Erin and son Connor, were hosting a get-together at their home in Ft. Collins. I looked forward to spending the day with my family. The drive to Ft. Collins was easy and I felt relaxed when we arrived. Randy and Erin had two amazing Great Danes and another medium-sized dog. Those dogs were such a part of their family. The Danes were quite tall and it took a little getting used to. Because of their size and loud bark, they could be a little intimidating. But once you saw the gentle look in their eyes, you knew they were friendly. It was a perfect day to be outdoors so we ventured out to their inviting patio; the dogs wasted no time in joining us. Pam and Tim arrived with Jason and Tyler, but our granddaughter (also named Erin) was away studying to become a Veterinary doctor. Our daughter-in-law's mother, Jan, and Erin's sister, Kate, were there as well. There was plenty to eat, with an array of yummy potluck dishes spread around the kitchen counter. Mother's Day has always been a special day in our family, and this Mother's Day 2009, was wonderful!

## Tasting Life

Shortly after Mother's Day, my son announced that he and Erin were going to move to Arizona. Randy had been travelling to Arizona almost weekly with his job, and he liked it and knew the area quite well. He said he looked forward to the warm winter climate and no snow. I was sad about my son moving away, but I offered words of encouragement. Most of my friend's adult children lived out of state. Why did I assume that my children would live near me forever? After thinking about it, I realized that Randy and his wife needed a fresh start. The state of Arizona has a lot to offer economically, and is also environmentally friendly with many adventurous things to do. One time when we visited Arizona, we went to the Grand Canyon and took a helicopter tour above that amazing canyon. We had visited Arizona several times in the past and now we would be going there more often.

In preparing for their move, Randy bought a well-used, well-loved RV camper for their trip to Arizona. The camper would provide shelter for them and their large dogs while on the road, and until they could get into a house in Arizona. The day of their departure, Dale and I drove up to Ft. Collins to see them off. They had everything planned out – Erin was going to drive the camper and Randy would drive the rental truck loaded with their furniture and one car. Son, Connor was going to drive the other car and help them unload when they got to Phoenix. They had sold their Ft. Collins house, and they were packed and ready to go when we arrived. I snapped a few pictures and we said our sad goodbyes. I couldn't help but shed a few tears.

The caravan embarked on their long journey. They travelled through mountain passes and across many miles. I had my reservations and concern about the old camper and that it might struggle getting over the mountains. Surely the person that sold it to them had been honest about the condition of the camper

## Chapter 13

engine. It had been about two days since Randy, Erin and Connor left and I assumed that things were going as planned. But that was not the case. When I picked up the phone and heard my son's voice, I could tell that something was wrong. He sounded very tired as he began telling me what had happened. They made it to Winslow, Arizona, and that's when the camper engine blew. Randy said it had been quite a hassle but he had things under control. They were tired and weary but okay, and he said they were in Scottsdale.

I felt sorry for my son as he continued to convey the chain of events. He said they transferred most of the items from the camper to a small space left in the U-Haul truck and they left the camper with the owner of a gas station in Winslow. The dogs rode in the truck and in the car for the remainder of the trip. Randy said it was a cramped situation, especially for the big dogs, but they dealt with it. He went on to say that he would be forever grateful to a friend and business acquaintance in Scottsdale. He was a kind man who offered them (and their dogs) a vacant house he owned in Scottsdale. The man said the house was just sitting there and they were welcome to stay there for a few days until they could get into the house in Peoria. After Randy finished telling me his story, I wanted to hug him. They had been so excited before they left Colorado, but their journey to Arizona was quite an ordeal. It sounded like a nightmare to me, but their resilience and positive attitude made it all work. And now, umpteen years later, they still live in Arizona. But they moved from the big city to a place just outside of Clarkdale, where they enjoy a quiet country setting, gorgeous mountain views, and the Arizona desert landscape.

After Randy and Erin moved away, we became regular visitors to the state of Arizona. We try to make it a practice to see each other at least once a year. During one of our visits, they took us to a place called Out of Africa Wildlife Park (Camp Verde) in the Verde Valley, which is located about thirty minutes from Sedona, Arizona. At that time, Erin was working at the park giving tours to customers for close-up viewing of the wild animals. She drove an open-air vehicle and she wanted to give us a "private tour." It was a perfectly warm Arizona day when we climbed aboard her vehicle and Erin began her tour. And, let me tell you, it was the ultimate private safari tour! Erin knew those wild beasts by name, and she knew the characteristics of each animal. She knew how to make it fun and it was an awesome experience!

During another visit to Arizona, Randy and Erin took us to the Verde Canyon Railroad, which is located in Clarkdale. We had reserved seating and rode the train into the gorgeous Verde Canyon. The train itself is a fun experience, and the beautiful scenery is unforgettable. The tracks follow the Verde River north and west of Clarkdale, Arizona, up through the canyon. The route is around twenty miles to the ghost town of Perkinsville. The excursion lasts about four hours round-trip. While on the train, we took advantage of the first-class tickets and enjoyed appetizers and drinks. It was well worth the extra cash! While waiting to board the train, it was interesting to look at the storyboards along the tracks and read the information about the history, the wildlife, and terrain of the Canyon. And while we were there, we browsed through the train museum where we saw many interesting artifacts reflective of a period of time over 100 years. I always enjoy a train ride, and I look forward to repeating this wonderful adventure sometime in the future.

## Determination and Amazing Skills

Time does not stand still. I know that, but sometimes it moves all too quickly. Our first grandson, Jason, was graduating

## Chapter 13

from college and I found myself wondering "Where have all the years gone?" Dale and I are lucky grandparents, living near our grandchildren during their growing up years. The big day arrived and I was excited about Jason's graduation. The ceremony was held at the CU Denver campus in downtown Denver. It was a beautiful day and I remember feeling the energy when riding the Hop on the Sixteenth Street Mall in getting to our destination. It was a wonderful day of celebration, and we couldn't have been prouder of our grandson when he received his degree in Musical Engineering – and then, he was honored with a special award. Jason is blessed with a charismatic personality and incredible abilities. He can build absolutely anything! The stunning renovation of the Dairy Arts Center in Boulder is one of Jason's most impressive accomplishments. He is skilled in so many ways and has progressed in his career as Head Superintendent for a large construction company. Beyond Jason's daily work, he has many other talents. In his spare time, he has built several beautifully crafted guitars, and one time he disassembled a non-working organ and completely rebuilt it. When Jason finished the work, he sat down to play the organ. I was more than impressed when I heard the beautiful sound – it was amazing! Jason never ceases to amaze me!

    Coloradans are enthusiastic about physical fitness and spending time in the great outdoors. I quickly observed this after moving to Colorado, and was impressed with the abundance of fitness centers and hiking trails. After moving into the Devils Thumb neighborhood in 1970, walking became part of my daily routine. I found it to be very invigorating, especially in such a beautiful area. After finishing a walk, my mind and body feels refreshed and energized. During the many years living on Briarwood Drive, my walking route usually took me south on Briarwood and out to Lehigh Street, then I circled around on Bear Mountain Drive and back to Briarwood. One time, while I was walking north on Lehigh, I noticed a police car at the cross street with a radar detector mounted on the vehicle. As I approached and started to cross the street, the police officer stuck his head out the window and shouted that he clocked me at four miles an hour. I turned around, chuckled and said, "I guess I better pick up my pace if I want to win the race." The officer laughed and wished me a good day. Nowadays, my walks take me around Waneka Lake. It's very peaceful there. When I reach the east side of the lake, I sometimes stop for a moment to enjoy the view across the lake to the snow-covered Rocky Mountains. It's quite beautiful! There are a number of memorial benches scattered around the lake and sometimes I like to sit, take some deep breaths, and enjoy the moment. On occasion, my dear friend Sandy drives from Niwot to my house and we walk together. The round-trip walk from my house is a little over two-miles. It's always a special time and gives us a chance to catch up on things.

Ouch! The Great Recession happened! It was during the period of time between 2007 and 2009. Oh, my goodness – the housing market and the U.S. economy went into a tailspin. This recession proved to be the most severe economic downward slope in the United States since the Great Depression of the 1930's. It was a period of general decline in national economics, primarily caused by the subprime mortgage crisis. Many people lost their homes to foreclosure, and it was a chaotic mess! My real estate work was difficult during that time and I learned how to work in a different economic environment. But eventually, the economy revived itself and moved forward on an upward trend. Fortunately, Boulder County real estate withstood the recession better than many other parts of the country.

## Chapter 14

## A New Decade – 2010 and Beyond

Burr – it's cold outside! It was the perfect time to escape the winter weather and head to Hawaii. It was January 2011, and our first stop was Maui where we enjoyed a fabulous week at the Kapalua Villas. We had been there before and it was nice to come back and explore Maui once again. We took our tennis racquets with us and enjoyed playing on the courts at the condo. Dale is a good tennis player and he was very patient with me as I tried to be competitive. We were having such a good time and I could have stayed right there, but we had reservations on the Big Island, and it was time to move on. After a leisurely breakfast outside on the lanai, we tidied the kitchen, packed up our things and left.

It was a gorgeous day in paradise and a warm gentle breeze brushed against my face as I climbed in the rental car. Dale and I were on our way to the airport for the short commuter flight to Kona on the Big Island. I didn't know it yet, but I would soon be wishing I was back in Maui. In planning our trip, I found a private listing for a furnished house in Kona, in the residential area in Waikoloa. The posting said that the house had been remodeled, and it had a pool. The on-line photos looked beautiful and we decided to book it. When we arrived at the house, the key was exactly where the owner said it would be. There were a few steps leading up to the double entry doors, and from the street, it looked like a normal residential home. Upon opening the front door to the house, I was puzzled. "Wow, this is different." I said as I looked at Dale. Instead of stepping into a room, lo and behold – we stood on the patio where the pool was located. It looked as though the owner had sawed off half of the house, and used the space to install a pool and patio.

We stood there looking around and realized that in order to get into the house, we had to walk along the patio and unlock another door. That door took us into the kitchen and family room. There was no bathroom in this area. Then we discovered the two bedrooms were located at the end of the structure, and yes, we had to go back outdoors from the kitchen to access the bedrooms, and each bedroom had its own door with entry from the outdoors. The bathrooms were located inside the bedrooms. So, in order to get from one room to the next, we had to go outdoors! Albeit, the house had been remodeled with a new kitchen, new bathrooms and so on, but this was a very strange floor plan! Strangely enough, it was quite chilly in Waikoloa, with the temp in the 60's, which is actually cold for Hawaii, and the house had no heat. There must have been a cold front moving through because the wind was howling and the outdoor patio area was in direct line of the cold wind. Consequently, having to go outdoors to get from one room to the next, we were cold and very uncomfortable – especially when we expected to find 85 degrees!

We quickly realized that this was not going to work for us and Dale called the owner. He expressed our disappointment and said the house had been misrepresented with no mention of having to go outdoors to get from one room to the next. Dale said we simply could not stay there and he asked for a refund. Of course, we had

## Chapter 14

paid in advance for the entire week. The owner said he was sorry that we didn't like it there and he agreed to refund half of our payment. Frankly, we felt fortunate to get half – we just wanted to get out of that place. But I needed to find lodging. In those days, I travelled with my computer and I opened it up and began searching on-line for another place to stay. And then, the Hilton Waikoloa Village Resort popped into my mind. We had stayed there on one of our prior visits to Kona, and I remembered it as a beautiful place with lush greenery, waterways running through the resort and small Venetian boats to escort guests around the resort. Then I thought about the dolphins at this resort, and that guests had the opportunity to get into the water for a dolphin experience. The resort was quite nice – why hadn't I booked a room at this place to start with? Hoping the hotel had space for us, I dialed the number. The receptionist connected me with reservations and luckily, they did have a room! We had not yet unpacked and were ready to go. I called the local manager to let him know we had spoken with the owner and we were leaving. We deposited the keys where we found them, and drove away from that awful house. The Hilton was about thirty minutes away and after checking in, we resumed our vacation. We still laugh about that house and our vacation experience.

Upon arriving in Denver, we were greeted with light snow. Was I surprised – did I think that winter had gone away during our time in Hawaii? If I closed my eyes, I could see the ocean and the colorful sunset; I could see the lush greenery we had just left behind. But we were home and who has time to worry about a little snow? During the ride home from the airport, I thought about an exciting event that would take place in the spring, something wonderful to look forward to. Our granddaughter, Erin, would be graduating from the School of Veterinary Medicine at Kansas State

University. After getting settled in at home, I made sure to reserve our flight to Manhattan, Kansas, and hotel accommodations well in advance.

## Special Events

It was a beautiful spring day when Dale and I arrived in Manhattan, Kansas. The fragrant scent of spring was in the air and trees were budding all around. It was the month of May 2011, and our first grandchild was celebrating. The merits of hard work came to fruition for Erin when she received her degree and became a Doctor of Veterinary Medicine! This was a huge accomplishment and I was extremely excited to be there for this special event. Pam and Tim arrived with the boys, Jason and Tyler, and I was so thrilled to have this opportunity to see the entire Kane family – Phyllis and Charlie, Tim's brothers Mike and Brian, and Tim's sister, Kitty – they were all there. And my sister, Paula and her husband Dick, also came to share in the celebration. Being together, sharing all those warm hugs – it was very special! Erin offered to show us around the teaching hospital where she had spent so much time over many years of study. The tour was very interesting and I was glad to walk in the space where Erin had given so much of herself to become a veterinarian doctor. My mind wandered back to the days when Erin was a little girl. She loved animals, and she loved riding horses.

Erin looked radiant as she walked across the stage, proudly wearing her cap and gown with significant ropes of designation draped over her shoulder. She graduated with high honors and was awarded her Doctor of Veterinary Medicine (DVM) Certification. Congratulations Dr. Kane! Dale and I couldn't have been any prouder of our granddaughter. The day was filled with celebration and excitement. After the graduation festivities, both

## Chapter 14

families gathered together that evening for a fabulous dinner at a local restaurant, compliments of Charlie Kane! Before flying back to Denver, Dale and I went to Kansas City and spent some quality time with Paula and Dick.

After years of study and hard work, Erin was ready for a little relaxation and took advantage of spending the summer months at home in Boulder. During her break, she was offered the opportunity to complete a one-year internship at a well-respected veterinary hospital in Coral Springs, Florida. Erin could have gone directly into veterinary practice, but she wanted the additional experience and felt the internship would enhance her degree. I think Erin was glad she made that choice, but her internship involved a grueling year of very long days filled with extremely hard work, and no time off. After completing her internship, she was offered a position close to home in Colorado. I was grateful that Erin found work in Colorado and would be close to her family. Many of my friends and neighbors have taken their pets to see Dr. Erin. I continually hear wonderful comments about Erin – how gentle and compassionate she is with the animals, and that she is an excellent doctor. A friend in my Book Club expressed how wonderful Erin was when her dog had to be euthanized. She told me that Dr. Erin came to her house to perform the procedure, and that she wouldn't have been able to get through it without Erin's help and kindness. I am not surprised by these nice comments because that's who Erin is – kind, considerate, compassionate, dedicated, hard-working, a very special person, and very beautiful inside and out!

It was summertime and our patio was open for guests. I hosted Father's Day brunch at our place, and Dale did a great job getting the patio ready. It had sort of become a tradition that I host Father's Day, and I thoroughly enjoyed doing it. And of course, there would be several impromptu BBQs throughout the summer and early fall. Gloria and Donald came for a visit that summer and they were with us for a few days. During their stay, Donald insisted on treating us to dinner at the Flagstaff House, and that's a special treat one doesn't forget. Then, we took them to lunch at Chautauqua Dining Hall. It was a gorgeous day, and we had a lovely table on the porch facing the mountains. Chautauqua is a very old landmark in Boulder, and the beautiful setting provides the perfect place to relax with friends. When Gloria and Donald left, we promised to visit them at their place, and we did! We have since visited them several times in the charming little town of Bigfork, Montana.

The Bensons were back in Colorado! Everybody loves Lorraine and Dick, and we were so happy to have them back in town. They had recently moved into a lovely townhouse in Legacy Ridge – one of my favorite neighborhoods. I looked forward to our get-togethers and invited them over to our place. Dick is a very entertaining fellow and easily makes people laugh. Lorraine always wears a beautiful smile and back in the day when she had the Cellar in her Boulder home, she invited the girls to her home to shop. It was the best shopping experience ever! If you shopped in the morning, you were treated to coffee and donuts, and if you shopped in the afternoon, Lorraine offered wine. It was great fun and I wish I had someplace like the Cellar to shop today! After being back in Colorado for a while, the Bensons decided to escape Colorado winters and away they went. They became snowbirds and spent the winter months in Scottsdale, Arizona. Eventually, they tired of going back-and-forth with the seasons and decided to make Scottsdale their permanent home. They asked me to sell their townhouse and I took great pride in marketing their lovely home. Lorraine had it decorated beautifully and it was already

## Chapter 14

staged to perfection. I miss Lorraine and Dick, but we stay in close contact and manage to see each other at least once a year.

My husband turned eighty that October! How could that be? He didn't look eighty, and he still had the gait of a young man! Dale did not want a party – no, no, no! So, our daughter suggested dinner at the Kane's – just the four of us. She told her dad he could at least do that and celebrate this milestone on October 4, 2011. In the meantime, Pam had something else up her sleeve and she talked to me about it later. "What do you think about a little surprise get-together at our house, with just a few friends who live close by?" I told Pam I thought that was a great idea, and I was on-board with it. Later that day, I began reminiscing about Dale's 60th birthday when the kids and I had a party for him. It wasn't a surprise party, but we did have something fun planned. I heard about a belly dancer that came to private parties, but I needed to ask about her routine; I didn't want anything risqué. She was very nice and assured me it would be in good taste. So Pam, Randy and I decided to ask her to arrive around eight o'clock, after guests had time to enjoy food and drinks. When the dancer arrived, Dale realized what was happening and he was somewhat embarrassed. I hadn't meant to embarrass him and momentarily wished we hadn't asked her to come. But Dale was a good sport and the guests were laughing so Dale began laughing too. The dancer's performance was very graceful, and it all turned out okay.

The scenic drive up the canyon to Pam and Tim's is always beautiful and enjoyable. It was Dale's 80th birthday, making it even more special! Dale was looking forward to a nice quiet dinner, just the four of us (or so he thought). During the drive, he commented that he was hungry. I wasn't sure if Pam had asked the guests to park their cars in the neighbor's driveway, but when we arrived, I didn't see any cars. Pam opened the door and greeted us with her beautiful smile. As we walked in, Dale was in total shock to hear the shouts of "Happy Birthday!" He was surprised to see Lorraine and Dick standing there to greet him, and Sandy and Doug were there, and the grandkids – just a nice small group of people. Dale was momentarily speechless, but excited to see dear friends and family. We hugged and greeted each other and were in the midst of a fun conversation when the biggest surprise of all was about to happen. I watched Dale as he turned sideways to say something to Dick, and that's when Dale saw his son walk down the stairs and he was overcome with surprise and joy. Dale and Randy held each other in a warm embrace, and I noticed they were both a little teary-eyed. Randy had flown in from Arizona to surprise his dad on his 80th birthday! What better gift could a father ask for? It was a wonderful evening with friends and family, and I knew that Dale felt the love.

That same year in 2011, my sister, Paula and husband Dick came for a visit. I was excited about their visit and wanted something fun and different to do during their stay. I had heard about the Wild Animal Sanctuary, located in Keenesburg, Colorado. It's about an hour's drive from our house. Dale and I hadn't been there and it sounded like a fun excursion. I asked Paula if they would be interested in going there and she didn't hesitate to say, "Absolutely!" The Sanctuary is situated on 790 wide-open acres. This large acreage provides a natural habitat for lions, tigers, bears, wolves and other rescued animals. The sanctuary specializes in rescuing and caring for large predators which have been mistreated, and might otherwise have been euthanized. The viewing walkways are structured above the open grazing area, well above any possible reach of the animals. And yes, there is boundary fencing along the perimeter of the large acreage. It was heartwarming to watch these wild animals graze on the open land where they can roam freely in

## Chapter 14

the fresh Colorado air. It was a wonderful experience and the four of us had a great time together.

### Girl's Trip to The Big Apple

A sense of anticipation swept over me – I was going to New York City with my daughter and my granddaughter! Three generations of "savvy, sexy women" as Pam put it, travelling to the Big Apple. It was 2013, and Pam had been talking about doing this trip in May. Lately, she had gotten more serious about it, and she was making plans. I was totally on board with it, but I had gotten so busy with work and it wasn't in the forefront of my mind. It was early morning when I answered the phone. Pam wasted no time in saying, "Okay, Mom, you have to decide. Erin and I are going to NYC, and we want you to go with us. I'm in the process of booking reservations." I had planned to go with them of course, and I was excited about the trip, but it seemed like we had just gotten home from our January trip to Central America. And Dale and I were scheduled for a big trip that July. I would need an agent to cover my work for that trip and the trip to New York. After a slight pause, I said "I'll call you back in ten minutes." I hung up the phone and stood there for a few seconds. All of a sudden, my thoughts were screaming at me. "What are you waiting for, you Dodo! You may never have this opportunity again – of course you'll go!" I told myself I would figure things out work-wise, and so what if I'm gone again in July! I rushed downstairs to talk to Dale. He was aware of the pending trip, so it was no big surprise. I simply said "This is the rare chance of a lifetime, the three of us girls – I have to go on this trip." Then I picked up the phone and called Pam.

I had travelled extensively with Dale, but it was rare that I got to do a girl's trip, or fly anywhere on my own. As I packed my bag, I found myself feeling very liberated. It was a five-day getaway to the city that never sleeps and I could hardly contain my excitement. It was time to leave and as I was kissing Dale goodbye, he made me promise that I wouldn't ride the subway in New York. I told him not to worry about things, I promised, and said "You know I'll be in good company." Pam, Erin and I boarded the airplane and we were on our way. The three of us were having fun and my insides felt a little giddy. Pam had done a great job planning the trip, and our schedule was packed full with adventure. Erin found the perfect place for us to stay. It was a fabulous hotel with a rooftop bar and a terrific view of the Empire State Building. Hotel Metro was lovely, and our suite had been beautifully updated – it was perfect for the three of us. It was located in Midtown Manhattan on West 35th Street, and just down the street from Harold Square.

Our first day in the Big Apple, we met up with Erin's friend, Greer. Greer lived in Brooklyn with her fiancé, and after she got off work, she joined us for happy hour at the rooftop bar. It was warm and sunny and I was comfortable dressed in a sleeveless top. That evening the four of us hailed a taxi and we went to a quaint restaurant for dinner. The next day, we were off to Times Square. How many times have I watched the ball drop on New Year's Eve at Times Square (on TV)? Now, there I was – in person, with Pam and Erin. My head was turning right, then left, then upward toward the sky, taking it all in. I was beyond excited! We went inside the huge Toys "R" Us store to see the 65-foot-tall Ferris wheel rotating indoors. It was amazing! Sadly, two years later, that Toys R Us store closed and the Ferris wheel was dismantled. We stopped for lunch at a cute little place in Times Square, where we ordered at the counter. In NYC, you can find anything you want to eat. The following day we visited the Empire State Building. We

## Chapter 14

went all the way to the top and from there we saw amazing views in every direction and below we could see the Hudson River. We saw skyscrapers close-up, rooftop water towers, and Central Park in the middle of it all! From there, we ventured down to street level and the subway below – how could I go to NYC, and not ride the subway? It's actually pretty incredible, very well organized, and the best way to get around in NYC.

Grand Central Station was remarkable and way beyond my imagination. It was filled with crowds of people and I found myself wondering if most were tourists like us, or if some were actually travelling. The three of us enjoyed a delightful lunch at the station. It was quite thrilling just being there among all the commotion. During our stay in NYC, we took the Circle-Line Cruise for close-up views of the Statue of Liberty, and Ellis Island. We crossed over the Brooklyn Bridge, we visited the 911 Memorial, we went to the Top of The Rock at Rockefeller Center for the night-time light display and spectacular views. The famous Metropolitan Museum of Art was the perfect place to visit on the wet rainy day we encountered. Greer joined us mid-day at the museum, and it was nice that Erin could spend time with her dear friend. One of the many highlights of our trip was the Gershwin Theatre, where we saw the live stage production of "Wicked." Our dinner reservation was six o'clock that evening, and we left the hotel in plenty of time to hail a taxi. But the taxis were busy and it was difficult getting their attention. After no luck holding our arms out and waiting, we decided to walk the fifteen blocks to the restaurant. We walked and walked – fast walking is what we did! But it was a lovely evening and we got there in plenty of time, in fact, a few minutes early for our reservation. It's amazing how easy it is to walk fast at sea level. Our dinner was wonderful and "Wicked" was magnificent – we loved it!

The entire evening was magical! After the play, we managed to hail a Pedicab for a ride back to Hotel Metro. It was fun being shuttled in the open-air bicycle carriage, and it was the perfect size for the three of us. The next day – our last day in NYC, we woke to a beautiful spring morning and we ventured out to Central Park. Flowers were in full bloom in the park and it was glorious! We took our time strolling through the park, stopping here and there for photos. Pam of course, was camera ready at every given moment. I was glad for the opportunity to see Strawberry Fields, John Lennon's "Imagine" Memorial. Visiting Central Park was the perfect ending to an exhilarating five-day adventure. Pam gave me a photo book on my birthday that year in memory of the trip, and in quoting Pam's words, "These three lovely ladies – Mother, Daughter, and Granddaughter – embraced the sights and sounds, tastes and smells, crowds and the excitement of the BIG APPLE. And they LOVED IT ALL !!"

## Randy and Erin's Visit

Springtime was lovely that year, and Dale's potted flowers were blooming beautifully. My life was happy and fulfilling, and my business was going well. That summer in 2013, Randy filled his mother's heart with joy when he called to say that he and Erin were coming to Colorado for a visit in late June. I quickly made plans for their visit and freshened up the guest room. In the meantime, I kept pace with my work as I anxiously awaited their arrival. I knew their visit would be short, and we made every minute count. Randy and Erin arrived earlier in the day on Friday, and that evening we took them to see the live stage performance of The Wizard of Oz. The Boulder Dinner Theatre is always a fun experience, and us adults had a blast watching the show. One might think The Wizard of Oz is more for kids, but the theatre was mostly filled with adults. The next day, I packed a picnic lunch and we drove up Flagstaff Road to Gross Reservoir. I was thrilled that Pam could join us, and it warmed my heart to see my two adult children together. In spite of the chilly, drizzly day, we found a nice picnic spot to eat our lunch in-between showers. Later that day, we revved up our adrenalin with a few games of pool in the lower-level rec room. Then on Sunday, Pam and Tim invited the whole gang up to their place for brunch, and that was wonderful! But the weekend sped by all too quickly, and it was time to head back to the airport. I savor the quality-time we have together and always look forward to the next time.

## Celebrating Sixty Years Together

That July, Dale and I celebrated our sixtieth wedding anniversary – I know, hard to believe! Being married to the same man all those years makes me feel very lucky and fortunate. Our life has certainly come a long way from where we began. Dale and I have had a wonderful life together and mostly good, but life doesn't always run on a smooth track. We have endured some tough times and some heartache along the way, but we weathered the rough patches, and we still love each other. The bond of love and marriage becomes stronger, and even more special, when you can do all that. And one more thing, always take time to enjoy the rainbows.

To commemorate our sixtieth, we booked an amazing cruise. The cruise began in Venice, Italy, and from there we travelled to many ports. After Venice, we visited Slovenia, then Croatia and Montenegro, five Greek islands, then Turkey. I was packed and ready for the trip and I felt comfortable about going away on vacation. I had taken care of any pending real estate and I had an excellent Realtor covering any upcoming business during my absence. Real estate is typically slow in July, and it seemed like good timing. The flight across the water was long but smooth, and I was beaming with excitement when the plane landed at the airport. I was never sure how far it was from Venice. Passage through customs was fairly quick and we proceeded to the passenger pickup area. The place was packed with people and I noticed the greeters standing around holding name signs above the crowd. Dale stood by our luggage as I walked back and forth searching for a sign that said "Rieger." We had transfer vouchers to our hotel, but where was our escort? Soon all the passengers had cleared out and there was no one there to pick us up. After waiting patiently for one hour, we came to the realization that we were on our own. I tried to find someone who spoke English, but no such luck. We left the terminal and went outside with our luggage in tow. I noticed some people walking and towing their luggage along a walkway. Then I saw the arrow sign that read "taxi d'acqua." I recognized the words "taxi" and "aqua" – meaning "water taxi." We followed the sign and followed the people.

It was very hot that day and felt like it must have been 100+ degrees. The walkway leading to the water taxi was rough and bumpy and I was concerned about our luggage wheels. We had several pieces of luggage and towing it in the heat was no easy task. By the time we reached the taxi station we were dripping in sweat and exhausted – I would take this matter up with our tour director! We found a water taxi and I asked the driver if he was familiar with the Molino Stucky Hotel. He shook his head "yes" and motioned us to climb in. Dale steadied my arm as I stepped into the wobbly boat, being careful to maintain my balance. I was grateful when the driver lifted our luggage into the boat. The water taxi reminded me of a speed boat. It moved swiftly through the Grand Canal, and within twenty minutes we arrived at our hotel.

## Chapter 14

The hotel was located on the Grand Canal, across from Venice. When we got to the check-in counter, I'm sure the clerk could see that we were travel weary. He was very kind and accommodating. The porter took charge of our luggage and we proceeded to our room. After freshening up, we got our second wind and went to the restaurant and bar the clerk told us about. After a relaxing dinner, we watched Venice come alive as its lights slowly began to shine – one by one, and soon the entire city was aglow. It was a sight to behold! We would be in Venice two days before boarding the cruise ship.

When I woke the next morning, I was filled with anticipation and I scrambled out of bed. I was anxious to explore this magical place. After breakfast, Dale and I were shuttled across the Canal and within a few minutes, we were standing in St Mark's Square! It was crowded with tourists and bustling with energy. We had been in Venice once before, but it was thirty-eight years ago in 1975, and I was ready to taste it all over again. We first set out to pursue a gondola ride on the Grand Canal. The gondolier rhythmically moved his rowing oar to slowly propel the gondola between the buildings and narrow passageways. We passed under The Bridge of Sighs on the Rio di Palazzo. I later learned about the theory that, if a couple were to sail under the bridge on a gondola and kiss, they would enjoy eternal love. The sighs are said to be from the couple drifting under the bridge below. I love that story – it is just so romantic! The old theory I heard about, when we visited Venice all those years ago, is depressing. It is believed that the sighs came from prisoners walking across the bridge on their way to prison. The first time we were in Venice, we toured Doge's Palace. And seeing the Venetian Gothic architecture of this grand structure for the second time was really quite amazing! We walked across the famous Ponte di Rialto Bridge, and we saw the beautiful Basilica di San Marco. We loved our many walks up and down the sweet little streets of Venice, and we stopped to shop here and there. We enjoyed wonderful food and relaxing drinks at the quaint restaurants and bars. We didn't miss a thing!

As we sailed away, the sun slowly edged its way downward, casting a warm glow on the Grand Canal. Dale and I stood on the deck of the Oceania Riviera cruise ship. It was time to say goodbye to Venice. There were many other passengers on deck, hands in the air waving, bidding farewell to Venice. Momentarily, I felt a little sad leaving Venice, but we were embarking on an amazing journey called "Paths of the Byzantines" and I was excited about the upcoming adventure. The ship cruised all night and our next port was Koper, Slovenia, then Croatia, and on to Montenegro. And from there, we travelled to the Greek islands, and Turkey. We visited five Greek islands with our first Greek port being Corfu, then Santorini, Crete, Rhodes, and Kavala. Corfu is situated in the north Ionian Sea, and is known as the Emerald Island because of its lush greenery, and is considered to have the most vegetation of the Greek islands. Sam was our guide and driver in Corfu. He was an excellent guide, making sure that we saw the entire thirty-six miles of this gorgeous island. He moved at a comfortable pace, allowing plenty of time for photos and stops along the way. Sam was probably in his mid-sixties. I sensed that he was sort of a romantic kind of guy because he went out of his way to show us the beautiful Bay of Paleokastritsa, where the view was spectacular! Dale and I stood admiring the view with our arms around each other when Sam told us that it was customary for couples to kiss atop this picturesque paradise – and so we did! Midway through our tour that day, Sam took us to a quaint village called "Bella Vista." By coincidence, we lived on a street by that same name many years ago. We stopped at an adorable little cafe where we

## Chapter 14

treated ourselves to THE BEST, most delicious baklava I have ever tasted!

I looked up at the huge ridgeline and towering cliffs – the cliffs were ginormous and looked as if they blended into the sky. Santorini was perched on top! The pathway leading to Santorini was interesting and a bit scary! We boarded the bus and away we went. I held onto Dale's hand as the bus took us up, up, up the narrow winding road. There was another bus travelling down the road and coming toward us. It didn't look like there would be enough room for the other bus to pass. The two buses slowed and the oncoming bus stopped as our driver carefully inched by. Whew! Our bus continued onward and upward along the winding road that didn't seem to end. Finally, we reached the top of those high cliffs and we were in Santorini. We were told that this extraordinary island is the fragmentary remains from one of the biggest volcanic eruptions in history, which happened around 1600 B.C. It was amazing to see the beautiful villages with white washed stucco-type houses staggered up and down the tiered cliffs. There were many monasteries in Santorini, with blue domed roofs. It was a sight to behold, and just as I had portrayed in my mind, a magical place. After spending the day in Santorini, we decided to ride the cable car down to the harbor. However, there were alternative exit options. Riding the bus down the narrow winding road was one option. Another option was walking 600 steps down, or you could ride the donkey down a narrow path in 100+ degrees! Dale and I were glad we chose the cable car option.

Our adventure continued into Turkey, where we had pre-arranged English-speaking guides. Engee was our guide during our stay in Ephesus. We were privileged to have the opportunity to visit The House of Virgin Mary, located on the top of the Bulbul Mountain near Ephesus. It was quite chilly when we reached the mountaintop and I was amazed at the temperature change. The house of Virgin Mary is quietly hidden among lush greenery, creating a feeling of serenity. It is said that Mary, mother of Jesus, spent the last years of her life in this small stone house, and that Saint John may have brought Mary to this house. As I stepped inside this little house, there was a feeling of calm and I sensed great respect. Dale and I remained silent while walking through the house, and I tried to imagine Mary living there. As we were leaving, I saw hundreds of thousands of prayer notes attached to a stone wall. Engee told us that people come from afar to leave a prayer note for the Virgin Mary.

After leaving the mountain top, Engee took us to see the Ephesus archaeological site. It was a very hot day in Ephesus, quite a change from the cool air we felt on top of Bulbul Mountain. There was no greenery at the ruins and no shade to shield us from the heat of the day, but we were determined to see this amazing place we had heard so much about. Our guide did an excellent job explaining everything to us. She told us that it is not certain who first founded Ephesus, or when the first information about this place came about from the year 2000 B.C. Using my imagination, I thought about the amazing city it must have been. Everything was stone and marble and amid the destruction, one could imagine it to have been of grand scale. Visiting Ephesus was a wonderful experience and I will always remember walking on the ancient streets paved in beautiful tile.

When we arrived in Istanbul, the cloudless sky was as blue as blue could be. We had three full days in Istanbul, and fortunately, we had a wonderful tour guide. Emi was a friendly young woman, very efficient, and she was with us every day. We provided Emi with our "must see" list and she pre-arranged our schedule to ensure seeing all the sights. Emi picked us up at our

## Chapter 14

hotel every morning at ten o'clock. The day we visited the famed Blue Mosque, I remember feeling a bit anxious and amazed. I think I was surprised that tourists were allowed to go inside. As we approached the entrance, I noticed long skirts were provided if covering was needed, but I had dressed accordingly that morning. To the left of the entrance, I saw a Muslim woman having her feet washed. Being respectful, I removed my shoes and covered my head and arms with a shawl. The Muslim men inside the Mosque wore long skirts and they were bent over as they chanted prayers. No one spoke and there was a feeling of calm. I left feeling grateful that I had been there. Before leaving the grounds, Emi snapped a photo of Dale and me standing in front of the Blue Mosque.

Our next adventure was very interesting and quite exciting. Our driver took us across an amazing suspension bridge, the Bosphorus Bridge, to the Asia side of Istanbul. This is where Istanbul straddles two continents – Europe and Asia. The Bosphorus Strait connects the Sea of Marmara with the Black Sea in the north, making Istanbul a city on two continents. The following day, we had the pleasure of visiting the Hagia Sophia Museum, located at the Sultanahmet Square. During our stay in Istanbul, Emi took us to Tevkifhane Sokak Open-air dining to relax and enjoy Turkish tea. This inviting place is located at the highest point in Istanbul, with the most amazing 360-degree views. We could see all of Istanbul and beyond! The following day, we visited the incredible Basilica Cistern. It is one of the largest of several hundred ancient cisterns that lie beneath the city of Istanbul. We also toured the beautiful Beylerbeyi Palace – so very old but beautifully preserved. And the gorgeous Topkapi Palace was also on our must-see list. We went to Taksim Square, and of course, we wouldn't miss seeing the amazing Grand Bazaar, and the Spice Market. Muslim people pray a lot and I remember hearing the calls to prayer during the night. Istanbul was way beyond my imagination, and definitely one of the highlights of the trip.

We had been on foreign soil for several weeks and it was time to head home. Dale and I explored many amazing places and I treasure all the wonderful memories of this adventure. Our 60th wedding anniversary was quite special, and how blessed we were to have the opportunity to celebrate in such an extraordinary way. We boarded our flight and settled into our seats for the long journey home. I laid my head back against the seatback and looked forward to being home. Coincidentally, the Bensons were staying at our house and that gave me peace of mind. It's interesting how this came about. A couple of months before leaving on our trip, I had the pleasure of listing Benson's townhouse in Westminster, and coordinating all details of the sale. Then when it came time to close, it just so happened that Dick and Lorraine would need a place to stay for a few weeks after moving out of their townhouse. That's when the light bulb went on in my head, and I said, "Hey, we'll be leaving on that trip about the same time you have to move out. You can stay at our house." It was actually the perfect situation for all. We left town, and Dick and Lorraine moved in with their adorable little dog named "Puff." What better house-sitter could a person have!

## Great Accomplishments

I watched this youngster grow up and now he's graduating from college. I am so lucky to have enjoyed all those tender years with my grandchildren. But I still seem to find myself wondering – where did the time go? After Tyler finished high school in 2009, he moved to the coastal city of Bellingham, Washington, to attend college at Western Washington University. Tyler had

## Chapter 14

studied Japanese in high school and he first thought he wanted to continue this line of study in college. But after a few months at Western Washington, he realized it was not the educational path he wanted. The following year, Tyler returned to Colorado to continue his education at the University of Colorado (CU), where he decided to pursue a degree in Geology.

CU had a large number of students graduating that December in 2013. It was an exciting day and I was so proud of Tyler! While getting dressed for the event, I let my thoughts drift back to the days when Tyler was a little tot. He was such an adorable little boy and had grown up to become a handsome young man. At a very young age, Tyler became interested in gymnastics, and I noticed how hard he worked at becoming an excellent athlete. During his elementary school years and throughout high school, Tyler competed statewide and beyond in Gymnastics championships. I loved watching him compete, and Dale and I attended his events at every opportunity. Sometimes when Tyler performed, I held my breath hoping for safe landings. I have many fond memories of Tyler's growing up years and here's a little story I'd like to share. I believe it was Tyler's 16th birthday when I asked him what he wanted for his birthday, and he promptly replied, "Well, Grandy, I would like to learn how to make a pie. Would you teach me?" I felt so honored and touched by his request, and I said, "I'd love to teach you how to make a pie, Tyler! Just let me know when you're available, then come over to the house and we'll make a pie." And he did just that. It was such a fun thing to do with Tyler – very special. And now, many years later, Tyler is a master at making pies and I love the fact that he can out-bake me!

Dale and I found our way to the Geology Department at CU, and took our seats. I had recently learned that Tyler didn't want to wear a cap and gown, which I'm told is not unusual in college graduation. He only wanted to attend the small department event. We were cool with that and it was good to know what to expect. There were only a few students graduating in the Geology Department that year, and let me tell you – these students are brilliant and my grandson tops the list! To our delight, but no surprise, Tyler graduated with honors and proudly received his degree in Geology. Dale and I were proud grandparents. After the ceremony, a lovely reception was held for the students and their guests. We had the opportunity to meet and visit with the professors, and that was nice. Then the whole family proceeded over to Brasserie Ten-Ten for lunch, and we continued celebrating Tyler.

The month of December was filled with exciting things – Tyler' graduation, Christmas – lots of celebrating. And now I was hanging a whole new 2014 calendar. Many times, during the month of January, Dale and I slipped away to Hawaii. I was ready to escape the cold of winter and enjoy the warm tropical breezes. The flight to the Hawaiian Islands is a bit long but well worth it because Hawaii is, quite simply, one of the most beautiful spots on earth! It was zero degrees the morning when we boarded the plane in Denver, but once I settled into my seat I forgot about the cold. We gained three hours of daylight with the time difference and arrived late afternoon on the Big Island.

One evening during our stay, Dale and I decided to have dinner at a popular restaurant on the island. It was their Tuesday Night Special! The place was packed with people and quite noisy, but we settled into the atmosphere. We had just placed our order when I felt my phone vibrate. I looked at the caller ID and saw that my granddaughter was calling. I knew that I wouldn't be able to hear anything in that noisy place, so I decided to go outdoors to call her back. I heard Erin's sweet voice say, "Hi, Grandy!" and she wasted

## Chapter 14

no time in saying, "I have some exciting news – I just got engaged! Blake asked me to marry him, and I said 'yes'!" Oh, my gosh, I was overjoyed and could hardly contain myself as I said "Oh, Erin, congratulations! This is wonderful news – I'm so happy for you and Blake." Erin told me that Blake had given her an engagement ring. She said they hadn't set a wedding date but she wanted to share the news of their engagement with me and Pappy. It warmed my heart that Erin wanted to be the one to tell us. As I rushed back inside the restaurant, I felt like jumping up and down. When I told Dale the news, he smiled broadly and said, "Well, how about that!" It was very exciting – our first grandchild was getting married! We drank a toast to Erin and Blake that evening.

When I woke up the following morning, I called Pam and of course, she and Tim already knew about the engagement. Pam shared with me that Blake was such a gentleman and that he had called to see if he could stop by their house. Pam said when Blake got there, he told them that he was planning to ask Erin to marry him and he was asking for Pam and Tim's blessing. I was so impressed – how many guys do this? But of course, Blake had their blessing. He swore them to secrecy and said he was off to buy an engagement ring. Blake had plans to take Erin out to dinner that very weekend and he wanted to surprise her with a ring. It was all so romantic! Erin and Blake had been dating for at least one year, maybe longer, and we had gotten to know him at family gatherings, and he seemed like part of the family. I already knew that I liked Blake, but all this told me he is a man of good character. As Pam and I talked, I could hear the excitement in her voice. She said she had been dying to tell me, but she had promised Blake. I started thinking back to the fun I had planning Pam and Tim's wedding – now it was my daughter's turn and I said, "Looks like your life is starting to go full-circle."

## Tasting Life

The morning air was cold and crisp when we arrived at the Denver Airport. I reached into my carry-on for the gloves I had stowed. I had slept a few hours on the plane and the overnight flight didn't seem so long. I was glad that we had arranged for town-car service back to Lafayette. Our driver was waiting for us curbside and it was comforting to step inside a nice warm car. Our two-week vacation in Hawaii was fabulous and very relaxing, but now I was back in the real world and it felt good to be heading home. As Dale and I made ourselves comfortable in the backseat, I began thinking about my work and the things that would need my attention when I returned to the office.

Life was moving along at a steady pace and I was busy with work. I was excited about a listing appointment in north Boulder. But the day of the appointment, I wasn't feeling very good and I should have rescheduled. I had been feeling a little off for a few weeks, not sure what was wrong and I had gone to see my doctor for a check-up. I complained to my doc about an area at the back of my head that felt a little sore, and tight muscles in my neck, and just overall not feeling myself. My primary doctor gave me the basic exam but didn't find anything wrong, so I figured it would work itself out.

It was mid-afternoon when I arrived for the appointment. I had known this potential client for a number of years and when they called, they told me that time had come for them to simplify their lives and down-size – they wanted to sell their home. They graciously invited me into their beautiful multi-million-dollar castle. The home was meticulously cared for and pride of ownership showed throughout the home. I took notes as I toured the home with the owner. It was a large home and the appointment took a bit longer than I had anticipated. As I finished up and prepared to leave, the owners seemed very

# Chapter 14

appreciative of my time and said they looked forward to my market analysis. They went on to say that they looked forward to working with me and I left feeling confident about the listing. I got in my car and headed home wondering what was wrong with me – why did I feel so crummy? I tried to shrug it off and told myself "I will feel better tomorrow and then I will work on the CMA." But the next day, I didn't feel better and the pain in my neck had intensified. I called my doctor's office and after another exam, the doctor said it could be a pinched nerve and she administered two injections into my neck. I went about my work and hoped the injections would take care of it.

## A Time to Hang in There

Just as I was getting ready for bed, the phone rang. When I heard my sister's emotional voice, I knew it was bad news – I had just lost another brother. "Mike just passed away" were Paula's words. Tears welled in my eyes and I looked at the calendar on my vanity. The date was March 28, 2014. Mike was only sixty-eight years old. While I expected the news, I felt stunned when I heard those words and my heart was saddened. Mike had throat cancer and had been fighting the disease for years. He used to call me quite often and he always made me laugh with a funny joke. But then one day, his phone calls stopped – the cancer had destroyed his vocal cords and he lost his ability to speak. I thought back to the last time I visited my brother in Texas. He could still talk but his eyes were sunken into his pale face. Mike could no longer swallow food and he had a feeding tube. I watched as he fed himself through the tube. He never complained; he just did what he needed to do. Mike loved life, he loved his family and he wanted to live. He fought a hard battle but had lost the war with cancer. Before Paula hung up, she asked if I would call our sister, Mary. When I talked to Mary, we shared a few stories about Mike, and chuckled about how cute he was with his curly blonde hair when he was a little boy. I was nine years old when Mike was born, and Mary and I were Mama's little helpers. We reminisced about changing Mike's diapers when he was a baby.

    I booked a flight and Dale, Pam and I left for Dallas a few days later. Mike and his family lived in Arlington, Texas, and that's where the service and burial took place. When we arrived at my brother's house, it was filled with family and many friends. It was nice visiting with everyone and sharing stories about Mike. Mike had requested a Catholic funeral and we all proceeded to the place of service. The chapel was packed with people and one could tell that my brother was well-loved by many. Mike served in the military when he was a young man and he was recognized for his patriotic service. The day after the funeral and burial, we headed back to Denver. I couldn't stop thinking about my two precious brothers who were no longer with us.

    After returning from Texas, I carried on with my work but I was in constant pain. Within the next two months I was in and out of doctor's offices and saw three more doctors. My health continued to decline and it seemed the doctors had given up on me. The injections did nothing for the pain and the recommended heat pad around my jaws was soothing but didn't help the intense pain. It was a few days before Memorial Day weekend when I ended up in the Emergency Room at Good Sam Hospital. The pain in my head, face, neck and jaws had become almost unbearable. I knew that something was seriously wrong with me. When the ER doctor came to the examination room, he was suited-up in full protective attire. But of course, he had to protect himself, in case I had an infectious disease. The doctor asked me to describe to him exactly how I felt. I explained my pain in detail and also told him

## Chapter 14

that I was losing weight rapidly. Dr. Cheek could tell that I was very sick, and he proceeded to order every possible test, including a test for Meningitis.

While lying in the ER waiting for test results, I reached up and put my hand on my forehead. My skin felt different – the veins in my forehead were protruding and swollen; they were actually bulging my skin. When Dr. Cheek returned to the exam room, I told him that my veins had become swollen just since arriving at the ER. He looked at me and he immediately said, "I think I know what is wrong with you. You most likely have Temporal Arteritis." I had never heard of that and asked, "What the heck is that?" Dr. Cheek went on to say, "It's an autoimmune disease, also called Giant Cells. But in order to know for sure, a biopsy of one of the veins in your head will need to be done; this involves a little surgical procedure." I was not familiar with autoimmune disease and the doctor explained that it occurs when the body's immune system attacks healthy cells in the body. It all sounded pretty weird and scary, but perhaps this doctor was on the right track and actually knew what was making me feel so bad. Dr. Cheek said that treatment for this disease is done by a Rheumatologist. Then he proceeded to refer me to a surgeon who specializes in the vein procedure. Dr. Cheek prescribed a drug called Prednisone, and said I should start taking it right away. I was so grateful for this doctor. He had been thorough and professional, and he was kind.

The morning air felt a bit chilly, but it was a pretty day in May. I was feeling a little anxious but ready for the procedure. I wanted to know if I had this strange disease called Temporal Arteritis. I had spent some time searching the internet trying to understand this disease. I certainly had many of the symptoms and I read that damage to the blood vessels could cause a stroke, and loss of vision is a common side effect. This was concerning.

Dale drove me to the medical center and I checked in. After a few minutes, a nurse came by and escorted me to the surgical room in the outpatient department. A nurse assisted me in getting situated on the surgical table, then another nurse came over and I noticed the razor in her hand. She pulled back my hair on the right-hand side near the temple area and said, "Don't worry, I'm only going to shave a small area." I wasn't worried – I just wanted to get it over with and hopefully find out what was wrong with me. Dr. Chew, the surgeon, came over to say hello. He was friendly and good natured, and I felt comfortable in his care. I was given a local anesthesia and I didn't feel a thing during the procedure. Dr. Chew said he had removed a vein and it would be sent to the lab right away. He said the lab would need a couple of days for their analysis and he would call me with the results. The nurse applied a small bandage to my head and advised me to keep it dry for a few days. I climbed down from the surgical table and the nurse escorted me to the reception area where Dale was waiting.

The procedure was done on Wednesday, and I hoped to get the results before the holiday weekend. I pulled my top hair over the bandage and went to the office to do some work. The Prednisone had started to give me some relief and I was grateful for that. I waited patiently for the phone call and soon it was Friday afternoon – the Friday of Memorial Day weekend. I left the office and headed home. Why did I think I would hear back from my doctor on Friday afternoon? It was five o'clock and I was about to give up when the phone rang. It was Dr. Chew calling and he said the lab confirmed my diagnosis; my vein tested positive for Temporal Arteritis. I didn't want that awful disease, but in a way, I was relieved to at least know what was wrong with me. Now I could move forward with treatment and hopefully, get well.

## Chapter 14

The following week I met with the Rheumatologist. When I met him, I realized that he and his wife had purchased one of my listings the prior year, and I thought that was coincidental. He was very professional and thorough in explaining Temporal Arteritis and the treatment I needed. He said the disease is an inflammation of the lining of the arteries in the head. He told me that my inflammation level was extremely high, and that I would need treatment for a minimum of one year to cure the disease, but said it could take longer. He prescribed a high dosage of Prednisone, along with several other medications. I left the Rheumatologist's office feeling encouraged and confident. Finally, after all these months, someone knew what was wrong and knew how to make me well. I began taking the higher dosage of Prednisone, and after a few days I felt much better. But the stronger drug left me feeling flighty and my hands were so shaky that I had difficulty buttoning my shirt. "Okay, I don't like the side effects," I thought to myself, "but I can learn to deal with it. At least the terrible pain in my neck and jaws had subsided." When I went to the office that day, I had a positive feeling that I would soon be back to normal.

What's that saying – "Life happens when you're busy planning something else." It's probably best that I didn't know what was ahead of me because this autoimmune disease wasn't done with me yet. While the Prednisone helped initially, the disease worsened and began attacking my body in various ways. I had severe bouts of colitis, my digestive tract wasn't working properly, my jaw muscles tightened and I could barely open my mouth wide enough to eat, I got shingles, I had sudden attacks of sharp pain in my esophagus; the disease caused me to become diabetic (which eventually reversed itself). Then, the unimaginable happened – I lost my body strength, and I lost all strength in my legs. I could only walk at a snail's pace, and I literally had to crawl up the stairs in my home. I became so weak that I could not turn over in bed. Feeling helpless and concerned, Dale called Pam many times and she rushed over to our house. Things seemed to go from bad to worse. I lost 16 pounds within a few weeks and barely weighed 100 pounds! During the course of this saga, I was in the ER five times and hospitalized twice.

It was around the middle of August, and I was very ill. My son, Randy, flew in from Arizona and arrived to find me in the hospital. My work had nearly come to a halt as I continued to refer my business to other Realtors. Pam had maintained her real estate license and she jumped-in to coordinate a pending closing. During this particular stay in the hospital, I was seen by an amazing hospital doctor. Her name was Dr. Sullivan. This doctor had studied my chart thoroughly and she knew everything about me and what I had been going through. Dr. Sullivan opened my chart and she immediately said, "I have conferred with the other doctors and we are going to cut 85 percent of your medications." Pam was there with me that morning and I remember Pam's response so well, "Dr. Sullivan, my dad would hug you if he were here. He has been saying that my mom has too much medication." A few days later I was discharged from the hospital. I had new hope.

One of my biggest fears through all of this was that I might not be well enough to attend my granddaughter's wedding. Erin and Blake were getting married September 27, 2014, and it was nearly the end of August. I was fighting hard to get well, but my balance was off and I felt unsteady on my feet. For a period of time, I wasn't well enough to drive, and my two-mile brisk walks had long-since vanished. One morning I woke to find a nice surprise on my front porch. My friends and past clients, Marilyn and Dale (coincidentally the same name as my husband),

## Chapter 14

surprised me with two trekking poles for walking. This was such a wonderful gift and just what I needed. They are lightweight and helped steady me as I tried to regain my balance and walking strength. I desperately wanted my life back; I wanted to go back to work, and I wanted to dance with Dale at my granddaughter's wedding. The dress I had chosen for the wedding was hanging in my closet, and on the shelf above were the gorgeous heels I had purchased for the occasion. My dress is a pretty shade of light gray with a short jacket and easy-flowing fabric. Earlier that year, Pam and I had such fun shopping for our dresses. I was determined to be present at the wedding and prayed to be well.

### A Joyful Event

I opened the window blind and noticed the autumn leaves glisten in the morning light. It was a beautiful fall day for Erin and Blake's wedding! And the historic Hotel Boulderado is the perfect place for a wedding. This hotel first opened its doors in downtown Boulder, with a gala ball on New Year's Eve in 1908. Erin and Blake would be married in this amazing place at 5:30 p.m. My sister, Paula, had arrived from Wichita the day before, and Randy, Erin and Connor had come from Arizona. I was so grateful to be feeling well that morning and to have most of my strength back. I looked in the mirror, hoping my face wasn't puffy from the Prednisone. "So far, so good." I thought. I slipped into my robe and made my way to the kitchen. I had ground the coffee beans and filled the water container the night before, so all I had to do was flip the switch. It wasn't long until Paula woke up, and the aroma of fresh brewed coffee led her to the kitchen. Her son, Steve, was coming by to take her out for breakfast and a little drive in the mountains. Whenever Paula came to Colorado, her favorite thing to do was go for a drive in the mountains.

After a while, Steve arrived and I wished them a fun morning together and reminded them to be back in time to get ready for the wedding. As they went out the door, Paula shouted back, "No worries, we'll be back in plenty of time." I enjoy having guests at our house and that particular day, everything felt relaxed and easy. Randy, Erin and Connor occupied the guest area downstairs, while Paula took a bedroom upstairs. Dale and I enjoyed a leisurely breakfast with Randy, Erin and Connor and we spent some nice quality time outside on the patio. After everyone was dressed for the wedding, I had fun taking a few photos. The morning seemed to slip away, and I was wishing Paula and Steve had been there, in fact, I was wondering where they were. I had prepared a light lunch and hoped that they would be back before I left for the hotel. Erin had invited me to join in the fun at the Bridal Suite that afternoon and I was excited to be included.

I glanced at my watch and decided to call Paula's cell phone. But about that time my phone rang and it was Paula. I was relieved to hear her voice but when I asked Paula where she was, she said she was at Boulder Community Hospital. I sucked in a deep breath and said, "Oh no, what happened?" Paula said she became ill after she and Steve had eaten at a restaurant in Nederland. She thought it might have been her heart, so Steve contacted an ambulance company which just happened to be in Nederland, and she was taken to the hospital. A few years before, Paula had suffered a major heart attack and she was lucky to have survived. Paula said, "Due to my past history, the ER doctor is checking everything and running tests, but now I'm feeling better." I told Paula I would come to the hospital but she said no, that she was sure they would release her soon and Steve would take her back to the house so she could get dressed for the wedding. I felt so sorry for Paula, and said how frightening it must have been for

## Chapter 14

her. She said she was okay and not to worry, that it was probably a combination of the altitude and the greasy food they served at that restaurant. Well, I did worry and I felt bummed about it. This was supposed to be a fun time for Paula. But she sounded okay, and she assured me that she would be at the wedding. I asked her to text me when she was on her way.

When I arrived at the hotel, I opted to ride the ancient elevator, rather than climb up the expansive stairway. I was feeling a bit anxious about Paula, and waited for her text. I tapped on the door to the Bridal Suite and Pam greeted me with a warm hug. The Victorian-style suite was quite spacious and luxurious. It included a large main room with the bedroom and connecting bath tucked away behind the main wall. The room was hustle-bustle with lots of activity. Erin's face radiated with joy. It warmed my heart to see her so happy. She rushed over to give me a hug and offered me food and a drink, but I was too excited to be hungry and grateful just being there. Erin was well-attended by her bridesmaids and maid of honor, and her hairdresser was just starting to put the finishing touches on her hair. She created a beautifully coiffed style for Erin, just perfect for her veil. It was fun watching all the activity in this room. Pam pinned on her corsage then she helped me with mine. We decided to wear them below our shoulders rather than on the wrist. I took a seat and sat back to watch as Erin stepped into her gorgeous wedding gown. Seeing her in that moment literally took my breath away. She looked so beautiful and radiant. As I watched Pam's expression, my thoughts drifted back to her wedding day and I knew that my daughter was feeling the same emotions I had when she got married. And now, my daughter is the mother of the bride.

The afternoon slipped away and I hadn't heard from Paula. After leaving the Bridal Suite, I checked my phone for messages but found no text and no phone message from Paula. I quickly tapped her name on my speed dial. Paula answered her phone and said, "Well, the ER doctor recommended that I stay overnight in the hospital, due to my past history." I thought Paula might cry. She was heartbroken to miss Erin and Blake's wedding, but she had decided to follow the doctor's advice. This was not what I wanted to hear, but I felt confident that my sister was in good hands and she was wise to follow the doctor's advice. I told Paula that I loved her, and how very sorry I was that this happened to her. Everyone would miss seeing her. My heart was saddened, but I knew that my sister felt even worse than I did.

I set out to find Dale and saw him chatting with Randy on the mezzanine. I walked over and we hung out a bit. Then I had an opportunity to visit with Blake's family and that was very nice. It wasn't long until the music prompted our attention and guests gathered 'round the railing of the mezzanine. About then I spotted Mary, my other sister, and went over to give her a hug. "Where's Paula?" she promptly asked. I didn't want to alarm her by telling her that she was in the hospital, so I softly replied, "Paula wasn't feeling well, probably an upset stomach." I had talked to Steve earlier and mentioned that perhaps it was best not to alarm everyone by saying that Paula was in the hospital, maybe wait until after the wedding, and he agreed. I was a little on edge, somewhat emotional, and I felt bad about Paula. But it was comforting standing close to my husband and I slipped my arm through his. Randy, Erin and Connor stood next to us, Mary was tucked in there too, and Pam and Tim on the other side of us. This was a very special day. Our granddaughter was about to be married!

The music played softly in the background and everyone stood watching and waiting. But soon I heard the quiet as the bridal

## Chapter 14

party slowly came down the stairs and took their places. Then Erin appeared at the top of the grand old staircase, escorted by her dad. She was stunningly gorgeous and her beauty left everyone breathless! The wedding march began and Erin gracefully descended the stairs to join her handsome groom. Blake stood waiting on the stairway landing beside his father. Blake's father, Tom Walters, wrote the eloquent wedding vows and he graciously officiated the ceremony. As Erin and Blake pledged their vows to each other, my eyes filled with tears and I began to cry. I noticed Pam was crying too, but our tears were emotional joy. The wedding was absolutely beautiful! After the ceremony, pictures were taken and then Erin and Blake left the hotel for a walk around the outdoor mall where more photos were taken. The social hour began, followed by a delicious dinner. Many toasts were made, and dancing followed into the late evening hours. My wish had been granted – Dale and I danced at our granddaughter's wedding!

The following morning, I was up early thinking about Paula. The minute I climbed out of bed, I called her. "How was the wedding?" she asked. "It was beautiful, Paula, but everyone asked about you and wanted to know why you weren't there." I thought about the worried expression on Erin's face, on Pam's face, on Mary's face and everyone else's concern when I told them that Paula was in the hospital. I told Paula that I explained to everyone what had happened. Then I asked, "The question is, how are you feeling?" Paula said she felt fine and she hadn't had any more symptoms. She said that she would be released from the hospital by early afternoon. Then I asked Paula, "Do you feel up for the brunch Pam and Tim are hosting for the family at the Cheesecake Factory? Maybe the doctor could release you sooner." Well, that didn't happen, and Paula missed the brunch too. It was such a bummer, but sometimes unexpected things happen and you just have to roll with it – and that's what we all did. After the brunch, Dale and I went directly to the hospital, and Pam and Tim were close behind. Paula always seems to have a ready grin or laugh, and when we walked into her hospital room, you guessed it – Paula had a grin on her face. She was such a good sport in spite of her eventful twenty-four hours. I had saved a piece of wedding cake for Paula, and when she finally got back to our house, she at least got to enjoy the delicious cake. Paula flew back to Wichita the following day.

It was the fourth quarter of 2014, and I was back at work. I was so grateful to have my life back. I sat down at my desk and began reviewing my client base and laid out a plan to get things moving. It was my 37th year in real estate and I was enthused about the future. The holidays were rapidly approaching and Pam and Tim had again offered to host Thanksgiving. It's always such a treat to spend Thanksgiving at Pam and Tim's house in the mountains. Randy and Erin were well-settled in Arizona, and I sure do miss sharing the holidays with them. Years ago, I designated the day before Thanksgiving as "pie day" and I usually bake a cherry pie and an apple pie. Then on Thanksgiving morning, I fix a large bowl of cranberry salad. I inherited the special cranberry salad recipe from Dale's mother. This yummy colorful salad is a nice complement to the turkey and everyone seems to love it. Pam carries the big job of preparing the turkey with all the trimmings, and she always sets a beautiful table for everyone to enjoy. Perhaps one day she will pass this job on to one of the grandkids.

Once again, the holidays came and went, leaving behind many happy memories. And now, it was time to bid farewell to the past year and welcome 2015. Dale and I stayed home on New Year's Eve, and watched the new year arrive on television. Many times, in our younger years, we celebrated the arrival of the New

## Chapter 14

Year by going out with friends or hosting a party at our house. It was always fun and I enjoyed the thrill of getting all fancied up to party and dance the night away. But as time went on, I actually preferred staying home on such a night. Sometimes, we invite another couple to come over and enjoy a casual quiet dinner at our house. So, 2015 arrived quietly and I looked forward to going away in January to enjoy a warmer climate. This particular January, we had plans to visit Marco Island.

Many years ago, Dale and I visited Marco Island and shared a condo with some friends. At that time, this island was so quiet that you could set your clock at 5:30 every evening when the senior citizens got in their cars to go out for dinner. I remember how the four of us laughed as we watched the seniors, slowly, ever so slowly, drive down the road, one by one. But it's 2015, and I find myself laughing again because I'm now a senior citizen! When we arrived in Marco Island, the bridge leading into the island looked familiar but this small place had grown so much that I hardly recognized it. The island size certainly hadn't changed but every piece of bare ground had been filled. There were new hotels, new high-rise condos, more restaurants, and new neighborhoods had sprung up here and there. The breeze drifting off the water kept the air on the chilly side. Naples is about twenty minutes away and it was a bit warmer there, so we ventured over to Naples several times during our stay. In year's past, we travelled to Naples and visited our dear friends, Gloria and Donald. But later on, they moved to that cute little place called Bigfork, Montana.

After returning from Florida, I jumped back into my work. I was filled with energy and excited about four new listings coming that spring. Flipping through my Day-Timer, I was reminded of the upcoming Continuing Education (CE) classes I needed to fulfill that year. Colorado Realtors are required to complete twenty-four hours of CE every three years before renewing their real estate license. Some classes are mandatory annually, such as the Annual Update class, while others are elective classes. I do appreciate the importance of keeping up-to-date on new regulations and contract changes. February was a busy month filled with market analysis appointments. In reviewing my marketing program, I realized it was time for a new photo. Coincidentally, the Boulder Area Realtor Association was hosting Realtor Day photos – perfect timing! My new head shot turned out great and fit nicely with my updated website. I worked on some new advertising designs for upcoming listings and was geared up and ready for the spring market.

After a full work day, I generally arrived home around seven o'clock in the evening. Sometimes I found myself wishing I had left the office earlier so I could have more evening time to relax on the patio. But the traffic going east out of Boulder had gotten much heavier, and if I headed home during the five to six o'clock rush, I usually sat in a line of cars. So, I decided it made sense to let the traffic clear while I caught up on some desk work before heading home. Dale always tried to make it easy for me and if I didn't have a dinner plan, he would suggest going out to a nearby restaurant for dinner. I never argued with that! In planning meals for the week, I like to fix a casserole or two, something easily warmed in the microwave; combine that with a salad, some French bread, and woo-hoo – dinner! Dale was my grocery shopper in those days, and every week I prepared a grocery list and Dale did the shopping. And he did it well, I might add. That's a job I did not miss!

"Good morning! This is Barbie." I chimed as I answered my phone. I had just walked into my office and pushed the button on my phone to receive calls. I recognized the eastern accent

## Chapter 14

immediately. My long-time clients from New Jersey were calling to let me know they wanted to sell their Gold Run condo. Many years ago, they travelled to Boulder in search of a nice condo for their son to live in while attending the University of Colorado. They were a darling couple and so nice to work with – and so very proud of their son. After showing them all the best condo options near the university, they decided on a third-floor condo in Gold Run. It was a cute place with a small balcony overlooking a seasonal stream. They had made a good choice.

I have to admit, the one thing I never learned to enjoy in real estate is the multi-story condo market. The density of condo buildings sometimes made it difficult to find the condo number on the building. After parking the car, I set out on foot with clients and in search of the condo unit. I found myself always looking up in search of the condo building number instead of watching where I was walking. In fact, I've had a few missteps over the years. One time, I sprained my ankle when I tripped on an uneven sidewalk. I proceeded to show the condo, but once inside I realized that my ankle was sprained and it began to swell. My clients helped retrieve some ice from the owner's refrigerator and we helped ourselves to a plastic bag. I left a note for the owner explaining why I had taken the ice and a plastic bag. The lady that owned the condo was so nice to follow up with a phone call to see how I was.

The clients from New Jersey had kept the condo after their son graduated. It had proven to be a solid investment for them, and never any vacancies. But now, they were ready to sell and use the money for their retirement. When their son graduated from CU, they invited me to share in their joy and they asked me to have brunch with them and their son at the Boulder Teahouse. They were proud parents and very excited to tell me about all of his accolades. I enjoyed spending time with this family and I felt honored that they chose to include me.

Living far away in New Jersey, my clients didn't want to make a trip to Colorado. They were relieved to hear that it wasn't necessary for them to come; things could be handled long distance, including the closing. Their condo was currently occupied and the tenants would be moving out at the end of the month. They asked me to look at the unit and let them know what needed to be done before putting it on the market. I scheduled an appointment with the tenant and when I arrived, a courteous young man greeted and invited me inside. He couldn't wait to tell me that the place is infested with bedbugs, and he proceeded to show me his arms where he had been bitten! He said that his girlfriend had even more bites! Well, I wasn't prepared for this news and I immediately started to feel itchy, but I kept myself in tow and tried not to show any emotion. I made note of it on my notepad and thanked the tenant for letting me know. I proceeded to walk through the unit while taking notes about repairs needed. I had completed my inspection. When I got downstairs to ground level, I stomped my feet on the concrete hoping I didn't have any little critters on my shoes. After I was back in my car, I phoned the owner to let them know about the bedbugs. I ran through my list of repairs and said I would email a copy. They were horrified to hear about the bedbugs and said they would call an exterminator immediately.

Thankfully, the exterminator did a fine job and those little pests were soon gone. I found myself wondering if any other units in that building had bedbugs. I reminded the owner to disclose the bugs on the Seller's Property Disclosure, and they did. The repairs and cleaning were completed in a timely manner, and the condo was ready for the market. Luckily, I received an acceptable

## Chapter 14

offer quickly with a 30-day close. The seller's settlement papers were sent to New Jersey ahead of the closing and my clients signed and returned the papers promptly. They were happy that they didn't have to travel to Colorado, and glad to save considerable money in travel expenses.

The long days of summer bring extra sunshine and warmth, and beautiful blue skies give pause to appreciate all the beauty the season brings. I absolutely love summer and I try to take advantage of those warm summer months before it fades away. Some of the activities that summer included celebrating Father's Day with a family get-together on our patio. Then July arrived, marking our 62nd wedding anniversary and we treated ourselves to a lovely dinner at the Flagstaff House. Another evening, we took in a play at Boulder Dinner Theatre. And we enjoyed having friends over for outdoor BBQ's. And then, I turned the calendar page to September – my birthday month! I do enjoy celebrating birthdays. My family helped me celebrate with an outdoor brunch at a delightful restaurant in Niwot called Colterra. The large patio at the restaurant was beautifully situated beneath huge old trees, and live music made it even more enjoyable. But that restaurant closed the following year due to a kitchen fire, and the building was later sold. While my real estate schedule kept me busy, I still managed to enjoy the wonderful summer activities.

That fall, Dale and I were off to Hawaii for two weeks in Maui. After celebrating Thanksgiving with the family, we boarded a direct flight on November 28, 2015. We reserved a condo at the Kapalua Villas where we had vacationed in the past and loved it. As a whole, we have been blessed with great weather in Hawaii. However, one time during a stay on the island of Maui, we encountered torrential downpours and it rained for three days straight. The streets were closed due to flooding and we were stuck indoors! But when the rain stopped and the sky turned blue, we had beautiful sunshine and enjoyed the rest of our time there. But on this visit to Maui, the weather was picture-perfect the entire two weeks. The condo we rented was lovely and the location was wonderful. The front entry was ground level – no stairs, and at the back of the condo we had a lovely lanai overlooking the golf course. And each morning, we enjoyed breakfast outside on the lanai. The colorful birds were delightful and added to the beautiful setting. I had fun watching as they perched themselves on the ledge of the lanai, hoping for a few crumbs. I have to admit, I couldn't resist giving them a few crumbs.

One day we hopped in our rental car and drove over to Lahaina for a water adventure on a glass bottom boat. The boat was called Reef Dancer. We climbed aboard and found two seats together at the lower part of the boat. I noticed a few divers on board and soon learned that they would be entertaining us below the surface. Once the boat was far enough from shore, the divers were in the water. Sadly, I had heard that the colorful coral had diminished over the years, so it was no surprise. However, we did see some beautiful fish. The divers swam here and there to fetch a few living creatures, such as a small octopus. Then they swam close to the windows of the boat and held the creatures close for the passengers to see. The diver then gently released the creature. This fun little adventure leisurely filled our afternoon.

The world-renowned PGA Golf Tournament is held in Maui every year at the Plantation Golf Club. One evening, Dale and I enjoyed a fabulous dinner at the Plantation House Restaurant. We were seated at a lovely table overlooking this famous golf course. We were not there during the tournament and didn't have to deal with crowds of people. While visiting Maui that year, I learned that Peter Merriman and his sister, Melanie, were launching their

## Chapter 14

new cookbook with a Launch Party at Merriman's Restaurant on December 11th. I wasted no time in making reservations. The event was held outdoors on the huge restaurant patio overlooking the ocean. The view was gorgeous and the event was spectacular. A sumptuous array of food was beautifully arranged on a multitude of tables. I was fascinated as I watched food prep demonstrations. I sampled the Wok-Charred Ahi and it was to die for – I had to go back for seconds! That evening, Dale and I had the opportunity to meet Peter and Melanie. They are gracious people, and it was such a pleasure to meet and visit with them. Peter noticed I was carrying his cookbook and offered to autograph it for me. I'm glad he said something because I almost forgot to ask. Our last evening in Maui, Dale and I stood at the edge of the beach watching a glowing sunset. As the sun slowly slipped away, a gentle breeze touched my face giving me a sense of calm.

During a prior visit to Hawaii in 2012, we explored the entire island of Oahu. There is a lot to see and do in Honolulu, and I don't think we left a stone unturned or missed seeing everything there is to see. This is a funny little story I'd like to share with you. In planning our day, Dale and I decided on a hike to the top of Diamond Head. Now, to all you serious hikers, I realize that Diamond Head is a baby mountain, or perhaps just a big hill. But for someone who loves to walk but doesn't do much hiking (that's me), it might be a challenge. I was nearing the summit, without any hitches I might add, when my cell phone rang – imagine that! I recognized the caller and touched 'accept call'. "Hi, Bonnie." It was Bonnie Burkhart, a realtor from my office. "Do you have a minute?" she asked. "Sure thing, but I don't know how good the reception is up here and I may lose you." Bonnie asked where I was and when I told her, she said, "Wow, you sound like you're right next door. Sorry to interrupt your hike, nothing important anyway. Enjoy your vacation." I told Bonnie I would call her later and we continued the upward climb. We made it to the summit! I felt very invigorated as I stood there surveying the view. Dale and I looked at each other and I knew he felt the same. After our descent, I was proud to say that I had hiked to the top of Diamond Head.

The house on Rimrock Circle: I have lived in that house longer than any other house. I feel well-nested, comfortable with my life, and I love my home. Starlight Ridge is a special neighborhood and I love that it's a well-balanced neighborhood. There are about seventy-six homes with a combination of young families, retirees, and we have a neighborhood book club. Starlight Ridge Book Club was established in 1999, and I am considered one of the founding mothers. As I recall, when we had our first meeting, there were about ten members. My, oh my, how this book club has grown. Today, there are about thirty members – amazing, intelligent, thoughtful women. I don't think we ever expected it would grow to this size, but we have never closed the membership. Over the years we have read hundreds of books, from fiction to non-fiction to historical fiction. Our very first book was Memoirs of a Geisha: A Novel by Arthur Golden. The Book Club meets on the last Thursday of each month around seven o'clock in the evening. We take turns hosting the meeting in our homes. I know what you are thinking – "How in the world do you manage thirty women in someone's home?" Well, not everyone attends, and we usually end up with fourteen to nineteen at each meeting. We now ask for volunteer co-hosts and this works pretty well and makes it easier for the host. We kick off each meeting with a fun social hour, yummy appetizers, soft drinks and there's always plenty of

## Chapter 14

wine. After the social hour, we find a place to sit in a circle and take a few minutes to discuss any business, then the facilitator starts our book discussion. We share thoughts about the book, likes and dislikes, and sometimes the book discussion leads to other topics, completely off the subject of the book. It's always a fun evening.

Who's turning eighty – Me? No way! Well anyway, "it's just a number!" I didn't feel eighty years old and I wondered how it had crept up on me like that. I continued doing what I loved to do – real estate, and I hadn't given any thought to aging, so I found it hard to put myself in the eighty-year-old category. Dale wanted to have a really big party for me. Pam wanted to help, so she and Dale planned the party together – and what a party it was! All I had to do was provide the guest list. They scheduled a birthday brunch at 95a Bistro – one of my favorite restaurants. At the time, 95a had a private dining room large enough to host the party. The dining room led out to a spacious patio and adjacent park – how perfect was that! My birthday is September 1st and that year it landed in the middle of the week so the party was held on Sunday, August 28, 2016.

When I woke up that morning, I was thrilled to find such a perfect summer day. I dressed in a casual off-white outfit, fixed my hair and was ready to go. I was bowled over when I walked into the reserved space at the restaurant and saw how nicely it was prepared. Dale and Pam had put so much effort and work into planning the party. The dining tables were beautifully set with white tablecloths, flowers on each table, and I was quite surprised to see the stand-up card in the middle of each table with my baby picture on it. It was pretty cute, I have to admit. And then I noticed something very interesting was printed on the card. Pam had researched "Notable Events in 1936" and here are the events listed on that card:

> Other notable events in 1936:
> FDR was president
> Jesse Owens won 4 Gold Medals at the Berlin Olympics
> Margaret Mitchell published Gone with the Wind
> The Hindenburg took its maiden flight
> Sunscreen was first invented
> Hoover Dam was completed
> The Rural Electrification Act became law
> The cost of gas was 10 cents per gallon
> A loaf of bread cost 8 cents
> Hamburger was 12 cents per pound
> You could buy a Studebaker for $665.00

Guests started to arrive and I was beyond excited. Seeing everyone and sharing hugs with family and friends was awesome. Randy and Erin had arrived from Arizona the day before and I was so glad they could be there. Their son, Connor, was sick with a flu bug and I felt a twitch of sadness that he would miss the party. Upon arrival, the guests were delighted to be offered a beverage. Many of the guests knew each other, but those who didn't were not bashful about meeting others. After the guests were seated and the food was being prepped for serving, Dale stood and said he would like to make a toast. Everyone raised their glass as Dale raised his. He looked at me and made such a lovely toast. I felt so honored and proud. Then Pam followed up and said she had a few things to say. She pulled out a piece of paper and began. Oh, my goodness, it was such a wonderful tribute to me, and I found myself sucking in a few deep breaths. A few days before the party,

# Chapter 14

I thought perhaps it would be appropriate for me to say a few words to the guests, and thank them for coming to my party. So, I jotted a few thoughts on a piece of paper. The morning of the party, I looked at my notes and I tucked the small piece of paper in my bag. The food was served and everyone seemed to be enjoying it. After a while, I turned to look around the room and could see that everyone seemed to be having a good time visiting with each other. It looked like they had finished eating, so I thought this might be a good time. I stood up and walked towards the middle of the room and Pam tapped her glass to draw attention.

"WOW . . . I never dreamed that turning eighty could be so much fun! I have to admit, this one snuck up on me, but I'm grateful to have the opportunity to celebrate this ginormous birthday. And having my family and friends here to help me celebrate fills my heart with overwhelming joy, and it just doesn't get any better than that." I paused for a moment to gather my thoughts, then I continued. "Recently I noticed an article in the AARP magazine that caught my eye. The article said, Age is what you decide you want it to be. Well, I know that life doesn't always work that way, so when my next birthday rolls around, I'll still say – It's just a number, and I hope to pile on many more numbers." I said a few other things and ended by saying how much it meant to me, having each and every one of them there.

The beautiful tiered three-layer cake was proudly displayed and waiting to be served. It was decorated with a special icing and pretty painted flowers in varied rainbow colors. I blew out the candles and I think everyone was singing "Happy Birthday, Barbie" but I was very excited so I'm not sure. The servers cut the cake and everyone got to enjoy a piece of the melt-in-your-mouth delicious cake. It was the perfect finish to a fabulous party. Many of the guests lingered about visiting on the outdoor patio. Blake set up his tripod in the park and the immediate family gathered 'round the park bench for a photo. Wow – what a special day!

## 2017 – An Eventful Year

My son-in-law, Tim, is a special man – a very special person in our lives. That January, we attended his retirement party. First of all, he is a wonderful husband to our daughter and they have been married over forty years. Tim can build just about anything, from houses to tall commercial buildings, hospitals, and everything in-between. After forty years as Head Superintendent, Tim retired from Wyatt Construction. Most of the beautiful stately buildings in downtown Boulder and beyond, were built by Tim Kane. He is amazing in his skill, but beyond that, he is an amazing person through and through. Pam hosted a retirement party for Tim at a brewery in Louisville. I took my camera to the party, and I'm glad I did. When Dale and I arrived, the place was packed with Tim's friends, and I started snapping photos. Pam had her camera too, but she was busy with guests and glad to see me taking pictures. A large video screen was flashing some of the many buildings that Tim had built. Tim has always been a hard-worker, and as a tribute to his excellent work he received many accolades over the years. I couldn't have wished for a better son-in-law, and I am so very proud of Tim.

Randy was full of excitement when he called to say he and Erin had found a house and they had signed a contract to buy it. "It's a cute little house with almost an acre of land," he beamed. "And wait 'till you see the view! It's just what we have been looking for, and I can't wait for you and Dad to see it." I told Randy I would start making plans for a visit. Dale and I talked about it and decided to go for a visit towards the end of April. The weather would be lovely in Arizona, and I scheduled a long

## Chapter 14

weekend get-away for April 29th. I couldn't wait to see their house and looked forward to seeing Randy and Erin.

Travel day arrived and I was up bright and early. My carryon bag was lightly packed with a few necessities, some spring tops, a pair of sandals and jeans. I zipped the bag closed and attached a twisty-tie to hold the zipper in place, then I sat it in the hallway next to Dale's bag. I finished my coffee and was ready to go. Everything seemed to be going so smooth that morning and both of us were ready earlier than anticipated. Dale had already loaded our bags in the car and we decided to go ahead and leave for the airport; we could take our time and not have to rush. I set the house alarm and off we went, headed for the express tollway. The tollway is such a great highway and we breezed along at seventy miles per hour without any stops.

We arrived at US Airport Parking and followed the arrows to the designated parking. The shuttle sat waiting to take us to the airport check-in. Now here's a funny story. When Dale opened the trunk of the car, OMG, it was empty – no luggage! I looked at Dale in disbelief and will never forget the look of shock on his face when he realized he had loaded our luggage in the wrong car! Our bags were at home! "Well, I guess we won't be on that flight." Dale exclaimed! "Yes, we will." I said, while still shaking my head in disbelief. "We still have plenty of time. Let's get back in the car and head for home to get our luggage." Away we went, back to the highway. Dale was kicking himself all the way home, convinced that we would never make it back to the airport in time to catch our flight. But, thanks to that great toll highway, we made it back to our house in about thirty minutes, driving at the speed limit. Dale rushed to open the trunk of the other car, fetched our bags and away we went back to the airport; however, this time we bypassed the shuttle parking and went directly to the airport close-in parking garage. Fortunately, I had taken care of early check-in the day before, and we had our boarding passes. Whew – we made it to our gate with time to spare! We laugh about this little travel incident every time one of us brings it up (and it's usually me), and I enjoy teasing Dale whenever we leave for a trip, asking the question, "Which car did you put our bags in?"

While the flight from Denver to Phoenix is an easy two hours, the commute from the airport to Clarkdale is over two hours. But the state of Arizona has good roads and we moved along steadily. I knew we had to be getting close to our destination but I lost track of the number of round-abouts at the edge of Clarkdale, so I called Randy on my cell for directions. I was focused straight ahead, watching for the street sign where we would turn left. But then, I glanced upward and noticed a man in the distance; he was standing on a hill. As we drew closer, he began waving his arms back and forth above his head, seemingly to get our attention. And then, I realized it was our son! "That's Randy!" I shouted. He had gone outside after we finished talking and walked over to the edge of the upper hillside where he could spot us on the road. Seeing Randy up on that hill was rather comical and I started laughing. Anyway, we followed the curve and turned left onto the road leading to Randy and Erin's house. "We made it!" I beamed – relieved and happy to be there.

When we pulled up to our son's house, I could readily see why he and Erin liked the location – the view is gorgeous! Their place is somewhat removed from town, more like a rural setting. Their close neighbor had two cows and chickens were roaming about. There was no HOA, and that suited them just fine. Their house has a stucco exterior with a tile roof – typical construction in Arizona. Randy took us inside and he and Erin showed us around. While their home is small with only 1,000 square feet, the contemporary design is bright and open with a feeling of spaciousness, and Erin has decorated it beautifully. The main level consists of a large great room, a bathroom, and the kitchen. Then downstairs you'll find their bedroom, a bathroom, and the laundry area. The lower-level walks out to a beautiful patio with heavenly views. It didn't take long for Randy to take over the two-car garage and turn it into his man cave and gym. Randy moved all of his workout equipment and heavy weights from Colorado, and the garage provided the perfect space for everything. Randy began lifting weights at a young age and he has been faithful to his workouts ever since.

The next morning, Randy fixed breakfast for us and later on, Erin prepared a lovely BBQ. We also went to some fun restaurants. They showed us many wonderful places and we enjoyed just being together. We spent the nights at a nearby hotel, and on Monday morning we drove back to Phoenix. Our weekend with Randy and Erin was wonderful. I know I've said this before, "Our goodbyes are always hard." Before turning in our rental car at the Phoenix Airport, we drove to Scottsdale to see Lorraine and Dick. They have the cutest condo with a cozy patio overlooking the swimming pool. The landscaping is lush and green and it feels similar to being at a resort. We had some nice quality time together and enjoyed a late lunch at one of their favorite restaurants where we could eat outdoors. While our visit was short, we had a lovely afternoon with our dear friends before heading back to Colorado.

In early August 2017, Dale and I flew to Wichita to visit Bud on his 90th birthday. Dale's brother lived in a very nice assisted living facility in east Wichita. When we arrived at the facility, the front entrance door was locked. That seemed strange to me but I guess for security purposes it was necessary. Anyway, I pushed the buzzer to alert security and it wasn't long until someone came to the door. We introduced ourselves and said we were there to visit Bud. We knew that Bud's health had been failing in recent months but I was still surprised when I saw him. I immediately noticed that his demeanor had changed. Bud was always a happy guy with a big robust smile and he had an amazing hearty laugh. But he did not smile when he greeted us. After visiting for a while, we offered to take him out for a ride but he did not want to go anywhere. The following day, we went back to the assisted living apartments to be with Bud. A nice birthday lunch had been arranged at the facility for Bud and his family. The lunch was lovely but Bud was somewhat quiet and we couldn't seem to cheer him up. We stayed with Bud until that evening. That was the last time Dale saw his brother.

After saying our goodbyes to Bud, we drove to Paula and Dick's house in west Wichita. Paula and I were so excited to see each other. When we went inside, I was pleasantly surprised and thrilled that Paula's first husband, Delbert and his wife Jacque were there. My nephew, Greg and wife Vicky and their two kids, Tyler and Kylee, were also there. It was awesome, and I was so happy to see all of them. It's amazing how Paula and Delbert managed to become friends, years after their divorce. And the good news is, the spouses were okay with the friendship. I had no idea that Paula had planned this little get together in honor of my upcoming September birthday. She even had a pretty birthday cake for me. I was so touched and it warmed my heart.

I was having a good time visiting with everyone and catching up on their lives when I noticed that Dale seemed anxious. He started pacing about and said he was ready to go. I asked him to be patient and said I would like to stay a while longer. We were leaving the next morning and I knew it would be a long time before I saw my sister and her family. We had barely finished

## Chapter 14

eating the delicious cake, and Dale became more anxious and said he wanted to go. It had started to rain and soon became a hard downpour. I thought we could surely wait until the rain let up, but Dale insisted on leaving. So, I said my goodbyes and made a mad dash for the car and we left in that rain storm. I wasn't sure why Dale was feeling so anxious; perhaps he was thinking about Bud, and having a rough time.

We arrived home on Sunday, and by Noon Tuesday, I knew that Dale had a problem. He was having stomach pains and he took a dose of his old standby, Alka Seltzer. That didn't seem to help, and he laid around all afternoon. I began feeling concerned and suggested we call his doctor but he didn't want to do that. Several hours passed and he said the pain was getting worse. By then, I was very worried and I had a strong feeling that Dale had another bowel obstruction. I urged him to let me take him to the ER, and it was around midnight when he finally agreed. I helped him to the car and off we went to Good Samaritan Hospital. Good Sam Hospital was only about ten minutes from our house and there was no traffic at that hour. I pulled up to the entrance and helped Dale to the check-in counter. The ER staff was very accommodating and wasted no time in getting Dale to an examination room. After the ER doctor examined Dale, he was given medication to ease his pain, and an MRI was ordered. I rushed back outside to move my car from the ER entrance. After a short wait, Dale was taken to Imaging for the MRI, which confirmed that Dale had an obstruction and he needed surgery. The ER doctor had already notified the surgeon. This was Dale's third obstruction, and each one required surgery. I couldn't help but wonder about the trip to Wichita. Could stress have caused the obstruction?

The nighttime hours passed slowly as Dale lay waiting for the surgeon. Thankfully, the medication had eased his pain. I glanced at the wall clock – it would soon be daylight. I decided to call Pam – she would want to know that her dad was going to surgery. Pam's voice sounded a little sleepy and I could tell she was still in bed. When I told her what was going on, she said she would scramble around and come to the hospital. Pam arrived a few minutes before her dad was taken to surgery. When Dale saw Pam walk in, his face brightened and I knew he was glad to see his daughter. I kissed Dale and gave a little wave as he was wheeled away. Pam and I were directed to the family waiting area where we found a place to sit, and then helped ourselves to coffee. Time always seems to pass slowly when waiting for news of a loved one, and I was glad that Pam was there with me. After the surgeon completed the procedure, he came to the waiting area. He said the surgery had gone well but Dale's affected intestine had already turned black, and he removed a twelve-inch section of intestines. I was extremely grateful for this surgeon and felt that he had saved my husband's life.

## Transitioning Forward

Transitioning – I like the sound of that, and really, that's what it would be. I didn't want to say that I was retiring from real estate. In fact, I used to say "I'll never retire." Why would I give up something I love so much? But my body was talking to me and telling me to slow down. Perhaps after forty years, it was time to transition out of marketing and sales. I was eighty-one years young at the time and if I couldn't continue at full speed and give 110 percent, maybe it was time to let go. But I had a plan. I would keep my real estate license current and active, maintain my continuing education and work as a referral agent. That would keep me in touch with past clients; I would help them connect with a realtor best suited to their needs, if and when the need arose.

My multimillion-dollar listing was coming up for renewal that September, and I had devised a plan to discuss with the

## Chapter 14

owner. So, I called them to schedule an appointment. It was a warm sunny day as I parked my car on the circle drive in front of this magnificent property. I grabbed my portfolio and walked up to the grand entrance. The owner invited me inside and after a little chit chat, we made ourselves comfortable and I began telling them about my plans. I told them I had decided to transition out of marketing and sales. "We had a feeling that you were going to tell us you're retiring." the wife said. "Actually, I prefer to think of it as 'transitioning'." I replied. The owner offered congratulations and said they were happy for me. I went on to say that it would become official January 1, 2018, and I went on to explain the plan I had in mind for their property. I proposed renewing the listing on their home through December, hoping to have it Under Contract before the end of the year. However, in the event their property wasn't under contract within that time frame, I would like to refer them to an excellent Realtor to take over the listing at the beginning of the new year – but of course, making sure they felt comfortable with the Realtor, and that it was a good fit for them and their property. These folks were long-time clients, going back many years, and they trusted me and my judgement. I was glad to hear them say that it sounded like a good plan.

The Annual Installation and Awards Ceremony of the Boulder Area Realtor Association was held on October 10, 2017. I was given a special invitation to attend, and was told that I would be honored at the event with the REALTOR Emeritus status from the NATIONAL ASSOCIATION of REALTORS (NAR). I had been a Realtor for forty years with continuous membership in NAR since 1977. The event was held at the Dairy Arts Center in Boulder, and that's interesting because my grandson, Jason, had recently completed the renovation of this wonderful place. I was very excited to attend and when I arrived, the reception area was already crowded with realtors. The social hour had just begun with drinks and hors d'oeuvres being served. It was nice seeing so many of my colleagues, many of whom I have worked with over the years. After socializing for a while, it was time for the ceremony to begin and we were given the signal to go to the theatre. I took a seat next to Mary, the VP and General Manager at WK Real Estate. The program began with a segment of entertainment, which was a new feature that year and very enjoyable. Then the new officers and directors were sworn in, and eventually it was time for the awards. My name was called and I was asked to come up onto the stage. I felt honored and very proud to be awarded the Realtor Emeritus status.

## Becoming Great-Grandy

Later that fall, something wonderful and exciting happened. I became a great-grandmother! When my children had their children, I became Grandy, and it was an amazing experience. With the joy of each new grandchild, our family circle grew. And now, oh my goodness, my granddaughter gave birth to a baby boy – our great-grandson, and the family circle continues to grow! Erin and Blake were very excited about their pregnancy and they were blessed with a beautiful, healthy baby boy. Lewis Kane Walters is his name and he was born on December 8, 2017. Dale and I were ecstatic about becoming great-grandparents, and we couldn't wait to meet the little guy! Pam and Tim were at the hospital when Lewis was born. I was very happy that they could be present for this precious moment in time. My thoughts travelled back to when Erin was born. Dale and I were invited to be present for the birth, and I ended up being Pam's labor coach. It was an unforgettable experience of sheer joy. And now, it was Pam and Tim's turn to become grandparents and I had to remind myself, "Remember to

## Chapter 14

stand back – It's Pam's turn to be a grandmother." The following day, Dale and I went to the hospital to meet Lewis. Erin was tired, but she welcomed us with open arms. The whole family showed up that day to meet the new member of the family. Pam and Tim were already there when we arrived, and Jason and Tyler (Erin's siblings) were there – it was a joyful event. I think everyone had followed the rules of hand-washing, and our vaccinations were up to date, so we all took turns holding baby Lewis. He was such a good baby and didn't mind being passed around. When it was my turn, I snuggled him close. He was so sweet and cuddly, and my heart strings were bursting with love for baby Lewis, my great-grandson. Once again, I had been truly blessed.

### The Clock was Ticking

Time has a way of flying by, and sometimes I want to say "Hey, wait up!" It was almost Christmas, the clock was ticking, and I was hoping for an offer on my multimillion-dollar listing before the end of the year. There had been two recent showings with some possible interest from one party. I had already introduced my clients to a Realtor I felt was best suited to take over the listing in January, but I remained hopeful that wouldn't be necessary. My clients liked the Realtor I had recommended and they felt comfortable with the transition. Well now, lo and behold, my wish had been granted – I received an offer shortly before Christmas! The offer was countered and we had been negotiating for a couple of days. Then a new counter was prepared and was awaiting the owner's signature. It was Christmas Eve and Dale and I were on our way to Pam and Tim's house when my cell phone rang. I recognized my client's number and I tapped the answer button. They were calling to say "Merry Christmas, Barbie! Thought you'd like to know that we just signed the counter." I was very excited about the call and said, "You just made my Christmas! Thanks for calling me on Christmas Eve, and Merry Christmas to you as well!" I called the Buyer's agent to let her know that the counter had been signed and we were Under Contract. The signed document was on its way to the agent's computer via DocuSign. Electronic signatures are efficient and very helpful for the Realtor and the client.

When we arrived at Pam and Tim's, we were greeted with Pam's beautiful smile and open arms. Tim wore a cheerful smile, and was waiting for his turn at hugs. There was a warm glowing fire in the fireplace and the sound of Christmas music could be heard in the background. It was all so cozy and welcoming and I made myself right at home. That year, our Christmas celebration was a little different from past years. With the new baby in the family, Erin and Blake chose to celebrate baby Lewis' first Christmas at their home in Longmont. Lewis was only seventeen days old, and being flu season, it was best to keep the baby at home to avoid any exposure. Of course, this made good sense and we applauded their decision. In Christmas' past I had always prepared dinner at our house, but after the grandkids grew up, Dale and I started a new tradition of treating the family to dinner at a nice restaurant. Then, after dinner the family came to our house (Grandy and Pappy's) for a gift exchange and dessert. Everyone seems to enjoy this, and we have since made it our new tradition. And the good news is, I don't have to cook. Instead, I can relax and enjoy my family and not miss out on the conversation.

Thinking about a nice getaway to the warmth of the desert was exciting. It would be a wonderful way to begin my transition. Dale and I had rented a place in Arizona for the entire month of January. Of course, that was before my most prized listing was Under Contract. But now, going away in January was out of the question and our nice plans went by the wayside. I didn't feel comfortable

## Chapter 14

handling this particular transaction long distance. I told Dale that we would have to cancel our trip. We were both disappointed, but Dale understood the importance of my being in town. I contacted the property owner in Arizona and explained my situation. She was very nice and understanding and she let us out of the rental. She said there were other people waiting and she was sure she could get it rented.

I hung the new 2018 Hawaiian calendar on the little nail. It was a brand-new year with a brand- new baby in the family and I had so much to be grateful for. During the last week in December, I began moving things out of my office at WK Real Estate. The large file cabinet needed to be emptied, plus the drawers in my desk. One by one, I emptied the drawers. I had a "trash pile" and a "to go" pile. I placed the "to go" files in boxes and the "trash pile" in a plastic bag. I closed my laptop computer and cleared the miscellaneous items from the top of my desk. I wiped all the surfaces clean. The office was spotless and ready for the next Realtor. Dale came to the office to load the heavy boxes into my car.

As I write about this today, it makes me feel a little sad. How did I bring myself to give up something I enjoyed so much? My body was talking to me, that's how. But on that move-out day, I didn't feel sad. I knew it was time and I was ready for the transition. I had been in real estate over forty years, and it was an amazing career! This was simply moving on to a new chapter in my life – I was transitioning, not retiring. I purchased a new L-shape desk for my home office, with nice file drawers – the works. Why hadn't I bought that desk years earlier? It would have been so convenient all those evenings working after hours at home, many times negotiating contracts during the evening hours while preparing documents on my home computer.

I had plans in place to transfer my real estate license from WK Real Estate, into my own name, but I would wait to do that until after the closing of my prized listing. The transaction was moving along on schedule and I hoped the inspection would go well. Overall, I was feeling positive about the transaction, and I was grateful to accomplish the sale of that property at that time. It would be the last big real estate sale of my career, and a nice feather in my cap – so to speak. The inspector said his inspection would last all day. That was not surprising since the house has 12,000 square feet, plus a five-car garage – not your average house! The inspection objection deadline date was on Friday – Friday the 13th. I was not superstitious so the date didn't matter to me.

It had been two days since the inspection was completed. Friday morning arrived and I hadn't heard anything from the Buyer's agent and I was thinking "No news is good news." The business day was drawing to a close and it was almost five o'clock on Friday the 13th. Since I hadn't heard anything, I was feeling confident the buyer must be happy with things. But then my cell phone rang and my caller ID told me it was the Buyer's agent. "Hopefully, she's calling to say that all is good." But that wasn't the case and the adrenalin drained from my body when I heard her say that the Buyer was giving Notice to Terminate the contract! Momentarily, I couldn't believe it. "What did you say?" I asked. "Does your buyer have any requests? What is their objection?" But she simply replied "No. There's nothing to discuss. They decided not to buy the property. I'm sending the Notice to Terminate over to you." I sat there stunned. How can this be happening after all the effort on everyone's part? Words cannot describe my disappointment and how bad I felt about the phone call I had to make. I tapped the speed-dial on my cell phone and called the owner.

The morning air was crisp and the wind had changed to a light breeze. It was a good day for a brisk walk. I bundled up, pulled my hat down over my ears and went outside to sit on the porch swing

## Chapter 14

and wait for my dear friend, Sandy. The drive from Sandy's house in Niwot is about ten-minutes. She is so sweet to drive over to my place, and I always look forward to our weekly morning walks. It wasn't long until she pulled up and parked out front. We gave each other a hug and off we went strolling to Waneka Lake Park. The lake was gorgeous that morning, with the snow-capped mountains looming in the background. Walking distance around the lake is one-mile, but counting the distance from my house, it becomes a good two-mile walk. The walk is very invigorating and it gives us girls a chance to catch up. We always have lots to talk about. Sandy is such a dear special friend. Our friendship goes beyond fifty years.

Cindy's Breakfast Club is a Wednesday morning delight! At nine o'clock every Wednesday, we meet at Le Peep's Restaurant in Boulder to enjoy breakfast together and share fun conversations. I absolutely adore these fun-loving, vibrant, amazing women. As we gather 'round the big table, the air suddenly fills with enthusiasm and chatter. We never lack for new and interesting things to talk about and discuss, and we usually leave with the name of a hot new book or tips on the latest new movies on Netflix. I first met Cindy at WK Real Estate. She was the best Relocation Director ever – until one day, sadly, she became quite ill and had to resign from her job. Cindy suffered through a very long period of struggling to get well. After her cancer surgery, she was given the news that she had six months to live. I was heartbroken to hear this sad news, as was everyone else. But Cindy was a fighter and she endured many weeks of Chemotherapy. And then, Cindy got some good news – she was approved for Clinical Trials treatment with a new test drug. The bad news was, she had to fly to Houston for treatment, but that did not deter Cindy. She was determined and never complained about the travel to Houston every three weeks. And then, a miracle happened – the test drug worked for Cindy, and her cancer went into remission! Breakfast Club was started because of Cindy. As one can imagine, Cindy's many friends wanted to visit her and offer support by stopping by her home or taking her to lunch or breakfast. She loved the attention, but after a while, it became a little overwhelming for her, and that's when she came up with the idea to start a Breakfast Club. And now, Cindy gets to see everyone at the same time – Wednesday mornings at Le Peep.

The simple things in life are so magnificent and usually are free – if only we take the time to notice the rainbows. Mother Nature is an amazing creature and she was hard at work. The trees had new buds and new growth was beginning to sprout. Tulips were pushing their way up through the soil ready to release their colorful blooms. Daylight Savings Time arrived and the days grew longer. I noticed how the sun remained higher in the sky; its bright rays no longer landed on my hardwood floor. We had guests coming that summer, and Dale and I were getting prepared. Dale opened up the patio in early spring, bringing all the patio cushions out of storage. Then he perfectly positioned his array of umbrellas around the patio. We would have plenty of shade on hot summer days. Our dear friend, Gloria had called to say that she and Donald would like to come for a visit. I was so very excited and began making plans. I wanted their visit to be special and started thinking about some fun things to do.

Gloria usually preferred to drive from Montana to our place, but this time she and Donald decided to fly. They were waiting curbside when we picked them up at DIA. It was wonderful to see them and share embracing hugs. Once we arrived at our house, I helped them get settled into the guest suite and after a while, we went outside to relax with a cool drink on the patio. I knew they would be tired from their travels, so I planned for a quiet dinner at our house that first evening. The following day we

## Chapter 14

ventured to Denver and the Museum of Nature and Science to see the amazing exhibit of the Dead Sea Scrolls. We saw ancient manuscripts including Biblical documents dating back over 2000 years! It was quite fascinating. Before heading home, we had a leisurely lunch in Denver.

The following morning, Gloria and I went for a walk around Waneka Lake, and that afternoon, the two of us did some girl shopping. The day slipped by all too quickly and soon it was time for dinner at Carelli's Italian Grill in Boulder. The ambiance and food is great, and we enjoyed a lovely dinner at Carelli's. I made reservations for the four of us to see a live Shakespeare play that evening, and we were off to the University of Colorado and the Mary Rippon Outdoor Theatre. Dale and I enjoy Shakespeare plays and we usually try to see at least one play each summer. I hoped that our friends would enjoy it too. We parked the car in the parking garage, making note of the parking space number. It's a bit of a walk from the garage to the outdoor theatre, and it hadn't entered my mind that it might be too much for Donald. We made it to the theatre just fine but getting to our reserved seats was a little tricky. Mind you, this outdoor theatre is very old and the steps are made of stone which are somewhat uneven. It never occurred to me that the steps would pose a problem for Donald, but I immediately noticed that he was not steady on his feet and he was having difficulty navigating these steps. But we made it to our seats and soon the play began.

It was the perfect evening for an outdoor play, but I was a little nervous about Donald. He wasn't as sturdy as he used to be and the Shakespeare plays are long. Perhaps it would be too much for him. I was wishing I had chosen a different venue for the evening. I quietly mentioned to Dale that perhaps we should leave during intermission, while it was still daylight. I was concerned about the walk back to the car in the dark. Dale agreed and I asked Gloria about it and she thought it was a good idea, so the four of us left during intermission. Now here's where it gets a bit comical – sort of! In past years, when the play is over, Dale and I simply follow the crowd back to the parking garage. However, this time there was no crowd to follow. After leaving the theatre, I led them in the direction I thought was the correct way to the garage, but I soon realized we were going the wrong way. So, we turned around and headed in the opposite direction. All the buildings looked alike and it felt like we were walking in circles – we were lost! I stood there looking around, and finally recovered my sense of direction. We got back on track and found the parking garage, and our car, right where we left it. We had a good laugh about it.

I was up early Sunday morning, getting things set up for breakfast outdoors on the patio. The sky was bright blue and it was a warm sunny day, just perfect to take Gloria and Donald for a drive in the mountains. After a leisurely breakfast, the four of us got in the car and drove up Boulder Canyon to Nederland, a quaint little town located near Barker Reservoir in the foothills of western Boulder County. The canyon is filled with beautiful rock outcroppings and lush mountain scenery and our friends thoroughly enjoyed the drive. When we arrived in Nederland, a surprise was in store for Gloria and Donald. Tucked in the center of Nederland, is a magical carousel called the Carousel of Happiness. This carousel is a menagerie of fifty-six whimsical, hand-carved animals on a restored 1910 merry-go-round – turning 'round and 'round to the music of a 1913 Wurlitzer band organ. Gloria and Donald were thrilled to see this delightful merry-go-round, and yes, we did take advantage of the $2.00 rides! As simple as it was, we had such fun and I think this might have been the highlight of their trip. But all good things must come to an end – so they

## Chapter 14

say. The following day, it was time to say goodbye and we took our dear friends to the airport. As we shared warm hugs, we began making plans for our next get-together.

Our grandson, Tyler, graduated with a Master of Science Degree from the Department of Geological Sciences at the University of Colorado. This was a huge accomplishment and Dale and I couldn't be prouder of Tyler! He studied and worked so hard to achieve this goal. The date was December 20, 2018. Tyler's dedication and devotion to geology is quite obvious. I quickly realize this whenever I ask him a question about his work at the United States Geological Survey (USGS). I always find his description quite interesting and mostly way above my head. Tyler's Thesis was: Mechanisms of Uranium Ore Passivation during in situ Phosphate Injections. (I learned that in situ means "to examine the phenomenon exactly in place where it occurs, i.e., without moving it to some special medium). Beyond Geology, Tyler has many other talents. First of all, he has a genuine, winning, lovable personality. During his leisure time, he occasionally plays in a band and performs locally at small restaurants and bars. Tyler can play a variety of musical instruments, plus he has an amazing voice and sings beautifully. In addition to all that, Tyler has built several musical instruments. This guy never ceases to amaze me and my heart bursts with love and pride when I think of Tyler. After the graduation ceremony, the family gathered together at a restaurant near CU, where we enjoyed great food and drinks as we continued celebrating Tyler.

A light dusting of snow clung to the grassy areas, but the cloudless sky was bright blue and the winter sun kept the air reasonably comfortable. I had planned to go for a walk that morning but after stepping outside on the porch, I noticed a few icy patches and decided to forgo the walk. Christmas was over and my thoughts drifted back a few days to our celebration with the family. Our great-grandson, Lewis, had his first birthday on December 8th. He made our Christmas especially fun this year. He has such a cute personality and was the center of attention. Just thinking about my wonderful family gives me an inner feeling of warmth and happiness.

I stood in the closet looking around and began sorting out a few things I wanted to take on the trip. I have a tendency to pack too many things and I told myself to be mindful of that. Dale and I were scheduled to leave on New Year's Day for a twelve-day Caribbean cruise with Oceania Cruise Lines. We had travelled to the Caribbean before and this particular cruise would take us to some of the same islands, but we didn't mind visiting those gorgeous places again. We just wanted a warm, sunny adventure on a cruise ship. Our travel day arrived and we flew to Miami where we spent the night in a hotel. Due to the tight flight schedule and the ship's departure, I thought it best to fly in the day before. It relieved the element of stress and I'm glad we did. The next afternoon, a taxi took us to Miami Harbor where we boarded Oceania's Riviera ship. I always get excited walking up the gangplank to board the ship. We found our stateroom and I walked over to the veranda and stepped outside to look around. The air was warm and summer-like. I quickly unpacked and stored my bag in the closet, then Dale and I went to the open-air restaurant and lounge to enjoy a nice beverage. After a while, the ship sailed away from Miami's harbor. I noticed how its skyline cast long interesting shadows from the late day sun.

The first port on this cruise was Great Stirrup Cay, Bahamas. The ship dropped anchor away from shore and we took a shuttle boat to this quiet little place. We explored around but there wasn't much there, mainly just a beach, but it was beautiful and we found a shady

## Chapter 14

spot to relax with a refreshing drink. The ship left port that evening and we cruised down to San Juan, Puerto Rico. San Juan was still in recovery from a devastating hurricane and some of the destruction was quite obvious as we strolled around this quaint town. Our next port was Philipsburg, St. Maarten. This island was also hit hard by that same hurricane and the people there said it would take years for it to fully recover. After leaving St. Maarten, we cruised over to St. John's, Antigua. From there we visited Gustavia, St. Lucia and St. Barts. I had pre-arranged for private tours in St. Maarten, St. John's, St. Lucia and St. Barts. The drivers were excellent and made every effort to take us to all of the places on our list. The cruise was lovely, the weather was perfect every day and our temperament, both mine and Dale's, must have been functioning under the same star because we agreed on everything the entire trip, and we had a wonderful time together.

How could it be? Our son would turn sixty that October. I called Randy to let him know that his dad and I wanted to be there to celebrate this special event. Ten years prior, we travelled to Arizona to celebrate Randy's 50th birthday. That was shortly after he and Erin moved to Arizona, and we wouldn't miss this milestone either. I booked the trip and we were all set. I was surprised and very pleased when Randy said he would pick us up at the Phoenix Airport. And in addition to that, he offered to let us use his car during our stay. Randy made our trip completely stress-free. Normally, the drive from Phoenix to Clarkdale is a little more than two hours, but that particular Saturday, the traffic was backed up and it took over three hours. When we finally arrived at their house, Erin had a lovely lunch ready for us. By that time, I was starving and Erin's lunch was delicious!

It was a beautiful Sunday afternoon in Clarkdale, just perfect for a barbecue. Randy invited his boss and wife to come over for the barbecue and I was so glad to have the opportunity to meet them. Randy has always spoken so highly of Richard and Dawn and after meeting them, I could see why. They are lovely people and so easy to be with. We spent the afternoon outside on Randy and Erin's beautiful patio and enjoyed a wonderful time together. The following day, Randy and Erin treated us to a Trolley Tour in Sedona. The tour was fabulous and I loved riding the trolley. The next day was Randy's BIG birthday. The day began with a casual stroll around the town of Clarkdale. Their dog, Willow, was happy and wagged her tail when she was invited to go along. Later that afternoon, we celebrated Randy's birthday at a famous restaurant in Sedona. I think we had the best table in the house because the view was spectacular! We enjoyed a leisurely happy hour with birthday toasts, then treated ourselves to a delicious meal. After a few pictures outside the restaurant, Randy and Erin dropped us off at the condo and we said our goodbyes – that's always the hard part.

Randy arranged for Quick Rides to take us back to the airport in Phoenix. He made everything so easy and convenient for us. The following morning, the Quick Rides driver picked us up at nine o'clock. We always try to visit Lorraine and Dick whenever we're in Arizona, and I had called Lorraine earlier to make sure they were home. I knew it would be a short visit but didn't want to miss the opportunity to see them and I asked the driver to take us to the Benson's condo in Scottsdale. As it turned out, we had just enough time for a nice lunch with them at Tommy Bahamas. Then we were off to the airport for the flight back to Denver.

## Chapter 15
## 2020 – A Doozy of a Year

When a new year rolls around, I'm usually excited about it. This particular new year was 2020 and I liked the sound of it. 2020 made me think of things being perfect, like 20/20 vision, and I had a feeling it would be a good year. Dale and I usually travel to a warm climate during the month of January, but that year we hadn't scheduled a trip and I don't know why. As it turned out, it was for the best because something very surreal was lurking in the atmosphere. I could not have imagined in my wildest dreams what the world would face in 2020. I first began to hear rumblings in the news during the month of January, about a life-threatening virus in China. Thousands of people in China had died from a highly contagious virus called COVID-19, also referred to as the Coronavirus. It was first said that China kept it a secret from the rest of the world and consequently, the world had no time to prepare. Travelers spread this horrible virus beyond China's borders and it didn't take long for COVID-19 to reach every continent in the world. It soon became a world-wide pandemic.

By mid-March, 2020, the United States was on lock-down; our country literally shut down. It was hard to comprehend what was happening – it was like a nightmare! Airline flights were cancelled, U.S. borders closed, and borders around the world closed. Social distancing was enforced and everyone was required to wear masks upon leaving their home. The hardest part – we couldn't hug our loved-ones in fear of being in contact with carriers of the virus. The death toll continued to climb, there was a shortage of ICU beds, respirators were in short supply and our health care system was being tested in unimaginable ways. By mid-March, Stay-at-Home orders were implemented. City and state offices closed, schools closed and children and teachers had to adapt to remote learning. Restaurants closed (many permanently) and thousands of wait staff lost their jobs. Banks locked their doors and customers had to schedule an appointment for any banking business. Shopping malls closed, churches were not allowed to hold services, movie theatres closed, hair salons closed, gyms closed, most businesses were ordered to close their doors and employees learned to work remotely at home. Millions of people were laid off from their jobs causing massive unemployment and a stressed economy. Every country in the world felt the effects of COVID-19 – it was as if the entire world had turned upside down.

## All Things Are Possible

During the pandemic and a suffering economy, many wondered how and why the real estate market remained strong. But buyers were in the marketplace amid a pent-up housing shortage, and home prices continued to soar. During the past few years, I had grown accustomed to multiple offers on listings, with buyers offering over list price, and that trend escalated during the pandemic. Towards the end of 2019, Dale and I decided to sell our last remaining investment property. The property needed some refurbishing to get it ready for the market, and fortunately, we

## Chapter 15

had started this process early in December of 2019, before the pandemic. We selected the carpet and appliances, and met with painting contractors for bids. We were fortunate that we could pre-purchase the appliances and carpet and the proprietors could warehouse the products until we were ready to install. The day after our tenant moved out, the painter began. Things moved forward like clock-work and luckily, the appliances were installed and all work was completed before March 16th, when businesses in the United States were ordered to shut down.

Real estate is considered an "essential" business, and therefore, Realtors were allowed to market listings and show homes – but only in compliance with COVID restrictions. Our rental property was ready for the market and it showed beautifully! I had already completed the listing paperwork and I submitted the listing to the Multiple Listing Service (MLS). Within a couple of days, I had multiple offers on our property, and we accepted an over-list offer. The buyer's home inspection was completed in a timely manner and we were set to close in April. This was my "first-ever" Curbside Closing! It was the craziest thing – the buyers sat in their car, parked in front of the title company building, while Dale and I sat in our car, all parties wearing masks, of course. The Escrow Officer from the title company also wore a mask, and personally carried the buyer's closing documents to the buyer's car. The Escrow Officer then did the same for Dale and me. All parties signed closing documents in their own car, using their own blue pens. It was such a bizarre experience, but it worked and we sold that property during the raging pandemic!

All things truly are possible, and something wonderful happened during the pandemic. Dale and I were blessed with another great-grandchild. Cooper Anthony Newt was born on March 16, 2020. Our step-grandson, Connor and his partner,

Kaylee, are the proud parents. As of this writing, I had not yet met Cooper, but I'm hoping to have that experience one day soon. The little family relocated from Denver after he was born and now live in a town near Austin, Texas. Cooper is an adorable happy baby with an amazing smile – just like his dad.

## Take Nothing for Granted

As COVID lingered and spread of the virus went from bad to worse, Dale and I became home-bodies. We curtailed all socializing with friends and family. Walking with my dear friend, Sandy, came to a halt. Our lives existed within the walls of our home. Something as simple as grocery shopping no longer felt safe. Consequently, I stopped all in-person shopping. Pam was wonderful in helping us out with grocery shopping, and then, our granddaughter, Erin, offered to take over the task and for many weeks she did the grocery shopping for us. This was a big task for Erin, considering she worked full time treating patients at the veterinary clinic, plus taking care of a toddler and maintaining her own life, but she did it with a smile. But then, I finally got my act together and discovered how easily I could shop on-line for groceries and have them delivered to our front door.

While being cooped-up at home, I tried to focus on the brighter side of things. Dale and I had each other to lean on during the pandemic. We had a way of building each other up when one of us was feeling down. I was thankful that no one in our family had fallen ill to COVID. And I thought about how fortunate I was to have a nice inviting patio – a place to hang-out on warm weather days. Occasionally, a family member or friend stopped by for an outdoor visit – social distancing of course, and all wearing masks. One warm sunny day in September, my friend, Pam Hill, stopped by my house for a little visit. I wanted

## Chapter 15

to hug my dear friend, but we obeyed the rules and maintained our distance of six feet apart. I later found myself remembering back to when I first met the Hills. Jim and Pam came into my life in 1984, when I had the pleasure of helping them with their real estate. Their two kids, Eric and Jeff, were young boys at the time. "What a nice family." I said to myself when we met. They fell in love with the Devils Thumb neighborhood and a house I was marketing. They bought that house and still live there after all these years.

That same summer of 2020, other friends came to visit. The Bensons were in town from Arizona, and I invited them to come for lunch. They were comfortable with the idea and we obeyed the rules – no hugging and we stayed outdoors. Our patio table is quite long so it was easy to place Dick and Lorraine at one end of the table while Dale and I sat at the opposite end, and we made sure to stay six feet apart. It seemed very bizarre, being so distant with dear friends, but we were all in the same boat and that's just the way life was in 2020.

Our new way of life was disturbing and I wondered if our old way of life would ever return – maybe not; perhaps it would return as a "new normal." The pandemic caused me to be mindful about all the things I took for granted. The spontaneous hugs from my family and friends – Oh, how I missed those hugs! I took for granted the simple pleasure of going out for an impromptu dinner with friends. I took for granted just going to the grocery store without fear of being contaminated with COVID-19. I took for granted a casual date night at the movies with my husband. I took for granted standing close to a friend or family member. I missed seeing my grandchildren. So many simple pleasures slipped away.

My saving grace during the pandemic was going for long walks where I could lose myself in nature. I had to wear a mask outdoors, but still, the fresh air energized my body and helped fill my mind with positive thoughts. I desperately needed those positive thoughts because I quickly became bored with my new full-time job of cooking and online shopping. If Dale needed something, he sat next to me at my computer as I scrolled through on-line items for him. He was always telling me, "Don't scroll so fast; I need to read about it." We became regulars for Curbside Pickup at McGuckin Hardware and Home Depot, while some items were shipped to us from Walgreens or department stores. We received packages several times each week! While I have always enjoyed cooking, I missed going out to eat like we used to do. Part of my new routine involved sorting through my multitude of cookbooks in search of new recipes – something different to keep the two of us interested in my cooking. Preparing weekly menus became time consuming. Okay, I know what you're thinking, "I probably had plenty of vacant time." But you see, I had to make sure I had all the necessary ingredients for the chosen recipes before preparing the shopping list. And that meant checking the pantry, the spice shelf and refrigerator, making sure to add the needed ingredients to the shopping list. Once my list was complete, I ordered groceries online for home delivery. Sounds simple. Right – but it wasn't how I wanted to spend my time.

But then, towards the end of that summer in 2020, Dale and I decided to let our guard down a little and venture out to explore outdoor patio dining at a few restaurants. Many of our friends had already done this and said they felt safe as long as they were dining outdoors. When restaurants were allowed to reopen, they had to comply with many new regulations including the number of people allowed to dine at one time. Tables had to be spaced six feet apart, including outdoor dining, and restaurant staff were required to wear face masks; customers had to wear a mask until

## Chapter 15

seated. We wanted to avoid going inside any buildings, so when I called to make a reservation, I asked if we could go directly to the patio without entering the restaurant building; they were happy to accommodate my request. Once seated, Dale and I removed our masks and I actually felt liberated. It was so good to be out and about, where we could see and hear the laughter of other humans. At 95a Bistro, there were no paper menus. I simply scanned my phone over the bar code provided on the table and the menu suddenly appeared on my phone. That was pretty cool, and we weren't touching a used menu. Whoever thought of that idea was brilliant! But then, after going out to eat a couple of times I started thinking – in reality, being outdoors is probably a false sense of safety because the wait staff handles other diner's dishware and then serves us, and I continued to hear that the COVID-19 virus germ can linger on surfaces for long periods of time. Then there was a spike in virus cases, so we stopped patio dining at the restaurants. It wasn't long until restaurants were once again ordered to discontinue indoor dining, but they could remain open for curbside pickup. That's when I began ordering curbside take-out at least once each week in support of our local restaurants.

Just when we thought things couldn't get any worse in 2020, massive forest fires erupted in Colorado. The summer months were extremely hot with little or no moisture, causing extended drought conditions. Strong winds encouraged the fires and sent sparks flying through the air, igniting more fires. And suddenly, Colorado was battling several forest fires at the same time in Boulder and Larimer counties. Flakes of ash filled the air, leaving unhealthy air quality for many weeks. Our grandson, Tyler, recently purchased a home in the Foothills near Gold Hill, and when a fire erupted in the area, he was ordered to evacuate. It was a scary time for Tyler, and many others. Fortunately, his house was spared from the fire and after one week, he was allowed to return home. And then, on a Saturday afternoon, October 17th, the Calwood fire erupted north of Boulder. The subdivision called Mountain Ridge was completely destroyed. There were nineteen homes nestled at the base of the Foothills, and every house burned to the ground. Some past real estate clients lived in that subdivision and their home was a total loss. I still remember the day, twenty-five years ago in 1995, when I drove Art and Betty to this neighborhood to look at homes. They fell in love with the area and purchased a home on Mountain Ridge Drive. My heart breaks for these people and hundreds more who lost their homes to devastating fires in Colorado during 2020. The Calwood fire had burned through 8,788 acres by Sunday afternoon. And then, the East Troublesome fire burned 12,655 acres near Granby, a popular tourist area. About the same time, the Lefthand Canyon fire started and burned hundreds of acres. And there's the Cameron Peak fire in Larimer County that began burning in August, and it was still burning in October.

In spite of the pandemic and the crazy year, it was the year I would say goodbye to my 44-year-old classic sports car. My 1976 Corvette Stingray looked good at her age with 110,000 miles, and her engine still had a nice hum. But I had stopped driving the car long ago when it was no longer practical for my real estate business. The Corvette sat low to the ground and getting in and out of the car was tough on my aging knees. Dale took her out for a spin now and then to keep her battery charged, and he always said he got thumbs-up whenever he drove it. But mostly, she just sat in the third bay of our garage consuming space. I wondered why I had hung onto her all those years. Some people get attached to cars and I have to say – back in the day, I loved

## Chapter 15

that car. It became my signature when I began my real estate career. But I had the perfect opportunity to sell my Corvette, without every Tom, Dick, and Harry wanting to take her out for a fun test drive.

Dale was anxious to trade his car for a new 2020 vehicle with all the latest safety features, but we were in the midst of the COVID-19 pandemic and visiting the dealerships was not an option. So Dale sat down with his iPad and began his research. Fortunately, he knew what he wanted in a car and searching the internet for availability was helpful. After finding what he wanted, he connected with a sales rep at a local dealership to get acquainted by phone. I emailed photos of Dale's trade-in vehicle and photos of my Corvette. The sales rep was impressed with my Corvette and Dale's vehicle, and we were able to agree on a price for both vehicles as partial payment for the new car. Due to the ongoing pandemic, the transaction was conducted by phone and email. The sales rep located the car Dale wanted and it was shipped to the dealership. After the new car arrived at the dealership and was prepared for delivery, the sales rep delivered the new car to our home. We were all wearing masks and invited him to our back yard where Dale and I reviewed the paperwork and paid for the new car. A very excited technician came with the sales rep. He had been chosen to drive the Corvette to the dealership in Boulder. I heard there was a drawing among the technicians to choose who got to drive the Corvette. As the technician drove away with my car, I stood in the driveway and waved goodbye while thinking "She's still a sassy-looking, lovable ride!"

### Zoom Thanksgiving

Whoever created Zoom, I'd like to say "Thank you." 2020 was the year of firsts. It was the first year ever for me to order

Thanksgiving Dinner. Dale and I did curbside pickup at the Boulder Cork. Then at two o'clock Thanksgiving Day, our family got together via Zoom. It was fun seeing everyone while chit-chatting back and forth. The CDC recommended that families consisting of more than two households should not congregate for Thanksgiving. Since our immediate family consists of five households, we felt it was best to cancel our traditional family Thanksgiving and Christmas celebrations that year. Skipping those traditions was a first for my family and very disappointing for all of us, but it was the right thing to do.

While many things were disappointing in 2020, most of us made the best of it with Zoom get-togethers – Zoom Book Club, Zoom Breakfast Club, and impromptu Zoom or FaceTime with family and friends, and we even had a lovely Zoom get-together at the end of the year with our friends in the U.K., Lisa and Nigel. For Christmas however, we did see Pam and Tim [in person]. They invited Dale and me to come to their house for dinner on Christmas Eve – just the four of us and no masks. They quarantined themselves for about two weeks to make sure they hadn't been exposed to anyone or anything. . . bless them for doing that. We had a wonderful time together that Christmas Eve. It was so exhilarating to share warm hugs and enjoy a meal together – it actually felt normal.

## Miracles Do Happen

As the COVID pandemic left its indelible mark on this century, scientists around the world worked tirelessly day and night to find a vaccine. The world rejoiced when announcements were made about several promising vaccines. Testing continued and the results proved to be effective. The world waited with rolled up sleeves. Then on December

## Chapter 15

14, 2020, the U.S. Food and Drug Administration issued an Emergency Use Authorization for the Pfizer/BioTech vaccine. And a few days later the Moderna vaccine received authorization. Then came the Johnson & Johnson vaccine approval for emergency distribution and this one required only one shot. This truly was like a miracle – discovering not just one, but several, much needed vaccines in less than one year! Many thanks to these amazing scientists!

As I say goodbye to 2020 and welcome in 2021, I say "Adios – Good riddance 2020." It was the year our lives were put on hold, and sadly, also the year that hundreds of thousands of lives were lost in the United States due to COVID. Some call it the "Lost year." But I have to say, I learned a lot that year and not all was lost. For one thing, I spent a good amount of time writing my life story, and that was time well spent. I learned that amid adversity, people found resilience and hope. I found people in general were more helpful, kinder and gentler. I am grateful that Dale and I received our first dose of the COVID vaccine on January 6, 2021, and the second shot on February 3rd. I rejoiced in getting the vaccine. It gave me a piece of my freedom back – freedom from the worry of exposure to COVID-19. And as our family members became vaccinated, we could hug again. I will never take those hugs for granted!

Life is truly a remarkable journey and as I reflect back, I realize what a wonderful life I've had, and continue to have – and so far, no complaints. I am still married to the love of my life and husband of sixty-eight years. We have travelled the world together, to places far and near, including five amazing continents. I've experienced the joys of having children and raising a family. I've enjoyed a fantastic career of forty-one years in real estate. I am blessed to have special friends in my life.

But my greatest accomplishment, my biggest joy, and what I am most proud of, is my family. Life is very precious, and during my eighty-four years of tasting life, I've discovered that the world offers a multitude of flavors – many of which I have already tasted and enjoyed, and others I've yet to explore.

# About the Author

Following 40 years of successfully navigating hundreds of real estate transactions, Barbie Rieger "transitioned" out of her Real Estate career at the age of 81. Retirement was never part of her plan so she "transitioned" instead. This led to new opportunities and time to write about her very interesting life story. Barbie continues to lead an active lifestyle, enjoying travel, gourmet cooking, and spending time with family and friends. Barbie lives with her husband in Lafayette, Colorado.

www.ingramcontent.com/pod-product-compliance
Lightning Source LLC
Chambersburg PA
CBHW071411070526
44578CB00003B/547